SHORT ESSAYS

FOURTH EDITION

Gerald Levin
The University of Akron

HBJ

HARCOURT BRACE JOVANOVICH, PUBLISHERS

San Diego   New York   Chicago   Atlanta   Washington, D.C.
London   Sydney   Toronto

Cover: John Singer Sargent, The Black Brook, The Tate Gallery, London

ISBN: 0-15-580918-0
Library of Congress Catalog Card Number: 85-81183
Printed in the United States of America

Preface

The majority of essays in the Fourth Edition are three to five pages long—about the length assigned in many composition courses. Matters of organization and development can be taught effectively through the short essay, allowing sufficient class time for discussion of composition and other matters. The book also contains longer essays by L. E. Sissman, John Gregory Dunne, Arthur L. Campa, Lewis Yablonsky, Robert J. White, and Joan Didion.

The Fourth Edition follows the earlier editions in presenting concrete, contemporary essays pertinent to the world and interests of students. The range of topics is wide, and each section of the book includes a variety of them. Changing values in American life and the problems of growing up continue to be important themes. New to this edition are various essays on fathers and children, animal experimentation, and the obligation of military service. Of the 66 essays in the book, 31 are new.

The basic plan of the book is that of earlier editions, but the Fourth Edition introduces expressive writing as a separate category. Part One discusses the organization of the essay, but the topics are reordered, beginning with unity and thesis and ending with coherence. Part Two now presents expressive writing with a focus on narrative, descriptive, and reflective essays.

The later sections have been rearranged. Part Three discusses expository writing, with a focus on example, process, comparison and contrast, cause and effect, definition, and classification and division. Part Four deals with argument and persuasion. A new section on strategies of persuasion includes a discussion of satire. The Fourth Edition retains paired essays on contemporary issues.

The final two parts of the book deal with sentences and diction. Part Five discusses effective sentences, with a focus on emphasis, parallelism, and sentence variety. Part Six explores effective diction, focusing on concreteness, figurative language, tone, and usage.

A new feature of the book is the extended analysis of a representative essay at the start of each part of the book. The analysis examines the essay in light of the various topics that follow. Part Four contains an analysis of both an argumentative essay and a persuasive essay.

Each essay is followed by a Comment on the rhetorical principles discussed at the start of each section. The Questions generally begin with the content and rhetoric of each essay, developing points in the Comment; they conclude with questions on the ideas of the essay. The Vocabulary Study supplements these questions, teaches the uses of the dictionary, and emphasizes the importance of context in reading and writing.

The text includes a thematic table of contents. Since each essay illustrates rhetorical topics other than the one it illustrates in the book, instructors may want to switch essay and topic to fit the needs of their classes. The Suggestions for Teaching and Suggestions for Writing in the Instructor's Manual offer alternatives for teaching.

I thank again Andrea A. Lunsford, University of British Columbia, and Ann Raimes, Hunter College of the City University of New York, for their contribution to the first edition. The following people suggested various changes for this revision: Dennis J. Hock, Central Washington University; George Miller, University of Delaware; Neil Nakadate, Iowa State University; and Mary K. Ruetten, University of New Orleans.

I owe special thanks to William Francis, Bruce Holland, Robert Holland, and Alice MacDonald of the University of Akron, who continue to discuss composition with me and made suggestions for this edition. Eben W. Ludlow encouraged this book from the start and has continued to give me strong support and friendship. My acquisitions editor, Tom Broadbent, spent many hours discussing this revision and, in particular, the present reordering of topics. To the permissions editor, Eleanor Garner, I am grateful for her many efforts on my behalf. I am especially fortunate to have had an outstanding manuscript editor, Audrey M. Thompson. My debt to my wife, Lillian Levin, is as strong as always.

GERALD LEVIN

Contents

Description   84

Reflection   105

PART 3   *Exposition*   123

Introduction and analysis of an essay:

Example   131

Process   144

Comparison and Contrast   169

Cause and Effect 191

Definition 211

Classification and Division 225

PART 4 *Argument and Persuasion 249*

Thematic Table of Contents

Introduction

This book introduces various kinds of writing and shows how they serve particular purposes. The purposes for which we write are so numerous that no one classification can account for all of them. One recent and important classification distinguishes four main purposes for writing: for personal expression, for reference or the giving of information, for creation of literary effect, and for persuasion. According to this classification, an essay may express the personal feelings or beliefs of the writer; or, as in a textbook, may give information about a particular subject; or, as in a play or novel, may generate laughter or pathos; or, as in a political speech, may seek to change opinion on an issue. These purposes are rarely exclusive of one another, for a piece of writing may have several purposes. For example, a satirical novel may simultaneously provide amusement, supply information about a contemporary issue, and seek to persuade its readers about the issue.

This book explores essays of personal expression, information, and persuasion. Informative essays are limited to "expository" writings, though this word more narrowly describes the general purpose of writing to provide information. The other three kinds of writing are narration, description, and argument. In writing home about your first week at college, you might use *narration* to give a chronological account of the events of the week, *description* to give details about your room, new friends, or classes, and *exposition* perhaps to explain the confusing registration process that made your first week of college a trying one. The exposition would explain the reasons for something that happens, describe processes, define terms, classify ideas, items, or events, and then perhaps compare and contrast the same.

A letter later in the year might be persuasive—its purpose to get approval for your decision to change schools. Persuasive essays use explanation, narration, and description, but they chiefly use *argument*. Argument is concerned with establishing the truth of statements; persuasion, with getting readers to accept these statements or to take action that the statements support.

Whatever their purpose, essays usually share certain features. They usually contain a central impression or central idea or *thesis*. Each paragraph, in addition, contains a *topic sentence* or statement of the subject or guiding idea. Like paragraphs, essays have some kind of organization or *order of ideas*. Important to the coherence of the essay are *transitions*—words, phrases, and other devices that link sentences and paragraphs. These features are the subject of this first part of the book. The questions and suggestions for writing that follow each selection will give you practice in these various elements.

Though knowledge of these elements alone will not make you a better writer, knowledge of how other writers develop their experiences and ideas will help you in drafting and revising your own essays. You will become a better writer only through constant writing and revising. The essays presented here are not "models" in the sense that they illustrate the only effective way of developing a paragraph, organizing an essay, constructing a sentence, or choosing the appropriate words. They are examples only of proven ways of organizing and developing essays. They show how a wide range of writers who differ in background and interests achieve their purpose in writing.

part one

Organizing the Essay

The word *essay* has various meanings. To many writers the word describes a short, carefully organized composition that develops a single idea or impression. To other writers the word describes a beginning, or trial attempt, in which the central idea or impression is explored rather than developed or analyzed completely. Thus Samuel Johnson, the great eighteenth-century writer, essayist, and lexicographer, referred to the essay as "an irregular undigested piece."

Johnson's definition fits many essays that have the informality of a first draft—those that state ideas and impressions with neither an immediate concern for their organization nor a central guiding idea or thesis. Informal letters are sometimes essays in this sense of the word. Like journal entries, trial essays help writers discover what they want to say. Much of your writing in your composition course may be trial essays of this kind.

Of course, upon revision the trial essay may become a carefully organized composition that focuses upon a single idea or impression. Though many of the essays in newspapers and magazines merely explore a topic, for example, others contain a central idea or thesis and a careful organization or order of ideas. A newspaper editorial that argues for energy conservation is one kind of essay; an ex-

1

tended magazine article that describes methods of energy conservation is another; a newspaper column that describes personal experiences with energy-saving devices creates yet a third angle on the topic.

The purpose of each essay is different, and so may be the organization. The editorial is persuasive in intent while the magazine article is informative. Both, however, organize the argument or exposition in ways that will best persuade or inform their respective readers. The personal column on energy-saving devices, in turn, may simply express amusement or frustration about electrical devices and may therefore organize its description or narration to generate laughter or some other effect from the reader.

The following essay by John Allen is neither chiefly persuasive nor chiefly informative. Though Allen does answer the question he poses in his opening paragraph, and he does tell us something about the world of Lincoln Center—the complex of arts buildings on Broadway and 67th Street, in New York City—his main purpose is to express and to share his interest and amusement at people. He watches the world of Lincoln Center and in particular is amused at the "theater of the absurd" that an observer would find at any hour of the day in a large city.

Allen expresses his sense of the absurd through a series of details. We might refer to this sense or impression as an *implied thesis*. Paragraph 2 states the central thesis: people carry objects because they are performers on the world's stage, and performers need props. They also need costumes, so clothing becomes the subject of paragraph 4. The paragraphs that follow describe both costumes and props. The transition to Allen's second idea occurs at the end of paragraph 5, in the reference to the "much more bizarre plot" his observations suggested to him. Allen presents his observations in the order they occurred, but he also builds to more odd sights—those of the "Theatre of the Absurd." In paragraph 12 he emphasizes that the last of the characters he observed was the "strangest."

The one-sentence concluding paragraph reminds us of Allen's purpose in writing this essay: to express his sense of interest and amusement at the world. In that sentence, Allen realizes that he is part of the very scene he observes, for he is carrying his own prop—the yellow pad on which he has jotted his observations. He, too, is a performer on the stage of Lincoln Center.

The word *thesis* seems too strong to describe the central idea of this kind of essay, for Allen is not arguing a proposition in a formal way. *Observation* is perhaps the better word. Like the central idea or thesis of a persuasive essay, however, the observation organizes the details and gives direction. Allen might have presented what he saw without making a point or drawing a conclusion. Had he done no more than this, we would still share his point of view and perhaps his sense of the world—of what a busy part of New York City can reveal to the interested onlooker late in the afternoon.

In writing your own essays, remember that few readers see the world exactly as you do. They may, indeed, concentrate on different aspects and may have different ideas and feelings about them. Whether your purpose is chiefly to express your own feelings or beliefs, or to give information about the world as you see it, or to persuade readers to accept a belief of yours, you must help your readers see the world as you do. You must also help them follow the flow of your observations and thoughts. The sections that follow discuss ways of doing so.

John L. Allen
Props and the Man

John L. Allen is a free-lance writer living in Muskegon, Michigan, the town where he was born. He has worked as an instructor at the University of Michigan, as Director of Humanities at the Cranbrook Academy of Art, and as a free-lance writer in New York City. For several years he has written reviews and a weekly arts column for the Muskegon *Chronicle*. He has contributed to *The Saturday Review, Ovation Magazine,* and *Arts in Society,* among other publications.

Why is it most people, most of the time, seem to be carrying things?   1

Perhaps we can settle for Shakespeare's explanation: "All   2

Reprinted by permission of John L. Allen.

the world's a stage, and all the men and women merely players." Obviously, what we are toting about with us all the time
are our props; those carry-on items which define our parts
and help our scenes along.

I thought about this recently during the afternoon rush   3
hour in New York City. I had a few minutes to spare, so I
sat down on a bench opposite Lincoln Center and noted the
props parading by—guessing at the plots and characters they
suggested.

Much of it was standard costuming, of course: sweaters,   4
coats, shawls, umbrellas and the like. They helped establish
the time of day: heated afternoon, following upon chillier
morning.

Most of the actresses lugged large purses about, tokens   5
of their busyness and organizational sense. Many of the ac-
tors carried their equivalent: a briefcase. The latter provided
far less diversity, unfortunately, than the former. Perhaps
someone is simply writing more interesting parts for women
these days than for men.

I did see two young men, however, who went by wear-   6
ing white shirts and ties, no jackets; their arms full of manila
envelopes. A last-minute dash to the post office on the boss's
orders, or hand delivery of important papers needed in the
opening scene of the next business day? I couldn't tell.

A young mother and very small daughter went by, each   7
carrying a violin case—scaled to match the bearer. The explanation seemed to be the nearness of the Juilliard School of
Music and a host of teachers; but a much more bizarre plot
also occurred to me: perhaps there's more to cloning than a
joke, after all.

Theatre of the Absurd provided a couple of entries. One   8
was a man with a huge suitcase-shaped bundle—carefully and
completely gift-wrapped in old newspapers, and slung in a
twine sling for easier toting. I wondered if Godot were waiting up the block for delivery. The other Absurdist entry consisted of a pair of young women lugging big brown bags with

hemp handles. The bags bore the deliciously redundant message, "BIG BROWN BAG."

In a few minutes' time most of the major department stores   9
had marched past, their names carried far and wide by oblig-
ing if burdened customers. A handy means of establishing the
sense of place if not the plot itself.

One harried-looking gentleman, a little stoop-shouldered   10
from the weight of the world, was all but dragging his particular item: a bouquet of bright flowers wrapped in green
tissue paper. This seemed a crucial prop on which a scene
might very likely hinge for better or worse. Doubtless a domestic comedy.

One fellow went by carrying license plates, and I hoped   11
this was not the signal of things to come. Having to apply
for—and pay for—a walker's license doesn't appeal to me. But
in these financially pressed times, there's no telling what a state
or city government might not think up as a way of increasing
needed revenues.

The last—and strangest—character I saw was a slightly   12
grubby fellow, ambling along with an uncovered plastic pitcher
full of water. I watched his balancing act avidly as he came
toward me, but resisted the impulse to follow and see where
he was headed. In some cases, the suspense is all, and the de-
nouement can't help but be a disappointment.

I picked up my yellow pad and exited stage right for home.   13

Questions for Study and Discussion

1. How different are the props Allen describes? What do these
   props tell you about the personality or concerns of their owners?
2. What feelings do the people and their props arouse in Allen?
   Does he state these feelings directly?
3. What does the essay reveal about Allen himself—his personality, his interests, possibly his habits?

4. Allen illustrates Shakespeare's statement, "All the world's a stage, and all the men and women merely players." What does this statement imply about the world and people in general? Does Allen have in mind any of the ideas that the speaker of these lines—Jaques, in Act 2, Scene 7 of *As You Like It*—presents in explanation?

Vocabulary Study

1. The following words refer to plays and performance. What do the words mean, and how do they apply to the people and sights described?
    a. paragraph 7: *plot*
    b. paragraph 10: *domestic comedy*
    c. paragraph 12: *denouement*
    d. paragraph 13: *exited stage right*
2. Consult the *Oxford Companion to the Theatre* and other books in the reference section of your library to explain Allen's references to the *Theatre of the Absurd* and *Godot* in paragraph 8.
3. What do the following words mean?
    a. paragraph 2: *toting*
    b. paragraph 7: *scaled, bizarre, cloning*
    c. paragraph 8: *redundant*
    d. paragraph 12: *ambling, avidly*

Suggestions for Writing

1. Develop Shakespeare's statement with your own observations, made at a particular place and time. As Allen does, specify the place and time. Build the essay to a concluding idea or reflection if you wish.
2. Develop one of the following phrases of Mark Twain through a series of examples or observations:
    a. An experienced, industrious, ambitious, and often quite picturesque liar.—*Private History of a Campaign That Failed*
    b. All the modern inconveniences.—*Life on the Mississippi*

Unity and
Thesis

In a unified essay all ideas and details connect to a central, or controlling, idea. The reader sees the connections at every point and experiences the essay as a unity—much as one experiences unity in music, in which different sounds heard together develop a single theme.

The central idea that organizes the many smaller ideas and details of an essay is called the *thesis*. Occasionally the thesis appears in the first sentence or very close to the beginning of an essay, as in many newspaper editorials or columns. The effect is likely to be dramatic:

> "Don't you want to be one of the Now people?" asks an ad for a new soft drink, going on to urge, "Become one of the Now generation!"

> The only thing I can think of that is worse than being one of the Now people is being one of the Then people. As a member of civilization in good standing, I reject both the *nowness* and the *thenness* of the generations. I opt for the *alwaysness.*—Sydney J. Harris, "Now People and Then People"

7

The newspaper or magazine reader generally expects to find the main ideas or details of the editorial or column in the opening sentences.

Beginning an essay or article directly with the thesis can seem abrupt, however, and often the thesis may not be quite clear to the reader without some background information first. So the essayist frequently builds to the thesis, as in the following example:

> The killing of 239 servicemen in Lebanon and the invasion of Grenada have reminded Americans of the military's role in pursuit of the nation's purposes and once again have raised the question of the citizen's obligation to do military service when called upon. This question still is before us because of continuing controversy over a law requiring students seeking Federal aid to register for the draft.
>
> It would seem obvious that in a world of independent and sovereign states that come into conflict and threaten one another's vital interests—sometimes even existence itself—citizens who choose to remain in a particular country are morally obligated to serve in its armed forces when the need arises.—Donald Kagan, "Military Service: A Moral Obligation"

Such introductory comments and details before the statement of the thesis help to place the reader in the world of the writer.

Sometimes the thesis is stated toward the end of the essay rather than toward the beginning. One reason for this delay is that the reader may not understand the thesis without examples and considerable explanation. Another reason is that the writer may want to make the reader receptive to a controversial thesis before stating it. A thesis is highlighted when it appears toward the end, particularly if the writer builds to it gradually but steadily.

In some essays—especially those that are mainly narrative (that recount a series of events) or descriptive—the thesis is implied rather than explicitly stated. That is, a carefully planned accumulation of details, rather than any single statement in the essay, conveys the main idea or impression the writer wishes to share with the reader. Obviously it is especially important, in the absence of a stated thesis, that the writer maintain a clear sense of purpose and a consistent point of view in presenting the details. The second essay in this section, "The Woolen Sarape" by Robert Ramirez, provides an example of the thesis placed at the end of an essay.

You will find that producing unified, well-developed essays of your own is almost always easier if you take the time to formulate a clear preliminary thesis statement for yourself before you begin to write (even if you then occasionally decide not to state the thesis explicitly in the essay). And here is a final bit of advice: once you have a thesis, always be prepared to change it and refocus your paper if, while you are writing, you discover a new thesis that interests you more. The act of writing is often an act of discovery—of finding meanings and ideas you could not anticipate at the start.

Jennifer S. Youngman
Father Used to Know Everything

Jennifer S. Youngman is a photographer and free-lance writer whose photographs, essays, and articles have been in national magazines and newspapers, including *Wilderness* and *Christian Science Monitor*. Her personal essay on childhood experiences shows how indispensable exact details are in evoking the past and characterizing an important person in one's life.

I stood silently, listening to the thunder of metal on metal, watching the shrieking riders streak by like lightning. Moist glimmers of nostalgia and surprise tickled the corners of my eyes. The structure was so small, not the least bit threatening. And the ordeal, interminable to one frightened child 10 years earlier, now lasted but a moment.

I turned my back on the scene of my last roller-coaster ride and walked away, no family at my side to guide me through the maze of rides this night.

It had come as a shock to discover that my father couldn't answer all of my questions anymore. I carried with me right into high school vestiges of that delightful delusion that parents know all. So when help was no longer instantly forth-coming on baffling homework assignments, I wavered between impatience and dismay.

When I dropped pig Latin as a second language and took   4
up French, my father couldn't share a tête-à-tête with me as before. "Illy'say alk-tay" was his *pièce de résistance.* And the changing methods of textbook math always require time to get acquainted. But I concluded that he was letting me down. He *used* to know everything.

I suspect that were I to recall those long-ago replies that   5
always satisfied, I would find them to have been affirmations of love, more than facts. There would have been laughter in his response, gentle encouragement, patient wisdom. But as the scope of my searching broadened, I treasured these jewels of character less. Perhaps, as I became increasingly aware that easy solutions rarely exist, I wanted them more.

And so, the only failing going on was that I failed to ad-   6
just to my own changing perspective. Houses, forests, roller coasters, which seemed so immense and terrifying when we were small, shock us with their diminutiveness, even inade-quacy, when we return to them later. But we're just a little bigger, a little brasher, than we used to be.

Even the most educated human mind doesn't in itself have   7
the answer to everything. But as my own knowledge grew, I thought my father's was shrinking. No schoolbook taught me that a man's wisdom is not to be measured in facts.

When I was small, after late-night drives, my father car-   8
ried me gently up the long flight of stairs and into my room. He never missed a step when my eyelid cracked open, expos-ing my pretense. When I was equally small, he hid me in our clothes hamper, dirty towels draped over my head, during a family game of hide-and-seek. He hid my brother's Easter basket on the roof of our house, my mother's chocolate bars in the cellar so they wouldn't disappear so quickly, and my own beloved "little pillow" in a place I can only guess, when he felt it was time I graduate to bigger things. He enthusi-

astically responded to our pleas to stop at A & W drive-ins for a little "boot reer." And once he thrilled my brother, sister, and me beyond our wildest imaginings by bringing home a *three*-gallon container of ice cream. Our eyes bulged as much as the freezer.

Later the trips upstairs with tired children in his arms ended, but his love never did. I asked for a perfect participle. I received a perfect response, sometimes without the participle, always sincere. I wanted a square root. His answers were rooted in affection, encircling me in love. Unswerving and sure, his tender care was the firm ground held out to me as I shrieked along on the ups and downs. It braced as it embraced. 9

It's a hard way to learn, by retrospect—a sort of roller coaster ride all its own. But now I see how much of a man my father never ceased to be. He wasn't failing. His love, his laughter teach me still, uninhibited by barriers of time or space, now when I'm finally ready to learn. 10

The roller coaster still looks small, but my father once again appears as grand as ever, strong, warmhearted, and wonderfully wise. 11

Comment

Thoughts about the roller coaster, which awakens in Youngman the memory of a ride ten years earlier, lead to an early statement of her central idea or thesis. She develops that idea through a series of experiences that bring her father to life. Then she repeats her thesis—"It's a hard way to learn, by retrospect" (paragraph 10)—and concludes with a summary of the qualities she has explored. The essay expresses personal thoughts that are impossible to convey without examples. Though the examples are brief, Youngman gives us enough details to recreate her father's character and to give her ideas substance.

Questions for Study and Discussion

1. Where is the thesis first stated? How does Youngman restate it in paragraph 10, through the repeated reference to the roller-coaster?
2. In what way was her life with her father like a ride on a roller-coaster?
3. What had come as a shock to Youngman earlier? To what does she attribute this shock in paragraphs 5 and 6?
4. What personal qualities emerge in Youngman's telling of her experiences? What qualities does she call to the attention of the reader?

Vocabulary Study

Explain the following words in their context: *vestiges* (paragraph 3); *tête-à-tête* (paragraph 4); *perspective, diminutiveness, brasher* (paragraph 6); *retrospect, uninhibited* (paragraph 10).

Suggestions for Writing

1. Portray your father or mother or another relative through experiences that define the person's special qualities. Use this characterization to state an idea, as Youngman does. State the idea early in the essay, and restate it at the end.
2. Recast your essay, building to your idea or thesis through the experiences that define the special qualities.
3. Discuss your feelings and thoughts on discovering that one of your parents could not answer all of your questions. Draw a conclusion from the experience.

Robert Ramirez
The Woolen Sarape

Robert Ramirez was born in Edinburg, Texas, in 1950. He graduated from Pan American College, where he later taught freshman composition. He also taught elementary school and has worked as a photographer, a reporter, and an announcer for a television news department in Texas.

The train, its metal wheels squealing as they spin along the silvery tracks, rolls slower now. Through the gaps between the cars blinks a streetlamp, and this pulsing light on a barrio streetcorner beats slower, like a weary heartbeat, until the train shudders to a halt, the light goes out, and the barrio is deep asleep. 1

Throughout Aztlán (the Nahuatl term meaning "land to the north"), trains grumble along the edges of a sleeping people. From Lower California, through the blistering Southwest, down the Rio Grande to the muddy Gulf, the darkness and mystery of dreams engulf communities fenced off by railroads, canals, and expressways. Paradoxical communities, isolated from the rest of the town by concrete columned monuments of progress, and yet stranded in the past. They are surrounded by change. It eludes their reach, in their own backyards, and the people, unable and unwilling to see the future, or even touch the present, perpetuate the past. 2

Leaning from the expressway or jolting across the tracks, one enters a different physical world permeated by a different attitude. The physical dimensions are impressive. It is a large section of town which extends for fifteen blocks north and south along the tracks, and then advances eastward, thinning into nothingness beyond the city limits. Within the invisible (yet sensible) walls of the barrio, are many, many people liv- 3

Reprinted by permission of Robert Ramirez.

ing in too few houses. The homes, however, are much more numerous than on the outside.

Members of the barrio describe the entire area as their home. It is a home, but it is more than this. The barrio is a refuge from the harshness and the coldness of the Anglo world. It is a forced refuge. The leprous people are isolated from the rest of the community and contained in their section of town. The stoical pariahs of the barrio accept their fate, and from the angry seeds of rejection grow the flowers of closeness between outcasts, not the thorns of bitterness and the mad desire to flee. There is no want to escape, for the feeling of the barrio is known only to its inhabitants, and the material needs of life can also be found here.   4

The *tortillería*[1] fires up its machinery three times a day, producing steaming, round, flat slices of barrio bread. In the winter, the warmth of the tortilla factory is a wool *sarape*[2] in the chilly morning hours, but in the summer, it unbearably toasts every noontime customer.   5

The *panadería*[3] sends its sweet messenger aroma down the dimly lit street, announcing the arrival of fresh, hot sugary *pan dulce*.[4]   6

The small corner grocery serves the meal-to-meal needs of customers, and the owner, a part of the neighborhood, willingly gives credit to people unable to pay cash for foodstuffs.   7

The barbershop is a living room with hydraulic chairs, radio, and television, where old friends meet and speak of life as their salted hair falls aimlessly about them.   8

The pool hall is a junior level country club where *'chucos*,[5] strangers in their own land, get together to shoot pool and rap, while veterans, unaware of the cracking, popping balls   9

---

[1] *tortillería:* tortilla bake shop
[2] *sarape:* blanket or shawl
[3] *panadería:* bakery
[4] *pan dulce:* sweet bread or roll
[5] *'chucos: pachuco,* or Mexican (derogatory term)

on the green felt, complacently play dominoes beneath rudely hung *Playboy* foldouts.

The *cantina*[6] is the night spot of the barrio. It is the country club and the den where the rites of puberty are enacted. Here the young become men. It is in the taverns that a young dude shows his *machismo*[7] through the quantity of beer he can hold, the stories of *rucas*[8] he has had, and his willingness and ability to defend his image against hardened and scarred old lions.

No, there is no frantic wish to flee. It would be absurd to leave the familiar and nervously step into the strange and cold Anglo community when the needs of the Chicano can be met in the barrio.

The barrio is closeness. From the family living unit, familial relationships stretch out to immediate neighbors, down the block, around the corner, and to all parts of the barrio. The feeling of family, a rare and treasurable sentiment, pervades and accounts for the inability of the people to leave. The barrio is this attitude manifested on the countenances of the people, on the faces of their homes, and in the gaiety of their gardens.

The color-splashed homes arrest your eyes, arouse your curiosity, and make you wonder what life scenes are being played out in them. The flimsy, brightly colored, wood-frame houses ignore no neon-brilliant color. Houses trimmed in orange, chartreuse, lime-green, yellow, and mixtures of these and other hues beckon the beholder to reflect on the peculiarity of each home. Passing through this land is refreshing like Brubeck, not narcoticizing like revolting rows of similar houses, which neither offend nor please.

In the evenings, the porches and front yards are occupied with men calmly talking over the noise of children playing baseball in the unpaved extension of the living room, while

---

[6] *cantina:* tavern or saloon
[7] *machismo:* manhood
[8] *rucas:* girls

the women cook supper or gossip with female neighbors as they water the *jardines*.[9] The gardens mutely echo the expressive verses of the colorful houses. The denseness of multi-colored plants and trees gives the house the appearance of an oasis or a tropical island hideaway, sheltered from the rest of the world.

Fences are common in the barrio, but they are fences and not the walls of the Anglo community. On the western side of town, the high wooden fences between houses are thick, impenetrable walls, built to keep the neighbors at bay. In the barrio, the fences may be rusty, wire contraptions or thick green shrubs. In either case you can see through them and feel no sense of intrusion when you cross them.   15

Many lower-income families of the barrio manage to maintain a comfortable standard of living through the communal action of family members who contribute their wages to the head of the family. Economic need creates interdependence and closeness. Small barefooted boys sell papers on cool, dark Sunday mornings, deny themselves pleasantries, and give their earnings to *mamá*. The older the child, the greater the responsibility to help the head of the household provide for the rest of the family.   16

There are those, too, who for a number of reasons have not achieved a relative sense of financial security. Perhaps it results from too many children too soon, but it is the homes of these people and their situation that numbs rather than charms. Their houses, aged and bent, oozing children, are fissures in the horn of plenty. Their wooden homes may have brick-pattern asbestos tile on the outer walls, but the tile is not convincing.   17

Unable to pay city taxes or incapable in influencing the city to live up to its duty to serve all the citizens, the poorer barrio families remain trapped in the nineteenth century and survive as best they can. The backyards have well-worn paths to the outhouses, which sit near the alley. Running water is   18

---

[9] *jardines:* gardens

considered a luxury in some parts of the barrio. Decent drainage is usually unknown, and when it rains, the water stands for days, an incubator of health hazards and an avoidable nuisance. Streets, costly to pave, remain rough, rocky trails. Tires do not last long, and the constant rattling and shaking grind away a car's life and spread dust through screen windows.

The houses and their *jardines,* the jollity of the people in   19
an adverse world, the brightly feathered alarm clock pecking away at supper and cautiously eyeing the children playing nearby, produce a mystifying sensation at finding the noble savage alive in the twentieth century. It is easy to look at the positive qualities of life in the barrio, and look at them with a distantly envious feeling. One wishes to experience the feelings of the barrio and not the hardships. Remembering the illness, the hunger, the feeling of time running out on you, the walls, both real and imagined, reflecting on living in the past, one finds his envy becoming more elusive, until it has vanished altogether.

Back now beyond the tracks, the train creaks and groans,   20
the cars jostle each other down the track, and as the light begins its pulsing, the barrio, with all its meanings, greets a new dawn with yawns and restless stretchings.

Comment

Ramirez achieves unity in his description of the barrio by letting us see the barrio as an actual observer would. Once he introduces that point of view, with the reference to the train that approaches the barrio, he does not stray from it, and each part of the scene he describes is dealt with in enough detail for him to develop his impression or idea before he turns to another part. Through this detail Ramirez defines not only a place but a culture: the quality of life that distinguishes the barrio from other cultural worlds in the United States.

Questions for Study and Discussion

1. What statements and details show that Ramirez is writing to an audience unfamiliar with the barrio?
2. What qualities do the people of the barrio share? Does Ramirez show qualities or attitudes that mark them as individuals— as separate people living in the same neighborhood?
3. How does he introduce these qualities without disturbing his focus on the physical qualities of the barrio?
4. In what order are those physical qualities presented? Once the physical point of view is established, how does Ramirez remind us of it as the essay progresses?
5. What details of barrio life do you recognize in your own neighborhood, town, or city? In general, what similarities and differences are there between the barrio and your world?

Vocabulary Study

Write sentences of your own, using the following words to reveal their dictionary meanings: *paradoxical, permeated, stoical, pariahs, mutely, adverse.*

Suggestions for Writing

1. Discuss how the title of the essay contributes to the overall tone and point of view. Then analyze the order of ideas and development of the thesis.
2. Describe the prevailing culture, or variety of cultures, in a neighborhood or community you know well. Include the extent to which people of the neighborhood share a common language, perhaps a slang that protects them from the world outside. Give particular attention to their feelings and attitudes toward that outside world.

Topic Sentence

The phrase *topic sentence* describes usually the main or central idea of the paragraph—the idea that organizes details and subordinate ideas:

> The competition between man and beast is keenest in an event called bulldogging [*topic sentence*]. Riding alongside a steer, a cowboy must jump upon him from his horse while all three creatures are in full motion. He must grab the steer by the horns, bring him to a halt, and wrestle him to the ground. Since the steer weighs three or four times as much as the man, this is no easy task. When one of the wrestlers gets hurt, it's usually not the steer. The cowboys in this event are always young and strong, as are those in the various bucking contests. Only in calf roping do the older cowboys get a chance to stay active in the rodeo.— Ray Raphael, *Edges*

Not all paragraphs begin with a generalization like the one above. Some begin with a transitional statement that connects the paragraph to the previous one in the essay. The following paragraph begins with a descriptive statement that introduces a series of visual observations of western Scotland:

> The train bucked and turned north at Arisaig. The bays were like crater crusts filled with water. And offshore islands: Rhum, Eigg, Muck, and Canna—names like items from a misspelled menu. The Scour of Eigg was a hatchet shape against the sky. And now beneath the train there was a basin of green fields for three miles to the Sound of Sleat—and above the train were mountains of cracked rock and swatches of purple heather. Suddenly a horse was silhouetted in the sun, cropping grass beside the sea.—Paul Theroux, *The Kingdom by the Sea*

Placed at the start of the paragraph, perhaps following a transitional sentence, the topic sentence guides the reader's attention. However, the topic sentence may appear anywhere in the paragraph—at the beginning, in the middle, or at the end. The following paragraph is typical of those which open with a series of facts or details and lead into a more significant fact—the topic idea or sentence:

> The first transcontinental New Year's excess occurred in 1894– 95 when Amos Alonzo Stagg took his University of Chicago team to Los Angeles to play Stanford. The trip served as a multifaceted precedent for intercollegiate football. The distance travelled (6,200 miles), the duration (three weeks) and the trip's national publicity all served to demonstrate the possibilities of such intercollegiate games. When the teams from the two young universities met at the turn of the year far from either campus and for no discernible educational purpose, the modern bowl concept was established [*topic sentence*].—Robin Lester, "The Bowl as Cathedral"

Beginning your paragraphs with the topic sentence will help you organize the details and the many ideas coherently. In writing or revising your paragraph, you may decide to restate the topic idea, for new details and ideas may occur to you in recording your experiences and thinking about their meaning.

Francine Prose

Gossip

Francine Prose was born in Brooklyn, New York, attended Rad-cliffe College, and taught creative writing at Harvard. Her arti-cles have appeared in *Mademoiselle, The Atlantic Monthly, The New York Times,* and other periodicals. Her many novels include *The Glorious Ones, Household Saints,* and *Judah the Pious* which re-ceived the Jewish Book Council Award. Her most recent novel is *Hungry Hearts* (1983). Her essay on gossip makes an interest-ing and unusual point about a much criticized activity.

Once I met a woman who grew up in the small North Carolina town to which Chang and Eng, the original Sia-mese twins, retired after their circus careers. When I asked her how the town reacted to the twins marrying local girls and setting up adjacent households, she laughed and said: "Honey, that was *nothing* compared to what happened *before* the twins got there. Get the good gossip on any little moun-tain town, scratch the surface and you'll find a snake pit!" ·

Surely she was exaggerating; one assumes the domestic arrangements of a pair of Siamese twins and their families would cause a few ripples anywhere. And yet the truth of what she said seemed less important than the glee with which she said it, her pride in the snake pit she'd come from, in its his-tory, its scandals, its legacy of "good gossip." Gossip, the jui-cier the better, was her heritage, her birthright; that town, with its social life freakish enough to make Chang and Eng's seem mundane, was part of who she was.

Gossip must be nearly as old as language itself. It was, I imagine, the earliest recreational use of the spoken word. First the cave man learned to describe the location of the plumpest

---

bison, then he began to report and speculate on the doings of his neighbors in the cave next door. And yet, for all its antiquity, gossip has rarely received its due; its very name connotes idleness, time-wasting, frivolity and worse. Gossip is the unacknowledged poor relative of civilized conversation: Almost everyone does it but hardly anyone will admit to or defend it; and of these only the smallest and most shameless fraction will own up to enjoying it.

My mother and her friends are eloquent on the subject   4
and on the distinction between gossiping and exchanging information: "John got a new job," is, they say, information. "Hey, did you hear John got fired?" is gossip; which is, they agree, predominantly scurrilous, mean-spirited. That's the conventional wisdom on gossip and why it's so tempting to disown. Not long ago I heard myself describe a friend, half-jokingly, as "a much better person than I am, that is, she doesn't gossip so much." I heard my voice distorted by that same false note that sometimes creeps into it when social strain and some misguided notion of amiability make me assent to opinions I don't really share. What in the world was I talking about?

I don't, of course, mean rumor-mongering, outright   5
slander, willful fabrication meant to damage and undermine. But rather, ordinary gossip, incidents from and analyses of the lives of our heroes and heroines, our relatives, acquaintances and friends. The fact is, I love gossip, and beyond that, I believe in it—in its purposes, its human uses.

I'm even fond of the word, its etymology, its origins in   6
the Anglo-Saxon term "godsibbe" for god-parent, relative, its meaning widening by the Renaissance to include friends, cronies and later what one *does* with one's cronies. One gossips. Paring away its less flattering modern connotations, we discover a kind of synonym for connection, for community, and this, it seems to me, is the primary function of gossip. It maps our ties, reminds us of what sort of people we know and what manner of lives they lead, confirms our sense of who we are, how we live and where we have come from. The roots of the

grapevine are inextricably entwined with our own. Who knows how much of our sense of the world has reached us on its branches, how often, as babies, we dropped off to sleep to the rhythms of family gossip? I've often thought that gossip's bad name might be cleared by calling it "oral tradition"; for what, after all, is an oral tradition but the stories of other lives, other eras, legends from a time when human traffic with spirits and gods was considered fit material for gossipy speculation?

Older children gossip; adolescents certainly do. Except in the case of those rare toddler-fabulists, enchanting parents and siblings with fairy tales made up on the spot, gossip may be the way that most of us learn to tell stories. And though, as Gertrude Stein is supposed to have told Hemingway, gossip is not literature, some similar criteria may apply to both. Pacing, tone, clarity and authenticity are as essential for the reportage of neighborhood news as they are for well-made fiction.

Perhaps more important is gossip's analytical component. Most people—I'm leaving out writers, psychologists and probably some large proportion of the academic and service professions—are, at least in theory, free to go about their lives without feeling the compulsion to endlessly dissect the minutiae of human motivation. They can indulge in this at their leisure, for pleasure, in their gossip. And while there are those who clearly believe that the sole aim of gossip is to criticize, to condemn (or, frequently, to titillate, to bask in the aura of scandal as if it were one's own), I prefer to see gossip as a tool of understanding. It only takes a moment to tell what someone did. Far more mileage—and more enjoyment—can be extracted from debating why he did it. Such questions, impossible to discuss without touching on matters of choice and consequence, responsibility and will, are, one might argue, the beginnings of moral inquiry, first steps toward a moral education. It has always seemed peculiar that a pastime so conducive to the moral life should be considered faintly immoral.

I don't mean to deny the role of plain nosiness in all this,   9
of unadorned curiosity about our neighbors' secrets. And curiosity (where would we be without it?) has, like gossip, come
in for some negative press. Still, it's understandable; everyone
wants to gossip, hardly anyone wants to be gossiped about.
What rankles is the fear that our secrets will be revealed, some
essential privacy stripped away and, of course, the lack of
control over what others say. Still, such talk is unavoidable;
it's part of human nature, of the human community. When
one asks, "What's the gossip?" it's that community that is being
affirmed.

So I continue to ask, mostly without apology and espe-   10
cially when I'm talking to friends who still live in places I've
moved away from. And when they answer—recalling the personalities, telling the stories, the news—I feel as close as I ever
will to the lives we shared, to what we know and remember
in common, to those much-missed, familiar and essentially
beneficent snake pits I've lived in and left behind.

Comment

Francine Prose builds to her topic sentences in her introductory paragraphs, but the remaining paragraphs begin with topic
sentences that state the subject of the paragraph, or its central or
topic idea. She also builds the opening paragraphs to a statement
of her general thesis in paragraph 3, in which she characterizes gossip. The topic sentences that follow fix our attention on this word.

Questions for Study and Discussion

1. Which are the topic sentences of paragraph 1 and 2? How does
   Prose begin these paragraphs?
2. Which topic sentences state only the subject of their paragraphs and which state the central or topic idea of the entire
   essay?
3. "Civilized" is the key word in Prose's thesis statement in para-

graph 3. How does her definition of gossip in paragraph 6 explain this word?

4. How is gossip different from "rumor-mongering" and slander, discussed in paragraph 5? Why would Prose consider these kinds of talk uncivilized?
5. How does the discussion of children and adolescents develop the thesis? Why does Prose make the point that gossip has the qualities of good fiction?
6. How does paragraph 8 explain the "analytical component" of gossip?
7. How does Prose explain the fact that gossip is considered "faintly immoral"(paragraph 8)? And how does her discussion of this point in paragraph 9 further develop her thesis?
8. How is the concluding paragraph related to the opening ones? What reminder of her thesis does she give the reader?

Vocabulary Study

1. Examine the history of the word *gossip* in the *Oxford English Dictionary*. What support does this history give to the points Prose makes about gossip?
2. Use your standard dictionary to distinguish gossip as Prose defines it from the following:
   a. rumor
   b. hearsay
   c. libel
   d. slander

Suggestions for Writing

1. Illustrate Prose's definition of gossip through your talk with friends and family. Distinguish the kinds of talk you engage in, using the words you looked up in your dictionary.
2. Prose states: "Older children gossip; adolescents certainly do." Discuss similarities or differences in the talk you have observed in children and adolescents. Draw a conclusion from your analysis—a thesis that the various ideas and details of your discussion develop. You might build to a statement of this thesis at the end, or you might place it in the opening paragraphs, as Prose does.

Michael Nelson
The Desk

Michael Nelson, born in 1951, has taught political science at
Vanderbilt University. He previously worked as a VISTA volunteer in the Georgia Legal Services Program, as television
moderator in Augusta, Georgia, and as editor of *The Washington
Monthly*. He has written numerous magazine articles on American government and politics, and is a frequent contributor to the
Washington Post Magazine and the *Baltimore Sun*.

When editorial writers and politicians discuss bureau-   1
cracy, they talk about it with a capital B—the massive, face-
less, redtape-clogged Bureaucracy of chamber of commerce
after-dinner speeches. But when I think of bureaucracy, I think
of Martha.

Martha is a retired woman who lives in Augusta, Ga. She   2
survives, but barely, on a small social-security retirement check.
A friend once told her that because her income was so low,
Martha was also eligible for Supplemental Security Income
(SSI). Reluctantly—she is a proud woman—Martha applied.

There is a desk in the Augusta Social Security Adminis-   3
tration office; Martha sat down on the "client's" side of it.
She was, she timidly told the caseworker who sat opposite
her, at her wit's end. She just couldn't make ends meet, not
with today's prices. She had never asked anyone for charity
before—he had to understand that—but she needed help and
had heard that she was entitled to some.

The caseworker understood. Gently, he asked Martha the   4
questions he needed to fill out her application. Everything was
in order—except why did she have this $2,000 savings ac-
count? For her burial, she told him. She had always dreaded
dying as a ward of the state, so for almost 50 years she had

saved—a dollar a week when she had it—to finance her own funeral.

But, the caseworker said, we aren't allowed to give SSI to people with more than $1,500 in the bank; that's the law. Don't be silly; the law couldn't apply to burial money, said Martha, scared and defensive in her embarrassment. The caseworker saw her point, but there was nothing he could do; the law did not—and realistically could not—distinguish between money for funerals and money for high living. Anxious to help, he advised her to go out and blow $500 on a color television—or anything—just to bring her savings down to $1,500. Then, he said, she would be eligible for SSI. Appalled by this perverse advice, Martha left.

Martha is one of several dozen people I have talked to over the past three years, ordinary people from a variety of regions, classes and backgrounds. I talked with them because, as a political scientist and a political journalist, I was interested in finding out what the world of government and politics looks like from the citizens'-eye view. To my surprise, that world contained little of the issues and personalities that pollsters ask about and pundits fulminate about. Instead, it was a world dominated by bureaucracy—not Bureaucracy, mind you, but rather the specific government agencies that these citizens had to deal with in their personal lives—too often, they felt, and with too little satisfaction.

Most ironic was the image of government that was born of these experiences. As any scholarly treatise on the subject will tell you, the great advantage bureaucracy is supposed to offer a complex, modern society like ours is efficient, rational, uniform and courteous treatment for the citizens it deals with. Yet not only did these qualities not come through to the people I talked with, it was their very opposites that seemed more characteristic. People of all classes—the rich man dealing with the Internal Revenue Service as well as the poor woman struggling with the welfare department—felt that the treatment they had received had been bungled, not efficient; unpredictable, not rational; discriminatory or idiosyncratic, not uniform; and, all too often, insensitive, rather than courteous. It was as if they had bought a big new car that not only did not run when they wanted it to, but periodically revved itself up and drove all around their yards.

Are they right? Would that things were that simple. But   8 we taxpayers can't even make up our minds what the problem is with bureaucrats: are they lazy do-nothings, snoozing afternoons away behind the sports section, or wild-eyed do-everythings who can't *ever* sleep unless they have forced some poor soul to rearrange his life to conform with one of their crazy social theories?

As for the bureaucrats, they seem no less blinded by an-   9 ger than we. Frequently, they dismiss the unhappy citizens they deal with as sufferers of what one political scientist calls "bureausis"—a childish inability to cope with even the simplest, most reasonable rules and regulations. Like children, they add, we demand a lot but expect somebody else to pay.

Yet there are no callous bureaucrats or "bureautics" in   10 Martha's story, nor were there in most of the stories I heard. What there is, though, is a desk. On one side of it sits the citizen—a whole person who wants to be treated as a whole person. Special consideration? Of course. Bend the rules a little? Certainly, I'm unique. And she is unique, as is every other person who approaches government from her side of the desk.

Across from her sits the bureaucrat. His perspective is   11 entirely different. He is there not as a friend or neighbor, but purely as the representative of his agency, an agency whose only business is to execute the law. His job is to fit this person across the desk into a category: legally eligible for the agency's services or not; if so, for what and on what terms? He cannot, *must* not, look at the whole person, but only at those features that enable him to transform her into a "case," a "file," a "client" for his agency. That way she can count on getting exactly what any other citizen in her category would get from the government—nothing more, nothing less. And do we really want it any different? Would we rather that low-level bureaucrats had the power to give or refuse public services purely as they saw fit?

The desk, whether physical or metaphorical, is there in 12 every encounter between Americans and their government. It turns unique and deserving citizens into snarling clients, and goodhearted civil servants into sullen automatons. More than anything else, I suspect, it explains why we and our government are at each other's throats—why taxpayers pass Proposition 13s and public employees strike like dock workers. *It is the bureaucracy problem, and if what I heard from the people I talked with is representative, the bureaucracy problem is the crisis of our age.*

I only wish I had the solution. 13

Comment

A reading of only the topic sentences will show that they contain the ideas of the essay in miniature: the reader discovers not only what the essay is about but also what conclusions Nelson draws from the episode he describes. The whole essay builds from an experience—which Nelson considers representative of bureaucracy and its effects—to general conclusions. Notice that he does not claim to have the solution to the problem of bureaucracy. Identifying the problem is sometimes a step toward a solution; such an identification is his purpose in writing.

Questions for Study and Discussion

1. Do any of the topic sentences state the thesis of the essay? What is that thesis?
2. How does Nelson establish his authority on the subject of bureaucracy? How does he seek to persuade you that Martha's experience is a typical one?
3. What does Nelson mean by *bureaucracy*? Does he define this word formally, or does the episode with Martha, together with other details in the essay, provide an indirect definition?

4. Look up the word *metaphorical*. What does Nelson mean by the statement that the desk is both physical and metaphorical?
5. What distinction is Nelson making in paragraph 6 between *bureaucracy* and *Bureaucracy*? What would the second kind of bureaucracy constitute?
6. Do you believe Nelson is right in saying that "the bureaucracy problem is the crisis of our age"? Have you personally experienced such a problem, whether in government or at school? Do you find similar bureaucratic actions or treatment in institutions outside the government—in school offices, or the public library, and the like?
7. What other current social or political issues has Nelson raised in the course of examining government bureaucracy?

Vocabulary Study

1. Explain the difference in the meaning in the contrasted words in the following sentence: "People of all classes—the rich man dealing with the Internal Revenue Service as well as the poor woman struggling with the welfare department—felt that the treatment they had received had been *bungled*, not *efficient; unpredictable*, not *rational; discriminatory* or *idiosyncratic*, not *uniform;* and, all too often, *insensitive*, rather than *courteous*."
2. Explain how the word in parentheses changes the meaning of the original sentence:
    a. "*Appalled* (surprised) by this *perverse* (mistaken) advice, Martha left."
    b. "Most *ironic* (contradictory) was the image of government that was born of these experiences."
    c. "Across from her sits the bureaucrat. His *perspective* (attitude) is entirely different."
    d. "It turns *unique* (special) and deserving citizens into *snarling* (angry) clients, and goodhearted civil servants into *sullen automatons* (sleepy officials)."

Suggestions for Writing

1. Describe an experience with a government agency or official that shaped or changed your attitude toward government in general. Build from the experience to a statement of its effect

on you. Draw some conclusions about the problem of government and the citizen, as Nelson does.

2. Describe a series of experiences that shaped your present attitude to the college you now attend. Vary these experiences as much as you can, instead of writing about only positive or only negative ones. Comment on the motives of the people you encountered.

3. Nelson does not state solutions for the problem, but he does imply some. Discuss what these solutions are—and also any other solutions you would propose.

Order of Ideas

Ideas in the paragraph as well as in the whole essay can be presented or ordered in various ways. Certain kinds of writing have their own order. Descriptions are *spatial*—perhaps moving from foreground to background, or from top to bottom, or from side to side:

> Once we even saw a giraffe, but miles, miles away from us, alone under the clear sky among the thorn trees on the horizon, and we could see its silhouetted head and long neck turned to watch us; it seemed very lonely, very small, and very far away on the yellow flats; when the noise of our trucks reached it, it was frightened and began to run, heaving itself up and down. It ran away from us for a long time and got even smaller but never out of sight. At last it reached the horizon.—Elizabeth Marshall Thomas, *The Harmless People*

Narrative presents events chronologically—in the order of *time*. The paragraph just quoted combines description with narrative: the writer presents the sighting of the giraffe, the movement of the trucks, the flight of the animal in their temporal order. In reporting an experience or explaining a process, the facts or steps are also presented as they occur. To a person learning to drive, for example, you would not explain how to turn corners until you had explained how to brake and steer.

In expository and persuasive writing ideas may be presented in numerous ways. The principle kind of order usually will depend on the reader's knowledge of the subject, the purpose of the paragraph or essay, and the subject itself. For example, in describing the care of an automobile, you would probably describe simple procedures before describing complex ones—especially if your readers are owners of new models. In training mechanics to repair a new kind of engine, you might proceed from the most common to the most unusual problems mechanics are likely to encounter.

In the following definition of the potlach, a ceremony in which Indians of the Northwest dispose of property, the author clearly has his readers in mind in presenting details of the ceremony in the order of *importance:*

> A proper potlach involved prodigious displays of eating, since it was a point of honor with the host to provide much more food than his guests could consume. The eating would last for days, interspersed with singing, belching, speech-making, dramatic performances and the ceremonial conferring of honorific names. But the vital part of the occasion was the bestowing of gifts— bowls, boxes, baskets, blankets, canoes, ornaments, sculptures— that the chief had collected among his people, from each according to his ability, and now distributed among his guests, to each according to his rank.—Frederic V. Grunfeld, "Indian Giving"

The greater the drama of the event, the greater our sense of *climax*—of increasing importance or intensity as the paragraph or essay moves to the end.

Some paragraphs (and essays) move from *question* to *answer:*

> How wide is the scope of physical law? Do life, thought, history fall within its orderly domain? Or does it describe only the inanimate, the remote and the very tiny? It is the claim of contemporary physics that its laws apply to all natural things, to atoms, stars and men. There are not two worlds: the cold, precise mechanical world of physics, and the surprising, disorderly and growing world of living things or of human existence. They are one.—Philip Morrison, "Cause, Chance and Creation"

A related order is the movement from *problem* to *solution*. The following paragraph explains why animals and plants vary the times of the day or night at which they perform activities:

> We think we have the answer to why the rhythms often appear to run fast or slow under these unchanging conditions. To the organism placed in the laboratory at a constant level of light and temperature these two factors will continue to have the most impact during the sensitive phase of its twenty-four-hour cycle of responsiveness to the environment. These two factors in effect will appear, therefore, to the organism to show a daily variation, but now the light and temperature cycles will seem to have become inverted. Thus, during the sensitive period of its cycle—which normally falls at night—it will interpret the increased effectiveness of the light and temperature as indicating daytime. Employing the same splendidly adaptive machinery it uses in nature to reset its rhythm until the sensitive portion comes to fall in the darker, cooler nighttime, the organism keeps resetting its sensitivity rhythm a little forward, or backward, regularly each day in a futile attempt to adjust to the illusory "day–night cycles."—Frank A. Brown, Jr., "Life's Mysterious Clocks"

Some paragraphs move from the *specific* to the *general,* as in Robin Lester's paragraph on bowl games quoted earlier (p. 20). However, paragraphs commonly open with a general idea and develop it through specific details:

> The barrio is closeness. From the family living unit, familial relationships stretch out to immediate neighbors, down the block, around the corner, and to all parts of the barrio. The feeling of family, a rare and treasurable sentiment, pervades and accounts for the inability of the people to leave. The barrio is this attitude manifested on the countenances of the people, on the faces of their homes, and in the gaiety of their gardens.—Robert Ramirez, "The Woolen Sarape"

As our first example shows, paragraphs usually combine various orders—the spatial arrangement of details with the chronological presentation of events. A paragraph may, in addition, show that the events increase in importance or intensity. In writing your own paragraphs and essays, you may discover better ways of presenting your details and ideas as you see the paragraph or essay take shape. Usually the order of ideas in a paragraph depends on the order you discover is best for the whole essay.

Sue Hubbell
Felling Trees

Sue Hubbell writes in this essay about outdoor life—in particular, the experience of cutting down trees for firewood. In describing the process of woodcutting, she tells us much about day-to-day country life and the chores at which everyone must be competent.

I was out in the woods early in the morning cutting firewood for the winter. I do that every day this time of year. For an hour or two I cut wood, load it into the pickup and carry it back to my cabin and stack it. It isn't such a tiring job when I do a bit of it each day, before it gets hot, and I like being out there at that hour, when the woods are fresh and fragrant. 1

This morning I finished sawing up a tree from the place where I had been cutting for the past week. In the process I lost my screwrench, part screwdriver, part wrench, that I use to make adjustments on my chain saw. I shouldn't carry it in my pocket, but the chain had been loose; I had tightened it and had not walked back to the truck to put the wrench away. Scolding myself for being so careless, I began looking for another tree to cut and found a big one that had recently died. 2

I like to cut the dead trees from my woodlot, leaving the ones still alive to flourish, but this one was bigger than I feel comfortable about felling. I've been running a chain saw and cutting my own firewood for six years now, but I am still awed by the size and weight of a tree as it crashes to the ground. I have to nerve myself to cut the really big ones. I wanted this tree to fall onto a stretch of open ground that was free of other trees and brush, so I cut a wedge-shaped notch on that side 3 of it. The theory is that the tree, thus weakened, will fall slowly on the side of the notch when the serious cut, slightly above the notch on the other side, is made. The trouble is that trees, particularly dead ones that may have rot on the inside, do not know the theory and may fall in an unexpected direction. That is the way accidents happen.

I was aware of that and was scared, besides, to be cutting   4
down such a big tree; as a result, perhaps, I cut too timid a wedge. I started sawing through on the other side, keeping an eye on the treetop to detect the characteristic tremble of a tree about to fall. I did not have time to jam the plastic wedge in my back pocket into the cut to hold it open because the tree began to sway and started to fall in my direction. I killed the engine on the saw and jumped out of the way.

There was no danger, however. Directly in back of where   5
I had been standing were a number of other trees, which was why I had wanted to have the dead one fall the other way, and as it started down, its top branches snagged. I had sawed completely through the tree, but now the butt end had trapped the saw against the stump. I had cut what is descriptively called a widow maker. If I had been cutting with someone else, we could have used the second saw to free mine and perhaps brought the tree down, but it is dangerous and I don't like to do it. I couldn't even free my saw by taking it apart, for I had lost my screwrench, so I drove back to the barn, gathered up the tools I needed, a socket wrench, chains and a portable winch known as a come-along.

The day was warming and I was sweating by the time I   6
got back to the woods, but I was determined to repair the botch I had made. Using the socket wrench, I removed the bar and chain from the saw and set the saw body aside. The weight of the saw gone, I worked the bar and chain free from under the butt of the tree. Then I spat and drank ice water from my thermos and figured out how I was going to pull down the tree with chain and winch.

The come-along is a cheery, sensible tool for a woman.   7
It has a big hook at one end and a hook connected to a steel

cable at the other. The cable is wound around a ratchet gear operated by a long handle to give leverage. It divides a heavy job into small, manageable bits that require no more than female strength, and I have used it many times to pull my pickup free from a mudhole. I decided that if I wound a chain around the butt of the widow maker and another chain around a nearby standing tree and connected the two with the comealong, I might be able to winch the felled tree to the ground. I attached the chains and come-along appropriately and began. Slowly, with each pump of the handle against the ratchet gear, the tree sank to the ground. The sun was high, the heat oppressive, and my sweatshirt was soaked with sweat, so I decided to leave the job of cutting up the tree to firewood lengths until tomorrow. I gathered up my tools and, in the process, found the screwrench almost hidden in leaf mold.

I am good friends with a woman who lives across the hollow. She and her husband sell cordwood to the charcoal factory in town. Her husband cuts the logs because a chain saw, in the Ozarks, is regarded as a man's tool, and she helps him load and unload the logs. Even though the wood is going to be turned into charcoal, it is traditional to cut it to four-foot lengths. A four-foot oak log is heavy; a strong man can lift it, but a woman has to use all her strength to do her part. My friend returns from her mornings sick with exhaustion, her head throbbing. She and I talk sometimes about how it would be if women were the woodcutters: the length would be less than four feet. Having to do work beyond her strength makes my friend feel weak, ineffectual, dependent and cross.

My friend, and other Ozark women, often ask me curiously about my chain saw. Most people out here heat with wood, and if families in the suburbs quarrel about taking out the garbage, here the source of squabbles is getting enough firewood cut early in the year so that it can season. Women usually help by carrying the cut wood to the truck, but it is the men who cut the wood, and since the women think they cannot cut it, they frequently worry and sometimes nag about it.

My female Ozark friends envy me having my firewood   10
supply under my own control, and they are interested when
I tell then that they have had the hardest part of the job anyway, carrying the wood to the trucks. Cutting the wood into
lengths with the chain saw is not hard work, although it does
require some skill. So far, however, my friends have not taken
up my offer to come over so that I can give them a lesson in
using a chain saw. Forty years ago chain saws were heavy
and certainly beyond the strength of a woman to use; today
they are much improved and light. My saw is a small, light
one, but with its 16-inch bar it is big enough to cut any tree
I want to fell.

I know that feeling of helplessness and irritation that my   11
friends have, for that is the way I used to be. Like many
women my age, I would stand back and let a man change a
flat tire. I could press a button on a washing machine but not
fix the machine if something failed. I felt uneasy with tools
other than a needle, a typewriter or kitchen utensils.

When I began living here alone I had to learn how to   12
break down work into parcels that I could perform with my
strength and I had to learn to use tools that I had never used
and use them easily. Either that, or I would have had to leave.
It was the hardest schooling I've ever taken but the most ex-
hilarating. When there were Things in the world too heavy
to move where I wanted them to be and too mysterious to
be kept doing what I wanted them to do, I was filled with
dissatisfaction and petulance. Those Things controlled me.

I prefer it the other way around.   13

Comment

The personal truth to which Hubbell builds her essay will have
no meaning for the reader without the extended example she gives
in her account of cutting firewood. To make her experiences clear
to the reader who knows nothing about woodcutting, she com-

bines several kinds of exposition: she defines the "come-along," describes the process of cutting down a tree, analyzes why trees fall in unexpected directions, and compares her woodcutting with that of the woman who lives nearby. For the reader experienced in woodcutting, she might have chosen another order of ideas.

Questions for Study and Discussion

1. What is the idea or truth that Hubbell illustrates through the felling of trees? How do the details of the essay illustrate this idea?
2. How different would the effect of the essay be if she had stated her purpose and central idea at the beginning?
3. Were the essay directed to readers experienced in woodcutting, what might Hubbell have omitted and how might she have reorganized the essay?
4. What personal qualities emerge in the course of the essay—particularly in the description of the tree cuttings? Which of these qualities stand out most?
5. Is Hubbell arguing for a change in attitude toward women like herself, or is she merely contrasting her own life with that of her female neighbors?

Vocabulary Study

Be ready to discuss how the details of the essay or the dictionary help you understand the following terms:

a. *widow maker*
b. *come-along*
c. *screwrench*

Suggestions for Writing

1. Develop the central idea of Hubbell's essay through an extended example of your own. You might build to the idea through your example as Hubbell does or begin the essay through a statement of the idea.
2. Develop one of the following through examples drawn from personal experience:
   a. I have known people to stop and buy an apple on the cor-

ner and then walk away as if they had solved the whole
unemployment problem.—Heywood Broun
b.   If you have to keep reminding yourself of a thing, perhaps
it isn't so.—Christopher Morley
c.   There is no substitute for talent. Industry and all the virtues are of no avail.—Aldous Huxley

Harold Krents
Darkness at Noon

Harold Krents graduated from Harvard College and later studied law at Oxford University and Harvard Law School. He has
been practising law since 1971. Krents was the prototype for the
blind boy in Leonard Gershe's play (and the later film) *Butterflies
Are Free*. His experiences at Harvard are the subject of the film
Riding on the Wind. Krents has long been active in organizations
and government agencies concerned with the employment of
handicapped people.

Blind from birth, I have never had the opportunity to see   1
myself and have been completely dependent on the image I
create in the eye of the observer. To date it has not been nar-
cissistic.

There are those who assume that since I can't see, I ob-   2
viously also cannot hear. Very often people will converse with
me at the top of their lungs, enunciating each word very carefully. Conversely, people will also often whisper, assuming that
since my eyes don't work, my ears don't either.

For example, when I go to the airport and ask the ticket   3
agent for assistance to the plane, he or she will invariably pick
up the phone, call a ground hostess and whisper: "Hi, Jane,
we've got a 76 here." I have concluded that the word "blind"

is not used for one of two reasons: Either they fear that if the dread word is spoken, the ticket agent's retina will immediately detach, or they are reluctant to inform me of my condition of which I may not have been previously aware.

On the other hand, others know that of course I can hear, but believe that I can't talk. Often, therefore, when my wife and I go out to dinner, a waiter or waitress will ask Kit if "*he* would like a drink" to which I respond that "indeed *he* would."

This point was graphically driven home to me while we were in England. I had been given a year's leave of absence from my Washington law firm to study for a diploma in law degree at Oxford University. During the year I became ill and was hospitalized. Immediately after admission, I was wheeled down to the X-ray room. Just at the door sat an elderly woman—elderly I would judge from the sound of her voice. "What is his name?" the woman asked the orderly who had been wheeling me.

"What's your name?" the orderly repeated to me.

"Harold Krents," I replied.

"Harold Krents," he repeated.

"When was he born?"

"When were you born?"

"November 5, 1944," I responded.

"November 5, 1944," the orderly intoned.

This procedure continued for approximately five minutes at which point even my saint-like disposition deserted me. "Look," I finally blurted out, "this is absolutely ridiculous. Okay, granted I can't see, but it's got to have become pretty clear to both of you that I don't need an interpreter."

"He says he doesn't need an interpreter," the orderly reported to the woman.

The toughest misconception of all is the view that because I can't see, I can't work. I was turned down by over forty law firms because of my blindness, even though my qualifications included a cum laude degree from Harvard College and a good ranking in my Harvard Law School class.

The attempt to find employment, the continuous frustration of being told that it was impossible for a blind person to practice law, the rejection letters, not based on my lack of ability but rather on my disability, will always remain one of the most disillusioning experiences of my life.

Fortunately, this view of limitation and exclusion is beginning to change. On April 16, the Department of Labor issued regulations that mandate equal-employment opportunities for the handicapped. By and large, the business community's response to offering employment to the disabled has been enthusiastic.   17

I therefore look forward to the day, with the expectation that it is certain to come, when employers will view their handicapped workers as a little child did me years ago when my family still lived in Scarsdale.   18

I was playing basketball with my father in our backyard according to procedures we had developed. My father would stand beneath the hoop, shout, and I would shoot over his head at the basket attached to our garage. Our next-door neighbor, aged five, wandered over into our yard with a playmate. "He's blind," our neighbor whispered to her friend in a voice that could be heard distinctly by Dad and me. Dad shot and missed; I did the same. Dad hit the rim: I missed entirely: Dad shot and missed the garage entirely. "Which one is blind?" whispered back the little friend.   19

I would hope that in the near future when a plant manager is touring the factory with the foreman and comes upon a handicapped and nonhandicapped person working together, his comment after watching them work will be, "Which one is disabled?"   20

Comment

Krents wants to do more than state and describe the difficulties of being blind: he wants his reader to understand these difficulties as fully as possible. The essay is organized with this purpose in mind.

The three misconceptions about blindness might have been presented in a different order: the order Krents chooses helps us to appreciate the bizarre situation of losing one's sight and being treated as if speech and hearing were lost too. Krents moves from problem to solution: this is the general principle of organization in the essay. A notable quality is the proportion of examples to discussion—just enough are provided to illustrate each of the ideas. Krents selects his details carefully, for they must be striking enough to make his points vividly and clearly.

Questions for Study and Discussion

1. In what paragraph does Krents state the basis for his ordering of the three misconceptions? How does this order help us to appreciate the bizarre situation created by blindness? How does the change in tone in paragraph 15 accord with the order of ideas?
2. What is his thesis? Does he state it directly, or is it implied?
3. What are the implied causes of the problems described? Does Krents state or imply a solution for them?
4. What attitudes and feelings does Krents express in the final anecdote?
5. Do you find the organization of ideas successful, or would you have organized them in a different way?

Vocabulary Study

Use your dictionary to distinguish the differences in meaning in the following series of words. Write a sentence using each of the words according to its dictionary meaning. The first word in each series is Krents's:

    a. *narcissistic* (paragraph 1), *vain, conceited, proud*
    b. *enunciating* (paragraph 2), *pronouncing*
    c. *graphically* (paragraph 5), *sharply, starkly, vividly*
    d. *disillusioning* (paragraph 16), *disappointing, frustrating*

Suggestions for Writing

1. Discuss the effect that a permanent or temporary handicap or disability has had on your life, or discuss problems you have

observed in the life of a disabled or handicapped friend or relative. You may want to organize your essay as Krents does—working from a problem to a solution. Note that the solution need not be complete or permanent; you may want to discuss the extent to which the problems described can be solved.

2. Krents writes about his blindness with humor. Discuss how he achieves that humor and what it tells you about his view of himself and people in general.

3. Describe an embarrassing experience of your own—how it came about, the persons involved in it, its outcome. Then discuss its causes, focusing on the most important of them.

James Thurber

The Princess and the Tin Box

James Thurber (1894–1961) was born in Columbus, Ohio. He attended Ohio State University for three years, and later worked for the U.S. State Department as a code clerk. From 1920 to 1925 he worked as a journalist on the *Columbus Dispatch* and *Chicago Tribune*. His long association with *The New Yorker* began in 1925, the year it began publication, and most of his stories, sketches, and cartoons appeared in that magazine. Thurber was a humorist and a satirist of many aspects of American life, in particular the relations of the sexes. His many books include *My Life and Hard Times* (1933), *Fables for Our Time* (1943), *The Thurber Carnival* (1945), and *Thurber Country* (1953).

Once upon a time, in a far country, there lived a king   1
whose daughter was the prettiest princess in the world. Her

From *The Beast in Me—and Other Animals* by James Thurber, published by Harcourt Brace Jovanovich. Copyright © 1948 James Thurber. Originally printed in *The New Yorker*.

eyes were like the cornflower, her hair was sweeter than the hyacinth, and her throat made the swan look dusty.

From the time she was a year old, the princess had been 2 showered with presents. Her nursery looked like Cartier's window. Her toys were all made of gold or platinum or diamonds or emeralds. She was not permitted to have wooden blocks or china dolls or rubber dogs or linen books, because such materials were considered cheap for the daughter of a king.

When she was seven, she was allowed to attend the wed- 3 ding of her brother and throw real pearls at the bride instead of rice. Only the nightingale, with his lyre of gold, was permitted to sing for the princess. The common blackbird, with his boxwood flute, was kept out of the palace grounds. She walked in silver-and-samite slippers to a sapphire-and-topaz bathroom and slept in an ivory bed inlaid with rubies.

On the day the princess was eighteen, the king sent a royal 4 ambassador to the courts of five neighboring kingdoms to announce that he would give his daughter's hand in marriage to the prince who brought her the gift she liked the most.

The first prince to arrive at the palace rode a swift white 5 stallion and laid at the feet of the princess an enormous apple made of solid gold which he had taken from a dragon who had guarded it for a thousand years. It was placed on a long ebony table set up to hold the gifts of the princess's suitors. The second prince, who came on a gray charger, brought her a nightingale made of a thousand diamonds, and it was placed beside the golden apple. The third prince, riding on a black horse, carried a great jewel box made of platinum and sapphires, and it was placed next to the diamond nightingale. The fourth prince, astride a fiery yellow horse, gave the princess a gigantic heart made of rubies and pierced by an emerald arrow. It was placed next to the platinum-and-sapphire jewel box.

Now the fifth prince was the strongest and handsomest 6 of all the five suitors, but he was the son of a poor king whose realm had been overrun by mice and locusts and wizards and mining engineers so that there was nothing much of value left in it. He came plodding up to the palace of the princess on a plow horse and he brought her a small tin box filled with mica and feldspar and hornblende which he had picked up on the way.

The other princes roared with disdainful laughter when 7 they saw the tawdry gift the fifth prince had brought to the princess. But she examined it with great interest and squealed with delight, for all her life she had been glutted with precious stones and priceless metals, but she had never seen tin before or mica or feldspar or hornblende. The tin box was placed next to the ruby heart pierced with an emerald arrow.

"Now," the king said to his daughter, "you must select 8 the gift you like best and marry the prince that brought it."

The princess smiled and walked up to the table and picked 9 up the present she liked the most. It was the platinum-and-sapphire jewel box, the gift of the third prince.

"The way I figure it," she said, "is this. It is a very large 10 and expensive box, and when I am married, I will meet many admirers who will give me precious gems with which to fill it to the top. Therefore, it is the most valuable of all the gifts my suitors have brought me and I like it the best."

The princess married the third prince that very day in the 11 midst of great merriment and high revelry. More than a hundred thousand pearls were thrown at her and she loved it.

Moral: All those who thought the princess was going to select 12 *the tin box filled with worthless stones instead of one of the other gifts will kindly stay after class and write one hundred times on the blackboard "I would rather have a hunk of aluminum silicate than a diamond necklace."*

Comment

The humor here derives from the ending, which is probably anticlimactic for the reader, but clearly not so for the princess. This disparity between what we expect to happen and what does happen is at *our* expense, as the moral shows. The order of ideas is thus essential to the effect. Much of the humor also arises from incongruity—a kingdom that contains wizards and mining engineers—and from the disparity between the setting and the language of this very modern girl. Disparities of this sort are a major source of irony. Many authors allow the irony to make its point without commenting on it. One delight in reading Thurber is in the discovery of those little deceptions that keep us feeling confident and pleased with ourselves.

Questions for Study and Discussion

1. How do the details of the first six paragraphs lead us to believe that the princess will choose the fifth prince? Is the order of these details important?
2. At what point does the reader discover the real character of the princess?
3. Thurber, in his moral, talks to us in a language different from that of the story. What exactly is this difference, and what humor arises from it?
4. What human frailties is Thurber satirizing? Is he satirizing the princess or the reader of the essay or possibly both?
5. Do you find Thurber's moral pertinent to the world today?

Vocabulary Study

Look up the following words: *parable, fairy tale, fable, allegory.* How closely does "The Princess and the Tin Box" fit the definitions you found?

Suggestions for Writing

1. Write a fairy tale or fable or parable of your own that uses the order of climax.
2. Write a non-satirical essay that examines the values Thurber writes about from your point of view and experience. If you take a different view of them, compare your view with Thurber's.

Coherence

An essay in which all of the details and ideas connect to a central idea or thesis has unity. To emphasize the unity, these details and ideas must obviously fit together into a whole: the reader must see how they cohere, or hold together. The ideas and details must seem to follow naturally.

Using pronoun reference and the repetition of key words and phrases are important ways to obtain coherence—ways that we depend upon with little if any thought. In the following paragraph, examples of key words have been italicized:

In the 40's my parents and I moved from Hillside Homes to a neighborhood in the Bronx that is now dominated by what was then known as the Einstein–Jacoby medical center. *It* was bordered by hundreds of acres of undeveloped land. What I remember most distinctly about *that land,* beyond a huge, flat-topped rock studded with a lifetime supply of mica chips, are the many hills that were covered by tiger lilies in the spring, poison sumac in the summer and perfect snow for sledding after any reasonable winter storm. Early on there were a few squatters farming land near *those hills;* later *they* disappeared. And early on I was content to stay in our beautiful new neighborhood, while later there wasn't enough there to hold me.—Judith Rossner, "The Dyre Avenue Shuttle"

Another important means of achieving coherence is through the use of parallel structure, the arrangement of similar words, phrases, and clauses to highlight similar ideas (again, examples have been italicized):

> Though perhaps Brooklyn is not quite a refuge anymore where sheep may safely graze, *there are places* there where you can listen in the dark of winter to the wind attacking from the Atlantic as moon-whitened waves break against the beach. *There are neighborhoods* of nations so alien and incredible that crossing into them mobilizes beyond any expectation both distance and time. *There are streets* where, on January nights, fires burn on every floor of every house, sending fragment smoke through the cold black trees. *There are meadows and fields, long rows of old oaks, bridges that sparkle from afar, ships about to leave for Asia, lakes, horses and islands in the marsh.*—Mark Helprin, "Brooklyn's Comforting Infinitude"

Where the natural course is clear through pronoun reference, repetition of key words and phrases, questions and parallel structure, no helping words or formal connectives are necessary. Sometimes, however, you will need transitional words and phrases when the connection of ideas or details is not immediately clear. If the steps of a process are presented chronologically and each step requires explanation, you may introduce the words *first, second,* and *third* to keep the steps distinct. You may also have to add the phrases *less important, just as important, more important* to show that you are presenting ideas in the order of importance. Connectives such as *thus, therefore, however, moreover,* and *nevertheless* show the logical relation of ideas. *Thus* and *therefore* show that one idea is the consequence of another or that certain conclusions can be drawn from the evidence presented. *However* and *nevertheless* show that one idea qualifies or contradicts another. *Moreover* shows addition.

Ellen Goodman

What Do You Teach a Person Aged 3?

Ellen Goodman wrote for *Newsweek* and the *Detroit Free Press* before joining the staff of *The Boston Globe* in 1967 as feature writer and columnist. She received the Pulitzer Prize for her commentary in 1980. Her columns on a wide range of social and political issues are collected in several books including *At Large*. Like Joshua Meyrowitz later in this text, Goodman discusses what our society teaches children.

My young friend does not need me to teach her how to   1
tie shoelaces. Between her first and third birthday, laces have
become nearly extinct on shoes her size. They were done in
by Velcro. The role that I had honed over years of teaching—left over right, under and pull—has also become extinct, done in by Velcro.

This girl won't experience the frustration or the accom-   2
plishment of learning this task. Nor will I experience the frustration or accomplishment of teaching it. But no matter. Life
is easier with Velcro.

My young friend does not need me to teach her to tell   3
time either. Children do not tell time anymore. They are told
it by the watches on their wrist. The big hands and little hands
that I had decoded with my child, nieces, cousins, and the
children of friends are being replaced inexorably with digits.
It is easier with digits.

I don't rail against these artifacts of progress. I am a fan   4
of Velcro, and absolutely neutral on the subject of digital

numbers. But the non-needs of my 3-year-old friend have given me some odd thoughts about old ties and old times. I feel suddenly like a loyal and competent employee whose work has been cyberneticized. I am skilled with skills that are unneeded.

I know there is something essentially modern in my dilemma of defunctness. Clocks and shoelaces are not major losses to me or to this little girl, but they are small examples of what happens routinely in our culture. Technology changes so quickly, we hardly have a chance to teach our children what we know before it becomes irrelevant.

Once, crafts were handed down from one generation to another until families were named after them—Millers, Smiths, Taylors. Now skills have a shelf-life shorter than our own. The state of the art is transient. So we have transformed the oldest kind of emotional relationship: the elder as guide, parent as teacher. We are no longer as sure that a younger generation can be prepared for the world by an elder generation.

In a dozen, hundred ways, "improvements" disrupt the lines of inheritance. In high-tech societies it is no longer the elders who hold the secrets, no longer the young who are to be initiated. Knowledge is more egalitarian. Indeed, in the Silicon Valleys of our culture, it is the young who decode mysteries.

I don't want to overstate my case of ties and times. Perhaps I cannot teach a 3-year-old shoe-tying, but I have a 16-year-old daughter with an automobile learner's permit. We practice hill starts as I once did with my parents, and still on a shift car. Most of us have taught someone younger how to throw a ball, bake cookies, hammer a nail or thread a needle.

Still it seems to me that discontinuity is a real tradition among us. The tradition of grandparents who are experts in the intricacies of carriage-driving just when cars appear. The tradition of elders who have mastered elegant script when typewriters are invented. Friends who are experts in multiplication tables when calculators become common.

We can all remember the catalog of 19th-century home-   10
making skills passed down from parent to child, and now reduced to a single lesson in comparison shopping.

Over time, how many of the functions of families were   11
whittled to a core? Families lost much of their economic glue,
the fierce tribal security need for staying together. Families
function now, for stronger and weaker, mostly as the emotional and caretaking center of our lives.

Similarly, less technical teaching goes on in familial ways.   12
We no longer really expect one generation to pass on its daily
technical curriculum to the next. The informal teaching that
goes on in our lives today is about subjects outside technology, and outside time.

We show our children, grandchildren, young friends how   13
to smell a ripe cantaloupe, pick up a frog, watch for poison
ivy, and understand each other. We learn to make generational ties by sharing ourselves rather than our crafts. The one
skill that is not obsolete is understanding of nature, especially
human nature. Most of the experts on human behavior are
amateurs.

So I won't teach my small friend how to tie shoes or tell   14
time this year. But maybe, by hanging out together, now and
again, I'll pass on to her what I learned from my elders: some
small things about connections that are timeless.

Comment

Journalistic essays like Goodman's often contain short paragraphs, each focusing on a main or a subordinate idea. Newspaper
stories are usually presented in short paragraphs to make the story
easier to read. The more paragraphs the essay contains, the greater
the need of transitions. For a succession of separate ideas and details may be difficult to follow, particularly if the author introduces
new ideas and builds them to increasingly broader conclusions as
Goodman does. Writing the essay for another periodical or for a

book, the author may choose to combine many of the short paragraphs—main and subordinate ideas—to form longer, more complex paragraphs.

Questions for Study and Discussion

1. One kind of transition makes reference to something in the
    preceding paragraph: the phrase *this girl* that opens paragraph
    2 refers to the three-year-old girl discussed in paragraph 1. What
    other paragraphs open with similar references?
2. What transitional ideas do the opening words of paragraphs 6,
    9, 11, 12, and 14 express?
3. What internal transitions do paragraphs 2, 6, 13, and 14 con-
    tain?
4. Which paragraphs might be combined to form longer and more
    complex paragraphs? What would be gained or lost through
    such revision?
5. What is Goodman's thesis, and where does she first state it?
    How does she restate this thesis as the essay progresses?
6. Goodman builds from concrete details to general conclusions.
    She also builds from the statement to a problem to a discus-
    sion of its consequences for parents and children. Does she
    merely explore these consequences, or does she suggest a so-
    lution?
7. Is Goodman writing to parents exclusively, or does she have a
    larger audience in mind? What features of the essay help you
    to define this audience?
8. Goodman states that "the one skill that is not obsolete is un-
    derstanding of nature, especially human nature." What might
    be some of the skills parents can teach children about human
    nature?

Vocabulary Study

Use your dictionary to supply synonyms for the following: *honed*
(paragraph 1); *inexorably* (paragraph 3); *cyberneticized* (paragraph 4);
defunctness (paragraph 5); *transient* (paragraph 6); *egalitarian*
(paragraph 7); *curriculum* (paragraph 12); *obsolete* (paragraph 13).

Suggestions for Writing

Discuss your agreement or disagreement with one of the following statements. Draw on your own experiences.

a. "We are no longer as sure that a younger generation can be prepared for the world by an elder generation."

b. "Still it seems to me that discontinuity is a real tradition among us."

c. "The one skill that is not obsolete is understanding of nature, especially human nature."

d. "Most of the experts on human behavior are amateurs."

L. E. Sissman
The Old Farmer's Almanac, 1872

L. E. Sissman, poet and essayist, collected his numerous poems in *Hello, Darkness* (1978) and other books. His personal essays for *The Atlantic Monthly* are collected in *Inner Bystander* (1975). Sissman wrote often about his boyhood in Detroit, and in this essay he compares our present world with the world described in an issue of a nineteenth-century farmer's almanac.

The homely publications of a hundred years ago have a 1 message for us. The *Official Railway Guide* of June, 1868, for example, tells me the disheartening news that my regular twenty-seven-mile commute took ten minutes less one hundred and four years ago than it does today. And the 1872 *Old Farmer's Almanac,* which I picked up in a New Hampshire secondhand store some years ago, bears even odder tidings.

If you consult the *Almanac* today, you know that behind 2

its familiar yellow cover is a thick pack of oddments—snippets of astrology, weather prognostications, old rhymes and jokes, a spate of small-space ads for trusses, roach-killer, and fish lures, and on pages that deal with the months of the year ahead, a series of nostalgic, neatly written "Farmer's Calendars."

Things were different in 1872. The *Almanac* was thin— 3 a mere fifty-two pages—and the only ads inside its peach covers (the original yellow was dropped for a time in the middle of the nineteenth century) touted Hallet & Davis pianos (endorsed by "F. Liszt, the First Pianist in the World"), Webb & Twombly's Premium Chocolates (which "have taken the highest award at every Fair in which they have been exhibited"), Wheeler & Wilson's Sewing Machines, Worcester's Quarto Dictionary (with a testimonial from Edward Everett), and the wares of Henry C. Sawyer, whose Waltham Book Store also sold stationery, wallpaper, silverplate, luggage, desks, Bibles, brushes, combs, perfumery, soap, pocket knives and scissors, fans for ladies, umbrellas, picture frames, and, of course, the *Almanac.*

But it is the editorial matter of the old *Almanac* that star- 4 tles the modern reader. Beginning soberly with a table of Meetings of Friends in New England and a list of salaries of executive officers of the United States ("Ulysses S. Grant, Ill., Pres., $25,000; Hamilton Fish, N.Y., Sec. State, $8,000"), it goes on through a page of astronomical data and rosters of New England colleges and registers in bankruptcy to an early crescendo: the spreads for the months of the year. Each is laid out much as it is today: a table of astronomical calculations on the left, a rather sketchy forecast and the "Farmer's Calendar" on the right. But these "Farmer's Calendars" are nothing like the rather bland, pleasant little essays of today. Each of them preaches and rails at the farmer to keep a better farm and live a better life; the Protestant ethic rears its minatory head in January and harangues the reader through the waxing and the waning year. The nameless scourge of slothful husbandmen begins the cycle, after a terse New Year's greeting, well into his evangelical stride: "Make up your mind therefore to be better and to do better, to aim higher and to have nobler ends in view. . . . Let us sit down by the crackling fire and lay out plans for the year. I suppose you have done the chores, of course, fed the cattle and the pigs, and cleaned up the barn. No use to sit down till the chores are done. . . ." In February, he has progressed a step further in his righteous indignation at his captive parishioners; now he begins by berating them: "Snug up about the barn this winter. Shut the door and the windows. Cold won't make cattle tough. . . . I wouldn't give a fig for a man who can't turn his mind to little things. All your luck in farming hangs on the chores at this season."

In March, he is quick to turn on the hapless, snowbound 5 farmer who grouses about the weather. "No use to fret about the storm and the snow. Keep your temper is a good rule on the farm. This way of finding fault with heaven and earth won't do. . . . It's a pity you don't raise more roots. Hadn't you better look about for a spot to put in an acre of mangolds and another of swedes?"

The Old Farmer takes the offensive early and keeps the 6 pressure up; the shiftless reader won't get a breather, even in springtime: "All plant life is on the spring now, and animal life too, as to that matter. And so you'd better spring around, John, if you want to see your barn well filled in the fall. Yoke up and go at it with your fine and sprightly team. . . . The fact is, there is no end to the work this month, and no time to lose in standing around or leaning over the wall with a gossiping neighbor." And: "It is of no use to find fault with work. We ought to thank our stars that we are able to work."

As the summer ends, the taskmaster's lips are thinner than 7 ever: "Now that the dog star rages, why don't you give the dog a bullet [presumably a pill of dog-days medicine], the boy a hoe, the girl the knitting needles. No work, no eating, is the rule, you know. Can't afford to keep drones on the farm." In September, to keep the enervated farmer on the qui vive, the *Almanac* lays out an impressive list of chores, including removing stones from fields to be tilled. "I hope you got out those rocks. . . . It is a shiftless way to lay down a lot with the bushes growing along the walls. Why don't you dig them out, and clean up the lot?" In October, he notes, with relish, that "there is enough to do to keep us on the jog all this month;" in November, after a peremptory reference to Thanksgiving, he's off again about stalling the cattle every night, fall sowing and plowing, and trimming the grapevines. Even in December—notably, there's no mention of Christmas—he's harping about the grapevines again, as well as pruning the fruit trees, making an inventory of stock and tools on the farm ("the sooner you set about it, the better you will be off"), and generally preparing for the worst: "Spruce up and get ready for a hard winter."

The rest of the *Almanac* is similarly grim; it dispels a number of common notions among farmers about cabbage, kitchen gardens, grass for horses, and food for stock, calls attention to the adulteration of commercial fertilizers, cautions the reader about transplanting evergreens ("it is a mistake to suppose that the same rules apply to evergreens as to deciduous trees"), and sagely discusses the pitfalls of stock-breeding farms. Then a little light relief: three pages of poetry, anecdotes, and puzzles, most of them not so light, at that. One poem, a tearjerker, was "found under the pillow of a soldier who died in a hospital near Port Royal, South Carolina." "Selections" includes Scott's "O, what a tangled web we weave/When first we practise to deceive;" the jokes include this epitaph: "I was well—wished to be better—read medical books—took medicine—and died."

The 1872 *Almanac* ends there, with the exception of a few population tables (according to the census of 1870, there were 38,555,983 people in the United States, of whom 942,292 lived in New York City and 4,382,759 in New York State; California could boast a mere 560,247), weather tables, tide tables, and post office regulations (first-class letters, 3 cents per half ounce). It ends with a sort of a whimper and a curious feeling of oppression in the reader, as if he had just been through that exhausting year with the poor, bone-weary farmer. It ends, finally, with a question forming in the modern reader's mind: Were the good old days that bad? In an age when we are daily and sorely tried by all sorts of mind-boggling disasters and injustices, when we daily repair to the past for reassurance and refreshment, is it possible that we are really better off than our forebears, and that our carefully cultivated nostalgia is founded on a mirage? On the evidence of the 1872 *Almanac,* that could well be. The stern preachments of the anonymous author of the "Farmer's Calendar" are not mere mouthings; it seems clear that the struggling farmer of a century ago really needed these appeals to his pride and his sense of duty in order to get on with the backbreaking, dawn-to-dusk job of cultivating his garden. It was a savage life of imponderables—blizzards, floods, crop failures, insect plagues, human and animal diseases for which there were no known cures—and only the most bitterly Calvinistic outlook could prepare one to compete in what had, eventually, to be a losing race. There was no social security in those days, no government price supports, no anesthesia, and above all no leisure. The farmer had literally nothing to look forward to except the fruits of a job well done and another day, week, month, and year of unremitting toil to keep ahead of a hostile nature.

To us, seated in our warm houses on our choreless days ¹⁰ off from work, knitted to all our friends by the telephone, possessed of cars to take us across the county or across the country as the whim strikes us, disposing of a hundred diversions to beguile our leisure, protected by effective medical care (for those, at least, who can afford it), assured of a cash competence in our retirement, this stark world of a hundred years ago is hard indeed to believe in—which is one of the reasons why we believe in a gilded age when all the world was young, when cares were few, when love was true, when, over the river and through the woods, grandmother's house was filled with goodwill, provender, and jollity. What a shame the truth was otherwise.

Comment

The opening topic sentences of paragraphs 1–8 refer to the central idea; the details in these paragraphs illustrate it in various ways. Paragraph 9 is organized in a different way: details of the final pages of the almanac lead into the topic sentence—the question "Were the good old days that bad?" The remaining sentences answer the question. In the concluding paragraph Sissman reflects upon the thesis of the essay.

To hold together the various details and ideas, Sissman depends on a number of devices. The opening sentences of some of the paragraphs make transitions to a new consideration or new stage of the analysis of the almanac. For example, the opening sentence of paragraph 4 marks the turn from advertisements to the editorial matter; the opening sentence of paragraph 6 shifts the discussion to the attitude of the Old Farmer toward his readers.

The long paragraphs (in marked contrast to the short paragraphs of Goodman) require careful transitions to mark turns of ideas—for example, in the following transitional sentence in paragraph 4:

> But these "Farmer's Calendars" are nothing like the rather bland, pleasant little essays of today.

Goodman's short paragraphs focus on a large number of ideas—none of which she develops in depth, perhaps because she is referring to facts familiar to her readers. Sissman, on the other hand, is describing a publication and a world unfamiliar to his readers, and he keeps his many details in focus through his much longer paragraphs, each devoted to one idea or feature of the almanac.

Questions for Study and Discussion

1. How late in the essay does Sissman state the thesis? What is gained by not stating it in the opening paragraph?
2. How are paragraphs 1–8 organized? Does Sissman describe the almanac cover to cover, or does he present the contents in a different order?
3. The "Protestant ethic" (paragraph 4) is the ideal of hard, unremitting work which exercises the virtues of the upright per-

son. How is this ideal related to the "Calvinistic outlook," referred to in paragraph 9? How does the discussion of the farmer's life throughout the essay explain these phrases?

4. Do you agree with Sissman's explanation of our romantic view of the American past? What additional or different reasons for this romantic attitude would you cite?

Vocabulary Study

Give the dictionary meanings of the following words. Then write an explanation of how the word is used in the particular sentence:

a. paragraph 1: *homely, tidings*
b. paragraph 2: *snippets, prognostications, spate, nostalgic*
c. paragraph 3: *touted*
d. paragraph 4: *bland, harangues, minatory, scourge, evangelical*
e. paragraph 7: *enervated, qui vive, peremptory*
f. paragraph 9: *anesthesia, unremitting*
g. paragraph 10: *beguile, competence, provender*

Suggestions for Writing

1. Examine an issue of a magazine published in the 1940s or the 1950s, and describe some of its contents. Organize your description to develop a thesis—perhaps a conclusion about the world of your parents or grandparents based on the evidence of the magazine.

2. Discuss how closely a recent movie about teenagers or young adults—for example, *The Breakfast Club* or *St. Elmo's Fire*—is true to your own experiences and observations. Restrict your discussion to one or two characters or episodes; don't try to discuss the whole movie. Build your discussion to a general conclusion or thesis suggested by the similarities or differences you note.

part two

Expressive Writing

You have probably scribbled words or made designs in your notebook in an absent moment at home or at school. Perhaps you doodle on the edges of a newspaper or magazine as you listen to the stereo or watch television. Like this absent-minded scrawling, much writing has the purpose of personal expression, the play of the mind for its own sake. For instance, a rambling letter from a friend may jump from one experience to another without obvious transition. Your friend wrote the letter to share feelings and thoughts of the moment, and you may do the same in responding.

Other kinds of expressive writing are more organized. A journal entry, a statement of personal belief, a letter of protest—these are different kinds of personal expression, and they may be organized in different ways for different purposes. For different audiences, you may choose a different order of ideas and details appropriate to a particular audience.

A journal entry, for example, is written for your own use, and that use determines the order in which you record impressions and ideas. You may keep the journal as a strictly chronological record of a trip or a loose compilation of facts collected for a paper. In contrast, a letter of protest is expressive in simply voicing your anger at an unjust law; the order of ideas and details will be shaped by your feelings of the moment—and would probably be quite different from a letter written to urge a change in the law. The statement of personal belief, too, will be shaped by the thoughts and feelings you want to stress as well as by considerations of audience. Writing to a familiar audience, you might include personal details that an unfamiliar audience might neither understand nor appreciate.

In the following essay, Gloria Emerson's purpose in describing her parachute jump is to share the pleasure and surprise of the experience: "Everyone at the center was pleased; in fact, I am sure they were surprised. Perhaps this is what I had in mind all the time." Her purpose is therefore expressive, though she does give us information about sky diving. She presents enough details about the jump to allow us to imagine the experience. But these details are not presented separately from her description of her feelings. The essay focuses on these feelings throughout. Had she wanted merely to give information about sky diving, the focus of her essay would have been different.

No doubt Emerson discovered new feelings and meanings as she wrote. In writing your own essays, you will probably make similar discoveries; indeed, you may discover a purpose you did not have in mind when you began writing. A piece of writing often changes in focus and organization as you put words on paper. Because expressive writing so often incorporates new discoveries and insights, this form of the essay is sometimes more open and organized more loosely than informative and persuasive essays. The writer of the expressive essay wishes to convey the openness of feeling and thought.

Gloria Emerson
Take the Plunge . . .

Gloria Emerson worked as a foreign correspondent for the *New York Times* from 1965 to 1972, reporting on Northern Ireland, on the Nigerian Civil War, and, from 1970 to 1972, on Vietnam. She received the 1971 George Polk Award for excellence in her reporting from Vietnam, and the 1978 National Book Award for her book about the Vietnam war, *Winners and Losers*. The feelings she describes in this essay on sky diving require the most careful mounting of detail, and that is what Emerson gives us.

It was usually men who asked me why I did it. Some were 1
amused, others puzzled. I didn't mind the jokes in the newspaper office where I worked about whether I left the building by window, roof or in the elevator. The truth is that I was an unlikely person to jump out of an airplane, being neither graceful, daring nor self-possessed. I had a bad back, uncertain ankles and could not drive with competence because of deficient depth perception and a fear of all buses coming toward me. A friend joked that if I broke my bones I would have to be shot because I would never mend.

I never knew why I did it. It was in May, a bright and 2
dull May, the last May that made me want to feel reckless. But there was nothing to do then at the beginning of a decade that changed almost everything. I could not wait that May for the Sixties to unroll. I worked in women's news; my stories came out like little cookies. I wanted to be brave about something, not just about love, or a root canal, or writing that the shoes at Arnold Constable looked strangely sad.

Once I read of men who had to run so far it burned their 3
chests to breathe. But I could not run very far. Jumping from a plane, which required no talent or endurance, seemed perfect. I wanted to feel the big, puzzling lump on my back that they promised was a parachute, to take serious strides in the absurd black boots that I believed all generals wore.

I wanted all of it: the rising of a tiny plane with the door 4
off, the earth rushing away, the plunge, the slap of the wind, my hands on the back straps, the huge curve of white silk above me, the drift through the space we call sky.

It looked pale green that morning I fell into it, not the 5 baby blue I expected. I must have been crying; my cheeks were wet. Only the thumps of a wild heart made noise; I did not know how to keep it quiet.

That May, that May my mind was as clear as clay. I did   6
not have the imagination to perceive the risks, to understand that if the wind grew nasty I might be electrocuted on high-tension wires, smashed on a roof, drowned in water, hanged in a tree. I was sure nothing would happen, because my intentions were so good, just as young soldiers start out certain of their safety because they know nothing.

Friends drove me to Orange, Massachusetts, seventy miles   7
west of Boston, for the opening of the first U.S. sports parachuting center, where I was to perform. It was the creation, the passion, of a Princetonian and ex-Marine named Jacques Istel, who organized the first U.S. jumping team in 1956. Parachuting was "as safe as swimming," he kept saying, calling it the "world's most stimulating and soul-satisfying sport." His center was for competitions and the teaching of skydiving. Instead of hurtling toward the earth, sky divers maintain a swan-dive position, using the air as a cushion to support them while they maneuver with leg and arm movements until the rip cord must be pulled.

None of that stuff was expected from any of us in the   8
little beginners class. We were only to jump, after brief but intense instruction, with Istel's newly designed parachute, to show that any dope could do it. It was a parachute with a thirty-two-foot canopy; a large cutout hole funneled escaping air. You steered with two wooden knobs instead of having to pull hard on the back straps, or risers. The new parachute increased lateral speed, slowed down the rate of descent, reduced oscillation. We were told we could even land standing up but that we should bend our knees and lean to one side. The beginners jumped at eight A.M., the expert sky divers performed their dazzling tricks later when a crowd came.

Two of us boarded a Cessna 180 that lovely morning,   9
the wind no more than a tickle. I was not myself, no longer thin and no longer fast. The jump suit, the equipment, the

helmet, the boots, had made me into someone thick and clumsy, moving as strangely as if they had put me underwater and said I must walk. It was hard to bend, to sit, to stand up. I did not like the man with me; he was eager and composed. I wanted to smoke, to go to the bathroom, but there were many straps around me that I did not understand. At twenty-three hundred feet, the hateful, happy man went out, making a dumb thumbs-up sign.

When my turn came, I suddenly felt a stab of pain for all   10
the forgotten soldiers who balked and were kicked out, per-haps shot, for their panic and for delaying the troops. I was hooked to a static line, an automatic opening device, which made it impossible to lie down or tie myself to something. The drillmaster could not hear all that I shouted at him. But he knew the signs of mutiny and removed my arms from his neck. He took me to the doorway, sat me down, and yelled "Go!" or "Now!" or "Out!" There was nothing to do but be punched by the wind, which knocked the spit from my mouth, reach for the wing strut, hold on hard, kick back the feet so weighted and helpless in those boots, and let go. The para-chute opened with a plop, as Istel had sworn to me that it would. When my eyelids opened as well, I saw the white gloves on my hands were old ones from Saks Fifth Avenue, gloves I wore with summer dresses. There was dribble on my chin; my eyes and nose were leaking. I wiped everything with the gloves.

There was no noise; the racket of the plane and wind had   11
gone away. The cold and sweet stillness seemed an astonish-ing, undreamed-of gift. Then I saw what I had never seen be-fore, will never see again; endless sky and earth in colors and textures no one had ever described. Only then did the para-chute become a most lovable and docile toy: this wooden knob to go left, this wooden knob to go right. The pleasure of being there, the drifting and the calm, rose to a fever; I wanted to stay pinned in the air and stop the ground from coming closer. The target was a huge arrow in a sandpit. I was cross to see it, afraid of nothing now, for even the wind was kind and the

trees looked soft. I landed on my feet in the pit with a bump, then sat down for a bit. Later that day I was taken over to meet General James Gavin, who had led the 82nd Airborne in the D-day landing at Normandy. Perhaps it was to prove to him that the least promising pupil, the gawkiest, could jump. It did not matter that I stumbled and fell before him in those boots, which walked with a will of their own. Later, Mr. Istel's mother wrote a charming note of congratulations. Everyone at the center was pleased; in fact, I am sure they were surprised. Perhaps this is what I had in mind all the time.

Questions for Study and Discussion

1. What is Emerson's purpose in writing? Does she state her purpose directly, or do you discover it from her approach to the subject and her focus? What were her motives in making the jump?
2. What details does she provide about the operation of the parachute, the descent, and the landing? How are these details fitted to the discussion of her feelings at various stages in her experience? What are these stages?
3. How does she maintain the focus on her feelings throughout the essay? Do these feelings change?
4. Would you have reacted to the parachute jump as Emerson did? What comparable experience aroused similar expectations and feelings in you?

Vocabulary Study

1. Emerson uses a number of technical terms, among them *rip cord, static line* and *wing strut*. See whether your dictionary—or an unabridged dictionary—contains these. If you do not find them listed, state how the essay clarifies their meaning. Notice that we do not always require a complete definition of a term to understand its purpose or role in the process. Is that true of these terms?

2. Explain the italicized words and phrases::
    a. "The truth is that I was an unlikely person to jump out of an airplane, being neither graceful, daring nor *self-possessed.*"
    b. "That May, that May my mind was as *clear as clay.*"
    c. "Instead of *hurtling* toward the earth, sky divers maintain a *swan-dive position,* using the air *as a cushion* to support them while they *maneuver with leg and arm movements* until the rip cord must be pulled."

Suggestions for Writing

1. Describe an experience with a complex piece of equipment like a parachute. You might discuss the problems encountered in assembling it, or other difficulties it created for you.
2. Describe an experience comparable to the one Emerson describes. Explain your motives in undertaking the experience, and trace the stages of the experience as Emerson does, giving an account of your feelings at each stage.

Narration

You are familiar with narration through works of fiction that present a series of events chronologically or weave past and present events into complex narratives or plots that explore the connection of events. Narratives are also basic in expository, persuasive, and expressive essays.

An essay tracing historical events may do so through narrative. The following paragraph describing the first landfall of Christopher Columbus in the Bahamas shows how a narrative may build to a climax:

> As the sun set under a clear horizon October 11, the northeast trade breezed up to gale force, and the three ships tore along at 9 knots. But Columbus refused to shorten sail, since his promised time was running out. He signaled everyone to keep a particularly sharp watch, and offered extra rewards for first landfall in addition to the year's pay promised by the Sovereigns. That night of destiny was clear and beautiful with a late rising moon, but the sea was the roughest of the entire passage. The men were tense and expectant, the officers testy and anxious, the Captain General serene in the confidence that presently God would re-

veal to him the promised Indies.—Samuel Eliot Morison, "First Crossing of the Atlantic"

Narrative of the same sort may serve persuasive writing. In the legal brief it serves an essential role in providing the background of the case—the events at issue. A simple argument may contain a supporting narrative of an event. A plea for a change in public policy may trace the consequences of present policy through a narrative illustrating them. We will consider examples in a later section.

Narrative is important, too, in expressive writing. Gloria Emerson's account of her parachute jump is a simple narrative. And Sue Hubbell begins her essay on woodcutting with a narrative of her experiences:

> This morning I finished sawing up a tree from the place where I had been cutting for the past week. In the process I lost my screwrench, part screwdriver, part wrench, that I use to make adjustments on my chain saw. I shouldn't carry it in my pocket, but the chain had been loose; I had tightened it and had not walked back to the truck to put the wrench away. Scolding myself for being so careless, I began looking for another tree to cut and found a big one that had recently died.

The essays that follow use narrative to express different feelings and attitudes.

In a narrative, the amount of detail you present depends on the knowledge of your readers. Since you usually cannot know how much knowledge each reader possesses about a subject, you will do best to include essential facts and to introduce those nonessential facts that will give the reader details about the world and the characters in your essay. It is important, however, not to give excessive detail, for this will often divert the reader from the central event. In the Columbus excerpt, Morison gives a necessary though brief description of the sailors and officers of the ship. To have described each of their reactions in detail would lessen the suspense and divert attention from Columbus himself, who is the actual focus of the narrative.

Edward Rivera
The Sociology Final

In *Family Installments*, his semi-autobiographical book on Spanish Harlem, Edward Rivera describes the experiences of a Puerto
Rican boy growing up in American society. The experience described in this excerpt—taking a final exam in a college course—
will be familiar to many students. Rivera writes about the exam
from an unusual perspective.

I took a cab up to school, but I was still late. On the way   1
there, I reviewed the "material" in my head: almost total confusion, a jumble of jargon, ordinary things passed off as pro-
fundities with the aid of "abstractionitis." ("The home then
is the specific zone of functional potency that grows about a
live parenthood . . . an active interfacial membrane or surface furthering exchange . . . a mutualizing membrane between the family and the society in which it lives. . . .")
    The classroom was packed for the first time since the   2
opening day of classes, and filled with smoke. Over forty students were bent over their examination booklets, most of them
looking confused by the questions. The professor, puffing an
immense pipe, was at his desk (manufactured by Vulcan),
reading Riesman on *The Lonely Crowd*, casually, as if it were
a murder mystery whose ending he had figured out back on
page one. He didn't look pleased when I stepped up to his
desk: another pair of lungs in a roomful of carbon dioxide
and cigarette smoke.
    "Yes?"   3
    I asked him for a question sheet and an examination   4
booklet. They were on the desk, weighted down with the
eighth edition of his anthology.

"Are you registered in this course?" he asked.   5

Yes, I was. He wanted to know my name. I told him. He   6
looked me up in his roll book. Had I been coming to class
regularly? Every time. How come I never spoke up in class?
Because I sat in the back. It was hard to be heard from back
there. I might try sitting up front, he said. I said I would. He
said it was a little late for that. For a moment I'd forgotten
what day this was. *Dies irae*, according to my paperback dictionary of foreign phrases. Do-or-die day.

There were no empty chairs, so I walked to the back of   7
the room and squatted in a corner, keeping my coat and scarf
on.

"Answer one from Part A, one from Part B, and one from   8
Part C." I had no trouble understanding that much. But my
mind blanked out on the choices in Parts A, B, and C. There
was something about "group membership as the source of individual morality and social health" (Durkheim? I couldn't
remember). I must have slept through that lecture, and I
couldn't remember any mention of it in the eighth edition.
Another one asked for something or other on Weber's contention that "minorities in 19th-century Europe—the Poles
in Russia, the Huguenots in France, the Noncomformists in
England, and the Jews in all countries—had offset their so-
cio-political exclusion by engaging in economic activity whereas
the Catholics had not." This one had to be explained in fifteen minutes. I got around it by drawing a blank.

The easiest choice in Part C asked for "a sociological au-   9
tobiography, demonstrating your command of certain relevant aspects in this course, as well as the terminology of
sociology."

"Terminology of sociology." That wasn't even a good   10
rhyme. It was also asking too much for fifteen minutes. It
wasn't even enough time for my nerves to calm down. Too
bad. I got up and left the room. No one noticed.

I went down to the student cafeteria for a cup of coffee,   11
and while I drank it, I read the opening chapter of Dr. A.
Alonso's *El Gibaro*, a Puerto Rican classic which I'd brought

with me to reread on the subway back home. "I am one of those," it went, "and this can't matter much to my readers, who are in the habit of not sleeping without first having read something"—another one, I thought, nineteenth-century version—"and this something must be of the sort that requires more than usual seclusion, order and meditation, since I think that at no time other than the night's silence can one withdraw from the real world, to elevate oneself into the imaginary; above all when the day has been spent without affliction, something that a young man achieves from time to time, before he becomes the head of a family, or while he does not have to govern, on his own, the vessel of his future."

In the examination blue book, which I hadn't bothered returning, I translated some of these long, rhythmic sentences as best I could (no dictionary on me, for one thing), just for practice, and then, when I'd finished a second cup of coffee, I shoved the Alonso and the blue book back inside my coat pocket and left for the subway.

12

Comment

"Let me tell you what the final was like," a friend says to you. The story she tells expresses various feelings—perhaps joy or anger or frustration. It may even develop a thesis—either an explicit or implicit point that your friend wants to make. You discover the implicit thesis largely through the tone of the narrative and the stress given particular details. Tone is an essential consideration, because it conveys the attitude of the narrator (see p. 410). These are matters to consider in Rivera's narrative of his sociology final.

The effectiveness of Rivera's narrative arises from the exactness of his detail. He does not tell us everything about the professor of the exam, but rather he selects the details that best convey the atmosphere of the classroom and that explain why he leaves without completing the exam. The episode is a small one, but it tells us much about the feelings of the outsider—of a Puerto Rican youth facing numerous barriers.

Questions for Study and Discussion

1. What are Rivera's feelings in arriving for the exam, in talking to the professor, in reading the questions, and in leaving the building?
2. How do the details of the professor and the exam help you to understand Rivera's feelings? What may be the significance of the title of the book the professor is reading? What is the general tone of his description?
3. What does the quotation from Alonso's *El Gibaro* tell you about Rivera's attitude? What is the general tone of paragraph 11?
4. Is Rivera merely expressing his feelings about the sociology exam, or is he in addition making a point? If so, what is that point or thesis?

Vocabulary Study

1. How do Rivera's examples explain the word *abstractionitis*?
2. The *Dies irae* ("Day of Wrath") is a hymn describing Judgment Day, sometimes included in masses for the dead. What is the point of the reference?

Suggestions for Writing

1. Describe an exam you took, or a similar experience, and convey your feelings through your details and the tone of your description. Remember that your tone need not be the same throughout the essay.
2. Rivera shows how language, like the jargon or the directions quoted, sometimes creates barriers or difficulties in everyday situations. Discuss a barrier or difficulty that jargon or unclear directions created for you.

Mashey M. Bernstein
The Birth of an American

Born in Dublin, Ireland, Mashey M. Bernstein emigrated to the United States and lives in Shawnee Mission, Kansas. His essay on becoming an American deals with American life from an unusual perspective—that of the immigrant whose view of the country had been earlier shaped by American movies. Bernstein raises interesting questions about the influence of movies and television on attitudes, and on values in general.

I am the only American filmmaker in exile. American films are my parents.—French film director Jean-Luc Godard

On May 17, 1985, I became an American citizen. I'm not sure who should take the credit for this major change in my life, but a large portion should go to the movies. Like other countries beginning with the letter "i" (Israel, India and Italy), Ireland, where I grew up, takes its moviegoing seriously. Because television did not begin to have an impact until I was already well into my teens, movies were my main form of escape. Moviegoing was not just another pastime; it was *the* pastime. I indulged frequently, going three or four times a week to our local cinema, where the bill of fare changed that often. In those days there seem to have been a lot more films to go round.

Movies, of course, meant American movies. All other kinds were "foreign," often with subtitles that made it difficult for a child to read, and much as I may have appreciated them later, to my youthful eye they appeared dark and dreary. On the other hand, American films were bright, uplifting and cheery. I loved them all—musicals like *Seven Brides for Seven Brothers*, hilarious comedies like *The Long, Long Trailer*, gangster parodies like *Some Like It Hot* and epics like *Gone With the Wind*, the greatest movie of them all. To this impressionable child, they pictured a land as wondrous and as magical as Dorothy had found in Oz. (Perhaps I had clicked my heels especially hard because here I am in Kansas!)

Growing up in a country with a history of traditional moral values, I found America's sense of cultural diversity, its desire for change and especially its sense of individuality puzzling yet attractive, intimidating yet almost sinfully alluring. Yet a chord had been struck. I can pinpoint the moments of my own changing awareness by the movies that I saw at the time. They remain signposts in my life. I entered traumatic adolescence with James Dean in *Rebel Without a Cause* and *East of Eden*; I danced into romance to *West Side Story* and grew into maturity with *Easy Rider*.

But the movies that affected me the most were the West- 4
erns. Critics have said that the Western is the only true American genre and, after having spent a large part of my youth watching them, it is a theory I can heartily support. I don't know if Hollywood fully comprehends what a powerful tool it has in the Western (which is making a minor comeback), but no other kind of movie quite captures the feel of a country the way the Western does of America. Watching Western after Western had, I am sure, a subtle effect on my psyche and made me feel like an American long before I ever touched these shores.

The best Westerns, like *Red River* and *Shane*, chronicled 5
a love for the land. They were hymns to the glory of the earth. Whether the characters were for the system or "agin" it, they rejoiced in the country's natural beauty and its wide-open spaces (something you could really appreciate if you lived on a smallish island). Furthermore, they had a goal, and in the darkened theater all shared in the quest: I could understand their desire for personal freedom and their voices, including John Wayne at his best, seemed to cry out, "Go West, young man, go West."

The voices went deep. As much as I enjoyed playing 6

cowboys and Indians like an American kid, I knew that I did not want to be a cowboy or a rancher, a sheriff or an outlaw; I was answering subtler messages. From movies like *Gun-fight at the O.K. Corral* and *High Noon*, I was learning about the mystique of wide-open spaces, that was sure, but also of the ability to formulate one's personal code and of the possibility to pursue one's chosen path—values I still consider to be the essential American message.

So when I came here, I was not rejecting the past, but rather I was looking for a way to live my life as I saw best. America offered me that opportunity. Still, Robin Williams in *Moscow on the Hudson*, as a Russian who speaks only broken English had an easier time adjusting to life here than I did. And I spoke English fluently. The first time I was asked if I wanted Italian, French, Russian or Thousand Island dressing on my salad, I had no idea what the waitress was talking about. I had heard only of oil and vinegar and I felt as frustrated as Jack Nicholson when he tried to get a simple sandwich in *Five Easy Pieces*.

There were too many choices here and, at first, like many aliens who are used to a tighter and more rigidly defined system, I was intimidated by the "looseness" in American arrangements. I mistook its liberty for a lack of responsibility, its obsession with change for a childish restlessness and its all too insistent belief in a better tomorrow for an unhealthy rejection of yesterday and even today. These initial impressions are still somewhat accurate; yet, as a new immigrant, I accepted even more heartily the credo of the American dream. The America I love and believe in is one of stark individuality, bold adventure and honest iconoclasm. It is an America comprised of Shane's defense of the innocent, Dorothy's sense of wonder, Dirty Harry's cockiness, Scarlett O'Hara's determinism, Mr. Smith's sense of right and wrong and Tom Joad's honesty in *The Grapes of Wrath*.

Therefore, when I stood in the Wyandotte County courthouse in Kansas City, Kansas, along with 88 others from 29 countries ranging from Asia to South America, from Europe to the Middle East, my true sponsors were those who in my youth had taught me the most about that particular American view of life, liberty and justice, and I count among them Henry Fonda's decency and compassion in *The Ox-Bow Incident*, those wry and offbeat Mr. Americas Peter Fonda and Dennis Hopper in *Easy Rider* and John Wayne in *The Searchers*. Together we all stood and took the oath of allegiance—and rode happily off into the West.

Comment

Though Bernstein does not develop his whole essay as a chronological narrative, he does use narrative to support his thesis. He does so by telling of his movie-going experiences in Ireland and his experiences on arriving in the United States. These experiences lead into his discussion of what he expected to find in America and what he did find. Bernstein introduces his thesis in the opening paragraph and refers to it in the opening sentences of each paragraph that follows. In his concluding paragraph, Bernstein completes his narrative and uses the details of his earlier narrative to restate his thesis.

Questions for Study and Discussion

1. What audience does Bernstein address in the essay? Does he assume his readers have all seen the movies mentioned? Does an understanding of the essay depend on having seen these movies?
2. Is Bernstein saying that the movies he saw presented an America different from the one he found? Did he feel misled and disillusioned? Or did his experiences on arrival confirm the "subtler messages" discussed in paragraph 6?
3. What differences between Ireland and America does Bernstein stress? Does an understanding of the essay depend on details about Irish life?
4. The movies mentioned by Bernstein are those of the 1970s and earlier decades. Do you believe the movies of the 1980s con-

tinue to depict "the glory of the earth" and express the same values Bernstein discusses in paragraphs 6 and 8?

Vocabulary Study

Explain the following words in their context in the paragraph:
a. paragraph 3: *intimidating, alluring, traumatic*
b. paragraph 4: *genre, psyche*
c. paragraph 6: *subtler, mystique*
d. paragraph 8: *obsession, credo*
e. paragraph 9: *wry, offbeat*

Suggestions for Writing

1. Discuss one movie or several movies of a particular genre (Westerns, police thrillers, musicals) that influenced your own values or views of America. Explain why these movies influenced you, and give sufficient details about them to support your ideas.
2. Bernstein refers in paragraph 8 to the American "obsession with change" and "its all too insistent belief in a better tomorrow." Discuss the extent to which you agree with this characterization of American life. Support your ideas with personal experiences and observations.

William Flynn
The Loving Walls of Grandma's Castle

At the time he wrote this memoir of his grandparents, William Flynn was a student at Westchester Community College, in Valhalla, New York. His essay vividly describes not just the apartment of his grandparents but also a boy's fascination with an exciting world.

One of my favorite places was my grandparents' apartment in a once all-Italian immigrant neighborhood, Park Hill in Yonkers. Spending the day with Grandma in her castle is a cherished memory.

I would dash up the stairs two at a time. By the time I reached the second floor, I would be out of breath, but the thick aroma of an Italian feast would make me run even faster up the next flight of stairs.

When I reached my grandmother's floor, her door was wide open because people from all over the neighborhood would stop in to visit her.

She would say, "Bella Grandma" (meaning "grandma's beautiful one") to me in a sweet Italian accent. Next would come a big kiss and hug. "In one hour, Sal and Grandpa will come home, and then we'll eat," she said.

While Grandma was busy preparing dinner, I would inspect her apartment. The first room was my grandmother's bedroom. It was a big room with a big double bed covered with a snow-white bedspread. On her dresser was a jewelry box I fancied going through. As what I thought were real diamonds, rubies and pearls ran through my fingers, I imagined myself a pirate finding a hidden treasure.

The next room was my Uncle Sal's room. Sal slept in a king-size bed because he was too big for a normal one. Sal's bureau was a mystery to me. I loved going through his top drawer and examining his prized possessions: jewelry, watches, wallets and dollar bills. A closet in Sal's room was another mystery to me. I would look through all his clothes, and I remember the distinctive moth-ball smell. I would put on Sal's long brown, leather jacket and don one of my grandfather's hats. Standing in front of the full-length mirror, I imagined myself a gangster walking down the street and everyone taking a step back as I came through. After fantasizing for a while, I would put everything back neatly.

Next was my favorite part of the house, the back room. The first thing I saw were all the barbells that had made my

Uncle Sal so big and strong—bench press, dumbbell, squatting racks and monstrous weights. I put two small weights on either side of an empty bar. I was looking in the mirror trying to get psyched for the big lift. I bent my knees and in one big jerk brought the weight up to my shoulders. I felt my muscles starting to tighten. Next, I noticed the veins in my neck bulge, and my face turned red. I started to push the weight up over my head. At first it felt like too much to handle, but I couldn't give up. I kept pushing for what seemed like forever, and finally my elbows locked over my head. I looked in the mirror satisfied, thinking that some day I'd be as big and strong as Sal.

After successfully pressing 50 pounds, I switched my attention to the most unusual item I knew: Grandma's old Singer sewing machine. I sat down on the chair and started pumping the pedal at the bottom of the machine with my foot. The pedal made the machine needle on top jolt up and down rapidly. The faster I pumped, the faster the needle moved. I was amazed, and I would spend 10 minutes just watching the needle "sew."

My grandmother would break my concentration by calling me to eat. I would rush into the kitchen and greet my grandfather and uncle. Then the time I'd been looking forward to would arrive. Time to eat. The food seemed as if it would last forever: spaghetti with thick rich tomato sauce, the tender veal cutlets, the sweet and hot sausages, the meatballs, red wine and salad. I would feel like a king. Dessert time was another experience in itself. First would come the canoli, éclairs, napoleons and finally the strawberry short cake, my favorite. By the time dinner was over, I would feel ready to burst.

After dinner, I would run downstairs to watch the older guys play stickball. "Hey, there's Sal's nephew," they would say. I knew most of their names but never could remember the guys with the funny sounding Italian names, like Nunzio or Guido.

At night, Grandma and a group of older Italian women

would sit on folding chairs in front of her apartment house, and they would talk in Italian. Grandma would send me over to the Italian cafe for another favorite, soft Italian ice.

When I returned, the women were ready to leave, and they all gave me a big kiss goodbye. I used to hate kissing all these strange women dressed in black, but pretended to like it.   12

The apartment house my grandparents lived in was a three-story, coldwater flat, and Grandma and Grandpa barely made enough to get by, but the warmth, love and comfort I felt with them in their castle is incomparable to any other feeling I have ever experienced. I shall always remember them, and the love and security I felt when I was with them.   13

Comment

Flynn's narrative gives the details of his visit to the apartment moment by moment. Notice how the opening topic sentences identify each stage and together form a summary of the essay. And notice how Flynn gives more details on some of his experiences than on others and how he tells the reader why the back room was his favorite in the apartment, and why he felt like a king at the dinner table. An especially fine feature of his essay is the characterization of people through the objects of their world—the objects in the uncle's and the grandmother's bedrooms, the contents of the back room, even the old Singer sewing machine.

Questions for Study and Discussion

1. In what sense of the word was the grandparents' apartment a castle? What experiences and words remind the reader that Flynn was the inhabitant of a castle during his visit?
2. Why was the back room his favorite, and why did he feel like a king at the dinner table?
3. Flynn states his central idea briefly in the opening paragraph and states it fully in the concluding paragraph. What is that

idea? Is Flynn implying anything in addition about his grand-parents' world?

4. How might Flynn have narrated the visit other than chrono-logically? What would be the advantage of a different order of events?

Suggestions for Writing

1. Narrate a childhood visit of your own to the home of a rela-tive. Give the setting and state the occasion in as few words as possible, giving most attention to the most important mo-ments. Use your narrative to develop a central impression or idea and state it in a prominent place in the essay—perhaps in the beginning or in the concluding paragraph.

2. Flynn characterizes his uncle through the details of his bed-room and those of the back room. Characterize a friend or a relative in the same way—through the details of this person's world.

Description

Usually a narrative contains description of people and places—a drawing in words of what they look like. The narrator may pause to draw this picture, sometimes doing so in a few words and sometimes at greater length. Description is always spatial—the scene is observed from a particular angle of vision. This viewing angle may remain fixed or it may change.

Robert Ramirez (p. 13) describes the barrio as an observer would see it, walking or driving through it at different times. Toward the beginning of his essay, he shows us the barrio as a whole—from a distant point of observation:

> Leaning from the expressway or jolting across the tracks, one enters a different physical world permeated by a different attitude. The physical dimensions are impressive. It is a large section of town which extends for fifteen blocks north and south along the tracks, and then advances eastward, thinning into nothingness beyond the city limits. Within the invisible (yet sensible) walls of the barrio, are many, many people living in too few houses. The homes, however, are much more numerous than on the outside.

This observation point changes in the course of the essay. In the following passage Ramirez shows us a neighborhood of the barrio at evening:

> In the evenings, the porches and front yards are occupied with men calmly talking over the noise of children playing baseball in the unpaved extension of the living room, while the women cook supper or gossip with female neighbors as they water the *jardines*. The gardens mutely echo the expressive verses of the colorful houses. The denseness of multicolored plants and trees gives the house the appearance of an oasis or a tropical island hideaway, sheltered from the rest of the world.

We are close to the houses of barrio—close enough to see what the people are doing—but in the concluding paragraph of the essay we once again return to the observation point of the beginning:

> Back now beyond the tracks, the train creaks and groans, the cars jostle each other down the track, and as the light begins its pulsing, the barrio, with all its meanings, greets a new dawn with yawns and restless stretchings.

Description is an essential part of every kind of writing. An expository essay on auto repair may include a description of some of the tools or the workplace. A persuasive essay may give us a picture of the people the writer wants us to help. In an expressive essay, description may be the dominant mode of presentation, for the writer often pauses to interpret the scene and describe his own feelings. The expressive essay centers on the writer primarily. A descriptive essay may also express the author's feelings.

Rachel Carson

Migrants of the Spring Sea

Rachel Carson (1907–1964) was one of the great writers on nature and ecology. She began her career on the zoology staff at

From *Under the Sea-Wind* by Rachel L. Carson. Copyright © 1941 by Rachel L. Carson. Reprinted by permission of Oxford University Press, Inc.

the University of Maryland, and from 1936 to 1952 she worked
for the U. S. Bureau of Fisheries as an aquatic biologist. Her
many books include *The Sea Around Us*, which won the National
Book Award in 1951, *Under the Sea-Wind, The Edge of the Sea*,
and *Silent Spring*, an influential book that warned of the dangers
of pesticides to the environment. The following essay—a chapter
from *Under the Sea-Wind*—is an example of Carson's immense
descriptive power.

Between the Chesapeake Capes and the elbow of Cape   1
Cod the place where the continent ends and the true sea begins lies from fifty to one hundred miles from the tide lines.
It is not the distance from shore, but the depth, that marks
the transition to the true sea; for wherever the gently sloping
sea bottom feels the weight of a hundred fathoms of water
above it, suddenly it begins to fall away in escarpments and
steep palisades, descending abruptly from twilight into darkness.

In the blue haze of the continent's edge the mackerel tribes   2
lie in torpor during the four coldest months of winter, resting from the eight months of strenuous life in the upper waters.
On the threshold of the deep sea they live on the fat stored
up from a summer's rich feeding, and toward the end of their
winter's sleep their bodies begin to grow heavy with spawn.

In the month of April the mackerel are roused from their   3
sleep as they lie at the edge of the continental shelf, off the
Capes of Virginia. Perhaps the currents that drift down to
bathe the resting places of the mackerel stir in the fish some
dim perception of the progress of the ocean's seasons—the
old, unchanging cycle of the sea. For weeks now the cold,
heavy surface water—the winter water—has been sinking,
slipping under and displacing the warmer bottom water. The
warm water is rising, carrying into the surface rich loads of
phosphates and nitrates from the bottom. Spring sun and fertile water are wakening the dormant plants to a burst of activity, of growth and multiplication. Spring comes to the land
with pale, green shoots and swelling buds; it brings to the
sea a great increase in the number of simple, one-celled plants

of microscopic size, the diatoms. Perhaps the currents bring down to the mackerel some awareness of the flourishing vegetation of the upper waters, of the rich pasturage for hordes of crustaceans that browse in the diatom meadows and in their turn fill the water with clouds of their goblin-headed young. Soon fishes of many kinds will be moving through the spring sea, to feed on the teeming life of the surface and to bring forth their own young.

Perhaps, also, the currents moving over the place where   4 the mackerel lie carry a message of the inpouring of fresh water as ice and snow dissolve in floods to rush down the coastal rivers to the sea, diminishing ever so slightly its bitter saltiness and attracting the spawn-laden fishes by the lesser density. But however the feeling of awakening spring comes to the dormant fishes, the mackerel stir in swift response. Their caravans begin to form and to move through the dim-lit water, and by thousands and hundreds of thousands they set out for the upper sea.

About a hundred miles beyond the place where the   5 mackerel winter, the sea rises out of the deep, dark bed of the open Atlantic and begins its own climb up over the muddy sides of the continental slope. In utter blackness and stillness the sea climbs those hundred miles, rising from depths of a mile or more until black begins to fade to purple, and purple to deep blue, and blue to azure.

At one hundred fathoms the sea rolls over a sharp edge—   6 the rim of the bowl formed by the foundations of the continent—and starts up the gentler acclivity of the continental shelf. Over the shelving edge of the continent, the sea contains for the first time roving herds of fishes that browse over the fertile undersea plains, for in the deep abyss there are only small, lean fishes hunting singly or in small bands for the sparse food. But here the fishes have rich pasturage—meadows of plantlike hydroids and moss animals, clams and cockles that lie passive in the sand; prawns and crabs that start up and dart away before the rooting snout of a fish, like a rabbit before a hound.

Now small, gasoline-engined fishing boats move over the   7
sea and here and there the water pours through the meshes
of miles of gill-net webbing suspended from floats or resists
the drag of otter trawls over the sandy floor beneath. And
now for the first time the gulls' white wings are patterned in
numbers on the sky above, for the gulls—except the kittiwakes—hug the fringes of the sea, feeling uneasy on the open
ocean.

As the sea comes in over the continental shelf it meets a   8
series of shoals that run parallel to the coast. In the fifty to
one hundred miles to tidewater the sea must hurdle each of
these shoals or chains of shoals, climbing up the sides of the
hills from the surrounding valleys to shelly plateaus a mile or
so wide, then on the shoreward side descending again into
the deeper shadows of another valley. The plateaus are more
fertile than the valleys in the thousand-odd kinds of back-
boneless animals that fishes live on, and so more and larger
fish herds browse on them. Often the water above the shoals
is especially rich in the moving clouds of small plants and animals of many different kinds that drift with the currents or
swim feebly about in search of food—the wanderers or
plankton of the sea.

The mackerel do not follow the road over the hills and   9
valleys of the sea's floor as they leave their wintering grounds
and turn shoreward. Instead, as though in eagerness to reach
at once the sun-lit upper water, they climb steeply the hundred-
fathom ascent to the surface. After four months in the gloom
of deep water the mackerel move in excitement through the
bright waters of the surface layers. They thrust their snouts
out of the water as they swim and behold once more the gray
expanse of sea cupped in the paleness of arching sky.

Where the mackerel come to the surface there is no sign   10
by which to distinguish the great sea out of which the sun
rises from the lesser sea into which it sets; but without hesi-
tation the schools turn from the deep-blue saline water of the
open sea and move toward the coastal waters, paled to green-
ness by the fresh inpouring of the rivers and bays. The place

they seek is a great, irregular patch of water that runs from south by west to north by east, from the Chesapeake Capes to southward of Nantucket. In some places it is only twenty miles from shore, in others fifty or more—the spawning grounds in which, from ancient times, the Atlantic mackerel have shed their eggs.

Throughout all the latter part of April mackerel are rising 11 from off the Virginia Capes and hurrying shoreward. There is a stir of excitement in the sea as the spring migration begins. Some of the schools are small; some are as much as a mile wide and several miles long. By day the sea birds watch them rolling landward like dark clouds across the green of the sea; but at night they pour through the water like molten metal, as by their movements they disturb the myriad luminescent animals of the plankton.

The mackerel are voiceless and they make no sound; yet 12 their passage creates a heavy disturbance in the water, so that schools of launce and anchovies must feel the vibrations of an approaching school a long way off and hurry in apprehension through the green distances of the sea; and it may be that the stir of their passage is felt on the shoals below—by the prawns and crabs that pick their way among the corals, by the starfish creeping over the rocks, by the sly hermit crabs,and by the pale flowers of the sea anemone.

As the mackerel hurry shoreward they swim in tier above 13 tier. Throughout those weeks when the fish are rolling in from the open sea the scattered shoals between the edge of the continent and the shore are often darkened as the earth was once dimmed by the passing of another living cloud— the flights of the passenger pigeons.

In time the shoreward-running mackerel reach the in- 14 shore waters, where they ease their bodies of their burden of eggs and milt. They leave in their wake a cloud of transparent spheres of infinitesimal size, a vast, sprawling river of life, the sea's counterpart of the river of stars that flows through the sky as the Milky Way. There are known to be hundreds of millions of eggs to the square mile, billions in an area a fishing vessel could cruise over in an hour, hundreds of trillions in the whole spawning area.

After spawning, the mackerel turn toward the rich feed-   15 ing grounds that lie to seaward of New England. Now the fish are bent only on reaching the waters they knew of old, where the small crustaceans called Calanus move in red clouds through the water. The sea will care for their young, as it cares for the young of all other fishes, and of oysters and crabs and starfish, of worms and jellyfish and barnacles.

Comment

Rachel Carson joins description with narrative in her account of the migration of mackerel inshore. The description is especially rich in detail, for Carson pauses at each stage of her account to describe the various worlds of the mackerel—from the deep ocean to the waters close to shore. Notice also how Carson joins the point of view of the marine biologist, observing the ocean from various angles, momentarily with that of the birds who watch the ocean from the sky and, in the following passage, with that of the fish: "They thrust their snouts out of the water as they swim and behold once more the gray expanse of sea cupped in the paleness of arching sky" (paragraph 9). Though Carson is writing an informative essay, she uses her description to express her wonder at a continuous process involving the seasons, ocean, plants, and animals.

Questions for Study and Discussion

1. Where does Carson show us the ocean from the viewpoint of birds and fish? Does she identify these viewpoints directly?
2. How does Carson establish the spatial dimension of her description of the ocean? How does she establish the temporal divisions of her narrative?
3. To make her description vivid, Carson often personifies the ocean, giving it the qualities of a living thing. What uses of personification do you find in paragraphs 3, 5, and 6?

4. Carson depends also on comparison and simile and metaphor—for example, she compares a mackerel to a rabbit (paragraph 6) and metaphorically equates small plants and animals to "moving clouds" (paragraph 8). What examples of simile and metaphor do you find in paragraphs 11–15?
5. Carson depends most of all on specific details of the world of the mackerel, as in the reference to the "blue haze of the continent's edge" in paragraph 2. Where else in the essay does she distinguish various colors, and for what purpose?

Vocabulary Study

1. Which terms in paragraphs 3 and 6 does Carson define formally? Does she define *shoal* formally in paragraph 8, or depend instead on context—the use of the word in the paragraph—to make its meaning clear?
2. What is the difference between an *escarpment*, a *palisade* (paragraph 1), a *slope* (paragraph 5), an *acclivity*, a *shelving edge* (paragraph 6), and a *plateau* (paragraph 8)?
3. Be ready to define the following:
    a. paragraph 1: *fathom*
    b. paragraph 2: *spawn*
    c. paragraph 3: *dormant, phosphates, nitrates, crustaceans*
    d. paragraph 5: *azure*
    e. paragraph 6: *hydroid*
    f. paragraph 7: *kittiwake*
    g. paragraph 8: *tidewater, plankton*
    h. paragraph 11: *myriad, luminescent*
    i. paragraph 12: *sea anemone*
    j. paragraph 14: *infinitesimal, milt*

Suggestions for Writing

1. Describe a body of water from the viewpoint of an observer standing on the shore or sitting in a boat. You might describe the water as it is seen at one time of the day or at various times. In giving the details of the scene, express the various feelings it arouses in you.
2. Describe the same body of water from the double viewpoint of an observer on the shore (or in a boat) and of a bird flying

over the water. Distinguish each viewpoint carefully as Carson does. Use your description to develop a central impression or idea.

3. Discuss the feelings that the sight of the ocean and the migration of the mackerel arouse in Carson. Explain how you discover these feelings in the course of the essay.

Maya Angelou
Picking Cotton

Maya Angelou was born in St. Louis in 1928, and grew up in Stamps, Arkansas, where she was raised by her grandmother, who operated the only black general store in town. In 1940 she moved to San Francisco to live with her mother. She later studied dancing and taught it in Italy and Israel, after performing professionally. Angelou has served as an official of the Southern Christian Leadership Conference, and she has traveled and lived in Africa, teaching school and writing for newspapers in Egypt and Ghana. Returning to the United States, she worked in the theater and taught writing. Her description of cotton pickers in Stamps is a complete section of an early chapter of her autobiography, *I Know Why the Caged Bird Sings* (1969). Angelou's other books include *The Heart of a Woman* (1981).

Each year I watched the field across from the Store turn caterpillar green, then gradually frosty white. I knew exactly how long it would be before the big wagons would pull into the front yard and load on the cotton pickers at daybreak to carry them to the remains of slavery's plantations. 1

During the picking season my grandmother would get out of bed at four o'clock (she never used an alarm clock) and creak down to her knees and chant in a sleep-filled voice, "Our Father, thank you for letting me see this New Day. Thank you 2 that you didn't allow the bed I lay on last night to be my cooling board, nor my blanket my winding sheet. Guide my feet this day along the straight and narrow, and help me to put a bridle on my tongue. Bless this house, and everybody in it. Thank you, in the name of your Son, Jesus Christ, Amen."

Before she had quite arisen, she called our names and is- 3
sued orders, and pushed her large feet into homemade slippers and across the bare lye-washed wooden floor to light the coal-oil lamp.

The lamplight in the Store gave a soft make-believe feel- 4
ing to our world which made me want to whisper and walk about on tiptoe. The odors of onions and oranges and kerosene had been mixing all night and wouldn't be disturbed until the wooded slat was removed from the door and the early morning air forced its way in with the bodies of people who had walked miles to reach the pickup place.

"Sister, I'll have two cans of sardines." 5

"I'm gonna work so fast today I'm gonna make you look 6
like you standing still."

"Lemme have a hunk uh cheese and some sody crackers." 7

"Just gimme a coupla them fat peanut paddies." That 8
would be from a picker who was taking his lunch. The greasy brown paper sack was stuck behind the bib of his overalls. He'd use the candy as a snack before the noon sun called the workers to rest.

In those tender mornings the Store was full of laughing, 9
joking, boasting and bragging. One man was going to pick two hundred pounds of cotton, and another three hundred. Even the children were promising to bring home fo' bits and six bits. The champion picker of the day before was the hero of the dawn. If he prophesied that the cotton in today's field was going to be sparse and stick to the bolls like glue, every listener would grunt a hearty agreement. The sound of the empty cotton sacks dragging over the floor and the murmurs of waking people were sliced by the cash register as we rang up the five-cent sales.

    If the morning sounds and smells were touched with the   10
supernatural, the late afternoon had all the features of the
normal Arkansas life. In the dying sunlight the people dragged,
rather than their empty cotton sacks. Brought back to the
Store, the pickers would step out of the backs of trucks and
fold down, dirt-disappointed, to the ground. No matter how
much they had picked, it wasn't enough. Their wages wouldn't
even get them out of debt to my grandmother, not to mention the staggering bill that waited on them at the white
commissary downtown.

    The sounds of the new morning had been replaced with   11
grumbles about cheating houses, weighted scales, snakes,
skimpy cotton and dusty rows. In later years I was to confront the stereotyped picture of gay song-singing cotton pickers
with such inordinate rage that I was told even by fellow Blacks
that my paranoia was embarrassing. But I had seen the fingers cut by the mean little cotton bolls, and I had witnessed
the backs and shoulders and arms and legs resisting any further demands.

    Some of the workers would leave their sacks at the Store   12
to be picked up the following morning, but a few had to take
them home for repairs. I winced to picture them sewing the
coarse material under a coal-oil lamp with fingers stiffening
from the day's work. In too few hours they would have to
walk back to Sister Henderson's Store, get vittles and load,
again, onto the trucks. Then they would face another day of
trying to earn enough for the whole year with the heavy
knowledge that they were going to end the season as they
started it. Without the money or credit necessary to sustain a
family for three months. In cotton-picking time the late afternoons revealed the harshness of Black Southern life, which in
the early morning had been softened by nature's blessing of
grogginess, forgetfulness and the soft lamplight.

Comment

Angelou combines narration with description, beginning with her grandmother's rising at four o'clock in the morning and ending with a picture of workers mending their sacks under coal-oil lamps at night. Descriptive details at the beginning suggest the "soft make-believe feeling": "The odors of onions and oranges and kerosene had been mixing all night and wouldn't be disturbed until the wooded slat was removed from the door"; the sounds and smells of morning "were touched with the supernatural," she tells us in a later passage. In contrast to the morning, the late afternoon is harsh and ordinary, and she gives details of that world in the remaining paragraphs. The concluding sentence of the essay combines these impressions to challenge a stereotype. Angelou is writing for an audience that perhaps holds a stereotype of the Southern black; this audience must be immersed in the sounds and feelings of the real Southern black world if it is to lose that stereotype.

Questions for Study and Discussion

1. How do you discover Angelou's purpose in writing the essay? Is her main purpose to challenge a stereotype?
2. What details in the essay suggest "nature's blessing of grogginess, forgetfulness and the soft lamplight"? Why are these a blessing? What other details suggest the "features of the normal Arkansas life"?
3. How does Angelou suggest the influence of that world on her feelings about her race?
4. How do the details contradict a stereotype of the Southern black? How does Angelou remind us of that stereotype? What other stereotypes is she possibly criticizing?
5. What personal qualities does Angelou stress in her description of her grandmother? What does this description contribute to the picture given of Southern black life?
6. What mistaken picture or stereotype of a group—perhaps teenagers or high-school athletes—could you correct through a similar description?
7. What impression do you get of Angelou as a person, judging from the qualities of people she writes about and the things in her world that catch her eye?

Vocabulary Study

1.   Which words in the essay are colloquial (words used conversationally and informally) and which are dialectal (words used by a particular group or part of the country)?
2.   What is *paranoia*, and how does Angelou use the word in paragraph 14?

Suggestions for Writing

1.   Describe an aspect of your childhood or adolescence that tells the reader something important about your upbringing. Build your details to a statement of your controlling idea as Angelou does.
2.   Describe one of your childhood or adolescent experiences from two points of view—that of the child and that of the young adult remembering the experience. Then comment on the differences between what the child or adolescent remembers and what the young adult understands. Use these differences to state a thesis.
3.   Discuss a stereotype that shaped your view of other people or of yourself. Explain how you came to hold the stereotype, and how you discovered its falseness.

Mary E. Mebane
The Rhythm of Life

Born in Durham, North Carolina, in 1933, Mary E. Mebane grew up in a segregated world in which her parents struggled to make

From *Mary, an Autobiography* by Mary E. Mebane. Copyright © 1981 by Mary E. Mebane. Reprinted by permission of Viking Penguin, Inc.

a living. Her mother worked in a tobacco factory and did housework; her father farmed and sold junk. Mebane tells us at the
end of her autobiography, *Mary*: "I made it the main aim of my
life to find someone who was understanding and sensitive, and
to find an environment in which I could develop and flourish.
Beyond me lay the great world, the white world, the world that
I had been taught was my implacable enemy. I didn't know how
I was going to get out, but I was going to try. I had to." Encouraged by her aunt, Mebane entered college in Durham, receiving a B.A. from North Carolina College. She later received
an M.A. and Ph.D. from the University of North Carolina at
Chapel Hill. Currently she teaches at the University of Wisconsin at Milwaukee. In this self-contained section from her autobiography, Mebane describes some of the happy experiences of
her childhood. Jesse was her older brother, Ruf Junior her younger
brother.

Life had a natural, inexorable rhythm. On weekdays, 1
Mama went to work at a tobacco factory. On Saturdays, early
in the morning, we washed clothes. We washed clothes out-
doors. First Mama and Jesse drew buckets of water from the
well and poured it into the washpot. It was a big iron pot
that stood on three legs and was very black from soot. Mama
put paper and twigs under it and poured kerosene on them.
They blazed up and soon there was blue smoke curling all
around the pot. She put all the "white" things in the pot—
sheets and pillowcases and underwear—and put Oxydol in with
the clothes. I was puzzled because most of the things she put
in with the "white" clothes were colored. Our sheets were made
from flour sacks and had red or green or blue patterns on them.
Some of the underwear was colored, too.

My job was to stand over the pot and "chunk" the clothes 2
down to keep the water from boiling over and putting out
the fire. I loved my job. I had a big stick, and sometimes I
stood there and "dobbed and dobbed" the clothes up and down
all the morning.

Then Mama and Jesse drew water and filled up two large 3
tin tubs. One was to wash clothes in; the other was the first

rinse. Then there was a foot tub that was for the second rinse, the one with the bluing in it. Sometimes Mama let me melt the bluing, which came in a long, flat cake.

Then there was an even smaller pot, full of starch—cooked 4 flour and water—with a heavy translucent skim on it. It was my job to skim it and throw the heavy part away. I loved that job, too.

After the clothes boiled and boiled, Mama would get a 5 big stick and carry them a few at a time from the washpot to the washing and rinsing tubs. Then she would put more clothes in the washpot, add water and more Oxydol, and I would dob some more. Sometimes instead of dobbing I "jugged" the clothes—that is, dobbed from side to side.

While the second pot of clothes was boiling, I helped 6 Mama with the wash. There was a big washboard in the first tub and a smaller one in the second tub (that was the first rinse). Mama washed with a big cake of lye soap that she had made, rubbing up and down on the washboard. The lye soap sometimes made tiny holes in her fingers. Then I rubbed the clothes up and down in the first rinse, which got the suds out; next I stirred them around and pulled them up and down in the bluing water. Then Mama wrung them out. Some things she starched. She hung them up high on the clothesline. By that time the second pot of boiling clothes was ready and we started all over again. Later in the morning she put in the "heavy things" to boil—overalls and her blue factory uniforms and the blankets. While they boiled, we ate dinner, the noon meal.

For dinner, Mama would send me to the field with a bas- 7 ket over my arm to get a dozen ears of corn, some cucumbers, and tomatoes. I would shuck the corn, pulling the long green hard leaves off, next the lighter-green inner leaves, then the silk in long yellow strands. Ruf Junior helped to silk it; then Mama would go over it again. She would let me slice the tomatoes and put mayonnaise on them, and slice the cucumbers and put vinegar, salt, and black pepper on them. But

I didn't want to slice the onions because they made me cry, so Mama would slice them in with the cucumbers herself. She sliced the corn off the cob into a big frying pan, full of hot grease. Then we ate the fried corn with tomatoes and cucumber and onions, and a hunk of corn bread, and a big mayonnaise jar full of buttermilk, and a piece of pork.

Sometimes Mama put on a "pot." It cooked a long time on the back of the wood stove. Sometimes it cooked all day. It cooked all the while we were washing, and when we came in we had a steaming plate of turnip greens with tomatoes and cucumbers and onions. Sometimes it was cabbage, yellow from having cooked so long. (I didn't like the yellowish cabbage or the orangey rutabagas.) Sometimes it was string beans. If we didn't have a pot, we had something quick, like fried squash with onions. Mama put on a pot of meat to go with the pot of vegetables. Often it was neck bones or pig feet or pig ears. Sometimes we had pork slices, swimming in red gravy. She would put on a pie at dinner, blackberry or apple, so it would be ready at suppertime; we had lemon meringue pie only on Sunday. We sometimes had sweet-potato custard through the week, also.

After dinner we went back out in the yard. By then the heavy things had boiled, and Mama took them on a large stick to the washtub. The water in the tub was gray now, with a high meringue of foam on it. But she rubbed and I rinsed, and she hung out the clothes high, but now she gave me the socks and sweaters to hang on the bushes. She sent me to see if any of the clothes were "hard," and I went to the line and lowered the stick that was holding it up. I took down the clothes that had been in the sun so long that they were dry and stiff. I took them in the house and put them on the bed. Then Mama went over to the field to look at her crop, leaving me to churn.

I put the gallon jars of sweet milk into the tall churn, using a stick shaped funny at the bottom. Then I jugged it up and down, up and down, looking every few minutes to see if

8

9

10

the butter had come. If it hadn't, I jugged some more. Mama would be over in the field a long time and then she would come and say, "The butter come yet?" And I'd look up and say, "No, ma'am," and churn some more. When the butter came, she scooped it up and shaped it into a cake.

For supper we had what was left in the pot from dinner, along with a pie Mama had put on then, and a glass of buttermilk, and corn bread. 11

Before supper, Mama would get out two heavy irons and put them on the hot part of the stove. Then she'd tell me to go sprinkle the clothes. I would take some water and wet the clothes down and then roll them into a ball. That would soften them up some and make the wrinkles come out easier. After supper, Mama would start to iron on a big ironing board that had burned places at the end where the iron stood. I couldn't lift the real heavy iron, but she would let me have the small iron and I would push it up and down a handkerchief or a pair of socks, glad to be a woman like Mama. 12

She would fold the clothes and put them in a drawer and put the sheets and pillowcases on the beds. By that time the flies and mosquitoes would be buzzing the lamp. When she finished she would go out on the porch and sit in the cool, with the basket of butter beans to be shelled for Sunday dinner. I would take a newspaper and shell right along with her, pausing occasionally to protest when Ruf Junior got a pod that I wanted. 13

After we finished shelling the beans, my eyes would have sand in them and Mama would tell me to go to bed. I would go into the house and fall asleep while I heard her still moving around. 14

I helped Mama pick the green tomatoes for chowchow. She cut up the green tomatoes, then a hill of onions while tears ran down her face. She put in green peppers and cup after cup of sugar and a bag of spice. Then she pushed the chowchow far back on the stove and let it cook. In a little while the kitchen and back porch smelled good. It was the chowchow cooking. Mama let it cook and cook until it "cooked 15 down." By nightfall she was ready to put it in the jars that Ruf Junior and I had washed.

She canned vegetables after she came home from work. There were tomatoes, which she put in hot water and scalded, then peeled; peas and corn; corn and okra; and butter beans and string beans. She put down cucumbers in a large stone jar and filled it with brine for pickles. After we finished eating watermelon, I peeled the rinds, front and back, and Mama cooked them with sugar and we had watermelon preserve. 16

I washed jars and Ruf Junior washed tops; and row after row of canned goods, looking just like pictures, formed on the shelves, around the sides of the back porch, and under the house. 17

When the truck came with the peaches, we stopped everything. If it was Saturday, we didn't wash anymore or gather vegetables; if it was during the week we worked until late at night. Everybody had to help because peaches spoiled so fast. Daddy and Jesse and even Aunt Jo helped. The grown folks and Jesse had big knives. Ruf Junior and I had small paring knives. Mama didn't like Ruf Junior and me to peel because she said we left more of the peach in the peel than we put in the pot. But she let us peel, too, because if she didn't we'd holler so loud and beg so hard that she wouldn't have any peace. She picked out the soft ones, near the bottom, that had bad places on them and let us peel those. We peeled and ate and peeled and ate and went to bed full of peaches, sometimes sick. 18

Slopping the hogs was Jesse's job when Daddy didn't do it. But sometimes if Jesse heard them squealing over in the pigpen before it was time, he'd let Ruf Junior and me take them something. We'd get water buckets; I'd take a full one and Ruf Junior would have half a one, and we'd carry slops— discarded vegetables cooked with "ship stuff," a coarse thickening substance about the consistency of sawdust. We'd pour it through the big spaces between the railings into the trough and watch them eat. There would always be four or five, and we'd beat the big ones away with sticks so the little ones could 19 eat. We were careful not to make too much noise because Daddy would wonder what was happening to the hogs if he heard them squealing too much.

Sometimes Mama would get after Ruf Junior and me   20
when she'd hear a chicken squawking and would look out to see a hen flying across the yard with Ruf Junior and me running after it. We didn't want to hurt her; we wanted to play with her; but she didn't understand that and went running for her life.

Daddy and Jesse plowed in the Bottom in the tobacco   21
and cotton. Mama and Aunt Jo hoed in the vegetables. I hoed until I started chopping up too many plants and Mama protested; then I joined Ruf Junior in running up and down the rows, feeling the hot sun on the dry dirt under my feet and the cool wet where the plow had just been. If Ruf Junior and I were good, we could go to the house and get cold water and bring it to the fields in half-gallon jars.

Comment

Autobiographical writing is expressive in purpose—the writer seeks to give us a sense of herself through the details of her world and often through the experiences of growing up. Like Maya Angelou, Mary Mebane in this autobiographical account gives us the details of the everyday world so exactly that we are not likely to forget them. She is writing for an audience that has probably never washed clothes in a pot or cooked chowchow. She is careful, therefore, to give necessary details, at the same time using these details to evoke the qualities and feelings of Southern life in the 1930s. Description and narrative combine in the essay, as they do in Angelou's.

Questions for Study and Discussion

1.   What are the qualities and feelings that Mebane evokes in her description of her childhood world? What is her attitude toward that world?

2. How does her description of washing, preparing food, and other activities illustrate the "natural, inexorable rhythm" of life? How does Mebane show that these activities are inexorable?
3. How different is the impression of Southern black life in Mebane's essay from that in Angelou's? Are there significant similarities?
4. How different from Mebane's was your participation in everyday family activities such as preparing food? Did life have less of a "natural, inexorable rhythm" in your growing up?

Vocabulary Study

1. Be ready to explain how Mebane helps us to discover the meaning of the following words: *chunk, dobbed* (paragraph 2); *bluing* (paragraph 3); *jugged* (paragraph 5); *shuck* (paragraph 7); *"pot"* (paragraph 8); *"hard"* (paragraph 9); *chowchow* (paragraph 15).
2. Examine the following reference books to find out how many of the above words are listed with the meaning they have in the essay:
    a. an unabridged dictionary
    b. *Dictionary of Americanisms on Historical Principles*
    c. *Dictionary of American Slang*
    d. *Dictionary of American English*

Suggestions for Writing

1. Write your own essay on the statement "Life had a natural, inexorable rhythm," drawing on your own childhood experiences. Make all of your details relate to this idea, and give your discussion unity by dealing with one experience at a time.
2. Like Angelou, Mebane tells us much about Southern life in general by focusing on a segment of that life and describing it in detail. Do the same with the world in which you grew up, focusing on a segment of it that you can describe fully in several pages. Define those terms and activities that your audience may not be familiar with.
3. Mebane describes the effect books, magazines, and radio programs had on her in high school: "I lived so intensely what I read in books and what I heard on the radio that even though

I knew that it wasn't everyday, it was more real than everyday." Discuss reading and television experiences that had an intense effect on you during high school, and draw a conclusion from these experiences. Choose a principle of order best suited to your audience and to developing this conclusion.

Reflection

The reflective essay is more open in its structure than essays bound by the requirements of narrative or exposition. For example, it occasionally follows the wanderings of the writer's thought, ending with neither a summary ending nor a completion of the idea or reflection. This kind of essay comes closest to the trial essay described in the introduction—the loosely organized essay that explores ideas without necessarily bringing the exploration to completion. The sixteenth-century French essayist Michael Montaigne defended these wanderings and unrevised thoughts in his essays, pointing out that his "understanding does not always advance, it also goes backwards. I do not distrust my thoughts less because they are the second or third, than because they are the first, or my present less than my past thoughts. Besides, we often correct ourselves as foolishly as we correct others."

Sometimes the reflective essay is tightly constructed, its ideas built carefully, without continuous revision or restatement. The structure and language of the essay depend on the writer's personality and characteristic manner of thinking. Montaigne describes his own. Writers like Montaigne think as they put words on paper; they revise and correct as they compose. Other writers choose to revise

105

the whole essay and present only their finished thoughts. The reflective essay, more so than other kinds of essays, takes the shape of the writer's thought and feeling.

Henry Beetle Hough
On Small Things

Henry Beetle Hough (1896–1985) was born in New Bedford, Massachusetts, and attended Columbia School of Journalism. For more than forty years he was editor and co-publisher (with his wife) of the *Vineyard Gazetta*, in Edgartown, Massachusetts. An early book, *History of Services Rendered by the American Press*, won the Pulitzer Prize in 1917. Hough is also the author of novels and nonfiction including his autobiography, *Mostly on Martha's Vineyard*. The essay reprinted here is an example of the reflective essay in which Hough excels.

August 7

Dear Jack,

When I dressed this morning I inadvertently put on an   1
old green shirt and the bright blue slacks I bought a few weeks ago at Dave Golart's because my waistline now rebels at the long-familiar Size 36, and because bright blue was about as modest a shade as I could find in this pigment-passionate age. My investment in Size 36 pants is dropping faster and I fear more permanently than the value of the stock portfolios of my betters.

I say this morning's color combination was inadvertent   2

because I think it was, and in that case it was a small thing. If it was not inadvertent, it was probably a big thing, dictate of some enormous reason I shall never learn. Green and bright blue look odd, I know, but they feel all right, and I shall not change until time for the bank directors' meeting this afternoon. The requirements for that are obviously severe.

Assuming my vagary in costume to be a small thing, I 3
remembered on my morning walk with Lochinvar something I had not thought of for years. I quote:

> "Neglect of small things is the rock on which the great majority of the human race has split."

I learned this, and the rest of the moral passage, now for- 4
gotten, in the Mary B. White School, a red brick building in a graveled yard which stood at the corner of Maxfield and Pleasant streets in New Bedford long ago. It was popularly but incorrectly known as the Maxfield Street School. There were four rooms, two downstairs and two upstairs, and I had a year's schooling in each room. The principal's office was in the turret which surmounted the outside stairs. All public buildings built of brick had turrets. I saw the principal's office only once, and I have forgotten the occasion.

The janitor was Mr. Cochrane. He had a red beard and 5
so far as I can remember always wore a business suit and a derby hat. The boys' urinal in the basement smelled so strong and frightful that I have hardly escaped from it yet, but I suppose Mr. Cochrane considered this normal and acceptable. I tried to hold my breath as I went through, but my lung capacity was usually insufficient.

Once we were let out of school to watch the circus pa- 6
rade pass by on Purchase Street, a block downhill from Pleasant. Across from the school an elderly woman sat on an uncommonly high porch platform attached to the front of a dun-colored house, and just as we were crossing the graveled yard the planks gave way and dropped the elderly woman and her chair ten or twelve feet to the ground. As I remember it, she landed upright, still sitting in the chair. Mr. Cochrane

set out on a dead run. I wondered what he was so excited about.

I have forgotten the circus parade in particular; I remember it only in an amalgamated succession of these wonders, mixed up with seeing the circus come in of an early morning at the Pearl Street railroad yards near the Wamsutta Mills. My brother and I used to see the stakes driven and the big tents raised in a lot at the North End near Brooklawn where Daniel Ricketson lived and where he entertained Henry Thoreau. Later the circus went to the West End or the South End, and I lost interest. When something is completely right and wonderful, it shouldn't be changed. 7

I remember that in my class at the Mary B. White School there were two boys with the given name of Byron. 8

These various details I supply because if one is going to write of the importance of little things, he had best show he is himself really attentive to them. Maybe the things I have drawn from memory, though small, may not be small enough to make the desired point. I can't tell. Everything one remembers long enough tends to become fascinating, though not to a wide public. 9

The passage I was required to learn, the first sentence of which I have quoted, was written by Dr. Samuel Smiles. He has seven lines and a fraction in the *Columbia Encyclopedia*, and I learn for the first time that he was Scottish, a physician, and that his books were mostly devoted to moral education. I think he is one of the writers of the past century (1812–1904) who has gone out, and I doubt if he will be back. There is no use whatever in putting the usual placard on the door, BACK IN TWENTY MINUTES or even BACK IN A HUNDRED YEARS. 10

I suppose the small things Dr. Smiles regarded as important were of an order now outdated: picking up odds and ends of string, washing behind the ears, painting the length of fence behind the lilac bush even though no one will see it, lifting one's hat clear from the scalp instead of merely tipping the brim, sweeping out the corners with conscience rather than 11 haste, and so on. It was Dr. Smiles who wrote, "A place for everything and everything in its place," but I never had to learn that. It was in Chapter 5 of a piece called *Thrift*.

This is all I shall say about Dr. Smiles, and it seems an 12 odd beginning for the defense of small things I have set out to make. He was so moral—so stuffy, I say—that I can hardly expect to lean upon him or his lavendered philosophy. I must start out for myself and may as well do so abruptly. I object to my life being portentous, and especially to the requirement that I pretend it to be.

Whatever comes up in the matter of ideas or enterprise, 13 someone says, "Let's broaden it." I don't want to broaden it. I prefer to narrow it. I can't paint, except for porches, walls, and things like that, but if I could I would not choose to paint on a large canvas. I probably wouldn't be able to reach the top or the sides, and I would only be an overblown, pretending artist, not a real one. Another thing—I don't want to be in the mainstream. The water is muddy, the pollution great, the vision limited, and too many people are trying to swim at once, each hitting another over the head.

I suppose what I am getting at principally is what I hope 14 is the small integrity of my point of view. It has to be small, because it is mine, and because I don't want to look out from way up there or way out yonder. I want to look out from here, and "here" happens to be an uncrowded place. Besides, if the ground on which I stand is too large or high I will surely be pushed over.

I think the small things now being importantly ne- 15 glected, that it is so much the fashion to neglect as routine and perfunctory, are the things generally that make life itself and in the end give it the meaning out of which new, fresh, or even grand ideas may spring. Information comes by radio, television, newspaper, magazine, and book, but these are not the country's thinking or the people's thinking. They may be stimulating and they may also be conforming. A man still needs his walking or hammering nails or chopping wood or bowling or shooting pool if he is really to find out what he thinks.

The sweeping concept is often not much by itself; it's like the wind that blew over last night, leaving a scatter of debris.

Thoreau said that a man was not born into the world to   16 do everything, but to do something. The opportunities of modern times, puffed and inflated by so many prophets, some real, some false, are over-appreciated; the limitations are undervalued a hundredfold, though they are the intimate companionship of our days and nights, our Sundays and our weekdays.

I suppose, too, that although limitations are generally what   17 they seem and no more, there is always a chance that they may nourish some particular fertility. Most great things nowadays are abstractions, and did not Dr. J. Robert Oppenheimer suggest that some of their puzzling relationships might be brought into understandable order through a small specific?

I argue that we, as ordinary people, ought to neglect great   18 things, even at the cost of appearing presumptuous. I am aware that Dr. Samuel Smiles (there he is again), if he could rise up from his serene bit of God's acre among the yews and willows beside the ivy-mantled church, would be bound to insist that this was not what he had in mind. Maybe, though, he could be persuaded.

I remember how David Copperfield, after his life with   19 Dora, declared that trifles make the sum of life. This is not what Dr. Smiles meant, either; his small things were not trifles. Not to him. But I am of David Copperfield's way of thinking. Life's trifles and trifling are not only its sum but its essence.

One small matter of doubt remains, rising from our ex-   20 perience in the newspaper profession. I remember Betty's intent pursuit of trifles: to keep Mrs. Duble's name from appearing in the *Gazette* as Mrs. Deeble, or vice versa; to defeat at all costs that persecuting vulgarity, "Rev. Smith"; to put the apostrophe in exactly and not approximately the correct place. So much of the good health of the paper lay here that, looking backward, I can almost accept the view that there are no minutiae.

As a last word in trying for an understanding or even for a compromise with Dr. Smiles, I suggest that if the great majority of the human race is going to split on the rock of neglect of small things, it will at least be too bad for so many of us to split on the rock of the wrong ones. 21

Yours, as ever,

Comment

Hough's letter has the openness and loose structure typical of much expressive writing. The miscellany of details that leads into paragraph 9 seems to illustrate Samuel Johnson's definition of the essay as an "irregular undigested piece." But the details have a purpose, as Hough directly states. That purpose is related to the statement of Samuel Smiles—first quoted in paragraph 3. Throughout the essay Hough gives us a sense of the reflective writer turning over the experiences and sayings that have mattered over a lifetime; Hough discovers a special meaning in writing about them. Out of seemingly small details and ideas concerned with everyday experiences come ideas about life itself.

Questions for Study and Discussion

1. What is the purpose of the miscellany of details that leads into paragraph 9?
2. What is the meaning of the quotation from Samuel Smiles in paragraph 3? How does Hough explain the statement in later paragraphs?
3. Hough discusses how people can live meaningful lives. What paragraphs introduce and develop these ideas?
4. Hough addresses his letter to "Jack"—a particular friend and reader of his newspaper. What features of the essay suggest that Hough has a larger audience in mind?

5. What impression do you get of Hough through his letter? What personal qualities most stand out? What kind of sense of humor does he have?

Vocabulary Study

1. Look up the following words and be ready to discuss how Hough uses them: paragraphs 1–2: *inadvertently, inadvertent;* paragraph 3: *vagary;* paragraph 7: *amalgamated;* paragraph 9: *attentive;* paragraph 12: *portentous;* paragraph 14: *integrity;* paragraph 15: *routine, perfunctory, concept;* paragraph 16: *intimate;* paragraph 18: *presumptuous;* paragraph 19: *trifles;* paragraph 20: *minutiae.*

2. The following words and phrases call a picture or smell to mind. What is that picture, and what does the word or phrase contribute to the meaning of the sentence?
   a. paragraph 12: *lavendered*
   b. paragraph 15: *scatter of debris*
   c. paragraph 16: *puffed, inflated*
   d. paragraph 21: *split, rock of neglect*

3. The words and phrases in question 2 above are metaphors— implied comparisons which attribute the qualities of one thing to another. In paragraph 13 Hough uses another metaphor, *mainstream,* and describes it: "The water is muddy, the pollution great, the vision limited, and too many people are trying to swim at once, each hitting another over the head." What is the implied comparison in *mainstream,* and what other comparisons is Hough making in the sentence?

Suggestion for Writing

Hough gives us a picture of himself through a miscellany of details. He draws no conclusion other than to say that he has paid attention to small details in his life:
   a. Write down quickly a scattering of details that give the reader a picture of your life and interests.
   b. Look carefully at the details, then write down one or two patterns that they suggest. Discuss one of these patterns in an additional paragraph.
   c. Your paragraph probably contains several ideas. Use one

of these ideas as the thesis of an essay that incorporates some or all of the details you recorded. You may wish to add others. Remember that a thesis organizes the details of the essay, giving them direction and purpose.

John Gregory Dunne
Quintana

After serving in the army, John Gregory Dunne worked for an advertising agency and a trade magazine in New York, and for five years worked as a staff writer for *Time Magazine*. He has written screenplays, numerous essays, and widely-read novels on Irish–American life, including *True Confessions* and *Dutch Shea, Jr.* His wife is the essayist and novelist Joan Didion (see p. 336). The unusual essay reprinted here describes his relationship with his adopted daughter, Quintana.

Quintana will be eleven this week. She approaches adolescence with what I can only describe as panache, but then watching her journey from infancy has always been like watching Sandy Koufax pitch or Bill Russell play basketball. There is the same casual arrogance, the implicit sense that no one has ever done it any better. And yet it is difficult for a father to watch a daughter grow up. With each birthday she becomes more like us, an adult, and what we cling to is the memory of the child. I remember the first time I saw her in the nursery at Saint John's Hospital. It was after visiting hours and my wife and I stood staring through the soundproof glass partition at the infants in their cribs, wondering which was ours. Then a nurse in a surgical mask appeared from a back room carrying a fierce, black-haired baby with a bow in her hair. She was just seventeen hours old and her face was still wrinkled and red and the identification beads on her wrist had not our name but only the letters "NI." "NI" stood for "No Information," the hospital's code for an infant to be placed for adoption. Quintana is adopted.

It has never been an effort to say those three words, even when they occasion the well-meaning but insensitive compliment, "You couldn't love her more if she were your own." At moments like that, my wife and I say nothing and smile through gritted teeth. And yet we are not unaware that sometime in the not too distant future we face a moment that only those of us who are adoptive parents will ever have to face—our daughter's decision to search or not to search for her natural parents.

I remember that when I was growing up, a staple of radio drama was the show built around adoption. Usually the dilemma involved a child who had just learned by accident that it was adopted. This information could only come accidentally, because in those days it was considered a radical departure from the norm to inform your son or daughter that he or she was not your own flesh and blood. If such information had to be revealed, it was often followed by the specious addendum that the natural parents had died when the child was an infant. An automobile accident was viewed as the most expeditious and efficient way to get rid of both parents at once. One of my contemporaries, then a young actress, was not told that she was adopted until she was twenty-two and the beneficiary of a small inheritance from her natural father's will. Her adoptive mother could not bring herself to tell her daughter the reason behind the bequest and entrusted the task to an agent from the William Morris office.

Today we are more enlightened, aware of the psychological evidence that such barbaric secrecy can only inflict hurt. When Quintana was born, she was offered to us privately by the gynecologist who delivered her. In California, such private adoptions are not only legal but in the mid-sixties, before legalized abortion and before the sexual revolution made it acceptable for an unwed mother to keep her child, were quite common. The night we went to see Quintana for the first time at Saint John's, there was a tacit agreement between us that "No Information" was only a bracelet. It was quite easy to congratulate ourselves for agreeing to be so open when the only information we had about her mother was her age, where she was from and a certified record of her good health. What we did not realize was that through one bureaucratic slipup we would learn her mother's name and that through another she would learn ours, and Quintana's.

From the day we brought Quintana home from the hospital, we tried never to equivocate. When she was little, we always had Spanish-speaking help and one of the first words she learned, long before she understood its import, was *adoptada*. As she grew older, she never tired of asking us how we happened to adopt her. We told her that we went to the hospital and were given our choice of any baby in the nursery. "No, not that baby," we had said, "not that baby, not that baby . . ." All this with full gestures of inspection, until finally: "That baby!" Her face would always light up and she would say: "Quintana." When she asked a question about her adoption, we answered, never volunteering more than she requested, convinced that as she grew her questions would become more searching and complicated. In terms I hoped she would understand, I tried to explain that adoption offered to a parent the possibility of escaping the prison of the genes, that no matter how perfect the natural child, the parent could not help acknowledging in black moments that some of his or her bad blood was bubbling around in the offspring; with an *adoptada*, we were innocent of any knowledge of bad blood.

In time Quintana began to intuit that our simple parable of free choice in the hospital nursery was somewhat more complex than we had indicated. She now knew that being adopted meant being born of another mother, and that person she began referring to as "my other mommy." How old, she asked, was my other mommy when I was born? Eighteen, we answered, and on her stubby little fingers she added on her own age, and with each birthday her other mommy became twenty-three, then twenty-five and twenty-eight. There was no obsessive interest, just occasional queries, some more difficult to answer than others. Why had her other mother given her up? We said that we did not know—which was true—and could only assume that it was because she was little more than a child herself, alone and without the resources to bring up a baby. The answer seemed to satisfy, at least until we became close friends with a young woman, unmarried, with a small child of her own. The contradiction was, of course, apparent to Quintana, and yet she seemed to understand, in the way that children do, that there had been a millennium's worth of social change in the years since her birth, that the pressures on a young unmarried mother were far more in 1966 than they were in 1973. (She did, after all, invariably refer to the man in the White House as President Nixon Vietnam Watergate, almost as if he had a three-tiered name like John Quincy Adams.) We were sure that she viewed her status with equanimity, but how much so we did not realize until her eighth birthday party. There were twenty little girls at the party, and as little girls do, they were discussing things gynecological, specifically the orifice in their mothers' bodies from which they had emerged at birth. "I didn't," Quintana said matter-of-factly. She was sitting in a large wicker fan chair and her pronouncement impelled the other children to silence. "I was adopted." We had often wondered how she would handle this moment with her peers, and we froze, but she pulled it off with such élan and aplomb that in moments the other children were bemoaning their own misfortune in not being adopted, one even claiming, "Well, I was almost adopted."

Because my wife and I both work at home, Quintana has never had any confusion about how we make our living. Our mindless staring at our respective typewriters means food on the table in a way the mysterious phrase "going to the office" never can. From the time she could walk, we have taken her to meetings whenever we were without help, and she has been a quick study on the nuances of our life. "She's remarkably well adjusted," my brother once said about her. "Considering that every time I see her she's in a different city." I think she could pick an agent out of a police lineup, and out of the blue one night at dinner she offered that all young movie directors were short and had frizzy hair and wore Ditto pants and wire glasses and shirts with three buttons opened. (As far as I know, she had never laid eyes on Bogdanovich, Spielberg or Scorsese.) Not long ago an actress received an award for a picture we had written for her. The actress's acceptance speech at the televised award ceremony drove Quintana into an absolute fury. "She never," Quintana reported, "thanked *us*." Since she not only identifies with our work but at times even considers herself an equal partner, I of course discussed this piece with her before I began working on it. I told her what it was about and said I would drop it if she would be embarrassed or if she thought the subject too private. She gave it some thought and finally said she wanted me to write it.

I must, however, try to explain and perhaps even try to justify my own motives. The week after *Roots* was televised, each child in Quintana's fifth-grade class was asked to trace a family tree. On my side Quintana went back to her great-grandfather Burns, who arrived from Ireland shortly after the Civil War, a ten-year-old refugee from the potato famine, and on her mother's side to her great-great-great-great-grand-mother Cornwall, who came west in a wagon train in 1846. As it happens, I have little interest in family beyond my immediate living relatives. (I can never remember the given names of my paternal grandparents and have never known my paternal grandmother's maiden name. This lack of interest mystifies my wife.) Yet I wanted Quintana to understand that if she wished, there were blood choices other than Dominick Burns and Nancy Hardin Cornwall. Over the past few years, there has been a growing body of literature about adoptees seeking their own roots. I am in general sympathetic to this quest, although not always to the dogged absolutism of the more militant seekers. But I would be remiss if I did not say that I am more than a little sensitive to the way the literature presents adoptive parents. We are usually shown as frozen in the postures of radio drama, untouched by the changes in attitudes of the last several generations. In point of fact we accept that our children might seek out their roots, even encourage it; we accept it as an adventure like life itself—perhaps painful, one hopes enriching. I know not one adoptive parent who does not feel this way. Yet in the literature there is the implicit assumption that we are threatened by the possibility of search, that we would consider it an act of disloyalty on the part of our children. The patronizing nature of this assumption is never noted in the literature. It is as if we were Hudson and Mrs. Bridges, below-stairs surrogates taking care of the wee one, and I don't like it one damn bit.

   Often these days I find myself thinking of Quintana's   9 natural mother. Both my wife and I admit more than a passing interest in the woman who produced this extraordinary child. (As far as we know, she never named the father, and even more interesting, Quintana has never asked about him.) When Quintana was small, and before the legalities of adoption were complete, we imagined her mother everywhere, a wraithlike presence staring through the chain-link fence at the blond infant sunbathing in the crib. Occasionally today we see a photograph of a young woman in a magazine—the mother as we imagine her to look—and we pass it to each other without comment. Once we even checked the name of a model in *Vogue* through her modeling agency; she turned out to be a Finn. I often wonder if she thinks of Quintana, or of us. (Remember, we know each other's names.) There is the possibility that having endured the twin traumas of birth and the giving up of a child, she blocked out the names the caseworker gave her, but I don't really believe it. I consider it more likely that she has followed the fairly well-documented passage of Quintana through childhood into adolescence. Writers are at least semipublic figures, and in the interest of commerce or selling a book or a movie, or even out of simple vanity, we allow interviews and photo layouts and look into television cameras; we even write about ourselves, and our children. I recall wondering how this sentient young woman of our imagination had reacted to four pages in *People*. It is possible, even likely, that she will read this piece. I know that it is an almost intolerable invasion of her privacy. I think it probable, however, that in the dark reaches of night she has considered the possibility of a further incursion, of opening a door one day and seeing a young woman who says, "Hello, Mother, I am your daughter."

Perhaps this is romantic fantasy. We know none of the circumstances of the woman's life, or even if she is still alive. We once suggested to our lawyer that we make a discreet inquiry and he quite firmly said that this was a quest that belonged only to Quintana, if she wished to make it, and not to us. What is not fantasy is that for the past year, Quintana has known the name of her natural mother. It was at dinner and she said that she would like to meet her one day, but that it would be hard, not knowing her name. There finally was the moment: we had never equivocated; did we begin now? We took a deep breath and told Quintana, then age ten, her mother's name. We also said that if she decided to search her out, we would help her in any way we could. (I must allow, however, that we would prefer she wait to make this decision until the Sturm and Drang of adolescence is past.) We then considered the possibility that her mother, for whatever good or circumstantial reasons of her own, might prefer not to see her. I am personally troubled by the militant contention that the natural mother has no right of choice in this matter. "I did not ask to be born," an adoptee once was quoted in a news story I read. "She has to see me." If only life were so simple, if only pain did not hurt. Yet we would never try to influence Quintana on this point. How important it is to know her parentage is a question only she can answer; it is her decision to make.

All parents realize, or should realize, that children are not possessions, but are only lent to us, angel boarders, as it were. Adoptive parents realize this earlier and perhaps more poignantly than others. I do not know the end of this story. It is possible that Quintana will find more reality in family commitment and cousins across the continent and heirloom orange spoons and pictures in an album and faded letters from Dominick Burns and diary entries from Nancy Hardin Cornwall than in the uncertainties of blood. It is equally possible that she will venture into the unknown. I once asked her what she would do if she met her natural mother. "I'd put one arm around Mom," she said, "and one arm around my other mommy, and I'd say, 'Hello, Mommies.'"

If that's the way it turns out, that is what she will do.   12

Comment

Though he introduces a central idea in the opening paragraph and builds to his final point that "children are not possessions," Dunne pauses for reflection on the way. He introduces ideas sometimes with formal transition—"Often these days I find myself thinking of Quintana's natural mother," he comments in paragraph 9—and in the preceding paragraph parenthetically mentions his inability to remember certain names. Dunne gives the essay the shape of his thinking and feeling about his adopted child. He shows that his feelings as well as thoughts are sometimes difficult to express. The essay images the writer in this way.

Questions for Study and Discussion

1. Where does Dunne first state the central idea of the essay? How often does he restate it in the whole essay?
2. Is the single-sentence paragraph that concludes the essay another restatement of the thesis, or is it a final reflection?
3. How does the discussion of Quintana's natural mother in paragraphs 9 and 10 develop the thesis?
4. Is Dunne writing to a general audience or to a special one—perhaps to adoptive parents or adopted children? What do you think is his purpose in writing?
5. Possibly we would agree that honesty should guide the rela-

tions of parents and children. Do you agree that total honesty is desirable with children of all ages? Is it desirable with adopted children in the circumstances Dunne describes?

Vocabulary Study

The context or surrounding sentences or text often suggests the meaning of an unfamiliar word or phrase. How much help does the context or use of the following words and phrases give you in understanding them? What additional help do you get from the dictionary?

a.   paragraph 1: *panache*
b.   paragraph 3: *dilemma, radical departure, specious addendum, expeditious and efficient*
c.   paragraph 5: *equivocate*
d.   paragraph 6: *parable*
e.   paragraph 8: *dogged absolutism, patronizing, surrogates*
f.   paragraph 9: *wraithlike, traumas, sentient*
g.   paragraph 10: *Sturm and Drang, militant contention*

Suggestions for Writing

1.   Dunne writes about parent and child as an adoptive parent and adult. Write an essay of your own on parents and children from your own experience. Limit your topic to a problem you can explore as fully as Dunne explores the problem he and his wife tried to solve. In writing your essay, make your topic sentences direct attention to your thesis as Dunne does.

2.   Dunne states in paragraph 11 that "All parents realize, or should realize, that children are not possessions, but are only lent to us, angel boarders, as it were." Use this sentence as the introduction to an essay on the consequences of looking at friends as possessions. Explore the problem before you attempt to state a thesis.

part three

Exposition

Much writing that you do is for the purpose of giving information. A recipe, directions on how to repair a tire, an explanation of how mules differ from horses, a definition of a molecule, an analysis of why the United States became engaged in Vietnam—all of these give information. We use the word *exposition*, meaning explanation or the unfolding or setting forth of an idea, to describe this kind of writing.

Exposition may use narration and description to develop the explanation. In explaining how to repair a tire, for example, you may describe the tire rim, the tire itself, and the tools needed to do the repair. In explaining Vietnam, you may narrate the events leading to the American engagement, including the defeat of the French in Indochina, later political events that led to decisions by President Eisenhower and President Kennedy, and the Gulf of Tonkin Congressional resolution.

Exposition, in turn, may serve other kinds of writing. Expressive writing often contains information of various kinds; a veteran's personal account of Vietnam probably will include informative details. Persuasive writing—for example, an essay arguing for or against

123

America's involvement in Vietnam—probably would include details of that involvement as well as an analysis of causes and effects.

The purposes of giving information are obviously many. In the following essay on the need of error in human life, Lewis Thomas is defining the word *human*. Thomas might have developed an abstract definition that a particular audience probably would understand without the observations and details he provides in the essay. Instead, he compares humans with computers and thus draws on experiences most readers have had. The technique of proceeding gradually from known experiences to complex and difficult ideas is a common method in exposition. Many essays do begin with abstract statements, but many essayists prefer to lead into abstract ideas gradually through concrete details. These generate interest in the subject, sometimes through historical background unfamiliar to most readers.

Thomas combines most of the kinds of exposition illustrated in the sections that follow. He bases his exposition on comparison with computers, using the similarities between computers and humans (in particular the programmed error in computers) to define the kind of error that makes human life possible. And he uses analogy, or a point-by-point comparison between unlike things—here a good laboratory and a good computer—to illustrate why error promotes increased inefficiency and thinking. He also uses contrast between humans and lower animals, which lack the "splendid freedom" of error, to explain why error is essential to human development. Throughout the essay Thomas is concerned with cause and effect—the cause of human progress, the effect of error.

Thomas introduces his thesis early in the essay, following his discussion of computers:

> Mistakes are at the very base of human thought, embedded there, feeding the structure like root nodules. If we were not provided with the knack of being wrong, we could never get anything useful done.

He restates his thesis in the course of his illustration and discussion:

> The capacity to leap across mountains of information to land lightly on the wrong side represents the highest of human endowments.

> What we need, then, for moving ahead, is a set of wrong alter-
> natives much longer and more interesting than the short list of
> mistaken courses that any of us can think up right now.

In this concluding restatement of the thesis, Thomas moves from
information to persuasion. But he stops short of developing pro-
posals—ways to encourage acceptance of error, the "splendid freedom" that he earlier suggested animals lack.

This analysis shows that Thomas is organizing the essay according to his judgment of his audience. He is writing as you would
converse with a friend—pausing to explain and illustrate ideas when
you see that you are not being understood. You repeat your main
point to give your explanation a frame but also to be persuasive even
when your main purpose is informative. In writing, you must make
a judgment about an audience and assess the kind of explanation
and information it needs to understand your main point or thesis.

Lewis Thomas

To Err Is Human

Lewis Thomas is a physician and is president of the Memorial
Sloan–Kettering Cancer Center in New York. After completing
his work at Princeton University and Harvard Medical School,
he served in a number of medical posts including chairman of
pathology and medicine and dean of New York University–
Bellevue Medical Center and chairman of pathology and dean of
Yale Medical School. His essays, which first appeared in the *New
England Journal of Medicine*, have been collected in *Lives of a Cell*
(1974) and *The Medusa and the Snail* (1979). Thomas writes about
scientific subjects in language that the general reader understands. As the essay reprinted here shows, his lucid style is ideal
for the exposition of complex ideas.

Everyone must have had at least one personal experience   1
with a computer error by this time. Bank balances are suddenly reported to have jumped from $379 into the millions,
appeals for charitable contributions are mailed over and over
to people with crazy-sounding names at your address, department stores send the wrong bills, utility companies write
that they're turning everything off, that sort of thing. If you
manage to get in touch with someone and complain, you then
get instantaneously typed, guilty letters from the same computer, saying, "Our computer was in error, and an adjustment is being made in your account."

These are supposed to be the sheerest, blindest accidents.   2
Mistakes are not believed to be part of the normal behavior
of a good machine. If things go wrong, it must be a personal,
human error, the result of fingering, tampering, a button getting stuck, someone hitting the wrong key. The computer, at
its normal best, is infallible.

I wonder whether this can be true. After all, the whole   3
point of computers is that they represent an extension of the
human brain, vastly improved upon but nonetheless human,
superhuman maybe. A good computer can think clearly and
quickly enough to beat you at chess, and some of them have
even been programmed to write obscure verse. They can do
anything we can do, and more besides.

It is not yet known whether a computer has its own con-   4
sciousness, and it would be hard to find out about this. When
you walk into one of those great halls now built for the huge
machines, and stand listening, it is easy to imagine that
the faint, distant noises are the sound of thinking, and the
turning of the spools gives them the look of wild creatures
rolling their eyes in the effort to concentrate, choking with
information. But real thinking, and dreaming, are other
matters.

On the other hand, the evidences of something like an   5
unconscious, equivalent to ours, are all around, in every mail.
As extensions of the human brain, they have been con-

structed with the same property of error, spontaneous, un-
controlled, and rich in possibilities.

Mistakes are at the very base of human thought, embed-   6
ded there, feeding the structure like root nodules. If we were
not provided with the knack of being wrong, we could never
get anything useful done. We think our way along by choosing between right and wrong alternatives, and the wrong
choices have to be made as frequently as the right ones. We
get along in life this way. We are built to make mistakes, coded
for error.

We learn, as we say, by "trial and error." Why do we al-   7
ways say that? Why not "trial and rightness" or "trial and
triumph"? The old phrase puts it that way because that is, in
real life, the way it is done.

A good laboratory, like a good bank or a corporation or   8
government, has to run like a computer. Almost everything
is done flawlessly, by the book, and all the numbers add up
to the predicted sums. The days go by. And then, if it is a
lucky day, and a lucky laboratory, somebody makes a mistake: the wrong buffer, something in one of the blanks, a
decimal misplaced in reading counts, the warm room off by
a degree and a half, a mouse out of his box, or just a misreading of the day's protocol. Whatever, when the results come
in, something is obviously screwed up, and then the action
can begin.

The misreading is not the important error; it opens the   9
way. The next step is the crucial one. If the investigator can
bring himself to say, "But even so, look at that!" then the new
finding, whatever it is, is ready for snatching. What is needed,
for progress to be made, is the move based on error.

Whenever new kinds of thinking are about to be accom-   10
plished, or new varieties of music, there has to be an argument beforehand. With two sides debating in the same mind,
haranguing, there is an amiable understanding that one is right
and the other wrong. Sooner or later the thing is settled, but
there can be no action at all if there are not the two sides,

and the argument. The hope is in the faculty of wrongness, the tendency toward error. The capacity to leap across mountains of information to land lightly on the wrong side represents the highest of human endowments.

It may be that this is a uniquely human gift, perhaps even 11
stipulated in our genetic instructions. Other creatures do not seem to have DNA sequences for making mistakes as a routine part of daily living, certainly not for programmed error as a guide for action.

We are at our human finest, dancing with our minds, when 12
there are more choices than two. Sometimes there are ten, even twenty different ways to go, all but one bound to be wrong, and the richness of selection in such situations can lift us onto totally new ground. This process is called exploration and is based on human fallibility. If we had only a single center in our brains, capable of responding only when a correct decision was to be made, instead of the jumble of different, credulous, easily conned clusters of neurones that provide for being flung off into blind alleys, up trees, down dead ends, out into blue sky, along wrong turnings, around bends, we could only stay the way we are today, stuck fast.

The lower animals do not have this splendid freedom. 13
They are limited, most of them, to absolute infallibility. Cats, for all their good side, never make mistakes. I have never seen a maladroit, clumsy, or blundering cat. Dogs are sometimes fallible, occasionally able to make charming minor mistakes, but they get this way by trying to mimic their masters. Fish are flawless in everything they do. Individual cells in a tissue are mindless machines, perfect in their performance, as absolutely inhuman as bees.

We should have this in mind as we become dependent 14
on more complex computers for the arrangement of our affairs. Give the computers their heads, I say; let them go their way. If we can learn to do this, turning our heads to one side and wincing while the work proceeds, the possibilities for the future of mankind, and computerkind, are limitless. Your average good computer can make calculations in an instant which

would take a lifetime of slide rules for any of us. Think of what we could gain from the near infinity of precise, machine-made miscomputation which is now so easily within our grasp. We would begin the solving of some of our hardest problems. How, for instance, should we go about organizing ourselves for social living on a planetary scale, now that we have become, as a plain fact of life, a single community? We can assume, as a working hypothesis, that all the right ways of doing this are unworkable. What we need, then, for moving ahead, is a set of wrong alternatives much longer and more interesting than the short list of mistaken courses that any of us can think up right now. We need, in fact, an infinite list, and when it is printed out we need the computer to turn on itself and select, at random, the next way to go. If it is a big enough mistake, we could find ourselves on a new level, stunned, out in the clear, ready to move again.

Questions for Study and Discussion

1. To what extent do computers resemble human beings? How does Thomas distinguish the reasoning of each?
2. What is gained in the exposition by the comparison with computers?
3. What consequences of the human kind of reasoning does Thomas explore?
4. What is the thesis of the essay, and where is it stated?
5. Does Thomas explicitly say that nonhuman beings or things cannot possess the human faculty of reasoning?

Vocabulary Study

1. Explain how the italicized words are used in each sentence. Then explain how the word in brackets changes or modifies the meaning:
   a. "The computer, at its *normal* [average] best, is *infallible* [reliable]."

130 Exposition

b. "After all, the whole point of computers is that they represent an *extension* [development] of the human brain. . . ."

c. "With two sides debating in the same mind, *haranguing* [arguing], there is an *amiable* [mutual] understanding that one is right and the other wrong."

d. "It may be that this is a uniquely human gift, perhaps even *stipulated* [arranged for] in our *genetic instructions* [brains]."

e. "[The lower animals] are limited, most of them, to absolute *infallibility* [predictability]."

f. "I have never seen a *maladroit* [awkward], clumsy, or *blundering* [muddling] cat."

g. "Think of what we could gain from the near *infinity* [immensity] of *precise* [exact], machine-made *miscomputation* [misconception] which is now so easily within our grasp."

2. Write a paraphrase of paragraph 12, giving particular attention to the metaphors of the final sentence.

Suggestions for Writing

1. Describe an experience of your own with a computer error. Use your description to develop your own conclusions about the impact of machines on our lives or about some other idea.

2. Discuss an important change that occurred in your life as a result of a mistake you made in thinking about people or about action you intended to take.

3. Explain what Thomas means by *unconscious* in paragraph 5. Then illustrate the point Thomas is making from your own experience.

4. Discuss the extent to which your own experience with dogs and cats supports the statements Thomas makes about them.

Example

An example is a picture or illustration of an idea. In explaining ideas, we fit our examples to the knowledge and experience of our readers or listeners. In explaining to a child that points of light in the night sky are really very large distant objects, we first have to explain why large objects can appear small. An example suited to the child's experience might be a ball that seems to get smaller as it flies through the air. In explaining to college physics students why the space of the universe is said to be "curved," the professor draws on mathematical formulas and scientific observations, but for the person who knows little or nothing about science, the professor would look for analogies in everyday experience.

The word *example* carries the meaning of typical: that is, the example represents the many occurrences or forms of the idea. Examples are essential in exposition, particularly to the explanation of complex ideas. For instance, it would be difficult to explain the following idea without an example:

> The attitude that produces the pseudo-technical tone is made up of a desire to dignify the subject and the writer, coupled with the belief that important matters require a special vocabulary.—Jacques Barzun, *Simple and Direct*

131

Barzun provides this example of pseudo-technical tone:

> I am sorry not to be able to accept the experience of more inten-
> sive interaction with your group and its constituency.

No amount of definition and descriptive detail can replace an effective example such as this. At the same time, many examples do require explanation or analysis, particularly when the idea is a complex
one.

Tom Wicker

"Court Day" in Moore
County, North Carolina

Tom Wicker was born and raised in Hamlet, North Carolina,
and studied journalism at the University of North Carolina,
graduating in 1946. He worked as a journalist and editor for
several Southern newspapers, including the *Nashville Tennessean,*
and in 1960 began working for the *New York Times.* From 1964
to 1968 he was the *Times* Washington bureau chief, and has been
associate editor of the newspaper since 1968. Recent books of
his include *A Time to Die* (1975) and *On Press* (1978), from which
this essay is reprinted.

Monday was "court day" in Moore County, North Car-   1
olina, in 1949, and I regularly spent it at the county seat,
Carthage, as correspondent for the *Sandhill Citizen,* of Ab-
erdeen, North Carolina (population 1603). I reserved most
of the afternoon for peddling ads—another of my duties—to
the Carthage merchants, in keen competition with the county

seat weekly, the *Moore County News*. On first arrival at the courthouse in the morning, I checked with the register of deeds, the clerk of court, the sheriff, and other officials for suits newly filed, big property transfers, scandalous foreclosures, heinous crimes, and the like; then I laboriously copied down births, deaths, and marriages of note. Later I hastened to the courtroom, where County Judge Leland McKeithen dispensed evenhanded justice, or something as close to it as anything I've seen since.

That courtroom was rank with the enduring follies and foibles of mankind. It was segregated still, and in the summer months sweltering in the harsh dry heat of the North Carolina Sandhills in the days before universal air conditioning. But it provided a generous education in human nature, lawyers' tricks, oratory, and the law itself—in roughly that order. I witnessed court actions involving murders, manslaughters, crimes of property too numerous to define, vagrancies, seductions, desertions, auto offenses of every variety, bitterly disputed wills, breaches of promise and peace, recoveries of damage, alienations of affection, assaults, rapes, batteries, break-ins, reckless endangerments, ad infinitum. It seemed natural enough to me in the South of the 1940s that most defendants, and most victims, were black.

One divorce case—that of a white couple—had a particular impact on me, although I scarcely recall its details. They involved one party futilely chasing the other with an ax. The story plaintively related from the witness stand by the complainant, a worn-out woman with a ZaSu Pitts voice, haggard eyes, and hair just beginning to go gray, was the human comedy at its most ribald and perverse—Moore County transported to Chaucer's time and *The Canterbury Tales*. The spectators scattered around the courtroom, the press—another reporter and I—at its privileged table, even occasionally Judge McKeithen, rocked with laughter. The conclusion was foregone—divorce granted, with a fine crack of the gavel.

That was Monday. That afternoon, I hawked the *Citizen*'s ad space, probably to no better effect than usual. The next day, armed with copious notes, I turned out a humorous account of the divorce case for my long lead over the agate type that summed up the other court cases ("Lonzo McNair, Star Route, Carthage, failure to observe stop sign, costs of court"; "A. C. Overby, Vermont Avenue, Southern Pines, aggravated assault, continued to Superior Court") and sent it back to the *Citizen*'s ever-clacking Linotype machine (in a small shop in the days before offset printing, it was mandatory to keep "the machine" running, both to make the thing pay and to keep the lead pot from "freezing").

On Thursday, putting on my editor's hat, I wrote a two-column head for my court story and scheduled it for page one, above the fold—top play in the *Citizen* as in any other newspaper. We went to press routinely that night, got the mail copies to the post office in the nick of time, and went off for a few late beers.   5

Working late justified sleeping late; and when I dragged myself into the *Citizen* office about noon that next day, I had a visitor: a worn-out looking woman with a ZaSu Pitts voice, but whose once-haggard eyes were blazing, whose fluttering hands were clenched into fists, and whose graying hair—I suddenly saw at range closer than that of the witness stand—was that of a woman not too many years older than I, who not too long before probably had been considered a peach by the boys in her high-school class.   6

"Mr. Wicker," she said without preamble, "why did you think you had the right to make fun out of me in your paper?"   7

I have never forgotten that question—and I still can't answer it. In 1949 I doubt if I even tried. I remember thinking I had not bargained for such awful moments when I had landed my first reporter's job a few months before. Accurate though my story had been, and based on a public record, it had nevertheless exploited human unhappiness for the amusement or titillation of others. I had made the woman in my office something less than what she was—a human being possessed, despite her misfortunes, of real dignity.   8

Seeing that, I saw too that I had not only done her an   9
injury but missed the story I should have written. This is one
of the besetting sins of journalism—sensationalism at the expense of the dignity and truth of the common human experience. I have been fortunate to have worked mostly for
publishers and editors who sought to avoid that sin—not always successfully. And reading some of the more lurid journals, I've often thought that sensationalism and gossip columns
tend to be techniques employed mostly by big-circulation
publications for an anonymous audience. Not many editors
and reporters would be callous or unseeing enough to engage
in them if they had to face the victims the next morning over
a battered desk in an office not much bigger than a closet.

Comment

Our understanding of the concluding paragraph depends on the
example Wicker develops: without it the "sensationalism" that he
refers to would be a vague term. In developing his example, Wicker
gives us the setting as well as some of the important details—enough
of them to make his point. Had he given all of them, the focus would
have shifted from his own experience as a young reporter to the
woman and the divorce hearing.

Questions for Study and Discussion

1. What information about the divorce does Wicker include, and
   what details show why he found it funny? What other aspects
   of the case might he have included had he wished to focus on
   its humor?
2. How does the episode reveal the "sensationalism" that Wicker
   refers to in the final paragraph?
3. What personal qualities does Wicker reveal in his account of
   the episode? Which of these qualities does he want to stress?
4. Is Wicker saying that the divorce was not newsworthy and
   should not have been reported?

Vocabulary Study

Use your dictionary to explain how Wicker uses the following words: paragraph 1: *heinous, dispensed;* paragraph 2: *foibles, sweltering, vagrancies;* paragraph 3: *ribald, perverse;* paragraph 4: *copious, linotype;* paragraph 8: *exploit, titillation;* paragraph 9: *lurid, callous.*

Suggestions for Writing

1. The character of a newspaper is often revealed by its front page—by what news, what pictures, what headlines the front page includes. Analyze the front page of a paper you read regularly to define its character. Do not try to describe everything on the page. Focus on key details.
2. We have all had experiences like Wicker's in which we made important discoveries about ourselves. Discuss one such experience of your own, giving enough details to let the reader discover what you did. Draw a conclusion from your example.

Pat Orvis
Fathers

Pat Orvis writes what is believed to be the first syndicated column by an American journalist on the people and the problems of Third World countries. She began investigating the Third World because, in her words, "she got tired of reading about anonymous starving masses." Instead, Orvis explores the very human side of Third World life. She is a Vermonter who "grew up poor, too" on a small farm in the Green Mountains. Her essay on fathers covers a wide range of people concisely and informatively.

UNITED NATIONS—Fathers have been rediscovered, as a fringe benefit of the women's liberation movement, a movement that is by now known (and usually condemned) in even the remotest hamlets.

"Women's lib! Women's lib! We've heard enough of it!" an old man hollered through the window as I interviewed his equally senior wife in the twilight of their courtyard in a distant Asian village. (I wasn't crusading: I had simply asked, at the end of a long interview about her daily life, whether she'd ever heard of the women's liberation movement.)

"My wife carried an entire tree home on her head just this morning for our cooking fires," the old man shouted. "What does she need with women's lib?" His wife nodded assent, smiling proudly.

But I also know a younger man—an African father with a Ph.D. and right to a chieftain's title—who baby-sits his kids, often does the washing, and every Saturday leads his family "as a team" in doing the weekly cleaning.

Sure, he lives in Queens, with a laundry room across the hall, and he would never admit to most other Africans that he does "women's work." But he likes it, he said, because it gives him the chance to influence the minds of his children.

In Greece, every Sunday afternoon, fathers can be seen, all dressed up, walking along the waterfront or down main street hand-in-hand with their children. (It's been a Greek tradition—in cities as well as villages—since well before women's lib.)

On the Israeli kibbutz, a father is considered to be his child's playmate, and arranges his work to spend as much time as possible, day and evening, with his offspring.

And as for life in the "unliberated" Third World, UNICEF turned up these surprising facts in a worldwide roundup on "fathering."

In Colombia, the village father stays home to help with household chores during the first week of his child's life—and has his boss's blessing.

In India, fathers are "indulgent with the infant, especially in the matter of giving small amounts of money."

In Bhutan, a man gives his newborn its first bath and (at

least in the case of boys) its first haircut, and some have been known—in the absence of a midwife—to deliver the baby. Couples there work very hard together in the fields. Bhu fathers also help with housework, cooking, and feeding.

"We have learned that the father is at least equally important as the mother as a source of stimulation—emotional and intellectual—and as a role model for both boys and girls," Dr. Hernan Montenegro of Chile's Ministry of Health told UNICEF.

Few fathers quoted in the UNICEF roundup came close to U. S. husband and writer David Brownell, who stays home to raise his daughter, Jean, so his wife, Sara Linnie, can continue her job as lighting designer for the San Francisco Ballet.

Sweden, however, has outpaced the United States in making shared parenting possible. Its "optional paternity leave" allows the new father 10 months from his job, which he can split with his wife or use entirely. Parents of pre-school children also can work part-time at their jobs without loss of status or benefits.

Anthropologist Margaret Mead said years ago, describing a tribal people in New Guinea:

> Fathers show as little embarrassment as mothers in disposing of the very young child's excreta, and as much patience as their wives in persuading a young child to eat soup from one of the clumsy coconut spoons that are always too large for the child's mouth.
>
> The minute day-by-day care of little children, with its routine, its exasperations, its wails of misery that cannot be correctly interpreted, these are as congenial to the Arapesh men as they are to the Arapesh women.
>
> And in recognition of this care, as well as in recognition of the father's initial contribution, if one comments upon a middleaged man as good-looking, the people answer, "Good looking? Ye-e-s? But you should have seen him before he bore all those children."

Comment

Perhaps the most common form of exposition is illustration—developing a thesis through one or more examples. Pat Orvis, in her journalistic essay, states a central idea in her opening paragraph and develops it through a series of far-ranging examples. These examples, including the long concluding quotation from the anthropologist Margaret Mead (whose essay on society's superstitions appears on p. 358), imply much about the effect of women's liberation on fathers themselves. Though she does comment on the African father living in Queens, and she quotes a Chilean official on the benefit of the change in parental roles, Orvis lets her examples make most of her points. The strength of the exposition depends, then, on the strength of the examples.

Questions for Study and Discussion

1. What does Orvis's interview with the Asian husband show? And what point is Orvis making implicitly about Greek and Israeli fathers?
2. Do the examples of Colombian, Indian, and Bhu fathers make the same point? Or are they random examples of worldwide attitudes and practices?
3. Why does Orvis conclude with the statement of Margaret Mead? What is the point of the concluding statement by the Arapesh people, quoted by Mead?
4. Is the essay persuasive as well as informative—that is, is Orvis promoting a certain view as well as informing us about fathers around the world?

Vocabulary Study

1. In the reference section of your college library, find a discussion of the Israeli kibbutz. How does the organization of work and the raising of children on the kibbutz help you to understand the everyday life of fathers and children referred to by Orvis?
2. Investigate the world of the Arapesh in Margaret Mead's

Growing Up in New Guinea or another book. How does the discussion illuminate the statement of Mead?

Suggestions for Writing

1. State an idea of your own related to changing relationships between parents and children. Develop the idea through a series of brief observations or personal experiences. Conclude your essay with the example that you consider most revealing or decisive.

2. Develop one of the following statements through a series of examples drawn from your observation and personal experience:
   a. The first week in a new school can be frustrating.
   b. Words often have different meanings for parents and children.
   c. Making friends is often hard work.

The New Yorker
Bad News

The New Yorker Magazine publishes some of the best and most influential social and political commentary of leading American writers. John Hersey's *Hiroshima*, Rachel Carson's *Silent Spring*, and Jonathan Schell's *The Fate of the Earth* first appeared in *The New Yorker*. Each issue opens with a section titled "The Talk of the Town"—a collection of short sketches and commentaries written by the staff of the magazine. E. B. White, John Updike, and Lillian Ross have written many of these. This commentary on reading the news is taken from "The Talk of the Town."

From time to time, people complain that the papers don't   1
print any good news. (Presidents, especially tend to complain

about this.) First off, it isn't entirely true. If we never see another story about a man who wins a million dollars playing
Lotto or Millionaire's Roulette or Lucky Bucks and is going
to keep his job at the post office because he likes to work but
maybe he'll buy an Oldsmobile—if we never see another story
like that, we won't kick. But, anyway, good news is not a
newspaper's job. We don't mean this the way it sounds, in
some civics-class, watchdog-of-the-democratic-process, Fourth
Estate sense. We mean that psychologically there is something reassuring about the newspaper *because* it is full of bad
news—the same bad news each morning. Not precisely the
same bad news, but close enough. On any given morning, the
front page of the *Times* should leave people in tears. As we
write this, we are looking at the top stories from last
Wednesday. The Soviet Union is reported overrunning a valley in Afghanistan after using high-altitude bombing to soften
up the resistance; talk continues about outer-space laser
weapons; in the Dominican Republic people are dying in riots
sparked by increases in food prices. We should be angry, sad,
and moved to action, but we are, at worst, mildly depressed
in a familiar, unfocussed way. Colonel Qaddafi says something evil, or was it Ayatollah Khomeini? There are thugs on
the F train; last week, they rode the No. 6. A house burns
down in Brooklyn, and another the next day, and two more
the day after that. There is no sense reacting, we think; this
is how the world is. Everything bad has already happened and
will happen again.

On slow news days—the days when the New York *Times* 2
actually leads with a story about something taking place in
New York—we sometimes feel a little uneasy. If not much is
going wrong this morning, what could be in store for tomorrow? And occasionally, when something does give us
pause, likely as not it's only because it is something freakish—something we hadn't worried about before—and we accept it into our picture of the inevitable world, and read about
it from then on with detachment. Last week, Kitty Wolf was
driving her grandson Robert to the airport so that he could

catch a flight back to school. When they were near Exit 13-A on the New Jersey Turnpike, more than a hundred ounce-and-a-half jars of Dickinson's Pure Fancy Sweet Orange Marmalade fell from the sky, shattering the windshield of the car but not hurting anyone seriously. The jellies apparently fell from a transcontinental airliner, but no one knows just how. "It's a puzzlement trying to find out how it happened," an airline spokesman told the *Times*. If every single morning, or even twice a month, you opened the paper to find an account of grocery items falling onto passing Volkswagens, Mrs. Wolf's travail would not be so arresting. But *marmalade*—marmalade, usually marvellously inert, an inmate of its jar until you choose otherwise and reach for a knife. Here it is, though, in the exit lane of the New Jersey Turnpike, an orange bolt from the blue. It is hard to imagine a more meaningless story; yet—and this is truly sad—it made us think twice as hard as any food riot in Santo Domingo.

Comment

"All news is bad news," you believe, and reading the daily newspaper seems to support that belief. *The New Yorker* shows how something unexpected or strange in the news forces a reaction—makes you think twice about what you have read. Without examples you would have at best a vague idea of what *The New Yorker* is saying. What is bad news to one reader is not bad news to another. The essay would therefore fail as exposition. It would also fail as a persuasive piece of writing. To hold the interest and gain the assent of readers, the essay must have the sense of truth. To gain that sense, readers must look closely at their own world and experience. The more interesting and vital the examples, the more readers will begin to think about their world.

Questions for Study and Discussion

1. *The New Yorker* tells us that "there is something reassuring about the newspaper *because* it is full of bad news—the same bad news

each morning." How does the first paragraph illustrate this thesis idea?

2. How does paragraph 2 illustrate the same idea?

3. Had *The New Yorker* wished to build to the thesis statement instead of introducing it early, how might the essay be reorganized?

4. Do you agree that "it is hard to imagine a more meaningless story" than that of the airborne marmalade? In general, do you find the examples effective in the two paragraphs?

Vocabulary Study

1. Words are often chosen for their connotations or associations. The connotation may be positive or pleasing, or it may be negative or unpleasant. The word may also call a picture to mind. What are the connotations of the italicized words?

   a. "*watchdog*-of-the democratic process"
   b. "high-altitude bombing to *soften up* the resistance"
   c. "*thugs* on the F train"
   d. "only because it is something *freakish*"
   e. "an *inmate* of its jar"

2. What synonyms, or words having approximately the same meaning, might substitute for these words and the phrase? What is gained or lost in meaning through the substitution?

Suggestions for Writing

1. Describe your own feelings in reading the front page of a newspaper on a particular day. Give details of what you found on the page, and use them to lead into an observation of your own.

2. Discuss your agreement or disagreement with the statement that "psychologically there is something reassuring about the newspaper *because* it is full of bad news. . . . " Provide your own examples from a recent issue.

3. Illustrate and discuss some of your reasons for reading a newspaper. Lead into a central idea or thesis suggested by these illustrations and reasons.

Process

Another important kind of informative writing is process analysis. A *process* is any activity or operation that contains steps which are usually performed in sequence. It may be a mechanical one, like changing a tire, or a natural one, like the circulation of the blood. The process referred to in the following statement is a natural one:

> Just as human individuals and populations undergo continual alteration in response to infectious disease, so also the various infectious organisms that provoke disease undergo a process of adaptation and adjustment to their environment.—William H. McNeill, *Plagues and Peoples*

These are the two common types of process analysis.

A third type of process analysis deals with a historical process—one that occurred in the past, and can occur again, according to identifiable causes and effects. In the following passage on bubonic plague, McNeill identifies both:

> First, the steamship network that arose in the 1870s was the vehicle that dispersed the infection around the globe, and did so, once the epidemic broke out in Canton and Hong Kong, with a speed that was limited only by the speed with which a ship could

144

carry its colony of infected rats and fleas to a new port. Speed was obviously decisive in allowing a chain of infection to remain unbroken from port to port. Since it creates immunities among survivors, *Pasteurella pestis* was, after all, certain to run out of susceptible hosts among a ship's company of rats, fleas, and men within a few weeks.

Whether mechanical, natural, or historical, the steps of a process are usually described chronologically. In mechanical processes, you may have a choice of procedures or tools, and you may decide to describe more than one of these—for example, you may discuss several kinds of tire jacks and how they work. In the course of explanation, you may have to define and illustrate key terms, make comparisons, and comment on the uses of the process.

Many processes like the transmission of plague are complex: they contain several related processes, each of which must be carefully distinguished. For example, the instruction book that gives directions for wiring a stereo receiver and a tape deck to a turntable and speakers describes each process step by step. Assembling a receiver from a kit is even more complex a procedure.

Jack Trueblood
For a Love of Fishing

Jack Trueblood is an outdoor and conservation writer, who for five years was a contributing editor to *Field and Stream Magazine*. A graduate of Boise State University, he writes frequently about southern Idaho where he lives. Trueblood's comments on how to teach children may be compared with the comments of Goodman and Meyrowitz.

Johnson Creek, where it flows into the North Fork of the   1
Boise River, was about three times as wide as a boy is tall

Originally published in *Field & Stream*, June 1983. Reprinted by permission of Jack Trueblood.

when I discovered it. It is a fast creek, cutting its path through granite mountains as it descends from lakes high in Idaho's Sawtooth Wilderness. There are log jams there that have made a great array of holes, pools, backwaters, and riffles, all hiding trout.

One day when we were about fourteen a friend and I   2
fished our way up Johnson Creek, working alternate pools and not concerned with much of anything except the absolute freedom of our situation and the knowledge that we had the ability to catch the wild little cutthroats. When the day was about half used we decided that lunch was in order, so we kept the next four fish and cleaned them while a smokeless willow-twig fire burned to coals on a gravel bar beside the water. Fresh coals were occasionally added from a small fire next to the broiling bed, and the trout we cooked on green willow branches were as good as any fine restaurant could serve. This was an annual event for several years, and the reason it became such a good memory, I think, was not because we could catch the fish, but because we didn't have to.

My parents provided me with the opportunity to be near   3
fishing water from an early age. If you would teach a child to love fishing, do *not* put a rod in his hand and insist that he follow along and imitate you. All too often you find that you have moved into water too rough for the kid to handle, or that the casts required are too long, or that there is nothing for him to do but watch.

Setting is the first necessity in helping a child learn to love   4
fishing. If you live in an area where camping requires a considerable amount of time, perhaps you can find a pond, lake, or creek nearby to use when teaching the elements of casting. If not, a big lawn will do, but a youngster is likely to become impatient and fiddle with the dandelions instead of the rod. Kids usually want to learn to fish, and the value of learning to cast well becomes obvious only after they need the skill.

I've used a fly rod from as early as I can remember, and   5
learned how to handle it while catching crappies from a lake with shores clear of brush. Crappies in season will keep even

a novice interested, and it's easy to catch enough to build your confidence. By the time I started fishing seriously on mountain streams I could cast a fly well enough to get by, knew what a strike felt like and how to set up my own tackle. In short, I had passed the primer course in fly fishing before I ever attempted fishing in rough terrain.

My introduction to trout was in places like Granite Creek   6
on the Boise River in Idaho. As trout streams go, Granite isn't much. It wouldn't get mentioned by most of the people who haunt Silver Creek or Henry's Fork of the Snake. But if you and your old man are crouched under willow branches at the edge of a tiny creek while he quietly explains where the trout will be and how to gently flip a fly so that it will pass over them, then Granite Creek is Henry's Fork. Or Silver Creek. Or the Madison. At that moment you are at the center of the world, and all things come to you.

There was a log bridge on Granite Creek, and it was pos-   7
sible for a greenhorn boy to catch wriggling cutthroats just by lying on the bridge and sneaking the tip of his rod over the edge, then easing line out until the fly danced on the water. I soon learned that the same type of sneaking will score on trout from streamside.

A prime ingredient of setting is what the child can do   8
when he tires of fishing. Logging hadn't reached Granite Creek yet, so the road was primitive and there was no traffic. My brother Dan and I were great explorers when we weren't fishing, and an old sheep corral near camp lent itself to all types of boyhood adventures.

My father, who had experience at being a boy, didn't get   9
upset when we wanted to go climbing around the fences rather than fish. Instead he went with us, explaining where the truck had unloaded the sheep and pointing out the trail they had taken into the high country. We were intrigued by his explanation of the nomadic life of a sheepherder and his pack string. The success of his teaching was in letting us pursue our interests.

My age at the time of that trip was less than nine. When   10

I got tired of fishing, there was always something else to do. The point is that you can't teach a kid to love fishing by taking him to a place that is desolate or boring or cold. Go to places that would be good to visit with your kids even if there were no fishing, because he or she is going to be a kid first and then a fisherman.

The abundance of fish is another big factor. Getting   11
enough pan-sized trout for a meal was no problem where we kids fished. In the summertime they weren't finicky feeders, and by the time I was fourteen and needed a license, I knew enough about flies to do quite well. It takes only a few times up a stream with an experienced fisherman for a youngster to learn the basics, and long before I learned about hatches and fly colors I knew that I should carry a few of different types: Black Gnat and Brown Hackle for the times when dark colors were winners, Renegade and Royal Coachman when a splash of white was important, a couple of light-colored dry flies, and a few wet flies. Armed with this selection of a dozen or so, a pocketknife, and a light rod, I soon learned that every likely looking spot usually does hold a trout.

The streams I fished as a boy were not too big to wade,   12
and that's the kind I take my kids to. Pick streams gentle enough that a child can wade across in most places. Of course there will be deep holes or rapids that might be dangerous, but most youngsters won't get foolhardy in these places if the rest of the stream is something they can handle.

Brush is a thing you should consider too. A kid will be   13
slapped in the face by brush adults can push aside. Streams completely enclosed by brush should be avoided because they are too hard for a youngster to approach or to fish.

The tackle a beginner uses is most often like that of his   14
teacher. I was brought up to use a fly rod, though most of my friends used spinning tackle. Whatever you decide to start your student with, a few general guidelines are in order.

To begin with, make it light. This will usually mean that   15
it will be more his or her size and less awkward or burdensome to carry, and that it will transmit the feel of the fish bet-

ter than a heavy outfit. Next, make it durable. Kids often forget about stubbing the rod tip when walking, or laying the rod down in a careless place. Also, keep it simple. This will help avoid backlash and tangle problems, and make it easier to sort out those that do occur. And finally, buy quality. A nice, well-balanced outfit purchased when a kid is twelve can be used for the rest of his life, whereas an awkward, poorly made one may discourage the beginner, and in any case, will have to be upgraded as he becomes a better caster.

When I was a youngster, my folks took my brother and me on a camping vacation every summer. The "boy trips," as they came to be called, were two weeks to a month and in some of the most scenic places imaginable. It was on these summertime trips that we both learned about trout fishing, with camping and mountain lore as an added bonus. 16

Our favorite stream meandered through willows and provided a multitude of good pools and cut banks in addition to beaver ponds. Kids can learn a lot about trout from beaver ponds because they can see the fish. I can remember finding out that trout are frightened by footsteps on quaky ground. Although it had been explained before, it wasn't quite believable until I could actually see them dart for cover. 17

Another thing you can teach a beginner on a beaver pond is how well trout can see. In still water you can point out how fish are frightened by the shadow of a line, and the impact of a heavy-handed cast is obvious. Kids learn how to make a fly drift gently to the water, or if spinning, how to cast beyond fish and bring the bait or lure to them instead of bonking them on the head with it. The novice soon realizes that fish can see better through and out of water than people can into it, and the lessons will carry over whether the water is rough or smooth. 18

After the beginner has learned the mechanics of using his tackle, about the best way to help is by leaving yours in camp. Now you have made him the center of attention, and he knows that you are really interested. When the youngster shows signs of tiredness or is catching so many trout that you just can't 19 stand it, ask if you might use his gear to fish the next hole. This makes a kid feel important—after all, the adult wants what he has for a change, instead of the other way around.

Another advantage of leaving your tackle is that you can   20 give hands-on aid to the beginner. Stand (kneel if your student is short) immediately behind the learner and grasp the rod grip just ahead of his hand. You do the work of casting and the learner just sort of coasts along and learns from the feel of your cast things that are difficult to put into words, like the amount of force used and the timing. The beginner should control the line, letting it out as you instruct him to. Soon you apply less and less force and he naturally puts a little more effort into it, until you just step back and leave him in control. This often works better than the clearest of instructions.

Children have an attention span that shortens in direct   21 proportion to their frustration. Probably the greatest frustration to a child is a forceful, nagging, angry teacher. Enjoyment, after all, is the basic reason for sport fishing, and you have to enjoy your companions as well as your sport.

You can't teach kids to appreciate fishing if you isolate   22 yourself in the adult world and leave them in the child's world. You must remember that you, too, have experience at being a boy or girl, and use that experience to communicate the quality of life that is available to you and your kids somewhere along the creek.

Comment

Though his essay is chiefly concerned with giving information about fishing, Trueblood expresses his own love of the sport and tells us much about his background and interests. He also has a point to make about the process he describes. Trueblood might have focused on one of the many topics he discusses—for example, casting on a still pond—and given many more details about this skill. He chooses instead to cover a few details only, presenting those that develop his central point.

Questions for Study and Discussion

1. What is the central point Trueblood is making about children and fishing? How does the process described develop this point?
2. What are the stages of the process? Which stages does Trueblood describe in the most detail, and why?
3. What do you discover about Trueblood as a person through his discussion of his childhood experiences and of fishing?

Vocabulary Study

Plain and untechnical as Trueblood's description of fishing is, some of the steps would require different language or additional details if the essay were addressed to children rather than to parents. Rewrite the following sentences in words children would understand:

a. "Crappies in season will keep even a novice interested and it's easy to catch enough to build your confidence." (paragraph 5)
b. "By the time I started fishing seriously on mountain streams I could cast a fly well enough to get by, knew what a strike felt like and how to set up my own tackle." (paragraph 5)
c. "Kids learn how to make a fly drift gently to the water, or if spinning, how to cast beyond fish and bring the bait or lure to them instead of bonking them on the head with it." (paragraph 18)

Suggestions for Writing

1. Describe how to teach children a skill similar to fishing. Explain why children will find this skill rewarding, and why it has been rewarding to you.
2. Describe a process you have performed many times—for example, changing a bicycle or an automobile tire or threading and operating a sewing machine. Assume that your reader knows nothing about the necessary tools or machinery. Before writ-

ing consider what details you must provide and what terms you
must define at each stage of the process.

3. Certain jobs can be performed in more than one way—for example, training a dog not to jump on people. Discuss various
ways of doing this or a similar job. Keep these ways distinct
for your reader.

4. Trace a historical process like making the decision to attend
college. Comment on the implications of some of the stages as
you describe the process.

John Jerome
The S-stroke

John Jerome has written numerous articles and books on a variety of sports. His books include *Skiing* (1971), *The Death of the
Automobile* (1972), *On Mountains* (1978), and *The Sweet Spot In
Time* (1980). His description of the S-stroke, originally addressed to readers of a science magazine, is more technical in its
details than it would be for the usual sports newspaper or magazine. Jerome succeeds in describing a difficult process to readers
unfamiliar with swimming as well as to those familiar with the
sport.

When the 1976 Montreal Olympics came to an end, there   1
was only one swimming world record left on the books that
was more than two months old. Mark Spitz's seven gold-medal
times at Munich in 1972 wouldn't even have qualified him
for the 1984 U.S. team tryouts. This remarkable transience
of swimming records cannot be attributed to a new diet or a
wonder drug. It's simpler than that: Swimmers have learned
how to use their hands, arms, and feet better.

It is true that some of the improvements in swimming performance have come from attention to external details. Water hasn't gotten any faster, but swimming pools have. It is turbulence that most interferes with fast swimming—choppy water on the surface, roiling minicurrents below—and when racers dive in eight abreast or hit the wall with flip turns virtually in unison, you get aquatic chaos. The new pools hold the water still. They are at least seven and a half feet deep to reduce the effects of waves rebounding off the bottom; their gutters swallow waves and give no turbulence back. Even the dividers between the racing lanes are strung with intricately finned disks to damp out wavelets.

Swimsuits are now made from exotic stretch nylons and Lycra—thinner, tighter, and slicker—to reduce drag. One new fabric is polymer-coated so the surface repels water; swimsuits made from it must be put on wet so the polymer coating won't split and so it seals around body contours. (The suit however, is not recommended for distances beyond 400 meters because perspiration under it can cause extra drag.)

Coaches also say that the pace of recordbreaking accelerated when swimmers started wearing racing goggles. By reducing eye irritation from pool chemicals, the goggles permit swimmers to put in two or three times more training yardage per workout. And to swimmers, training yardage is like money in the bank.

But it is in the biomechanics and biochemistry of swimming that more profound discoveries are being made. It turns out that what a good swimmer does is quite different not only from what he appears to be doing but usually from what he thinks he is doing.

For example, in the freestyle, backstroke, and butterfly— strokes in which the arms move forward above the water—a good swimmer's hand may come out of the water ahead of where it entered. "Basically, the swimmer is anchoring the hand in the water, then pulling the body past it," says Ernest Maglischo of Bakersfield State College in California. "When the hand first enters the water, it slips forward for quite a distance, so by the time it comes out, it's still ahead of where it went in."

Swimmers themselves have trouble believing this. They 7 have the impression that they're pulling their hand through the water like a canoe paddle. Inexperienced swimmers try to swim this way, pulling the arm and hand in a straight line beneath the body. This is not only ineffective but difficult to do: Water pressure makes the hand and arm dart from side to side, and it takes a great deal of muscle to overcome this darting motion. When powerful swimmers pull hard, the hands seem naturally to pursue an S-shaped path. Until the mid-1960s, this S-curve was regarded as a technical flaw, and worldclass racers struggled to erase it from their strokes. But it kept winning races.

Maglischo, a swim coach and exercise physiologist, has 8 shown why. The hand and forearm, he says, are used less as paddles than as propeller blades. In the swimming stroke, the hand and the forearm form a plane. As this plane slides through the water, the fluid is divided into two streams. The stream that goes over the curved back of the hand (the top of an airplane wing or the front of a propeller blade) must travel faster than the stream over the palm of the hand (or the back of the blade). This creates less pressure on the top of the hand and more pressure on the palm, generating a force akin to the lift generated by an airplane wing.

A paddle pulls straight back, its blade at right angles to 9 a boat's motion. The boat is pushed forward because water resists the movement of the blade. Propellers, on the other hand, are pitched to thrust water back, producing a lift that pushes the boat forward—a more efficient means of propulsion. "I give a little demonstration to my swimmers at the beginning of a season," says Maglischo. "I put a toy paddle boat and a propeller boat in the water. The propeller boat beats the hell out of the paddle boat every time."

Thus the search for swimming efficiency is a search for 10 angles of attack by the hands, arms, and even the feet that will provide the greatest forward pressure for the energy put into them. Since we can't rotate the hands and feet like propeller blades, we must generate forward pressure in other ways. The S-curve is the best other way. In sweeping the hand through its S, the swimmer's cue that he is getting the best pull is the resistance of the water to the hand. But sometimes the most resistance comes when the pull is slightly misaligned, dragging or pushing the body off-line. The swimmer must learn to sense the tiniest deflections from the ideal straight line forward and adjust the pitch of the hand.

Even a mechanically perfect stroke won't win any races without the strength and endurance to keep the arms stroking. That's why Maglischo and exercise physiologist David Costill, director of the Human Performance Lab at Indiana's Ball State University, are not just interested in how to swim but in how much. It is a question that has usually been answered with the theory that more just had to be better.   11

Top-level swimmers are gluttons for work, regularly putting in six to nine miles of training per day. Swimming burns energy at about four times the rate of running; an eight-mile swim is roughly equivalent to a 32-mile run. This conversion is not perfectly linear, of course, and some advantages go to the swimmer: The water is an automatic cooling system, and there's no wear and tear on the body from hitting the ground. Runners who overtrain eventually injure their ankles or knees or shins; when swimmers train themselves into debilitation, they tend to suffer from depression, insomnia, and overexhaustion. These in turn may lead to a rash of physical symptoms that mimic flu and can turn into something very much like mononucleosis.   12

To find out how hard swimmers can train without breakdown, Costill corrals tired swimmers during and after practice and measures the levels of lactic acid and blood pH. High lactic acid and low pH inhibit muscle action, and their levels indicate how tired the muscles are and what they're capable of. Or he checks the levels of glycogen—the muscle fuel of   13 long-distance swimming—for signs of depletion. From this research Costill has set a level of training intensity below which a swimmer can work out several days in a row without beginning to break down. A workout above that intensity, he says, should be followed by a day off—or at the very least, by a less demanding practice.

Swimming races of more than 200 meters in length are mostly aerobic in nature, the muscles getting the bulk of their energy from consumption of oxygen in the blood. Most swimming races, however, are 200 meters or shorter, and highly anaerobic. The muscles in these events are powered primarily by a metabolic pathway that doesn't use oxygen, building up an oxygen debt that will be paid back only after the event is over. "Most exercise research in recent years has been on aerobic metabolism," Costill says. "But most of swim racing is highly anaerobic. There's a lot we don't yet know about the anaerobic side of things." No doubt just the things that will make the human propellers even faster. 14

Comment

Though Jerome is describing the overall process of becoming a successful long-distance swimmer, he focuses on one stage of this process—improving the swimming stroke. His description of the S-stroke depends on a special kind of comparison—analogy. The point-by-point comparison begins in paragraph 8 with the comparison of the hand and forearms to propeller blades, then in paragraph 9 he compares them to paddles. The difficulty of this stage of the process invites these analogies. Though the swimmer will profit from Jerome's explanation, Jerome is addressing a general audience; he explains terms and gives certain details that a special audience of swimmers would not require. As in Trueblood's discussion of fishing, a clearly-defined point of view is essential.

Questions for Study and Discussion

1. How do you discover the purpose of the essay? Does Jerome state his purpose directly, or does he imply it?
2. Why does Jerome focus on the S-stroke?
3. What are the points of similarity between hand and forearm and the propeller blade? And under circumstances would hand and forearm resemble the paddle?
4. What other stages of the process does Jerome discuss? Which does he give the least attention, and why?
5. What stages or details would require the least discussion (or no discussion) if Jerome were writing to swimmers only? Would his use of analogy have been appropriate for this audience as well as for a general audience?
6. From what physical point of view does Jerome describe the S-stroke—from that of an onlooker at the edge of the pool or from that of a swimming coach standing in the pool?

Vocabulary Study

Define the following technical terms: *flip turns, dividers* (paragraph 2); *polymer coating* (paragraph 3); *biomechanics, biochemistry* (paragraph 5); *freestyle, backstroke, butterfly* (paragraph 6); *conversion, linear, mononucleosis* (paragraph 12); *lactic acid, blood pH, glycogen* (paragraph 13); *aerobic, anaerobic, metabolic pathway* (paragraph 14).

Suggestions for Writing

1. Explain the S-stroke in your own words, without using the analogies of paragraphs 8–10. Then discuss the problems you encountered in making your explanation.
2. Describe one of the swimming strokes Jerome mentions, or another activity, in language appropriate to a general audience.

L. *Rust Hills*
How to Eat
an Ice-Cream Cone

Rust Hills was born in 1924 in Brooklyn, New York, and attended the United States Merchant Marine Academy and Wesleyan University. He was fiction editor of *Esquire* and *The Saturday
Evening Post,* has taught writing, and is now a freelance writer.
His books include *How to Do Things Right* (1972), *How to Retire
at 41* (1973), and *How to Be Good* (1976).

Before you even get the cone, you have to do a lot of   1
planning about it. We'll assume that you lost the argument
in the car and that the family has decided to break the automobile journey and stop at an ice-cream stand for cones. Get
things straight with them right from the start. Tell them that
after they have their cones there will be an imaginary circle
six feet away from the car and that no one—man, woman, or
especially child—will be allowed to cross the line and reenter
the car until his ice-cream cone has been entirely consumed
and he has cleaned himself up. Emphasize: Automobiles and
ice-cream cones don't mix. Explain: Melted ice cream, children, is a fluid that is eternally sticky. One drop of it on a
car-door handle spreads to the seat covers, to trousers, to
hands, and thence to the steering wheel, the gearshift, the
rearview mirror, all the knobs of the dashboard—spreads
everywhere and lasts *forever,* spreads from a nice old car like
this, which might have to be abandoned because of sticki-
ness, right into a nasty new car, in secret ways that even scientists don't understand. If necessary, even make a joke: "The
family that eats ice-cream cones together sticks together." Then

From *How to Do Things Right* by L. Rust Hills. Reprinted by permission of L. Rust
Hills.

let their mother explain the joke and tell them you don't mean half of what you say, and no, we won't be getting a new car.

Blessed are the children who always eat the same flavor   2 of ice cream or always know beforehand what kind they will want. Such good children should be quarantined from those who want to "wait and see what flavors there are." It's a sad thing to observe a beautiful young child who has always been perfectly happy with a plain vanilla ice-cream cone being subverted by a young schoolmate who has been invited along for the weekend—a pleasant and polite visitor, perhaps, but spoiled by permissive parents and scarred by an overactive imagination. This schoolmate has a flair for contingency planning: "Well, I'll have banana if they have banana, but if they don't have banana then I'll have peach, if it's fresh peach, and if they don't have banana or fresh peach I'll see what else they have that's like that, like maybe fresh strawberry or something, and if they don't have that or anything like that that's good I'll just have chocolate marshmallow chip or chocolate ripple or something like that." Then—turning to one's own once simple and innocent child, now already corrupt and thinking fast— the schoolmate invites a similar rigmarole. "What kind are *you* going to have?"

I'm a great believer in contingency planning, but none of   3 this is realistic. Few adults, and even fewer children, are able to make up their minds beforehand what kind of ice-cream cone they'll want. It would be nice if they could all be lined up in front of the man who is making up the cones and just snap smartly when their turn came, "Strawberry, please," "Vanilla, please," "Chocolate, please." But of course it never happens like that. There is always a great discussion, a great jostling and craning of necks and leaning over the counter to see down into the tubs of ice cream, and much interpersonal consultation—"What kind are *you* having?"—back and forth, as if that should make any difference. Until finally the first child's turn comes and he asks the man, "What kinds do you have?"

Now, this is the stupidest question in the world, because   4 there is always a sign posted saying what kinds of ice cream they have. As I tell the children, that's what they put the sign up there for—so you won't have to ask what kinds of ice cream they have. The man gets sick of telling everybody all the different kinds of ice cream they have, so they put a sign up there that *says*. You're supposed to read it, not ask the man.

"All right, but the sign doesn't say strawberry."   5

"Well, that means they don't have strawberry."   6

"But there *is* strawberry, right there."   7

"That must be raspberry or something." (Look again at   8
the sign. Raspberry isn't there, either.)

When the child's turn actually comes, he says, "Do you   9
have strawberry?"

"Sure."   10

"What other kinds do you have?"   11

The trouble is, of course, that they put up that sign say-   12
ing what flavors they have, with little cardboard inserts to put in or take out flavors, way back when they first opened the store. But they never change the sign—or not often enough. They always have flavors that aren't on the list, and often they don't have flavors that *are* on the list. Children know this—whether innately or from earliest experience it would be hard to say. The ice-cream man knows it, too. Even grownups learn it eventually. There will always be chaos and confusion and mind-changing and general uproar when ice-cream cones are being ordered, and there has not been, is not, and will never be any way to avoid it.

Human beings are incorrigibly restless and dissatisfied,   13
always in search of new experiences and sensations, seldom content with the familiar. It is this, I think, that accounts for people wanting to have a taste of your cone, and wanting you to have a taste of theirs. "*Do* have a taste of this fresh peach—it's delicious," my wife used to say to me, very much (I suppose) the way Eve wanted Adam to taste her delicious apple. An insinuating look of calculating curiosity would film my wife's eyes—the same look those beautiful, scary women in those depraved Italian films give a man they're interested in.

"How's *yours*?" she would say. For this reason, I always order chocolate chip now. Down through the years, all those close enough to me to feel entitled to ask for a taste of my cone—namely, my wife and children—have learned what chocolate chip tastes like, so they have no legitimate reason to ask me for a taste. As for tasting other people's cones, never do it. The reasoning here is that if it tastes good, you'll wish you'd had it; if it tastes bad, you'll have had a taste of something that tastes bad; if it doesn't taste either good or bad, then you won't have missed anything. Of course no person in his right mind ever *would* want to taste anyone else's cone, but it is useful to have good, logical reasons for hating the thought of it.

Another important thing. Never let the man hand you the ice-cream cones for the whole group. There is no sight more pathetic than some bumbling disorganized papa holding four ice-cream cones in two hands, with his money still in his pocket, when the man says, "Eighty cents." What does he do then? He can't hand the cones back to the man to hold while he fishes in his pocket for the money, for the man has just given them to *him*. He can start passing them out to the kids, but at least one of them will have gone back to the car to see how the dog is doing, or have been sent round in back by his mother to wash his hands or something. And even if papa does get them distributed, he's still going to be left with his own cone in one hand while he tries to get his money with the other. Meanwhile, of course, the man is very impatient, and the next group is asking him, "What flavors do you have?"

No, never let the man hand you the cones of others. Make him hand them out to each kid in turn. That way, too, you won't get those disgusting blobs of butter pecan and black raspberry on your own chocolate chip. And insist that he tell you how much it all costs and settle with him *before* he hands you your own cone. Make sure everyone has got paper napkins and everything *before* he hands you your own cone. Get *everything* straight before he hands you your own cone. Then, as he hands you your own cone, reach out and take it from him. Strange, magical, dangerous moment! It shares something of the mysterious, sick thrill that soldiers are said to feel on the eve of a great battle.

Now, consider for a moment just exactly what it is that you are about to be handed. It is a huge, irregular mass of ice cream, faintly domed at the top from the metal scoop, which has first produced it and then insecurely balanced it on the uneven top edge of a hollow inverted cone made out of the most brittle and fragile of materials. Clumps of ice cream hang over the side, very loosely attached to the main body. There is always much more ice cream than the cone could hold, even if the ice cream were tamped down into the cone, which of course it isn't. And the essence of ice cream is that it melts. It doesn't just stay there teetering in this irregular, top-heavy mass; it also melts. And it melts *fast*. And it doesn't just melt— it melts into a sticky fluid that *cannot* be wiped off. The only thing one person could hand to another that might possibly be more dangerous is a live hand grenade from which the pin had been pulled five seconds earlier. And of course if anybody offered you that, you could say, "Oh. Uh, well—no thanks."

Ice-cream men handle cones routinely, and are inured. They are like professionals who are used to handling sticks of TNT; their movements are quick and skillful. An ice-cream man will pass a cone to you casually, almost carelessly. Never accept a cone on this basis! Too many brittle sugar cones (the only good kind) are crushed or chipped or their ice-cream tops knocked askew, by this casual sort of transfer from hand to hand. If the ice-cream man is attempting this kind of brusque transfer, keep your hands at your side, no matter what effort it may cost you to overcome the instinct by which everyone's hand goes out, almost automatically, whenever he is proffered something delicious and expected. Keep your hands at your side, and the ice-cream man will look up at you, startled, questioning. Lock his eyes with your own, and *then*, slowly, calmly, and above all deliberately, take the cone from him.

Grasp the cone with the right hand firmly but gently be- 18 tween thumb and at least one but not more than three fingers, two-thirds of the way up the cone. Then dart swiftly away to an open area, away from the jostling crowd at the stand. Now take up the classic ice-cream-cone-eating stance: feet from one to two feet apart, body bent forward from the waist at a twenty-five-degree angle, right elbow well up, right forearm horizontal, at a level with your collarbone and about twelve inches from it. But don't start eating yet! Check first to see what emergency repairs may be necessary. Sometimes a sugar cone will be so crushed or broken or cracked that all one can do is gulp at the thing like a savage, getting what he can of it and letting the rest drop to the ground, and then evacuating the area of catastrophe as quickly as possible. Checking the cone for possible trouble can be done in a second or two, if one knows where to look and does it systematically. A trouble spot some people overlook is the bottom tip of the cone. This may have been broken off. Or the flap of the cone material at the bottom, usually wrapped over itself in that funny spiral construction, may be folded in a way that is imperfect and leaves an opening. No need to say that through this opening—in a matter of perhaps thirty or, at most, ninety seconds—will begin to pour hundreds of thousands of sticky molecules of melted ice cream. You know in this case that you must instantly get the paper napkin in your left hand under and around the bottom of the cone to stem the forthcoming flow, or else be doomed to eat the cone far too rapidly. It is a grim moment. No one wants to eat a cone under that kind of pressure, but neither does anyone want to end up with the bottom of the cone stuck to a messy napkin. There's one other alternative—one that takes both skill and courage: Forgoing any cradling action, grasp the cone more firmly between thumb and forefinger and extend the other fingers so that they are out of the way of the dripping from the bottom, then increase the waist-bend angle from twenty-five degrees to thirty-five degrees, and then eat the cone, *allowing* it to drip out of the bottom onto the ground in front of you! Experienced and thoughtful cone-eaters enjoy facing up to this kind of sudden challenge.

So far, we have been concentrating on cone problems, but of course there is the ice cream to worry about, too. In this area, immediate action is sometimes needed on three fronts at once. Frequently the ice cream will be mounted on the cone in a way that is perilously lopsided. This requires immediate corrective action to move it back into balance—a slight pressure downward with the teeth and lips to seat the ice cream more firmly in and on the cone, but not so hard, of course, as to break the cone. On other occasions, gobs of ice cream will be hanging loosely from the main body, about to fall to the ground (bad) or onto one's hand (far, far worse). This requires instant action, too; one must snap at the gobs like a frog in a swarm of flies. Sometimes, trickles of ice cream will already (already!) be running down the cone toward one's fingers, and one must quickly raise the cone, tilting one's face skyward, and lick with an upward motion that pushes the trickles away from the fingers and (as much as possible) into one's mouth. Every ice-cream cone is like every other ice-cream cone in that it potentially can present all of these problems, but each ice-cream cone is paradoxically unique in that it will present the problems in a different order of emergency and degree of severity. It is, thank God, a rare ice-cream cone that

will present all three kinds of problems in exactly the same degree of emergency. With each cone, it is necessary to make an instantaneous judgment as to where the greatest danger is, and to *act!* A moment's delay, and the whole thing will be a mess before you've even tasted it *(Fig. 1)*. If it isn't possible to decide between any two of the three basic emergency problems (i.e., lopsided mount, dangling gobs, running trickles),

Fig. 1

19

allow yourself to make an arbitrary adjudication; assign a "heads" value to one and a "tails" value to the other, then flip a coin to decide which is to be tended to first. Don't, for heaven's sake, *actually* flip a coin—you'd have to dig in your pocket for it, or else have it ready in your hand before you were handed the cone. There isn't remotely enough time for anything like that. Just decide *in your mind* which came up, heads or tails, and then try to remember as fast as you can which of the problems you had assigned to the winning side of the coin. Probably, though, there isn't time for any of this. Just do something, however arbitrary. Act! *Eat!*

In trying to make wise and correct decisions about the 20 ice-cream cone in your hand, you should always keep the objectives in mind. The main objective, of course, is to get the cone under control. Secondarily, one will want to eat the cone calmly and with pleasure. Real pleasure lies not simply in eating the cone but in eating it *right*. Let us assume that you have darted to your open space and made your necessary emergency repairs. The cone is still dangerous—still, so to speak, "live." But you can now proceed with it in an orderly fashion. First, revolve the cone through the full three hundred and sixty degrees, snapping at the loose gobs of ice cream; turn the cone by moving the thumb away from you and the forefinger toward you, so the cone moves counterclockwise. Then, with the cone still "wound," which will require the wrist to be bent at the full right angle toward you, apply pressure with the mouth and tongue to accomplish overall realignment, straightening and settling the whole mess. Then, unwinding the cone back through the full three hundred and sixty degrees, remove any trickles of ice cream. From here on, some supplementary repairs may be necessary, but the cone is now defused.

At this point, you can risk a glance around you. How 21 badly the others are doing with their cones! Now you can settle down to eating yours. This is done by eating the ice cream off the top. At each bite, you must press down cautiously, so that the ice cream settles farther and farther into

Fig. 2

the cone. Be very careful not to break the cone. Of course, you never take so much ice cream into your mouth at once that it hurts your teeth; for the same reason, you never let unmelted ice cream into the back of your mouth. If all these procedures are followed correctly, you should shortly arrive at the ideal—the way an ice-cream cone is always pictured but never actually is when it is handed to you *(Fig. 2)*. The ice cream should now form a small dome whose circumference exactly coincides with the large circumference of the cone itself—a small skullcap that fits exactly on top of a larger, inverted dunce cap. You have made order out of chaos; you are an artist. You have taken an unnatural, abhorrent, irregular, chaotic form, and from it you have sculpted an ordered, ideal shape that might be envied by Praxiteles or even Euclid.

Now at last you can begin to take little nibbles of the cone itself, being very careful not to crack it. Revolve the cone so that its rim remains smooth and level as you eat both ice cream and cone in the same ratio. Because of the geometrical nature of things, a constantly reduced inverted cone still remains a perfect inverted cone no matter how small it grows, just as a constantly reduced dome held within a cone retains *its* shape. Because you are constantly reshaping the dome of ice cream with your tongue and nibbling at the cone, it follows in logic— and in actual practice, if you are skillful and careful—that the cone will continue to look exactly the same, except for its size, as you eat it down, so that at the very end you will hold between your thumb and forefinger a tiny, idealized replica of an ice-cream cone, a thing perhaps one inch high. Then, while the others are licking their sticky fingers, preparatory to wiping them on their clothes, or going back to the ice-cream stand for more paper napkins to try to clean themselves up—*then* you can hold the miniature cone up for everyone to see, and pop it gently into your mouth.

Comment

Hills is writing about the joys of eating ice-cream cones, and he is writing humorously. The problems he describes are real ones, but these are part of the fun of eating ice-cream cones, and he knows that his readers will share this view. Though he gives instructions for each stage in the process, he also knows that his readers are probably familiar with all of the details. The purpose of the essay, then, is to give the pleasure of recognition. The many kinds of analysis—from comparison and contrast to process—can be used for many different purposes, as this delightful essay shows.

Questions for Study and Discussion

1. What in the description of the process depends on the reader's recognition of the problems? How does Hills remind the reader of these problems?
2. What explains the order of the steps in the process? Is Hills moving from the easier to the more difficult steps, or has he chosen another principle of order?
3. What is the overall tone of the essay? How do the drawings contribute to it.?
4. Are the various statements about human nature to be taken seriously, though they are presented humorously?
5. The most effective humor develops out of genuine problems and observations—not out of invented ones. Is this true of the humor of this essay?
6. What impression do you get of the writer—his personality, his outlook on life, his sense of humor?

Vocabulary Study

Formal words will often seem humorous in an informal setting: "This schoolmate has a flair for *contingency* planning. . . ." Identify formal words of this sort in the essay, and explain the humor they provide.

Suggestions for Writing

1. Write a humorous description of a process similar to eating an ice-cream cone—perhaps wrapping a large gift, or eating an

unfamiliar food for the first time. Let your details reveal something unusual and important about human beings.

2. Write a set of instructions for a job that involves a number of related processes, for example, changing a flat tire. Keep each of the processes distinct, and be careful to define important terms for the person who has not performed the process before.

Comparison
and Contrast

Like definition and division, comparison and contrast is an important method of analysis in exposition. *Comparison* deals with similarities, *contrast* with differences. In comparing, you show what two or more people or objects or places have in common; in contrasting, how they are unlike. There are many ways of organizing paragraphs or essays of comparison or contrast. One way is the block listing of the qualities of the first person or place, then the block listing of the qualities of the second—in the same order:

> Chicago, at the southern tip of Lake Michigan, is a port city and an important commercial and industrial center of the Middle West. It is also an important educational, cultural, and recreational center, drawing thousands to its concert halls, art museum, and sports arenas. Cleveland, on the south shore of Lake Erie, is similarly a port city and a commercial and industrial center important to its area. Like Chicago, it has several important colleges and universities, a distinguished symphony orchestra, one of the fine art museums of the world, and many recreational centers. The location of the two cities undoubtedly contributed to their growth, but this similarity is not sufficient to explain their wide cultural diversity. (paragraph of comparison)

169

A second way is an alternating comparison or contrast, point by point:

> Chicago is the southern tip of Lake Michigan; Cleveland, on the south shore of Lake Erie. Both are important commercial and industrial centers of the Middle West, and both offer a wide range of educational, cultural, and recreational activities.

In developing such paragraphs or essays, transitions like *similarly, likewise, by comparison,* and *by contrast* may be needed to clarify the organization. The purpose of comparison and contrast is usually to provide a relative estimate: you discover the qualities of the first person or object or place *through* the qualities of the second (or third). If Cleveland and Chicago share these characteristics and have the same history of growth, we are better able to understand the causes that shape cities. A contrast with Atlanta or Omaha—large inland cities—would clarify these causes further through a similar relative estimate.

Sydney J. Harris
Now People and Then People

Sydney J. Harris was born in London in 1917. After attending the University of Chicago and Central College in Chicago, he was employed in public relations for the legal division of the City of Chicago. He has been a journalist most of his life, and began a column for the *Chicago Daily News* in 1941. His columns have been collected into numerous books, including *Majority of One* (1957), *Last Things First* (1961), *On the Contrary* (1964), and *For the Time Being* (1972).

"Don't you want to be one of the Now people?" asks an ad for a new soft drink, going on to urge, "Become one of the Now generation!"

The only thing I can think of that is worse than being one of the Now people is being one of the Then people. As a member of civilization in good standing, I reject both the *nowness* and the *thenness* of the generations. I opt for the *alwaysness*.

To be a Now person means to be wholly concerned with the present and the immediate future; to be involved in fads, sensations and the whole pulsating ephemera of what's-going-on; to be perpetually on the *qui vive* for the newest, the latest, the coolest, the in. It also means to be insensitive to the past, to cut oneself off from the roots of tradition, to favor the sensory and the subjective over the rational and the real, to become a new kind of technological barbarian, which is more frightening than the old kind of preliterate barbarian.

To be a Then person means to cling to the past for its own sake, to apply lessons that are not relevant today, to engage in a mixture of nostalgia, envy, rage and fear toward "modern youth," and to imagine that twentieth-century problems can be solved by sixteenth-century moralism or eighteenth-century politics.

These are false alternatives, for they are not exclusive alternatives. There is a better way than either: and that is to be an Always person, transcending both the frantic cult of the new and the feeble cult of the old. This means selecting from both what is valuable, and discarding what is useless or harmful—which, of course, implies the ability to make such judgments. It means, further, learning to discriminate between values that are permanent and universal and mere matters of convention or taste or the times.

The Always person does not throw out the baby with the bath water as the Now person does—who thinks that because we have had a false and hypocritical morality in the past that therefore *all* morality is merely a matter of taste or preference. Nor does he, like the Then person, operate on the basis that *everything* that was true for previous generations is equally true and relevant today.

Life is primarily the art of selecting and combining, not   7
accepting or rejecting any philosophy in toto. The Now generation rejects the past too categorically, just as the Then generation embraces it too hysterically. To be an authentic person, in any age, means in some way to surmount the age and stand for the kind of order that permits and encourages graceful change.

Comment

Harris contrasts three kinds of people and briefly compares two of them to argue a thesis. This thesis takes the form of a definition, presented in the concluding paragraph. The argument Harris presents is a special one—a refutation of, or answer to, a false dilemma popular in advertising: we are either "Now" people, in fashion and in step with our times, or "Then" people, old-fashioned and out of step. Harris builds through his contrast to a third possibility, argued in the remaining paragraphs.

Questions for Study and Discussion

1. What are the points of contrast or the differences between Now people and Then people? And what are the differences between Always people and Now and Then people?
2. What is the similarity between Now and Then people that Harris stresses in the concluding paragraph? Why does he save this similarity for the conclusion?
3. How does he use comparison and contrast to reach a definition of the "authentic person"?

Vocabulary Study

Suggest synonyms for the following words: *opt* (paragraph 2); *ephemera, qui vive*—the sentry's challenge in French: "Who goes there?" (paragraph 3); *nostalgia* (paragraph 4); *transcending, dis-*

criminate (paragraph 5); *hypocritical, relevant* (paragraph 6); *in toto*—Latin: "as a whole"; *authentic* (paragraph 7).

Suggestions for Writing

1. Discuss another false dilemma or pair of alternatives promoted by advertising or by people you know. Contrast the alternatives as Harris does before suggesting a third possibility that offers a way out of the dilemma.
2. Compare two of your friends to determine how closely they fit any of the types Harris discusses. Consider both similarities and differences.

Don Richard Cox
Barbie and Her Playmates

> Don Richard Cox was born in Wichita, Kansas, in 1943, and was educated at Wichita State University and the University of Missouri, where he received the Outstanding Graduate Student Teacher Award in 1975. He is the author of two textbooks, *Emblems of Reality* (1973) and *The Technical Reader* (1980), and he now teaches at the University of Tennessee in Knoxville.

The Mattel Corporation's wonder doll, Barbie, is undoubtedly one of the toy phenomena of the second half of the twentieth century. The first of her kind, Barbie helped create a whole new breed of dolls—the fashion dolls. These dolls, all of whom are about eleven or twelve inches tall, are intended to represent attractive, apparently teenaged girls, who, like most teenaged girls, require large wardrobes. These

Reprinted by permission of *Journal of Popular Culture* and Don Richard Cox.

wardrobes are purchased separately from the dolls, of course, and initially most of Barbie's appeal to young purchasers involved the seemingly endless supply of fashions that Barbie and her friends could wear.

One did not simply buy a Barbie doll and stop, for Barbie was not an end in herself but an avenue to a whole world of Barbie accessories. The concept of a doll being primarily a vehicle for the future sale of related merchandise rather than being a terminal product whose marketing success ends with its sale is a concept that has caused Barbie to have the tremendous impact upon the toy industry that she has had and allowed her to survive in a doll market where the average product remains popular only a few years. Barbie's primary and social importance as a toy stems from the fact that she is different from the dolls that preceded her; this difference has reshaped our culture's way of looking at dolls and the way children now define their relationship to these dolls that sell in the millions. The sales figures alone are proof of Barbie's attractiveness. There is no doubt that Barbie and her friends have been accepted; they seem to have become a permanent part of twentieth-century life. But now that we have welcomed Barbie into our homes and placed her in our children's bedrooms, we should stop and examine what her presence there means, and what effect it may have.

Barbie was first introduced to sell clothes, but her initial role as a vehicle for doll fashions was soon expanded. For example, Barbie's size made her either too large or too small for the conventional doll furniture that had existed, so a new line of doll furniture tailored to her dimensions was created. Barbie's "Dream House" then became one of her first "non-fashion" accessories. Because Barbie was a young and presumably active young lady, her merchandise took on a distinctive character. Barbie was not a "baby" doll and she had no need for baby cribs, high chairs, or other "baby" furniture. So Barbie acquired recreational equipment—a dune buggy, a Volkswagen van, a swimming pool. She also acquired some friends—P.J. and Skipper—and most important of all Barbie found a boyfriend—Ken. With the addition of these friends to share her fun Barbie's need for equipment became as unlimited as the needs of any modern consumer. Barbie could ski, camp, swim, skate, cycle, perform gymnastics, boat, dance, shop, have her hair styled, or just entertain friends in her studio bedroom, her country home, or her penthouse apartment. Almost any activity open to today's teenagers became available to Barbie, and by extension became available to those who brought Barbie into their lives.

The success of the total Barbie market helped initiate several new series of dolls all of whom parlayed the Barbie format to success. Many of these dolls, drawing upon the interest Barbie's Ken had aroused in young boys, turned to a relatively untapped doll market—dolls for the male population. Selling dolls to young boys, however, necessitated a basic change in terminology. Boys' dolls were not called *dolls,* because that word has a distinctly feminine ring. Accordingly we find today that young males are interested in *action figures,* male dolls who are supposedly basically rugged individuals devoted to an outdoor life. "Big Jim," "Johnny West," and most notably "G.I. Joe," all belong to this exclusive club of adventurous spirits who demand enough dune buggies, jeeps, motorcycles, planes, boats, and helicopters to outfit a small mercenary force. Once again we can see that what is essentially being marketed here is a sophisticated type of doll "furniture," merchandise that surrounds and supports the original doll vehicles.

The major appeal of the action figures lies in the variety of accessories that can be adapted to them; like Barbie they are not terminal products. The action figures for boys, however, although they represent a direct result of Barbie's impact upon the toy market, do not necessitate a redefinition of the male role in play situations in the same way that Barbie has redefined the female role in these situations. The action figures are distinctly male and they inhabit a world that is exclusively male. A young boy will have to borrow his sister's fashion doll if he wants any feminine intruders invading his all-male play world. In this respect the male action figures do not require an adjustment in the masculine play role. Although we can label a boy's action figures "dolls," we should understand that as a collection of adult male dolls they might also be seen as simply elaborate toy soldiers, a traditional plaything of boys for generations. Young girls, however, have had their feminine play roles changed significantly by Barbie. Because the consequences of that redefinition could alter a child's basic attitudes toward sex, marriage, or a career, let us examine more closely the value structure implicit in Barbie's world.

We should begin by noting that Barbie's age is not com-   6
pletely clear. Ostensibly she is a teenager and therefore is no more than nineteen years old. Physically, however, as many people have pointed out, Barbie is a rather fully endowed and curvaceous woman possessing a figure few nineteen-year-olds have. Barbie is of course single so her friend Ken is just that— a boyfriend not a husband. Barbie's exact relationship with Ken is noticeably loose. She apparently is free to embark unescorted on all kinds of outings with Ken, including camping overnight (they each have their own sleeping bags, however). Barbie seemingly lives alone in all of her plushly furnished homes although there are certainly enough chairs, couches, and beds to accommodate overnight guests. Again, Ken is free to visit any time he wishes. The point here is not that Barbie is a doll of questionable morals, but we should note that her lifestyle is remarkably uncluttered and free of such complications as nosey little brothers or nagging parents.

Barbie's life is that of the ultimate swinging single. Al-   7
though she has no parents to cast shadows into her life of constant boating, skiing, and camping, she also does not seem to have a need for them. Total independence is a central characteristic of Barbie. Although she owns an extensive amount of sporting equipment, Barbie seemingly has no need for employment that allows her to purchase this merchandise. There is no such thing as a Barbie office in any of the Barbie equip-

ment, nor are there accessories that remotely suggest a job situation for this carefree doll; although Barbie might be in high school or college there are no accessories that hint at her having to endure the boredom of education. Life for Barbie appears to be a kind of endless summer vacation, an extended tour of summer homes and resorts, free from school, family, and financial worries.

Barbie's influence upon the minds of the children who share their play hours with her and her expensive wardrobe and recreation equipment is potentially a very strong one. Barbie provides a means of vicarious escape to her young female playmates—a glittering jet trip into a world of leisure and luxury that very few of her young friends will ever actually know. We can see that Barbie is a symbolic escape vehicle, a vicarious toy that encourages fantasy rather than a toy that encourages behavior imitative of normal living patterns.

The dolls that survive outside of the category of fashion dolls are still basically the kind of dolls that existed before Barbie and the fashion dolls came on the scene. These dolls are mostly "baby" dolls, dolls that require young mothers to feed and diaper them. A child who owns such a doll usually assumes a play role that is imitative of her own mother's role. The babies can be loved and cuddled, or punished and put to bed at a young mother's whim. In this play role the child assumes an adult personality, dominating the inferior doll-child just as the youngster herself is dominated. Obviously the work and responsibility involved in being a mother receives a good share of the child's attention in this particular situation. And, although a certain amount of fantasy is involved, presumably these fantasies will one day become more or less true when the child experiences motherhood herself. She in essence is only rehearsing for a future real-life role.

The play role initiated in a child's relationship with Barbie differs considerably from the play role required by a conventional baby doll. First of all Barbie is obviously not a child. She is a teenager and therefore is usually "older" than the child who owns her. The child's personality then is not necessarily

8

9

10

a dominant one when she relates with Barbie. Barbie has the clothes, sporting equipment, and most important, freedom, to do as she pleases. The child only directs Barbie in activities that the child herself may not be able to experience. The mother-child relationship that is an inherent part of owning a baby doll is considerably altered. One does not necessarily cuddle or punish a Barbie doll any more than one allows her mother to sit on her lap, or sends her mother to bed without dinner. Barbie's stature in this psychological relationship is not so great that she dominates the child; she does not become a symbolic parent in spite of her independent superiority.

Barbie's independence in fact is just what prevents her from becoming a miniature parent to the child. There are no children in Barbie's life; children, after all, involve responsibility and Barbie is not one to be burdened by such responsibilities. Instead of assuming the duties and pressures of adulthood, Barbie retains the worry-free aura of childhood, becoming a kind of surrogate big sister to the child. This relationship, the interaction between sisters at play, is fundamentally different from the mother-child relationship, and the values inculcated by this interaction are plainly different also.   11

As a model sister, Barbie, who leads a life free from responsibility, is able to stimulate a similar desire for independence in her owners. The degree to which her influence has actually affected children in the sixties and seventies needs to be investigated more closely. Of interest also is Barbie's impact upon future families, the families formed by the young girls of the "Barbie generation." Will they, like Barbie, resist the responsibility of having children, or, following Barbie's lead even more completely, resist the responsibility of marriage and family altogether? There is also the question of the sexual mores of today's Barbie owners. Barbie is a physically attractive woman with no visible permanent attachments. Will she produce a generation of sexually liberated playmates intent on jetting from resort to resort? Will these same playmates become a group of frustrated cynics if their private   12

Barbie fantasies do not come true? Older sisters often set social and marital patterns that their younger sisters attempt to
emulate; Barbie is capable of being a dominant model for all
her young sisters in this respect.

Certainly Barbie's dream world has already affected the   13
sexual lives of her playmates in one way: she has caused girls
as young as five or six to confront the problems of teenagers.
Very young children, children who might once have been
content to feed bottles to their infant dolls, are now exposed
to the dating experience. Girls who once spent the second
grade believing that boys were generally unpleasant creatures
now spend their days escorting Barbie and Ken through idyllic afternoons. Dating and the opposite sex—"those awful
boys"—have now become familiar experiences to jaded nine-
year-olds who have "accompanied" their "big sister" and her
boyfriend on unchaperoned camping trips many times. The
accelerating interest of big business in "pre-teenagers" (presumably those children between the ages of seven and twelve)
as a potential market for cosmetics, magazines, and phono-
graph records, is a positive indication of a budding sexual
awareness in this age group. The girls who screamed for Elvis
in the fifties were seventeen; those who now swoon at Donny
Osmond are eleven.

The total impact of Barbie should now begin to make it-   14
self visible in her playmates. As each generation finds its own
particular fantasy of escape the values of that fantasy become
imprinted in the generation itself. Motion pictures, the great
escape of the forties and early fifties, provided Hollywood's
vision of life for those who grew up munching popcorn in
dark theaters. Similarly, it has been proposed that many of
the youth protests of the late sixties reflected the desires of a
generation that was used to seeing life neatly resolved in sixty-
minute segments on a flickering tube. Barbie and her glittering accessories have now been purchased by a generation of
children; her fantasy world becomes steadily more elaborate.
If Barbie has indeed provided a behavioral model for a seg-

ment of the population, the values instilled in her miniature utopia will play an increasing role in the lives of those children who buy her version of the American Dream.

Comment

Cox develops a number of important ideas, all of them related to the impact of the Barbie doll on the girls who own them. These ideas grow out of specific details and analysis, as in paragraph 8: "We can see that Barbie is a symbolic escape vehicle, a vicarious toy that encourages fantasy rather than a toy that encourages behavior imitative of normal patterns." Cox builds these ideas to an encompassing generalization in his concluding paragraph: "As each generation finds its own particular fantasy of escape the values of that fantasy become imprinted in the generation itself." One way that Cox develops this and the other ideas of the essay is through comparison with other kinds of dolls—those designed for boys, for example. The relative estimate that emerges from this comparison tells us something important about the cultural attitudes that produced these various dolls and in turn are influenced by them.

Questions for Study and Discussion

1. What background does Cox provide for the reader unacquainted with the Barbie doll? How early does he state the purpose of his analysis?
2. What similarities and differences between Barbie and Ken does Cox discuss and illustrate? What central idea emerges from this relative estimate?
3. What is the point of the comparison with other kinds of dolls? What is gained by building to the comparison instead of introducing it at the beginning of the essay?
4. What have been the effects on children of the Barbie doll, according to Cox? How does he demonstrate these effects?
5. What is the overall tone of the essay? Does Cox write as a neutral observer? Or is he obviously approving or disapproving or sarcastic?

6.   Cox does not focus on male and female stereotypes, but his essay deals with this idea in the course of the analysis. What other ideas does he deal with indirectly?
7.   Do you agree with the conclusion Cox reaches about the impact of the Barbie doll on adolescents? Why or why not?

Vocabulary Study

Explain how the second word in each pair differs from the first, which is Cox's, and how it would change the meaning of the sentence in the paragraph cited:

a.   *concept* (paragraph 2), *idea*
b.   *terminal* (paragraph 2), *final*
c.   *initial* (paragraph 3), *first*
d.   *conventional* (paragraph 3), *customary*
e.   *necessitated* (paragraph 4), *required*
f.   *adapted* (paragraph 5), *fitted*
g.   *vicarious* (paragraph 8), *surrogate*
h.   *miniature* (paragraph 11), *small*
i.   *emulate* (paragraph 12), *imitate*
j.   *mores* (paragraph 12), *habits*
k.   *unchaperoned* (paragraph 13), *unaccompanied*
l.   *idyllic* (paragraph 13), *happy*

Suggestions for Writing

1.   Analyze the appeals made in advertisements for cosmetics or clothes of another class of product in a magazine directed to adolescents. Then discuss what similarities and differences you find. Use your analysis to reach a conclusion about the implied values you find or the attitude toward teenagers—their interests and tastes.
2.   Compare two magazines—one addressed to adolescents, the second to adults—to determine how different the ads for the same product are. Give particular attention to assumptions these ads make about the values, tastes, and interests of their audiences.
3.   Test Cox's conclusion that toys promote sexual stereotypes by comparing advertisements for the same class of product— sporting equipment or clothing, for example—in magazines di-

rected to girls and boys, or by comparing books or magazine stories.

Arthur L. Campa
Anglo vs. Chicano: Why?

Arthur L. Campa (1905–1978) was chairman of the Department of Modern Languages at the University of Denver and the director of the Center of Latin American Studies from 1946 to 1978. He served in the U.S. Air Force and the Peace Corps. His several books on Hispanic–American culture include *Treasure of the Sangre de Cristos* and *Hispanic Culture in the Southwest*.

The cultural differences between Hispanic and Anglo-American people have been dwelt upon by so many writers that we should all be well informed about the values of both. But audiences are usually of the same persuasion as the speakers, and those who consult published works are for the most part specialists looking for affirmation of what they believe. So, let us consider the same subject, exploring briefly some of the basic cultural differences that cause conflict in the Southwest, where Hispanic and Anglo-American cultures meet.

Cultural differences are implicit in the conceptual content of the languages of these two civilizations, and their value systems stem from a long series of historical circumstances. Therefore, it may be well to consider some of the English and Spanish cultural configurations before these Europeans set foot on American soil. English culture was basically insular, geographically and ideologically; was more integrated on the

First published in *Western Review*, Vol. IX (Spring 1972). Reprinted by permission of Mrs. Arthur L. Campa.

whole, except for some strong theological differences; and was particularly zealous of its racial purity. Spanish culture was peninsular, a geographical circumstance that made it a catch-all of Mediterranean, central European and north African peoples. The composite nature of the population produced a market regionalism that prevented close integration, except for religion, and led to a strong sense of individualism. These differences were reflected in the colonizing enterprise of the two cultures. The English isolated themselves from the Indians physically and culturally; the Spanish, who had strong notions about *pureza de sangre* [purity of blood] among the nobility, were not collectively averse to adding one more strain to their racial cocktail. Cortés led the way by siring the first *mestizo* in North America, and the rest of the conquistadores followed suit. The ultimate products of these two orientations meet today in the Southwest.

Anglo-American culture was absolutist at the onset; that is, all the dominant values were considered identical for all, regardless of time and place. Such values as justice, charity, honesty were considered the superior social order for all men and were later embodied in the American Constitution. The Spaniard brought with him a relativistic viewpoint and saw fewer moral implications in man's actions. Values were looked upon as the result of social and economic conditions. 3

The motives that brought Spaniards and Englishmen to America also differed. The former came on an enterprise of discovery, searching for a new route to India initially, and later for new lands to conquer, the fountain of youth, minerals, the Seven Cities of Cíbola and, in the case of the missionaries, new souls to win for the Kingdom of Heaven. The English came to escape religious persecution, and once having found a haven, they settled down to cultivate the soil and establish their homes. Since the Spaniards were not seeking a refuge or running away from anything, they continued their explorations and circled the globe twenty-five years after the discovery of the New World. 4

This peripatetic tendency of the Spaniard may be ac- 5

counted for in part by the fact that he was the product of an equestrian culture. Men on foot do not venture far into the unknown. It was almost a century after the landing on Plymouth Rock that Governor Alexander Spotswood of Virginia crossed the Blue Ridge Mountains, and it was not until the nineteenth century that the Anglo-Americans began to move west of the Mississippi.

The Spaniard's equestrian role meant that he was not close   6
to the soil, as was the Anglo-American pioneer, who tilled the land and built the greatest agricultural industry in history. The Spaniard cultivated the land only when he had Indians available to do it for him. The uses to which the horse was put also varied. The Spanish horse was essentially a mount, while the more robust English horse was used in cultivating the soil. It is therefore not surprising that the viewpoints of these two cultures should differ when we consider that the pioneer is looking at the world at the level of his eyes while the *caballero* [horseman] is looking beyond and down at the rest of the world.

One of the most commonly quoted, and often misinter-   7
preted, characteristics of Hispanic peoples is the deeply ingrained individualism in all walks of life. Hispanic individualism is a revolt against the incursion of collectivity, strongly asserted when it is felt that the ego is being fenced in. This attitude leads to a deficiency in those social qualities based on collective standards, an attitude that Hispanos do not consider negative because it manifests a measure of resistance to standardization in order to achieve a measure of individual freedom. Naturally, such an attitude has no *reglas fijas* [fixed rules].

Anglo-Americans who achieve a measure of success and   8
security through institutional guidance not only do not mind a few fixed rules but demand them. The lack of a concerted plan of action, whether in business or in politics, appears unreasonable to Anglo-Americans. They have a sense of individualism, but they achieve it through action and self-determination. Spanish individualism is based on feeling, on

something that is the result not of rules and collective standards but of a person's momentary, emotional reaction. And it is subject to change when the mood changes. In contrast to Spanish emotional individualism, the Anglo-American strives for objectivity when choosing a course of action or making a decision.

The Southwestern Hispanos voiced strong objections to the lack of courtesy of the Anglo-Americans when they first met them in the early days of the Sante Fe trade. The same accusation is leveled at the *Americanos* today in many quarters of the Hispanic world. Some of this results from their different conceptions of polite behavior. Here too one can say that the Spanish have no *reglas fijas* because for them courtesy is simply an expression of the way one person feels toward another. To some they extend the hand, to some they bow and for the more *intimos* there is the well-known *abrazo*. The concepts of "good or bad" or "right and wrong" in polite behavior are moral considerations of an absolutist culture. 9

Another cultural contrast appears in the way both cultures share part of their material substance with others. The pragmatic Anglo-American contributes regularly to such institutions as the Red Cross, the United Fund and a myriad of associations. He also establishes foundations and quite often leaves millions to such institutions. The Hispano prefers to give his contribution directly to the recipient so he can see the person he is helping. 10

A century of association has inevitably acculturated both Hispanos and Anglo-Americans to some extent, but there still persist a number of culture traits that neither group has relinquished altogether. Nothing is more disquieting to an Anglo-American who believes that time is money than the time perspective of Hispanos. They usually refer to this attitude as the *"mañana* psychology." Actually, it is more of a "today psychology," because Hispanos cultivate the present to the exclusion of the future; because the latter has not arrived yet, it is not a reality. They are reluctant to relinquish the present, so they hold on to it until it becomes the past. To an His- 11 pano, nine is nine until it is ten, so when he arrives at nine-thirty, he jubilantly exclaims: *"¡Justo!"* [right on time]. This may be why the clock is slowed down to a walk in Spanish while in English it runs. In the United States, our future-oriented civilization plans our lives so far in advance that the present loses its meaning. January magazine issues [including IDs] are out in December; 1973 cars have been out since October; cemetery plots and even funeral arrangements are bought on the installment plan. To a person engrossed in living today the very idea of planning his funeral sounds like the tolling of the bells.

It is a natural corollary that a person who is present oriented should be compensated by being good at improvising. An Anglo-American is told in advance to prepare for an "impromptu speech," but an Hispano usually can improvise a speech because *"Nosotros lo improvisamos todo"* [we improvise everything].   12

Another source of cultural conflict arises from the difference between *being* and *doing*. Even when trying to be individualistic, the Anglo-American achieves it by what he does. Today's young generation decided to be themselves, to get away from standardization, so they let their hair grow, wore ragged clothes and even went barefoot in order to be different from the Establishment. As a result they all ended up doing the same things and created another stereotype. The freedom enjoyed by the individuality of *being* makes it unnecessary for Hispanos to strive to be different.   13

In 1963 a team of psychologists from the University of Guadalajara in Mexico and the University of Michigan compared 74 upper-middle-class students from each university. Individualism and personalism were found to be central values for the Mexican students. This was explained by saying that a Mexican's value as a person lies in his *being* rather than, as is the case of the Anglo-Americans, in concrete accomplishments. Efficiency and accomplishments are derived characteristics that do not affect worthiness in the Mexican, whereas in the American it is equated with success, a value of highest   14 priority in the American culture. Hispanic people disassociate themselves from material things or from actions that may impugn a person's sense of being, but the Anglo-American shows great concern for material things and assumes responsibility for his actions. This is expressed in the language of each culture. In Spanish one says, *"Se me cayó la taza"* [the cup fell away from me] instead of "I dropped the cup."

In English, one speaks of money, cash and all related transactions with frankness because material things of this high order do not trouble Anglo-Americans. In Spanish such materialistic concepts are circumvented by referring to cash as *efectivo* [effective] and when buying or selling as something *al contado* [counted out], and when without it by saying *No tengo fondos* [I have no funds]. This disassociation from material things is what produces *sobriedad* [sobriety] in the Spaniard according to Miguel de Unamuno, but in the Southwest the disassociation from materialism leads to *dejadez* [lassitude] and *desprendimiento* [disinterestedness]. A man may lose his life defending his honor but is unconcerned about the lack of material things. *Desprendimiento* causes a man to spend his last cent on a friend, which when added to lack of concern for the future may mean that tomorrow he will eat beans as a result of today's binge.

The implicit differences in words that appear to be identical in meaning are astonishing. Versatile is a compliment in English and an insult in Spanish. An Hispano student who is told to apologize cannot do it, because the word doesn't exist in Spanish. *Apología* means words in praise of a person. The Anglo-American either apologizes, which is a form of retraction abhorrent in Spanish, or compromises, another concept foreign to Hispanic culture. *Compromiso* means a date, not a compromise. In colonial Mexico City, two hidalgos once entered a narrow street from opposite sides, and when they could not go around, they sat in their coaches for three days until the viceroy ordered them to back out. All this because they could not work out a compromise.

It was that way then and to some extent now. Many of

15

16

17

today's conflicts in the Southwest have their roots in polar-
ized cultural differences, which need not be irreconcilable when
approached with mutual respect and understanding.

Comment

Campa states the subject of his essay in his opening paragraph—the "basic cultural differences that cause conflict in the
Southwest." And he states his thesis at the start of his second: "Cultural differences are implicit in the conceptual content of the languages of these two civilizations, and their value systems stem from
a long series of historical circumstances." Paragraphs 2–6 deal with
the second part of this statement, identifying important Hispanic
and Anglo-American values and historical circumstances. Paragraphs 7–17 explore related values and connect these values to the
conceptual contents of Hispanic and Anglo-American words and
phrases.

Campa depends on formal transitions throughout, sometimes
using the opening sentences of his paragraphs as signposts to show
the major turns in his analysis:

A century of association has inevitably acculturated both Hispanos and Anglo-Americans to some extent, but there still persist
a number of culture traits that neither group has relinquished altogether. (paragraph 11)

The topic sentence of the paragraph immediately follows:

Nothing is more disquieting to an Anglo-American who believes
that time is money than the time perspective of Hispanos.

Both the transitional and the topic sentences here mark the contrasts Campa is developing. Campa gives emphasis to these contrasts in the opening sentences of most of the paragraphs.

Questions for Study and Discussion

1. What topic does Campa begin his analysis with in paragraph
    2? What topic does he turn to in paragraph 3?
2. Campa turns in paragraph 4 to the first of several historical cir-

cumstances. Which circumstance does he begin with? How are the circumstances discussed in paragraphs 5 and 6 related to that of paragraph 4?

3. How is Hispanic individualism—introduced in paragraph 7 and explored by contrast in paragraph 8—suggested by the Hispanic equestrian role discussed in paragraph 6?

4. Paragraph 9, which illustrates the differences in Hispanic and Anglo-American individualism, introduces differences in the conceptual content of Spanish and English. What are these concepts?

5. What different values does Campa explore in paragraph 10? How are the different values discussed in paragraph 11 related to these? How does Campa illustrate the differences in these paragraphs? How does paragraph 12 develop the difference discussed in paragraph 11?

6. How do previous differences help to explain that discussed and illustrated in paragraphs 13–15?

7. What is the function of paragraphs 16 and 17?

8. Campa develops his essay chiefly by contrast. Which paragraphs open with transitional sentences that mark major turns in the analysis?

9. Are any of the values Campa discusses your own? Is your ethnic background chiefly responsible for them?

Vocabulary Study

1. Find synonyms for the following words. Be ready to discuss what the etymology of the word contributes to your understanding of its use in the paragraph:
   a. paragraph 2: *conceptual, configurations, insular, peninsular, conquistador*
   b. paragraph 5: *peripatetic, equestrian*
   c. paragraph 7: *incursion*
   d. paragraph 10: *pragmatic, myriad*
   e. paragraph 12: *corollary, improvising, impromptu*
   f. paragraph 15: *circumvented, lassitude, disinterestedness*
   g. paragraph 16: *abhorrent*

2. What are the meanings of the words *absolutist* and *relativistic* in paragraphs 3 and 9? What dictionary meanings do these words not have in the essay?

Suggestions for Writing

1. Contrast values of your own with those of a friend, perhaps referring to some of the values identified by Campa. Then discuss the possible causes of these differences—upbringing, ethnic background, friends, school. Refer to ideas of Campa if these help explain the differences.

2. Campa states: "Even when trying to be individualistic, the Anglo-American achieves it by what he does." Discuss the extent to which this statement describes your way of being an individual. Compare or contrast your individualism with that of one or more friends. Use your analysis to verify or challenge Campa's analysis of American values.

3. Contrast the meaning you give particular words relating to money or success with the meaning given them by friends, parents, or teachers. Try to explain these different uses, referring to ideas of Campa if you find them useful.

Cause and Effect

Reasoning about *cause and effect* is often a simple matter of connecting two events. When I get wet during a thunderstorm, I know that rain is the cause. But making other connections is usually not this simple. If I catch a cold the same day, I may blame it on the rain. However, I might have caught cold even if I had stayed indoors; and if I had been in the rain, the rain alone may not have been the single cause. A number of conditions together probably produced the cold: a run-down state arising from overwork or lack of sleep, poor eating habits, getting wet—these may have triggered a virus in the body.

The sum of these conditions is generally what we mean by *cause*. We ordinarily speak loosely of one of these conditions as the cause. Except where an immediate action (exposure to the storm) produces a direct consequence (getting wet), my reasoning about cause and effect is probable rather than certain. Having identified conditions that produced colds in the past, I cannot be sure that they *must* produce one in the present. The identical conditions may be present, without producing a cold.

All discussions of cause and effect, formal and informal, include hidden or unstated assumptions or beliefs about people, society, the ways things happen in nature—human beings are naturally aggressive, adolescents are naturally rebellious, the Irish have hot tempers, the English are cold and reserved, opposites attract. Many who hold these beliefs unquestioningly seldom think about them, nor do they feel it necessary to test them through observation. In cause-and-effect reasoning such assumptions are hidden in the explanation and may be decisive.

Appletree Rodden

Why Smaller Refrigerators Can Preserve the Human Race

Appletree Rodden did research in biochemistry at Stanford University and has been a member of the Staatstheater Ballet Company, in West Germany. His essay, first published in *Harper's* in 1974, is as timely today as it was when Americans were becoming aware of "the energy crisis."

Once, long ago, people had special little boxes called re-   1
frigerators in which milk, meat, and eggs could be kept cool. The grandchildren of these simple devices are large enough to store whole cows, and they reach temperatures comparable to those at the South Pole. Their operating costs increase each year, and they are so complicated that few home handymen attempt to repair them on their own.

Why has this change in size and complexity occurred in   2

America? It has not taken place in many areas of the technologically advanced world (the average West German refrigerator is about a yard high and less than a yard wide, yet refrigeration technology in Germany is quite advanced). Do we really need (or even want) all that space and cold?

3   The benefits of a large refrigerator are apparent: a saving of time (one grocery-shopping trip a week instead of several), a saving of money (the ability to buy expensive, perishable items in larger, cheaper quantities), a feeling of security (if the car breaks down or if famine strikes, the refrigerator is well stocked). The costs are there, too, but they are not so obvious.

4   Cost number one is psychological. Ever since the refrigerator began to grow, food has increasingly become something we buy to store rather than to eat. Few families go to market daily for their daily bread. The manna in the wilderness could be gathered for only one day at a time. The ancient distaste for making food a storage item is echoed by many modern psychiatrists who suggest that such psychosomatic disorders as obesity are often due to the patient's inability to come to terms with the basic transitoriness of life. Research into a relationship between excessive corpulence and the size of one's refrigerator has not been extensive, but we might suspect one to be there.

5   Another cost is aesthetic. In most of Europe, where grocery marketing is still a part of the daily rhythm, one can buy tomatoes, lettuce, and the like picked on the day of purchase. Many European families have modest refrigerators for storing small items (eggs, milk, butter) for a couple of days, but the concept of buying large quantities of food to store in the refrigerator is not widely accepted. Since fresh produce is easily available in Europe, most people buy it daily.

6   Which brings to mind another price the large refrigerator has cost us: the friendly neighborhood market. In America, time is money. A large refrigerator means fewer time-consuming trips to the grocery store. One member of a deep-freeze-owning family can do the grocery shopping once

or twice a month rather than daily. Since shopping trips are infrequent, most people have been willing to forego the amenities of the little store around the corner in favor of the lower prices found in the supermarket.

If refrigerators weren't so large—that is, if grocery marketing were a daily affair—the "entertainment surcharge" of buying farm fresh food in a smaller, more intimate setting might carry some weight. But as it is, there is not really that much difference between eggs bought from Farmer Brown's wife and eggs bought from the supermarket which in turn bought them from Eggs Incorporated, a firm operated out of Los Angeles that produces 200,000 eggs a day from chickens that are kept in gigantic warehouses lighted artificially on an eighteen-hour light-and-dark cycle and produce one-and-a-half times as many eggs—a special breed of chickens who die young and insane. Not much difference if you don't mind eating eggs from crazy chickens. 7

Chalk up Farmer and Mrs. Brown as cost number four of the big refrigerator. The small farmer can't make it in a society dominated by supermarkets and big refrigerators; make way for superfarmers, super yields, and pesticides (cost number five). 8

Cost number six of the big refrigerator has been the diminution of regional food differences. Of course the homogenization of American fare cannot be blamed solely on the availability of frozen food. Nonetheless, were it not for the trend toward turning regional specialties into frozen dinners, it might still be possible to experience novelty closer to home. 9

So much for the disadvantages of the big refrigerator. What about the advantages of the small one? First of all, it would help us to "think small," which is what we must learn anyway if the scary predictions of the Club of Rome *(The Limits of Growth)* are true. The advent of smaller refrigerators would set the stage for reversing the "big-thinking" trends brought on with the big refrigerator, and would eventually change our lives. 10

Ivan Illich makes the point in *Tools for Conviviality* that   11
any tool we use (the automobile, standardized public education, public-health care, the refrigerator) influences the individual, his society, and the relationship between the two. A
person's automobile is a part of his identity. The average
Volkswagen owner has a variety of characteristics (income, age,
occupation) significantly different from those of the average
Cadillac owner. American society, with more parking lots than
parks, and with gridded streets rather than winding lanes,
would be vastly different without the private automobile.
Similar conclusions can be drawn about any of the tools we
use. They change us. They change our society. Therefore, it
behooves us to think well before we decide which tool to use
to accomplish a given task. Do we want tools that usurp power
unto themselves, the ones called "non-convivial" by Illich?

The telephone, a "convivial tool," has remained under   12
control; it has not impinged itself on society or on the individual. Each year it has become more efficient, and it has not
prevented other forms of communication (letter writing, visits). The world might be poorer without the telephone, but
it would not be grossly different. Telephones do not pollute,
are not status symbols, and interact only slightly (if at all) with
one's self-image.

So what about the refrigerator? Or back to the more ba-   13
sic problem to which the refrigerator was a partial answer:
what about our supply of food? When did we decide to convert the emotion-laden threat of starvation from a shared
community problem (of societal structure: farm-market-home)
to a personal one (of storage)? How did we decide to accept
a thawed block taken from a supermarket's freezer as a substitute for the voluptuous shapes, smells, and textures of fresh
fruits and vegetables obtained from complex individual sources?

The decision for larger refrigerators has been consistent   14
with a change in food-supply routes from highly diversified
"trails" (from small farms to neighborhood markets) to uniform, standardized highways (from large farms to centrally

located supermarkets). Desirable meals are quick and easy rather than rich and leisurely. Culinary artistry has given way to efficiency, the efficiency of the big refrigerator.

People have a natural propensity for running good things   15
into the ground. Mass production has been a boon to mankind, but its reliance on homogeneity precludes its being a paradigm for all areas of human life. Our forebears and contemporaries have made it possible to mass-produce almost anything. An equally challenging task now lies with us: to choose which things of this world should be mass-produced, and how the standards of mass production should influence other standards we hold dear.

Should houses be mass-produced? Should education?   16
Should food? Which brings us back to refrigerators. How does one decide how large a refrigerator to buy, considering one's life, one's society, and the world, and not simply the question of food storage?

As similar questions are asked about more and more of   17
the things we mass-produce, mass production will become less of a problem and more of a blessing. As cost begins to be measured not only in dollars spent and minutes saved, but in total richness acquired, perhaps smaller refrigerators will again make good sense. A small step backward along some of the roads of "technological progress" might be a large step forward for mankind, and one our age is uniquely qualified to make.

Comment

If Rodden were trying to persuade West German readers to buy large refrigerators, the benefits they provide would be emphasized. Writing to persuade Americans to give up large refrigerators, he focuses on one cause of their preference for them, the attitude that "time is money." If this attitude is one necessary condition of the American preference—that is, a condition that must be present for this preference to exist—attacking the attitude may help to diminish the incentive. Rodden attacks this attitude by showing the disadvantages of thinking about life in this way; these include the sacrifice of fresh food and the fun of buying it, the gradual disappearance of the small farmer, the use of dangerous pesticides—in general, the limits of choice imposed by technology. There may be other necessary conditions, but Rodden need not identify all of them and does not claim to have done so. The "natural propensity for running good things into the ground" is a necessary condition that would be difficult to eliminate. Writers seldom try to identify all the causes of a situation or attitude—not only because it would be difficult to do so, but because they need not do so to make their point.

Questions for Study and Discussion

1. In what order does Rodden present the costs of large refrigerators?
2. What other causes does Rodden state or imply for the American preference? What is the thesis of the essay, and where is it first stated?
3. Does Rodden explain why Europeans prefer small refrigerators? Is Rodden implying that Americans are more easily captivated by "technological progress"?
4. What in Rodden's comments on storing food and the problem of obesity shows that he is stating some of the reasons for practices and attitudes, not all of them?
5. Does Rodden assert or imply that the greater efficiency a tool has, the greater control it exerts over people?
6. Do you agree that the telephone is a "convivial tool" and do you agree with Rodden's theory of tools?
7. How formal are the transitions of the essay? What is the overall tone? Do you find shifts in tone?

Vocabulary Study

Find synonyms for the following words: *psychosomatic, transitoriness, corpulence, aesthetic, amenities, homogenization, convivial, usurp, culinary, propensity.*

Suggestions for Writing

1. Analyze your preference for a certain make or size of automobile, or your opinion about the role of the telephone or a comparable tool. Discuss as many causes of your preference or opinion as you can, and present them in the order of their importance.
2. Discuss your eating habits, or those of your family, with attention to the role of the refrigerator in shaping these habits.
3. Discuss a possible change in American eating or consumption habits or recreation that in your opinion would improve the quality of American life. Explain your reasons as Rodden does.

John Garvey

Thinking in Packages

John Garvey was a columnist for *Commonweal* for many years. Born in 1944 in Decatur, Illinois, he attended Notre Dame University, and after college taught high school and worked as an editor. Garvey writes about contemporary religious and social issues in his column. "There are true and false things," he has said, "and choices which align you with or against the universe." His essay discusses how we think about these things and the dangers of thinking too narrowly.

There is a grave problem which faces those of us who care about ideas. (Notice how I have gathered us all together in a noble little bunch.) It is something I have been paying attention to in a half-conscious way ever since I first started arguing with people, but it has only recently surfaced in all its silly array, probably because Ronald Reagan was elected president. It has to do not so much with ideas as with the way we relate to them. What I have noticed at long last, after years of doing all the wrong things, is embarrassing. It makes me think that everyone—every anarchist, libertarian, conservative, radical, and socialist—ought to take a vow of emotional poverty where ideas are concerned.

We have an investment in our ideas which has nothing to do with the particular worth of our ideas. Our ideas are like clan totems or old school ties. We tend to think that our ideas make us decent. If we have the right opinion about something, it means that we ourselves must be basically good folks; and the other side of this is that those who do not share our feelings on any particular subject are indecent, even perverse. Our ideas become tokens which we shove across the table at one another during conversations to show who we are. They are signals to people we often don't know very well, which we send through the space between us to let them know what to expect of us, and we are delighted when their response is approving: it means they are our sort. If they bat our tokens back at us with a cool stare or, more politely, through careful disagreement, our first impulse is often to assume that their motive for doing so must be base.

I believe, for example, that the arms race is suicidal and that it is almost certainly bound to end in such destruction as the world has never seen. I am putting this as mildly as I can. I also believe that to accept it as a tactical necessity means assuming something which is morally indefensible: the military use of civilian populations, and the willingness to hold them hostage to possible annihilation. I have noticed that people who disagree with me assume all sorts of things I not only have not said, but which I definitely do not believe. They assume that I believe the Soviet Union to be basically trustworthy and decent, not at all bad politically; they assume that I do not object to totalitarianism, and in fact have some sneaky attachment to it, and that I think of America as the world's greatest evil.

The problem is that people on my side of this life and death question do the same sort of thing. Because I agree with them, I tend to forgive them more easily for the moves which, coming from the other side, properly infuriate me. One problem I have always had with *Dr. Strangelove,* much as I enjoyed it, was the sickly consolation it gave to liberals with all of its easy targets. The assumption was that those crazy hawks enjoyed destruction, that they had a romance going with Armageddon. They—our ideological opponents—couldn't honestly believe that unless we met and overtook the Soviets weapon for weapon, we would be faced with a situation in which we might really be forced to accept the domination of a group of people who believe that the Gulag is the proper answer to dissent. They must have a darker reason, something to do with their being anal sorts. They must have had a dreadful relationship with their fathers, or they must have been sexually confused. They couldn't have an honestly different view of the world, a different reading of the same facts.

I disagree with a view of the world which can envision a   5 situation in which our superior strength will force our enemies to back down; we wouldn't be cowed so easily, and it seems naive to suppose that they are that much unlike us. I not only disagree with that view. I think that if it does not kill me off, it will kill my children or grandchildren. Or it may keep them from being killed—at the expense of other people's children and grandchildren. Even if those who defend the arms race as a necessary evil were right in their predictions, I would have to oppose them.

But it is too easy, too self-satisfying, to assume that our   6 own motives in this argument are pure while our opponents are indecent. They are wrong, I think; but to think that they are simply base (or even complicatedly base) involves us in doing several false things. We assume an ulterior motive, which handily keeps us from having to consider seriously the possibility that our opponents could be right. We assume that no other vision of the world could possibly have anything to recommend it, which keeps us from having to examine our own assumptions very closely. And we assume that our having the right idea, which is usually projected at people who already agree with us anyway, ought to gain us support, applause, and moral approval. We do this whether we are on the left or right. And by offering package deals we make it all easier for ourselves. A woman who knew that I opposed the war in Vietnam was shocked to learn that I opposed abortion, because in her package-deal way of thinking a person who opposed war must be in favor of abortion. The left is assumed by its enemies to be predictable, and so is the right. Both sides are right too often. Left and right *are* both pretty predictable, nearly tribal, and ideas and opinions are frequently waved around as signs of respectability within the tribe, as if language had nothing to do with exploring, or with moving towards a truth in a tentative way, or with being doubtful, or with taking a chance at the edge—which means being willing not only to be wrong, because the only thing at stake here is not whether an opinion falls into the true or false column, but also takes into account the possibility that your opponent is a human being as richly complicated and oddly formed as you are.

That does not make your opponent right. One must firmly 7
believe that there are ideas beyond decent debate. Genocide and child molestation are closed issues, I think. It is wrong not to be passionate about the things we care for deeply. I feel as strongly about nuclear war as I do about abortion, and find it difficult to have much sympathy with defenders of capital punishment. If Matthew 25 is right and what is done to the least human being is done to Christ, then capital punishment, abortion, the notion of a war in which whole populations may be destroyed, and the idea that hunger is in some circumstances acceptable, are all under a terrible judgment. But to think of those whose disagreements with us are deep as indecent or base is to put ourselves under the same judgment. An idea must bear fruit; a Christian perception is meant to go out from itself. If we see it as a personal possession we are on the wrong track. As a possession it is something we have to get rid of.

The Quaker saint John Woolman opposed slaveholders 8

and the men who were about to make the Revolutionary War. He thought that their decisions were profoundly wrong, and he let them know that. His life was a lived disagreement— but he always assumed that he was talking to a human being, one loved by God. Even where we believe that there is no room for debate, we must have compassion—which means *suffering with,* which means understanding how, a person could arrive at the place where he is—and we must realize that we share the disease of the heart which allows people to wound one another in the name of truth. Erasmus once wrote about one aspect of this universal problem: "There is great obscurity in many matters, and man suffers from this almost congenital disease, that he will not give in once a controversy is started, and after he is warmed up he regards as absolutely true that which he began to sponsor quite casually."

The point is not to become less committed, or to assume   9
that all ideas are of equal merit, but to be as clear as we can about our own motives, and to approach those who disagree with us the way Woolman did. We should not allow ourselves the luxury of thinking that our ideas have anything at all to do with our decency. We should realize that Matthew 25 applies to our judgments: the least of the brethren includes our opponents.

Comment

Garvey focuses his discussion on both the causes and effects of "thinking in packages." He begins with causes, as in these sentences of paragraph 2: "Our ideas are like clan totems or old school ties. We tend to think that our ideas make us decent." The transition to the effects occurs in paragraph 6: "but to think that they are simply base (or even complicatedly base) involves us in doing several false things." The concluding paragraphs present a solution to the problem. The basic organization, then, is a movement from problem to solution.

Garvey analyzes causes and effects informally, as we would in ordinary conversation. Indeed, that is how he addresses the reader—as a friend with whom he might on another occasion engage in argument. He talks to the reader as he would like to in an argument: casually, amiably, without heat, and without such a narrow focus on the issues that understanding or honest concession become impossible.

Questions for Study and Discussion

1.   In what ways are "our ideas . . . like clan totems or old school ties"? How does Garvey develop these similes?
2.   How does he illustrate the causes identified in paragraphs 4–6?
3.   What are the effects—the "several false things"—that result from "thinking in packages"?
4.   Garvey refers in paragraph 6 to the need of examining our assumptions closely. What is an assumption in thinking, and how does Garvey explain and illustrate the term?
5.   If there are "ideas beyond decent debate," how can and should they be discussed with those who hold opposite opinions? How does the statement of Erasmus help Garvey to deal with this question? And what use does he make of Matthew 25?

Vocabulary Study

1.   Explain the difference between the following words. The first word in each pair is Garvey's:
     a.   *investment* (paragraph 2), *interest*
     b.   *tactical* (paragraph 3), *diplomatic*
     c.   *totalitarianism* (paragraph 3), *dictatorship*
     d.   *hawks* (paragraph 4), *fanatics*
     e.   *ulterior* (paragraph 6), *deceitful*
     f.   *opponents* (paragraph 6), *enemies*
     g.   *genocide* (paragraph 7), *murder*
     h.   *obscurity* (paragraph 8), *misunderstanding*
     i.   *congenital* (paragraph 8), *inborn*
2.   Be ready to distinguish between the following words in paragraph 1: *anarchist, libertarian, conservative, radical, socialist.*

Suggestions for Writing

1. Analyze an editorial in a newspaper or newsmagazine, or a letter to the editor, to determine whether the writer is "thinking in packages." In the course of your analysis, explain what Garvey means by this term and what his ideas on thinking are as a whole.

2. Develop one of the following statements from your own experience and point of view. If you disagree with the statement, explain why you do:

    a. "We have an investment in our ideas which has nothing to do with the particular worth of our ideas."

    b. "Our ideas are like clan totems or old school ties. We tend to think that our ideas make us decent."

    c. "And by offering package deals we make it all easier for ourselves."

    d. "It is wrong not to be passionate about the things we care for deeply. . . . But to think of those whose disagreements with us are deep as indecent or base is to put ourselves under the same judgment."

K. C. Cole
Women and Physics

K. C. Cole is a journalist whose essays on science and on various aspects of the women's movement have appeared in *Newsday,* the *New York Times,* and other publications. *Between the Lines,* a collection of her essays, was published in 1982.

I know few other women who do what I do. What I do   1
is write about science, mainly physics. And to do that, I spend
a lot of time reading about science, talking to scientists and

struggling to understand physics. In fact, most of the women (and men) I know think me quite queer for actually liking physics. "How can you write about that stuff?" they ask, always somewhat askance. "I could never understand that in a million years." Or more simply, "I hate science."

I didn't realize what an odd creature a woman interested 2 in physics was until a few years ago when a science magazine sent me to Johns Hopkins University in Baltimore for a conference on an electrical phenomenon known as the Hall effect. We sat in a huge lecture hall and listened as physicists talked about things engineers didn't understand, and engineers talked about things physicists didn't understand. What *I* didn't understand was why, out of several hundred young students of physics and engineering in the room, less than a handful were women.

Some time later, I found myself at the California Insti- 3 tute of Technology reporting on the search for the origins of the universe. I interviewed physicist after physicist, man after man. I asked one young administrator why none of the physicists were women. And he answered: "I don't know, but I suppose it must be something innate. My 7-year-old daughter doesn't seem to be much interested in science."

It was with that experience fresh in my mind that I at- 4 tended a conference in Cambridge, Massachusetts, on science literacy, or rather the worrisome lack of it in this country today. We three women—a science teacher, a young chemist and myself—sat surrounded by a company of august men. The chemist, I think first tentatively raised the issue of science illiteracy in women. It seemed like an obvious point. After all, everyone had agreed over and over again that scientific knowledge these days was a key factor in economic power. But as soon as she made the point, it became clear that we women had committed a grievous social error. Our genders were suddenly showing; we had interrupted the serious talk with a subject unforgivably silly.

For the first time, I stopped being puzzled about why there 5 weren't any women in science and began to be angry. Because if science is a search for answers to fundamental questions then it hardly seems frivolous to find out why women are excluded. Never mind the economic consequences.

A lot of the reasons why women are excluded are spelled out by the Massachusetts Institute of Technology experimental physicist Vera Kistiakowsky in a recent article in *Physics Today* called "Women in Physics: Unnecessary, Injurious and Out of Place?". The title was taken from a 19th-century essay written in opposition to the appointment of a female mathematician to a professorship at the University of Stockholm. "As decidedly as two and two make four," a woman in mathematics is a "monstrosity," concluded the writer of the essay.   6

Dr. Kistiakowsky went on to discuss the factors that make women in science today, if not monstrosities, at least oddities. Contrary to much popular opinion, one of those is *not* an innate difference in the scientific ability of boys and girls. But early conditioning does play a stubborn and subtle role. A recent Nova program, "The Pinks and the Blues," documented how girls and boys are treated differently from birth— the boys always encouraged in more physical kinds of play, more active explorations of their environments. Sheila Tobias, in her book, *Math Anxiety,* showed how the games boys play help them to develop an intuitive understanding of speed, motion and mass. The main sorting out of the girls from the boys in science seems to happen in junior high school. As a friend who teaches in a science museum said, "By the time we get to electricity, the boys already have had some experience with it. But it's unfamiliar to the girls." Science books draw on boys' experiences. "The examples are all about throwing a baseball at such and such a speed," said my stepdaughter, who barely escaped being a science drop-out.   7

The most obvious reason there are not many more women in science is that women are discriminated against as a class, in promotions, salaries and hirings, a conclusion reached by a recent analysis by the National Academy of Sciences.   8

Finally, said Dr. Kistiakowsky, women are simply made to feel out of place in science. Her conclusion was supported   9 by a Ford Foundation study by Lynn H. Fox on the problems of women in mathematics. When students were asked to choose among six reasons accounting for girls' lack of interest in math, the girls rated this statement second: "Men do not want girls in the mathematical occupations."

A friend of mine remembers winning a Bronxwide mathematics competition in the second grade. Her friends—both boys and girls—warned her that she shouldn't be good at math: "You'll never find a boy who likes you." My friend continued nevertheless to excel in math and science, won many awards during her years at the Bronx High School of Science, and then earned a full scholarship to Harvard. After one year of Harvard science, she decided to major in English.

When I asked her why, she mentioned what she called the "macho mores" of science. "It would have been O.K. if I'd had someone to talk to," she said. "But the rules of comportment were such that you never admitted you didn't understand. I later realized that even the boys didn't get everything clearly right away. You had to stick with it until it had time to sink in. But for the boys, there was a payoff in suffering through the hard times, and a kind of punishment—a shame—if they didn't. For the girls it was O.K. not to get it, and the only payoff for sticking it out was that you'd be considered a freak."

Science is undeniably hard. Often, it can seem quite boring. It is unfortunately too often presented as laws to be memorized instead of mysteries to be explored. It is too often kept a secret that science, like art, takes a well developed esthetic sense. Women aren't the only ones who say, "I hate science." That's why everyone who goes into science needs a little help from friends. For the past ten years, I have been getting more than a little help from a friend who is a physicist. But my stepdaughter—who earned the highest grades ever recorded in her California high school on the math Scholastic Aptitude Test—flunked calculus in her first year at Harvard. When my friend the physicist heard about it, he said, "Harvard should be ashamed of itself."

What he meant was that she needed that little extra en-   13
couragement that makes all the difference. Instead, she got
that little extra discouragement that makes all the difference.
"In the first place, all the math teachers are men," she explained. "In the second place, when I met a boy I liked and
told him I was taking chemistry, he immediately said: 'Oh,
you're one of those science types.' In the third place, it's just
a kind of social thing. The math clubs are full of boys and
you don't feel comfortable joining."

In other words, she was made to feel unnecessary, and   14
out of place.

A few months ago, I accompanied a male colleague from   15
the science museum where I sometimes work to a lunch of
the history of science faculty at the University of California.
I was the only woman there, and my presence for the most
part was obviously and rudely ignored. I was so surprised and
hurt by this that I made an extra effort to speak knowledge-
ably and well. At the end of the lunch, one of the professors
turned to me in all seriousness and said: "Well, K. C., what
do the women think of Carl Sagan?" I replied that I had no
idea what "the women" thought about anything. But now I
know what I should have said: I should have told him that
his comment was unnecessary, injurious and out of place.

Comment

The issue that Cole explores—whether women lack ability in
science and mathematics—is related to a broader issue considered
briefly in paragraphs 6 and 7. This is whether males and females
differ innately in scientific ability. Cole reviews some recent evidence, then presents personal experiences that support the view that
social conditioning plays a decisive role; she wishes to show, mainly,
that girls are discouraged from excelling in science and mathematics. The evidence she presents is not, and cannot be, conclusive; but
it is strong enough to answer the question she poses at the begin-

ning of the essay—"why, out of several hundred young students of physics and engineering in the room, less than a handful were women." Her question cannot yet be answered definitely, but the evidence she assembles from various sources provides what she believes is a highly probable answer.

Questions for Study and Discussion

1. How various is the evidence Cole presents for the conclusion she reaches? Where does she state that conclusion?
2. How many causes does she distinguish for the failure of many women to excel in science and mathematics?
3. Does Cole say that innate differences in scientific ability do not exist between males and females, or does she reach a limited or qualified conclusion?
4. What other kind of evidence might be presented in consideration of the issue of innate scientific ability? For what kind of audience would this evidence have to be presented? For what audience is Cole writing?
5. Does your personal experience support the idea that ability in science and mathematics depends on encouragement and social conditions? Or do you have reason to believe that such ability is inborn?
6. How persuasive do you find the evidence Cole presents in support of her ideas?

Vocabulary Study

Explain the specific use Cole makes of the italicized words:

a. "Our *genders* were suddenly showing; we had interrupted the serious talk with a subject unforgivably *silly*" (paragraph 4).
b. "Dr. Kistiakowsky went on to discuss the *factors* that make women in science today, if not *monstrosities*, at least *oddities*" (paragraph 7).
c. "When I asked her why, she mentioned what she called the *'macho mores'* of science" (paragraph 11).
d. "But the rules of *comportment* were such that you never admitted you didn't understand" (paragraph 11).

Suggestions for Writing

1. Discuss your own experiences in learning science and mathematics, giving attention to the conditioning and encouragement you received, and in general the reasons for your good or bad or just average performance in them. Use your discussion to reach a limited conclusion or opinion on the issue Cole discusses.

2. Discuss the extent to which your personal experience supports one of the following statements:

    a. "The games boys play help them to develop an intuitive understanding of speed, motion and mass."

    b. "The main sorting out of the girls from the boys in science seems to happen in junior high school."

    c. "But the rules of comportment were such that you never admitted you didn't understand."

    d. "Science is undeniably hard. Often, it can seem quite boring. It is unfortunately too often presented as laws to be memorized instead of mysteries to be explored."

Definition

There are many ways to define a word, each depending on your purpose in writing and on the knowledge of your readers. In defining a cow for a child, it may be enough to point to one in a pasture or picture book. In a formal discussion you may point to a cow through words: first by relating it to the class *animal,* then stating the *specific differences* between the cow and all other animals: "the mature female of domestic cattle (genus *Bos*)" *(Webster's New World Dictionary)*. Also, you could explain that *cow* can refer to the female elephant or whale and other female animals.

These definitions are called *denotative* because they point to the object or single it out from all others. *Connotative* definitions by contrast refer to ideas and feelings associated with the word. Denotative definitions are the same for everyone; connotative definitions are not. To some people *cow* suggests laziness, or stupidity; others may associate a cow with feelings of nourishment and contentment.

If you want to explain the origin or derivation of a word, perhaps for the purpose of explaining current meanings, you may state its etymology. The word *coward* derives from the idea of an animal whose tail hangs between its legs. The etymology illuminates one

211

or more connotations of the word. You may, if you wish, propose or stipulate a new word for an idea or discovery. In the thirties Congressman Maury Maverick proposed the word *gobbledygook* as a description for pretentious, involved official writing. Such definitions may gain general acceptance. Some definitions remain in use for years, only to fall into disuse as new discoveries are made and new ideas appear, and better terms are invented to describe them.

How full the definition is depends on its purpose in the essay, as well as on the reader. For one kind of reader it may not be necessary to point to or single out an object: the writer will assume that the reader knows what the object is, and needs only to be told how it works. Parts of the object (the blade casing of a manual lawn mower) may be defined fully in the course of describing how to care for or fix it; other parts may not be defined because they are unimportant to the process. It may be enough to tell readers of novels written about the twenties that the Pierce-Arrow is an expensive automobile, or you may give one or two distinctive qualities of the Pierce-Arrow to explain an allusion to it.

Hilary DeVries
Real Yuppies

Hilary DeVries, a staff writer for the *Christian Science Monitor*, graduated from Ohio Wesleyan University in 1976. In 1983 she was named Magazine Writer of the Year by the New England Women's Press Association. The term *yuppie* became popular in the 1984 presidential election through its association with the primary candidate Senator Gary Hart. DeVries writes humorously about her efforts to join the ranks of yuppies.

Yup. I was proud not to be saddled with an acronym. 1
Pleased that I nimbly sidestepped the plethora of life-style

First published in the *Christian Science Monitor*, October 11, 1984. Reprinted by permission of Hilary DeVries.

manuals. "The Official Preppy Handbook," "Real Women Don't Pump Gas," and the rest of that know-thyself paperback pack. I was poised in the face of Woodstock's 15th anniversary; I had spent the Age of Aquarius trying to ace English in a public high school in Illinois.

Yet, despite my best efforts to avoid being pegged to a 2 generational trait, I find the term "Yuppie" not only unwithered but, like so much gourmet wheat germ, still sprouting. Even though Gary Hart, the true Yuppie hero, has come and gone.

If I am to believe what I hear during the waning days of 3 this campaign, I remain a political wooee, an assimilator of food processors, and unbearably upwardly mobile—the latter tips me into yet another socioeconomic category, that of the Yumpie, or "young upwardly mobile professional," in layman's lingo.

Much of this is news to me, not to mention my parents. 4 As far as I can tell, I still write rent-controlled rent checks every month and coddle along a car that is my college graduation present.

But in a sociological nutshell, it seems that we babyboomers have come of age—not by virtue of our achievements, rather by the extent of our style. Make that Style. Brunch has become a rite of passage and an MBA an almost requisite coat of arms.

Apparently we of the Me generation have decided that, 6 if we can't have it all, we can at least have it all First Class. A sort of "I strive, therefore I am." Our goals lie somewhere in the realm of inputtable data: a six-figure salary, live-in help, and the ability to snare the best tables at the city's top restaurants. All of it apparently reflects our insatiable taste for the good life.

As a newly christened Yuppie—an unutterably pert term 7 to my way of thinking—I find my native tongue has undergone some rehabbing. "Mesquite" and "dhurrie" are all linguistically right on, at least for the moment, unlike the already déclassé "Fettuccine Alfredo," "networking," and "cash machine." No one has to tell Yuppies the times, they are a-changing. An appetite for affluence is now the unwritten acme of good taste. A far cry from the creeds of the beads and flowers hippies.

Hence, as a true YUP, I will never, according to certain   8
codes of behavior, drink anything instant, cancel reserved tennis court time, or pay cash. I am supposed to be too busy patronizing those restaurants displaying a requisite amount of ferns, brass, and marble, where I never eat macaroni and cheese or tuna on white. I am too busy stoking up on sushi, gravlax, and gourmet chocolates.

And there is more to this way of life style.   9

I am supposed to do aerobics in the morning, jog at noon,   10
and meet at the health club after work. I am meant to work— better if I can "bill"—60-plus hours a week. But I must never tire and while away the down time in front of the TV. Excuse me, but I think I hear my arugula calling.

If my furniture doesn't float in my loft, if my cookware   11
(and it must be "cookware," not pots and pans) doesn't require copper cleanser or a small loan to finance, if I do not possess multiple vinegars or a particular make of German car, I will be suspected of being out of step. Or, more's the pity, I will miss becoming my own role model.

Yet, in a braver moment, I cannot resist testing the waters.   12
I had successfully brunched in the past, so I picked the yuppiest restaurant I could find and blithely booked a table for four. On the site of a humble eatery where I had previously reveled in plates of meat loaf, mashed potatoes, and brown gravy when I felt nostalgic for Mom-type cooking. I picked my way into a stark art deco wonder in order to see if I wore my socioeconomic label well. If I could hold my own with those who knew their way around a wedge of Brie.

I was in for trouble the minute I crossed the polished   13
threshold. Getting a meal here turned out to be as intimidating as applying for a bank loan or country club membership. The menu was as elliptical as a French symbolist poem—perfectly designed to make one feel simple-minded should a par-

ticular quail item need explication. Maybe I wasn't a true blue Yuppie after all. Not that I trembled in the face of "lightly oiled pasta," but others in the place seemed so at home, as if they had been weaned on warm lamb salad and not Bosco. My quartet stumbled through the ordering process, selecting the most familiar dishes with a relief not felt since getting out of grad school. It looked like a long evening.

Ironically, rescue came in the form of our busboy, a 14 pleasant-looking lad who had geometrically shaped hair, wore an earring, and clearly noticed our consternation. As he re-filled water glasses and passed out plates of bread and ceramic tubs of pale butter, he murmured without our even asking, "Land o' Lakes served in a ramekin." It was a clear tone of self-mockery totally out of synch with the industrial carpeting and bird-of-paradise flower arrangements. I glanced up. Sure enough, there was a wry twinkle in the busboy's eye not quite obscured by the new-wave coiffure.

Comment

Hilary DeVries is writing both informatively and expressively in defining the Yuppie. She does so through a series of humorous examples that show us what codes Yuppies obey, what games they play, how they eat, and what restaurants they patronize. But being a Yuppie is more than the sum of things Yuppies do. It is a state of mind that DeVries must attain. The language of the essay tries to capture both that state of mind and the anxious realization that she is missing the Yuppie style. Though her essay is humorous, De-Vries is making a serious point about values in America today.

Questions for Study and Discussion

1. The Yuppie is materialistic, DeVries shows. But does the Yuppie want to acquire things for their own sake, or does acquisition satisfy other needs?
2. What does DeVries mean by the statement that "I will miss becoming my own role model" (paragraph 11)?

3. What state of mind characterizes the Yuppie, and how does DeVries illustrate it?
4. Is DeVries saying or implying in the concluding episode that she has succeeded in becoming a Yuppie or instead that she has failed?

Vocabulary Study

The informal definition developed in the essay is largely connotative: DeVries depends on the associations of words to convey the feelings and style that mark the yuppie. Give both the denotative and the connotative meanings of the following words—the things the words represent, the feelings and images these words convey— and be ready to discuss their contribution to the essay: *Woodstock's 15th anniversary, Age of Aquarius, brunch, gourmet chocolates, aerobics, arugula, cookware, Bosco, new-wave coiffure.*

Suggestions for Writing

1. In a short paragraph write a formal definition of *yuppie* that summarizes the attitudes and behavior described by DeVries.
2. Define one of the following through the connotations or associations the word or phrase has for you. Where possible, illustrate the association through images or brief episodes as DeVries does:
    a. adolescence
    b. life style
    c. nerdish
    d. macho

August Heckscher
Doing Chores

August Heckscher, born in 1913 in Huntington, New York, worked for many years as a newspaper editor and as an editorial writer for the *New York Tribune.* He has served as director of the Twentieth Century Fund, president of the Woodrow Wilson

Foundation, and administrator of recreation and cultural affairs
for New York City. His writings include numerous essays and
books on public affairs, including *Open Spaces: The Life of American Cities* (1977) and *When LaGuardia Was Mayor: New York's
Legendary Years* (1978). His essay on chores is one of several essays in this text concerning the nature of work.

I have been doing chores, being for a brief spell alone in
a house that recently was astir with bustle and echoed with
the voices of a gathered family. For those, who may be in
some doubt as to the nature of chores, their variety, their
pleasures and their drudgery, I am prepared to deliver a short
disquisition.

The first point about chores is that they are repetitive. They
come every day or thereabouts, and once done they require
after a certain time to be done again. In this regard a chore
is the very opposite of a "happening"—that strange sort of
event which a few years back was so much in fashion. For a
happening was in essence unrepeatable; it came about in ways
no one could predict, taking form from vaporous imaginings
or sudden impulse. Chores, by contrast, can be foreseen in
advance; for better or worse, I know that tomorrow I must
be re-enacting the same small round of ritualistic deeds; and
they arise, moreover, from practical necessities, not from poetic flights.

A second point about chores is that they leave no visible
mark of improvement or progress behind them. When I am
finished, things will be precisely as they were before—except
that the fires will have been set, the garbage disposed of, and
the garden weeded. In this, they are different from the works
which optimistically I undertake. Ozymandias may have been
presumptuous, but he was essentially right when he looked
about him and said: *"See how my works endure!"* A work, once
achieved, leaves a mark upon the world; nothing is ever quite
the same again. The page of a book may have been printed
or a page of manuscript written; a sketch, a poem, a song
composed; or perhaps some happy achievement reached in one
of the more evanescent art forms like the dance or cooking.
All these have an existence of their own, outside of time, and

at least for a little while live on in the mind of their creator and perhaps a few of his friends.

The well-meaning wife, seeing her husband about his chores, will miss the character of his performance. "Henry loves to cut wood," she will say; "he positively dotes on controlling the flow of waste from dinner-table to compost heap." The wife is perhaps trying to appease an unnecessary sense of guilt at seeing her spouse engaged in mundane efforts. The fact is, he doesn't love doing chores. But neither does he feel humiliated or out of sorts for having to do them. The nature of a chore is that it is neither pleasant nor unpleasant in itself; it is entirely neutral—but it is obligatory.   4

Neutral—and yet I must confess that with their repetition, and perhaps because of their very inconsequence, chores can in the end evoke a mild sort of satisfaction. Here, as in more heroic fields of endeavor, a certain basic craft asserts itself. To do what must be done neatly, efficiently, expeditiously—"without rest and without haste"—lights a small fire deep in the interior being and puts a man in good humor with the world. Santayana described leisure as "being at home among manageable things"; and if he was right we who are the chore-doers of the world are the true leisure classes. At least one can be sure that no chore will defeat us; none will raise insuperable obstacles, or leave us deflated as when the divine muse abandons her devotee.   5

A man I know became seduced by the minor pleasure of doing chores—or at any rate by the absence of pain which they involve—and could be seen from morning till nightfall trotting about his small domain, putting everything in order, setting everything to rights that the slow process of time had disturbed. He was perhaps going too far. To season chores with work, and to intersperse them with a few happenings, is the secret of a contented existence. Fortunate the man or woman who achieves a just balance between these three types of activity—as I have been able to do by good chance, and for a little space of time.   6

Comment

Where Angelou writes concretely about the experience of work in an Alabama community, Heckscher writes in general terms. His purpose is to define one kind of happiness. That definition, coming in the final paragraph, takes the form of a general comment on the three activities discussed in the essay—chores, work, and happenings: "To season chores with work, and to intersperse them with a few happenings, is the secret of a contented existence." Heckscher builds to this thesis instead of beginning with it, because his point about these activities would not be clear without his having defined and illustrated them.

Questions for Study and Discussion

1. What are the differences between chores and work? Has Heckscher given a meaning to *work* different from your own? Do you ordinarily describe chores as work?
2. How does Heckscher introduce the essay? Does he merely state the subject—or does he also hint at his thesis?
3. Could the second point about chores (paragraph 3) have been discussed before the first?
4. Is Heckscher writing to a general audience or to a special one—perhaps husbands who perform weekend chores? What is his purpose in writing—to reflect on his personal experience, to inform his readers about work and chores, or to persuade them to change their thinking about work or their way of performing it?
5. Do you agree that chores can provide "a mild sort of satisfaction"?

Vocabulary Study

1. Read Shelley's poem "Ozymandias," and in a short paragraph discuss Heckscher's use of it in his essay.
2. Compare the dictionary meaning of the italicized word with the word following it in parentheses. Be ready to explain how the parenthesized word changes the meaning of the sentence:
   a. paragraph 1: *disquisition* (sermon)
   b. paragraph 2: *ritualistic* (habitual)

   c.   paragraph 3: *presumptuous* (conceited)
   d.   paragraph 3: *evanescent* (changing)
   e.   paragraph 4: *dotes on* (enjoys)
   f.   paragraph 4: *mundane* (ordinary)
   g.   paragraph 4: *neutral* (uninteresting)
   h.   paragraph 5: *expeditiously* (speedily)
   i.   paragraph 5: *deflated* (tired); *devotee* (fan)
   j.   paragraph 6: *domain* (household)

Suggestions for Writing

1. Discuss how accurately Heckscher's definitions fit the various kinds of work you perform at home. In the course of your essay, discuss how closely your idea of happiness agrees with Heckscher's.
2. Discuss daily activities at home and at school that you do not consider chores, and explain why.
3. About chores, Heckscher states: "Here, as in more heroic fields of endeavor, a certain basic craft asserts itself." Discuss the "basic craft" of a chore that you perform regularly. Contrast this "craft" with work that you also perform regularly.
4. Write your own definition of a contented existence, comparing your ideas and experiences with Heckscher's if you wish.

Charles Osgood
"Real" Men and Women

Charles Osgood was born in New York City in 1933 and graduated from Fordham University in 1954. He worked in radio as a reporter and program director before joining CBS News in 1972. He is seen frequently on the CBS Evening News as a special commentator, often giving his ideas in the form of poetry. His essay on man and woman has the concision and sharp focus that we expect of journalism; Osgood combines these qualities with considerable depth and force.

Helene, a young friend of mine, has been assigned a theme in English composition class. She can take her choice: "What is a *real* man?" or, if she wishes, "What is a *real* woman?" Seems the instructor has some strong ideas on these subjects. Helene says she doesn't know which choice to make. "I could go the women's-lib route," she says, "but I don't think he'd like that. I started in on that one once in a class, and it didn't go over too well." So, what is a real man and what is a real woman?   1

"As opposed to what?" I asked.   2

"I don't know, as opposed to unreal men and women, I suppose. Got any ideas?"   3

Yes, it just so happens I do. Let's start with the assumption that reality is that which is, as opposed to that which somebody would like, or something that is imagined or idealized. Let's assume that all human beings who are alive, therefore, are real human beings, who can be divided into two categories: real men and real women. A man who exists is a real man. His reality is in no way lessened by his race, his nationality, political affiliation, financial status, religious persuasion, or personal proclivities. All men are real men. All women are real women.   4

The first thing you do if you want to destroy somebody is to rob him of his humanity. If you can persuade yourself that someone is a gook and therefore not a real person, you can kill him rather more easily, burn down his home, separate him from his family. If you can persuade yourself that someone is not really a person but a spade, a Wasp, a kike, a wop, a mick, a fag, a dike, and therefore not a real man or woman, you can more easily hate and hurt him.   5

People who go around making rules, setting standards that   6
other people are supposed to meet in order to qualify as real,
are real pains in the neck—and worse, they are real threats to
the rest of us. They use their own definitions of real and unreal to filter out unpleasant facts. To them, things like crime,
drugs, decay, pollution, slums, et cetera, are not the real
America. In the same way, they can look at a man and say he
is not a real man because he doesn't give a hang about pro
football and would rather chase butterflies than a golf ball; or
they can look at a woman and say she is not a real woman
because she drives a cab or would rather change the world
than change diapers.

To say that someone is not a real man or woman is to   7
say that they are something less than, and therefore not entitled to the same consideration as, real people. Therefore,
Helene, contained within the questions "What is a real man?"
and "What is a real woman?" are the seeds of discrimination
and of murders, big and little. Each of us has his own reality,
and nobody has the right to limit or qualify that—not even
English composition instructors.

Comment

Where August Heckscher was able to give us an objective definition of *chore*, Osgood cannot give us one of a "real" man or woman
that does the same. He is writing about connotations that some
people make but others do not. In opposition to these, he gives the
minimum denotative definition. The dictionary does occasionally give
us connotations that are widely held or even inherent in a word—
objective connotations, as in the definition of *coward*. But these are
usually conventional connotations, not personal or subjective ones
such as Osgood writes about. Notice, too, that Osgood is using exposition for a persuasive purpose: he wants to change the way people think about men and women. He is attacking a common
stereotype.

Questions for Study and Discussion

1. How does Osgood identify the audience he wants most to reach?
2. What formal definition of a "real"man or woman does he give? How does he defend this definition?
3. What other stereotypes does he attack? What do they have in common with the stereotypes of men and women?
4. What meanings does the word "real" gather as the essay builds to the concluding sentence?
5. Do you agree that "masculine" and "feminine" are not descriptive of interests and behavior—that men and women cannot be typed in this way? If not, on what do you base your disagreement?

Vocabulary Study

1. The items in the following synonym group share certain meanings with each other, but each word also has its own meanings. Use your dictionary to distinguish the two kinds of meanings. The first word in each group is used by Osgood:
   a. *idealized* (paragraph 4), *romanticized*
   b. *exists* (paragraph 4), *lives*
   c. *proclivities* (paragraph 4), *preferences*
   d. *discrimination* (paragraph 7), *prejudice, bias*
2. How many of the derogatory words given in paragraph 5 are defined in your college dictionary? What does the etymology of those given tell you about the current meaning of the word, if one is given?
3. The following words are mainly connotative in their meanings. Write definitions for two of them, distinguishing their objective from their subjective connotations—that is, the general associations that everyone makes from the special associations some people make: *cute, cool, flip, crazy, silly, flaky.*

Suggestions for Writing

Use one of the following statements as the basis for an essay of your own. You may wish to agree with the statement and illustrate it from your own experience. Or you may wish to disagree with it, providing counterexamples or ideas:

a. "People who go around making rules, setting standards that other people are supposed to meet in order to qualify as real, are real pains in the neck—and worse, they are real threats to the rest of us."

b. "The first thing you do if you want to destroy somebody is to rob him of his humanity."

c. "They use their own definitions of real and unreal to filter out unpleasant facts."

d. "Each of us has his own reality, and nobody has the right to limit or qualify that—not even English composition instructors."

Classification
and Division

Classification and division are important methods of analysis in exposition. Repair manuals classify various tools into broad groups like drills, then explain the uses of individual drills. When you classify you arrange individual objects into groups or classes. Hardware stores, for example, shelve tools according to classes—hammers, drills, wrenches, pliers, and so on.

Division arranges the members of a general class into subclasses according to various principles. The division may be formal or scientific, as in the textbook or dictionary division of fleshy fruits like apples and oranges, drupaceous fruits (those with pits at the center) like cherries and peaches, and dry fruits like peas and nuts. The class to be divided may be as broad as *fruit* or as narrow as *apples* (a member of one of the subclasses of fruit).

The division of the class into groups is made on a single basis or principle. For example, apples can be divided informally according to color, use, variety, or taste, to cite a few possible divisions:

by color: red apples, green apples, yellow apples, and so on
by use: eating apples, cooking apples, and so on
by variety: Golden Delicious, Jonathan, Winesap, and so on
by taste: sweet, tart, winy, and so on

The principle of division depends on the purpose of the analysis. In instructing people what apples to buy for baking pies, you would divide apples according to variety, then perhaps according to taste. The color of the skin would not be important.

The division need be only as complete as your purpose requires: you might only distinguish tart from sweet and winy apples without naming the varieties. It is sometimes important to note that the division is not exhaustive. You might mention one or two varieties of tart apples like Jonathans and Granny Smiths, noting that other tart varieties are out of season. If you divide in more than one way (for example, dividing according to taste as well as variety), each division should be separate.

Lewis Yablonsky

The Violent Gang

Lewis Yablonsky has written much about juvenile crime. He was born in 1924 in Irvington, New Jersey, and studied at Rutgers and New York University, where he received his Ph.D. in 1957. He has taught at several universities, including the University of Massachusetts and the University of California at Los Angeles, and he is now professor of sociology at California State University in Northridge. This essay was first published in 1960.

It is a truism that criminal organizations and criminal activities tend to reflect social conditions. Just as surely as the Bowery gang mirrored aspects of the 1900's, the Capone mob aspects of the twenties, and the youth gangs of the depression elements of the thirties, so do the delinquent gangs that have developed since the 1940's in the United States reflect certain patterns of our own society.

The following quotations indicate the tone and ethos of a representative gang of today, the so-called Egyptian Kings, whose members beat and stabbed to death a fifteen-year-old boy named Michael Farmer in a New York City park not long ago. Michael Farmer, who had been crippled by polio, was not known to the Kings before the killing, nor had he been acquainted with any members of the gang.

> He couldn't run any way, 'cause we were all around him. So then I said, "You're a Jester," and he said "Yeah," and I punched him in the face. And then somebody hit him with a bat over the head. And then I kept punchin' him. Some of them were too scared to do anything. They were just standin' there, lookin'.

> I was watchin' him. I didn't wanna hit him, at first. Then I kicked him twice. He was layin' on the ground, lookin' up at us. I kicked him on the jaw, or some place; then I kicked him in the stomach. That was the least I could do, was kick 'im.

> I was aimin' to hit him, but I didn't get a chance to hit him. There was so many guys on him—I got scared when I saw the knife go into the guy, and I ran right there. After everybody ran, this guy stayed, and started hittin' him with a machete.

> Somebody yelled out, "Grab him. He's a Jester." So then they grabbed him. Magician grabbed him, he turned around and stabbed him in the back. I was . . . I was stunned. I couldn't do nuthin'. And then Magician—he went like that and he pulled . . . he had a switch blade and he said, "You're gonna hit him with the bat or I'll stab you." So I just hit him lightly with the bat.

> Magician stabbed him and the guy he . . . like hunched over. He's standin' up and I knock him down. Then he was down on the ground, everybody was kickin' him, stompin' him, punchin' him, stabbin' him so he tried to get back up and I knock him down again. Then the guy stabbed him in the back with a bread knife.

The attitudes toward homicide and violence that emerge from these statements led to eleven gang killings last summer and can be expected to produce an even greater number from now on.

One important difference between the gangs of the past   3
and those that now operate on our city streets is the preva-
lence of the psychopathic element in the latter. The violent
gangs of the twenties contained psychopaths, but they were
used to further the profitmaking goal of the gang, and were
themselves paid for their violence. Here, for example, is how
Abe "Kid Twist" Reles—who informed on Murder, Inc., and
confessed to having committed over eighteen murders himself—described the activities of the Crime Trust to a writer in
the *Nation:*

> The Crime Trust, Reles insists, never commits murders out of
> passion, excitement, jealousy, personal revenge, or any of the usual
> motives which prompt private unorganized murders. It kills im-
> personally and solely for business considerations. No gangster may
> kill on his own initiative; every murder must be ordered by the
> leaders at the top, and it must serve the welfare of the organi-
> zation. . . . Any member of the mob would dare kill on his own
> initiative or for his own profit would be executed. . . . The Crime
> Trust insists that murder must be a business matter organized by
> the chiefs in conference and carried out in a disciplined way.

Frederic Thrasher's famous analysis of Chicago gangs in   4
the mid-twenties describes another group that bears only a
limited resemblance to the violent gangs of today. Thrasher's
gangs

> . . . broke into box cars and "robbed" bacon and other mer-
> chandise. They cut out wire cables to sell as junk. They broke
> open telephone boxes. They took autos for joy-riding. They pur-
> loined several quarts of whiskey from a brewery to drink in their
> shack. . . .

Nor do the gangs of the thirties and early forties de-   5
scribed by W. F. Whyte in *Street Corner Society* bear much resemblance to the violent gang of today. The difference becomes
strikingly evident when we compare the following comments
by two Egyptian Kings with those of Doc, the leader of
Whyte's Norton Street gang.

> I just went like that, and I stabbed him with the bread knife.
> You know I was drunk so I stabbed him. [*Laughs*] He was

screamin' like a dog. He was screamin' there. And then I took the knife out and told the other guys to run. . . .

The guy that stabbed him in the back with the bread knife, he told me that when he took the knife out o' his back, he said, "Thank you."

Now Doc, leader of the Norton Street gang:

Nutsy was a cocky kid before I beat him up. . . . After that, he seemed to lose his pride. I would talk to him and try to get him to buck up. . . . I walloped every kid in my gang at some time. We had one Sicilian kid on my street. When I walloped him, he told his father and the father came out looking for me. I hid up on a roof, and Nutsy told me when the father had gone. When I saw the kid next, I walloped him again—for telling his father on me. . . . But I wasn't such a tough kid, Bill. I was always sorry after I walloped him.

Doc's comments about beating up Nutsy—"I would talk to him and try to buck him up"—or about fighting the other kids—"I was always sorry after I walloped them"—are in sharp contrast to the post-assault comments of the Egyptian Kings. Here is how one of the Kings who stabbed Farmer replied to my questions about his part in the homicide. The interview took place in a reformatory.

> KING: "I stab him with the butcher—I mean the bread-knife and then I took it out."
>
> QUESTION: "What were you thinking about at the time, right then?"
>
> KING: "What was I thinking? [*Laughs*] I was thinking whether to do it again."
>
> QUESTION: "Are you sorry about what happened?"
>
> KING: "Am I sorry? Are you nuts; of course, I'm sorry. You think I like being locked up?"

The element of friendship and camaraderie—one might almost call it cooperativeness—that was central to the Norton Street gang and others like it during the depression is entirely absent from the violent gang of today. To be sure, "candy store" or corner hang-out groups similar to those described by Whyte still exist, but it is not such groups who are responsible for the killings and assaults that have caused so much concern in our major cities in recent years.

Today's violent gang is, above all, characterized by flux. It lacks all the features of an organized group, having neither a definite number of members, nor specific membership roles, nor a consensus of expected norms, nor a leader who supplies directive for action. It is a moblike collectivity which forms around violence in a spontaneous fashion, moving into action—often on the spur of an evening's boredom—in search of "kicks." Violence ranks extremely high in the loose scheme of values on which such gangs are based. To some boys it acts as a kind of existential validation, proving (since they are not sure) that they are alive. Others, clinging to membership in this marginal and amorphous organization, employ violence to demonstrate they are "somebody." But most members of the gang use violence to acquire prestige or to raise their "rep."

> I didn't want to be like . . . you know, different from the other guys. Like they hit him, I hit him. In other words, I didn't want to show myself as a punk. You know, ya always talkin', "Oh, man, when I catch a guy, I'll beat him up," and all of that, you know. And after you go out and you catch a guy, and you don't do nothin' they say, "Oh, man, he can't belong to no gang, because he ain't gonna do nothin'."

> Momentarily I started to thinking about it inside: I have my mind made up I'm not going to be in no gang. Then I go on inside. Something comes up, den here come all my friends coming to me. Like I said before, I'm intelligent and so forth. They be coming to me—then they talk to me about what they gonna do. Like, "Man, we'll go out here and kill this cat." I say, "Yeah." They kept on talkin'. I said, "Man, I just gotta go with you." Myself, I don't want to go, but when they start talkin' about what they gonna do, I say, "So, he isn't gonna take over my rep. I ain't gonna let him be known more than me." And I go ahead just for selfishness.

If I would of got the knife, I would have stabbed him. That would
have gave me more of a build-up. People would have respected
me for what I've done and things like that. They would say, "There
goes a cold killer."

It makes you feel like a big shot. You know some guys think
they're big shots and all that. They think, like you know, they
got the power to do everything they feel like doing. They say,
like, "I wanna stab a guy," and then the other guy says, "Oh, I
wouldn't dare to do that." You know, he thinks I'm acting like
a big shot. That's the way he feels. He probably thinks in his
mind, "Oh, he probably won't do that." Then, when we go to
fight, you know, he finds out what I do.

The structure of the violent gang can be analyzed into   8
three different levels. At the center, on the first level, are the
leaders, who—contrary to the popular idea that they could
become "captains of industry if only their energies were re-
directed"—are the most psychologically disturbed of all the
members. These youths (who are usually between eighteen and
twenty-five years old) need the gang more than anyone else,
and it is they who provide it with whatever cohesive force it
has. In a gang of some thirty boys there may be five or six
such leaders who desperately rely on the gang to build and
maintain a "rep," and they are always working to keep the
gang together and in action. They enlist new members (by
force), plot, and talk gang warfare most of their waking hours.

At the second level, there are youths who claim affiliation   9
to the gang but only participate in it sporadically. For example, one of the Egyptian Kings told me that if his father had
not given him a "bad time" and kicked him out of the house
the night of the homicide, he would not have gone to the
corner and become involved in the Michael Farmer killing.
The gang was for this boy, on that night, a vehicle for acting
out aggressions related to another area of his life. Such a
"temporal" gang need, however, is a common phenomenon.

At the third level are boys who occasionally join in with   10
gang activity but seldom identify themselves as members of

the gang at any other time. One boy, for instance, went along with the Egyptian Kings and participated in the Farmer killing, as he put it, "for old time's sake." He never really "belonged" to the gang: he just happened to be around that night and had nothing else to do.

The "size" of violent gangs is often impossible to determine. If a leader feels particularly hemmed in at a given moment, he will say—and believe—that his gang is very large. But when he is feeling more secure, he will include in his account of the gang's size only those members he actually knows personally. In the course of a one-hour interview, for example, a gang leader variously estimated the size, affiliations, and territory of his gang as follows: membership jumped from one hundred to four thousand, affiliation from five brother gangs or alliances to sixty, and territorial control from about ten square blocks to jurisdiction over the boroughs of New York City, New Jersey, and part of Philadelphia. To be sure, gangs will often contact one another to discuss alliances, and during the street-corner "negotiations," the leaders will brag of their ability to mobilize vast forces in case of a fight. On a rare occasion, these forces will actually be produced, but they generally appear quite spontaneously—the youths who participate in such alliances have very little understanding of what they are doing.

The meaning of gang membership also changes according to a boy's needs of the moment. A youth will belong one day and quit the next without necessarily telling any other member. To ask certain gang boys from day to day whether they are Dragons or Kings is comparable to asking them, "How do you feel today?" So, too, with the question of role. Some boys say that the gang is organized for protection and that one role of a gang member is to fight—how, when, whom, and for what reason he is to fight are seldom clear, and answers vary from member to member. One gang boy may define himself more specifically as a protector of the younger boys in the neighborhood. Another will define his role in the gang by the statement, "We are going to get all those guys who call us Spics." Still others say their participation in the gang was forced upon them against their will.

Despite these differences, however, all gang members be-   13
lieve that through their participation they will acquire prestige and status; and it is quite clear, furthermore, that the
vagueness which surrounds various aspects of gang life and
organization only enables the gang to stimulate such expectations and, in some respects, actually helps it to fulfill them.
Similarly, if qualifications for membership were more exact,
then most gang members would not be able to participate,
for they lack the ability to assume the responsibilities of more
structured organizations.

The background out of which the violent gang has   14
emerged is fairly easy to sketch. In contemporary American
society, youth is constantly bombarded by images—from the
media, schools, and parents—of a life of ownership and consumption, but for the great majority of young people in this
country, and especially for those from depressed social and
economic backgrounds, the means of acquiring such objectives are slim. Yet something more definite than class position or the inadequate relation between means and ends
disturbs young people. It is the very fact of their youth which
places them at an immediate disadvantage; objects and goals
that adults take for granted are, for them, clearly unattaina-
ble. As a consequence, many young people step beyond the
accepted social boundaries in an attempt to find through deviant means a dramatic short-cut to an immediate feeling of
success.*

Drugs and alcohol are two possible short cuts; another   15
characteristic deviant path is the search for thrills or "kicks."
The violent gang, especially because it is both flexibly organized and amenable to the distortions of fantasy, is an obvious vehicle for acting out the desire for ownership and status.

---

*This statement is a gross oversimplification of conceptual developments of Emile
Durkheim, Robert Merton, and others, who have examined the means-goal dislo-
cation.

In the gang, a youth can be "president" and control vast domains, while the members can reinforce one another's fantasies of power—"Don't call my bluff and I won't call yours." In the gang, it is only necessary to talk big and support the talk with some violent action in order to become a "success," the possessor of power and status: "We would talk a lot and like that, but I never thought it would be like this. Me here in jail. It was just like fun and kidding around and acting big."

The choice of violence as a means toward achieving "social" success seems to be the result in part of the past two decades of war as well as the international unrest that filters down to the gang boy and gives him the same feelings of uneasiness that the average citizen experiences. At this level of analysis, direct casual relations are by *no means* precise; yet a number of connections do seem apparent. 16

A considerable amount of explicit data indicates that recent wars and current international machinations serve as models for gang warfare. For example, one form of gang battle is called a "Jap": "a quick stomp where a group of guys go into an enemy's territory, beat up some of their guys and get out fast. The thing is not to get caught." "Drafting" members is another common gang practice. The boys themselves freely use such terms as "drafting," "allies" (brother gangs), "war counselor," "peace treaty," etc., and they often refer, both directly and indirectly, to more complex patterns of conflict and structure. Here is one Egyptian King talking about a territorial dispute: 17

> You have a certain piece of land, so another club wants to take over your land, in order to have more space, and so forth. They'll fight you for it. If you win, you got your land; if you don't win, then they get your land. The person that loses is gonna get up another group, to help out, and then it starts all over again. Fight for the land again.

Here is another discussing gang organization:

> First, there's the president. He got the whole gang; then there comes the vice president, he's second in command; then there's the war counselor, war lord, whatever you're gonna call it—that's

the one that starts the fights; then there's the prime minister—
you know, he goes along with the war counselor to see when
they're gonna fight, where they're gonna fight. And after that,
just club members.

Murder, Inc., Thrasher's gangs, and Whyte's Norton Street
gang did not have the "divisions," "war lords," and "allies"
typical of the contemporary violent gang.

In addition to this international model, it is important to [18]
note that many weapons now used by gangs were brought to
this country by veterans of recent wars. Where in former years,
gang wars were more likely to be fought with sticks, stones,
and fists, today abandoned World War II weapons such as
machetes (one was used in the Michael Farmer killing) and
Lugers consistently turn up. The returning soldiers also
brought back stories of violence to accompany the weapons.
War and violence dominated not only the front pages of the
press, but everyday family discussion, and often it was a father,
an uncle, or an older brother whose violent exploits were ex-
tolled.

Another aspect of international events which gang youths [19]
may have absorbed, and which they certainly now emulate, is
the authoritarian-dictatorial concept of leadership. Earlier gangs
sometimes utilized democratic processes in appointing leaders. But, today, in the violent gang, the leader is usually su-
preme and gang members tend to follow him slavishly. In
recent years, in fact, there have been many abortive attempts—several on the Upper West Side of New York City—
to pattern gangs specifically upon the model of Hitler and the
Nazi party.

What finally confronts the youth of today is the possibil- [20]
ity of total destruction by atomic power—everyone is aware
of this on some level of consciousness—and the possibility of
induction into the army at a point when he might be establishing himself in the labor force. In short, the recent history
of international violence, the consequences of the past war,
and the chance of total annihilation, establish a framework
which may not only stimulate the formation of gangs but in

some respects may determine its mode of behavior—in other words, its violence.

But such background factors, however much they create $_{21}$ an atmosphere that gives implicit social approval to the use of violence, cannot actually explain how violence functions for the gang boy. As I have already indicated, gang youths feel extremely helpless in their relations to the "outside" world. The gang boy considers himself incapable of functioning in any group other than the gang, and is afraid to attempt anything beyond the minimal demands of gang life. One interesting indication of this is the way gang boys respond to flattery. They invariably become flustered and confused if they are complimented, for the suggestion that they are capable of more constructive activity upsets their conviction of being unfit for the hazards of a life outside the protective circle of the gang.

Given this low self-estimate, the gang boy has carved out $_{22}$ a world and a system of values which entail only the kind of demands he can easily meet. Inverting society's norms to suit himself and the limits of his partly imagined and partly real potential, he has made lying, assault, theft, and unprovoked violence—and especially violence—the major activities of his life.

The very fact that it is *senseless* rather than premeditated $_{23}$ violence which is more highly prized by the gang, tells us a great deal about the role violence plays for the gang boy. He is looking for a quick, almost magical way of achieving power and prestige, and in a single act of unpremeditated intensity he at once establishes a sense of his own existence and impresses this existence on others. No special ability is required—not even a plan—and the anxiety attendant upon executing a premeditated (or "rational") act of violence is minimized in the ideal of a swift, sudden, and "meaningless" outbreak. (To some extent, the public's reaction to this violence, a reaction, most obviously of horror, also expresses a sort of covert aggrandizement—and this the gang boy instinctively understands.)

Thus the violent gang provides an alternative world for
the disturbed young who are ill-equipped for success in a society which in any case blocks their upward mobility. The irony
is that this world with its nightmare inversion of the official
values of our society is nevertheless constructed out of elements that are implicitly (or unconsciously) approved—especially in the mass media—and that its purpose is to help
the gang boy achieve the major value of respectable society:
success. "I'm not going to let anybody be better than me and
steal my 'rep' . . . when I go to a gang fight, I punch, stomp,
and stab harder than anyone."

Comment

Yablonsky uses division in two ways in the course of the essay.
First he classifies gangs of the past and gangs of the present, then
defines their purpose and structure. Second, he divides gangs of the
present—the violent street gangs—according to their "levels." This
division is, in fact, a more detailed analysis of the structure of the
gang, for Yablonsky's earlier discussion of that structure is concerned only with its general features. The three levels reveal the various motives of the gang members. Reflecting the values of the fifties,
the violent gang shows how people are directed by forces beyond
their control. Yablonsky's concern over the death of Michael Farmer
is in part a concern over wanton acts by boys who did not know
their victim or themselves. He returns to this point at the end. His
essay shows how an episode (the murder of Michael Farmer) can
be used to say much about a society—its values, its structure, the
motives of acts that seem "senseless."

Questions for Study and Discussion

1. How does Yablonsky explain the difference between gangs of
   the past and the violent gang of the fifties?
2. By what other principles might the violent gang be divided?
   To what use could these divisions be put in another essay?
3. Yablonsky states: "In contemporary American society, youth is

constantly bombarded by images—from the media, schools, and parents," and he identifies those images and their effect. Yablonsky was writing in 1960. Do you believe youth in the late seventies is bombarded by the same images? Are the effects of images the same today?

4. What does Yablonsky mean in paragraph 14 by "the inadequate relation between means and ends"? How does the context of the statement help to explain it?

5. Yablonsky cites the Second World War and the atomic bomb as causes of certain attitudes and behavior in youth of the fifties. Do you believe war and fear of destruction are a major cause of juvenile crime today? Do you believe the pressures to conform are as strong today as they were in the fifties?

6. The phrase "society's norms" (paragraph 22) refers to the values or standards by which people live. How does Yablonsky show that not all of these "norms" are admitted or recognized by the people who live by them?

7. What is Yablonsky's thesis and where is it first stated? How does he restate it in the course of the essay?

8. To what extent does Yablonsky depend on formal transitions?

Vocabulary Study

Complete the following sentences, using the italicized word according to one of its dictionary meanings:

a. It is a *truism* of life that
b. One *aspect* of the energy crisis is
c. There was no *consensus*
d. The *phenomenon* of flying saucer reports
e. The teacher was *amenable* to
f. She could distinguish between *fantasy* and
g. They could not *emulate*
h. The contract *entails*
i. There was a *covert* recognition

Suggestions for Writing

1. Analyze the "levels" of a group you belong to, or divide the group by another principle. Use your analysis to develop a the-

sis or to support or argue against one of Yablonsky's conclusions.
2. Make a list of principles of division for each of the following.
    Then write an essay on one of them, employing a single prin-
    ciple of division:
    a. recreational vehicles
    b. health fads
    c. exercise enthusiasts
    d. animal lovers

Susan Allen Toth
Cinematypes

Susan Allen Toth was born in Ames, Iowa, and attended Smith
College, the University of California at Berkeley, and the University of Minnesota. She has taught English at Macalester College in St. Paul, Minnesota, since 1969. As a writer, she is
particularly interested in the education and changing roles of
American women, subjects of her books, *Blooming: A Small-Town
Girlhood* (1981) and *Ivy Days: Making My Way Out East* (1985).

Aaron takes me only to art films. That's what I call them, 1
anyway: strange movies with vague poetic images I don't always understand, long dreamy movies about a distant Technicolor past, even longer black-and-white movies about the
general meaninglessness of life. We do not go unless at least
one reputable critic has found the cinematography superb. We
went to *The Devil's Eye,* and Aaron turned to me in the middle and said, "My God, this is *funny.*" I do not think he was
pleased.

When Aaron and I go to the movies, we drive our cars 2

separately and meet by the box office. Inside the theater he sits tentatively in his seat, ready to move if he can't see well, poised to leave if the film is disappointing. He leans away from me, careful not to touch the bare flesh of his arm against the bare flesh of mine. Sometimes he leans so far I am afraid he may be touching the woman on his other side. If the movie is very good, he leans forward, too, peering between the heads of the couple in front of us. The light from the screen bounces off his glasses; he gleams with intensity, sitting there on the edge of his seat, watching the screen. Once I tapped him on the arm so I could whisper a comment in his ear. He jumped.

After *Belle de Jour* Aaron said he wanted to ask me if he   3
could stay overnight. "But I can't," he shook his head mournfully before I had a chance to answer, "because I know I never sleep well in strange beds." Then he apologized for asking. "It's just that after a film like that," he said, "I feel the need to assert myself."

Pete takes me only to movies that he thinks have redeem-   4
ing social value. He doesn't call them "films." They tend to be about poverty, war, injustice, political corruption, struggling unions in the 1930s, and the military-industrial complex. Pete doesn't like propaganda movies, though, and he doesn't like to be too depressed, either. We stayed away from *The Sorrow and the Pity;* it would be, he said, just too much. Besides, he assured me, things are never that hopeless. So most of the movies we see are made in Hollywood. Because they are always topical, these movies offer what Pete calls "food for thought." When we saw *Coming Home,* Pete's jaw set so firmly with the first half-hour that I knew we would end up at Poppin' Fresh Pies afterward.

When Pete and I go to the movies, we take turns driving   5
so no one owes anyone else anything. We leave the car far from the theater so we don't have to pay for a parking space. If it's raining or snowing, Pete offers to let me off at the door, but I can tell he'll feel better if I go with him while he finds a spot, so we share the walk too. Inside the theater Pete will hold my hand when I get scared if I ask him. He puts my

hand firmly on his knee and covers it completely with his own hand. His knee never twitches. After a while, when the scary part is past, he loosens his hand slightly and I know that is a signal to take mine away. He sits companionably close, letting his jacket just touch my sweater, but he does not infringe. He thinks I ought to know he is there if I need him.

One night, after *The China Syndrome,* I asked Pete if he 6 wouldn't like to say for a second drink, even though it was past midnight. He thought a while about that, considering my offer from all possible angles, but finally he said no. Relationships today, he said, have a tendency to move too quickly.

Sam likes movies that are entertaining. By that he means 7 movies that Will Jones in the *Minneapolis Tribune* loved and either *Time* or *Newsweek* rather liked; also movies that do not have sappy love stories, are not musicals, do not have subtitles, and will not force him to think. He does not go to movies to think. He liked *California Suite* and *The Seduction of Joe Tynan,* though the plots he said, could have been zippier. He saw it all coming too far in advance, and that took the fun out. He doesn't like to know what is going to happen. "I just want my brain to be tickled," he says. It is very hard for me to pick out movies for Sam.

When Sam takes me to the movies, he pays for every- 8 thing. He thinks that's what a man ought to do. But I buy my own popcorn, because he doesn't approve of it; the grease might smear his flannel slacks. Inside the theater, Sam makes himself comfortable. He takes off his jacket, puts one arm around me, and all during the movie he plays with my hand, stroking my palm, beating a small tattoo on my wrist. Although he watches the movie intently, his body operates on instinct. Once I inclined my head and kissed him lightly just behind his ear. He beat a faster tattoo on my wrist, quick and musical, but he didn't look away from the screen.

When Sam takes me home from the movies, he stands 9 outside my door and kisses me long and hard. He would like to come in, he says regretfully, but his steady girlfriend in Duluth wouldn't like it. When the *Tribune* gives a movie four stars, he has to save it to see with her. Otherwise her feelings might be hurt.

I go to some movies by myself. On rainy Sunday after-   10
noons I often sneak into a revival house or a college auditorium for old Technicolor musicals, *Kiss Me Kate, Seven Brides for Seven Brothers, Calamity Jane,* even, once, *The Sound of Music.* Wearing saggy jeans so I can prop my feet on the seat in front, I sit toward the rear where no one will see me. I eat large handfuls of popcorn with double butter. Once the movie starts, I feel completely at home. Howard Keel and I are old friends; I grin back at him on the screen. I know the sound tracks by heart. Sometimes when I get really carried away I hum along with Kathryn Grayson, remembering how I once thought I would fill out a formal like that. I am rather glad now I never did. Skirts whirl, feet tap, acrobatic young men perform impossible feats, and then the camera dissolves into a dream sequence I know I can comfortably follow. It is not, thank God, Bergman.

If I can't find an old musical, I settle for Hepburn and   11
Tracy, vintage Grant or Gable, on adventurous days Claudette Colbert or James Stewart. Before I buy my ticket I make sure it will all end happily. If necessary, I ask the girl at the box office. I have never seen *Stella Dallas* or *Intermezzo.* Over the years I have developed other peccadilloes: I will, for example, see anything that is redeemed by Thelma Ritter. At the end of *Daddy Long Legs* I wait happily for the scene when Fred Clark, no longer angry, at last pours Thelma a convivial drink. They smile at each other, I smile at them, I feel they are smiling at me. In the movies I go to by myself, the men and women always like each other.

Comment

Toth does not tell us she will distinguish the types of men who take her to the movies—that is, use division as an organizing principle—but this is how she develops her simple, richly detailed essay. And she does not tell us that she will use this division to make a subtle point about these men. We discover her intention as her division and contrast proceed: out of the contrast emerges a similarity—a quality shared by these men—that Toth hints at in her concluding statements. The humor of the essay arises in part from our not immediately realizing what she is doing, and in part from the details of her experiences. Toth shows how a great deal can be said through a careful selection of detail and its arrangement.

Questions for Study and Discussion

1. What are the differences that Toth stresses in the male "cinematypes" she describes? What do we discover at the end of the essay that they have in common?
2. How does Toth use contrast with her own movie-going to lead up to this similarity? What is this point or thesis?
3. The class that Toth divides is *cinematypes*. What is her principle of division?
4. What does Toth gain by omitting a formal introduction and formal transitions?
5. Given what she says and shows about the men who take her to the movies, do you think Toth would agree with Osgood on the issue of "real" men and women?
6. Has Toth exhausted the types of movie-goers, or are there others she might have included?

Vocabulary Study

1. What is the difference for some people between *films* and *movies,* and what point is Toth making about this distinction?
2. What is the tone of the following sentence—"We do not go unless at least one reputable critic has found the cinematography superb"? What does the word *cinematography* contribute to the tone?
3. What words in paragraph 6 contribute most to the tone? What is that tone?
4. Toth says in paragraph 11: "Over the years I have developed other peccadilloes." How would the meaning change if she had "developed other bad habits" instead?

Suggestions for Writing

1. Write an essay dividing one of the following classes, illustrating each type in your division simply but in detail, as Toth does, and using your analysis to develop a point or thesis. Save this thesis for later in the essay, perhaps building to it as Toth does. Divide the class consistently, in a single way:
    a. concert-goers
    b. party-givers
    c. television addicts
    d. boyfriends
    e. girlfriends
2. Divide one of the following in more than one way—for example, by variety and use. Then use your analysis to make a point:
    a. musical comedies
    b. horror movies
    c. romantic comedies
    d. soap operas
    e. adventure or detective movies

Michele Huzicka

On Waiting in Line

Michele Huzicka wrote the following essay in her first year at the University of Akron. She uses informal division simply and effectively, distinguishing types of students and experiences she encountered at various times of the day.

At one time or another, in the course of an average day, all of us must wait in some sort of line. In these lines we can learn much about ourselves and one another before we reach   1

Reprinted by permission of Michele Huzicka.

our destination. I wait in line often on campus—most often at meal time in the dining room.

As we all know, there are those who can be called 2 "morning people" and there are those who cannot. Morning people don't mind getting up early. They are cheery, pleasant, organized, and attentive—all without a hair out of place or the least bit of sleep left in their eyes. The non-morning people loathe the morning people for these qualities. When the two come together in a line for breakfast, turbulent feelings may arise. For this reason the breakfast line is relatively quiet, compared to other lines. People would rather not run the risk of sparking ill-feelings so early in the morning. However, if the same people were to meet later in the day, the situation would probably be entirely different.

The lunch line is probably the most pleasant of all the 3 lines we must cope with on campus. The majority of students are now fully awake. The non-morning people no longer feel muddled or groggy; they are now simply "people"—people waiting in line. Idle chatter about one's next class or one's hometown or mutual friends is a good distraction from what would otherwise be a very boring wait. It is here at lunch that we are forced to break away from our little cliques and explore the possibility that there are people different from ourselves. So we meet new people and learn about different classes on campus and about different towns and cities in Ohio. We even listen to trivial details just for the sake of having something to do.

In the dinner line I can see people once again returning 4 to the security of their friends as I join mine. It is always this line that seems to move the fastest as we recap the day's events, gossip about friends, analyze new boyfriends, and plan for the evening ahead. It is not surprising to look around and see other little groups doing very much the same thing. Talk of this sort is the most entertaining of the day.

Other lines, too, weave their way into our everyday lives. 5 Depending upon their location and the time of day, they can most definitely be quite uncomfortable and dull, or they can be adventurous discoveries about other people. Waiting in line at any time of day, we constantly learn new things about ourselves and other people. We are forced to be with masses of people who share one common goal—getting to the start of the line.

Comment

Michele Huzicka might have chosen another basis of division in her essay. Had she noticed differences in how students wait in different kinds of lines, for instance, she might have divided on that basis. Those waiting to register for classes perhaps behave differently from those waiting in a cafeteria. Huzicka began writing her essay with an observation that she wanted to develop and a sense of college life that she wanted to express. Her thesis occurred to her in the act of reporting that observation. At another time, she might have begun her essay with a general idea or thesis that she wished to illustrate and then searched her experience for examples.

Questions for Study and Discussion

1. How does Huzicka introduce her subject? How early in the essay does she state her thesis?
2. Huzicka writes both informatively and expressively. What does she reveal about her personality and interests in characterizing people and lines?
3. In what other ways might Huzicka have divided students standing in line? What other purposes might such divisions have?

Suggestions for Writing

1. Write an essay of your own on the same topic—on standing in line. Use classification or division at some point in the essay or throughout. Use your discussion to develop an idea as Huzicka does.
2. John Allen (p. 3) characterizes people not on the basis of how they stand in line but on the basis of the props they carry

during the day. Write an essay characterizing people on another basis, drawing on your personal experience. Use classification or division to develop your essay.

3.   Use classification or division to develop an essay on one of the following topics:
     a.   On writing essays
     b.   On sitting in college classes
     c.   On first living away from home
     d.   On riding the subway or bus

part four

Argument and Persuasion

Argument, or proof, is different from exposition, but the two usually occur together in essays. Most arguments require the explanation or illustration that exposition provides, and many explanations seem to be proving an idea.

Arguments seek to establish the truth or falseness of a statement. They often have different purposes and use different kinds of evidence. A lawyer in a court trial may argue the innocence of his client on the basis of eyewitness testimony and supporting circumstantial evidence. A scientist may argue on the basis of repeated experiments that heredity plays a role in some kinds of cancer. A newspaper editorial may argue for equal educational opportunity for the handicapped through an appeal to constitutional precedents.

Arguments are classified as either *inductive* or *deductive* on the basis of the kind of evidence used to rationalize the conclusion. In the examples above, the lawyer and the scientist are developing inductive arguments that reason from observation and personal experience; the editorialist is developing a deductive argument that reasons from given truths or principles. Many writers use both kinds of reasoning to prove various ideas that together form the essay.

An essay that contains argument usually does more than prove or demonstrate the truth of a statement. In developing the argument, the writer usually is trying to change the thinking of people on an issue or is trying to encourage them to take some kind of action. The purpose of the argument in these instances is persuasive. But not all persuasive writing uses formal argument. Political cartoons are persuasive without being argumentative, for example. So are satirical essays and poems. In this part of the book, we will discuss argument and persuasion separately, though some of the essays in the two sections illustrate both.

Inductive Argument

When you reason from facts, statistics, observations, or personal experience, you are reasoning inductively. You would be doing so if you were to predict that it will rain on the upcoming Fourth of July because it has rained on previous Fourths. A scientist would do so by reasoning that the success of vaccines in combatting polio, smallpox, and rabies suggests that vaccines would also be effective in fighting new viral diseases.

Inductive arguments make predictions about the future on the basis of past and present experience. The prediction or conclusion of an inductive argument cannot go beyond the particular evidence presented. It may rain this Fourth of July, but you cannot conclude it will rain on other holidays, too. The success in treating viral disease suggests that vaccines may be effective in fighting new viral diseases; it does not prove that vaccination is the only effective method, or that it may be effective with all infectious diseases.

In the upcoming essay on children, Joshua Meyrowitz makes a prediction based on personal experience and observation and argues that childhood and adulthood have merged in recent years:

251

Given this analysis, it is not surprising that the first widespread rejection of both traditional child and traditional adult behavior occurred in the late 1960s among the first generation of Americans to have grown up with television.

The cause-and-effect reasoning described in the previous section is one form of inductive argument: identifying the "conditions" that produce an event is the same as drawing a conclusion from particulars of experience. Meyrowitz uses causal analysis, in company with statistical evidence, to argue that television is responsible for the change in children. And he supports this argument with inductive generalizations of social scientists who observe social behavior—generalizations based on accumulated facts, statistics, and observations:

> Human development is based not only on innate biological stages, but also on patterns of access to social knowledge. Movement from one social role to another usually involves learning the secrets of the new status.

Meyrowitz thus draws upon several kinds of inductive evidence in reaching his conclusion that television changed the behavior of children and adults in the 1960s.

An *analogy* is a point by point comparison used to prove a thesis. An argument from analogy is inductive because it makes an appeal to experience. For example, you might argue that a senator running for the presidency should be elected because of resemblances to an admired former president. The analogy covers a range of resemblances in personality, traits of character, policies, and governmental acts. In an effective argument from analogy, the points of similarity must be pertinent to the issue—here, the qualifications for the presidency. It would be immaterial to the argument if the candidate were shorter than the former president. Important differences would weaken the analogy: it would be a material difference if the candidate had no previous governmental experience. If the similarities noted are genuine and if no significant differences weaken the analogy, it can be argued that the senator probably would make a good president.

Notice the qualification *probably*. The analogy cannot say with certainty that the senator *will* make a good president. Inductive arguments are probable only. For we can never be certain that we have discovered all the facts—that an exception may not exist to the conclusion drawn from the evidence. In inductive arguments, the major problem is not to claim more in the conclusion than the evidence warrants. The conclusion must be limited properly.

Joshua Meyrowitz
Where Have the Children Gone?

Joshua Meyrowitz teaches communication at the University of New Hampshire. He is the author of *No Sense of Place: The Impact of Electronic Media on Social Behavior* (1985). His essay on the "merging of childhood and adulthood" raises important questions about the role of television on children today.

About six years ago I was eating lunch in a diner in New York City when a woman and a young boy sat down in the next booth. I couldn't help overhearing parts of their conversation. At one point the woman asked: "So, how have you been?" And the boy—who could not have been more than seven or eight years old—replied, "Frankly, I've been feeling a little depressed lately." 1

This incident stuck in my mind because it confirmed my growing belief that children are changing. As far as I can remember, my friends and I didn't find out we were "depressed" until we were in high school. 2

The evidence of a change in children has increased steadily in recent years. Children don't seem childlike anymore. Children speak more like adults, dress more like adults and behave more like adults than they used to. The reverse is also true: adults have begun to speak, dress and act more like overgrown children. 3

It is not unusual to see children wearing three-piece suits 4
or designer dresses, or adults in Mickey Mouse T shirts, jeans
and sneakers. Adults now wear what were once considered
play clothes to many work locations, including the White
House.

Education, career choice and developmental stages were 5
once discussed primarily in relation to children and adolescents. Now an increasing number of adults are enrolling in
adult-education programs, changing careers in midlife and
becoming concerned with their "life stages." Meanwhile, al-
coholism, suicide, drug addiction and abortion have become
children's issues. Children also commit adult crimes such as
armed robbery and murder.

The merging of childhood and adulthood is reflected in 6
the shifting image of children in entertainment. The Shirley
Temple character of the past was a cute and outspoken child.
Current child stars, such as Brooke Shields and Gary Cole-
man, seem to be adults imprisoned in children's bodies.

Whether this is good or bad is difficult to say, but it cer- 7
tainly is different. Childhood as it once was no longer exists.
Why?

Human development is based not only on innate biolog- 8
ical states, but also on patterns of access to social knowledge.
Movement from one social role to another usually involves
learning the secrets of the new status. Children have always
been taught adult secrets, but slowly and in stages: traditionally, we tell sixth graders things we keep hidden from fifth
graders.

In the last 30 years, however, a secret-revelation machine 9
has been installed in 98 percent of American homes. It is called
television.

Communication through print allows for a great deal of 10
control over the social information to which children have
access. Reading and writing involve a complex code of symbols that must be memorized and practiced. Children must
read simple books before they can read adult books.

On TV, however, there is no complex code to exclude 11

young viewers. There is no sharp distinction between the information available to the fifth grader, the high-school student and the adult. Even two-year-old children, unable to read or write their own names, find television accessible and absorbing. They watch over 27 hours a week.

While adults often demand more children's programming, children themselves prefer adult programs. In fact, everyone, regardless of age, tends to watch similar programs. In 1980, for example, "Dallas," "The Dukes of Hazzard," "Love Boat" and "The Muppets" were among the most popular programs in *all* age groups in the country, including ages 2 to 11.

The world of children's books can be insulated to present kids with an idealized view of adulthood. But television news and entertainment presents children with images of adults who lie, drink, cheat and murder.

Reading skill no longer determines the sequence in which social information is revealed to children. Through books, adults could communicate among themselves without being overheard by children. Advice books for parents, for example, can refer them to books that would be inappropriate for children. Similar attempts on television are relatively useless because they are as open to children as they are to adults. Advisory warnings on television often have a boomerang effect by *increasing* children's interest in what follows.

Even early conservative programs such as "Father Knows Best" and "Leave It to Beaver" reveal important social secrets to children. They portray adults behaving one way in front of children and another way when alone. "Father Knows Best," for example, reveals to the child viewer the ways in which a father hides his doubts and manipulates his behavior to make it appear to his children that he knows best.

Such programs teach children that adults play roles for their benefit and that the behavior adults exhibit to children is not necessarily their real or only behavior. Television not only exposes adult secrets, it also exposes the secret of secrecy. As a result, children become more suspicious of adults and adults may feel it no longer makes sense to try to keep some things hidden from children. Television undermines behavioral distinctions because it encompasses both children and adults in a single informational sphere or environment.

Many formal reciprocal roles rely on lack of intimate 17
knowledge of the other. If the mystery and mystification disappear, so do the formal behaviors. Stylized courtship behaviors, for example, must quickly fade in the day-to-day intimacy of marriage. Similarly, television's involvement of children in adult affairs undermines many traditional adult-child roles.

Given this analysis, it is not surprising that the first wide- 18
spread rejection of both traditional child and traditional adult behavior occurred in the late 1960s among the first generation of Americans to have grown up with television. In the shared environment of television, children and adults know a great deal about each other's behavior and social knowledge—too much, in fact, for them to play out the traditional complementary roles of innocence versus omnipotence.

Questions for Study and Discussion

1. Meyrowitz draws on several kinds of evidence, beginning with observation, to establish his thesis. Does he emphasize one kind of evidence over other kinds?
2. Where does he first state his thesis? Where does he restate it in the course of the essay?
3. How do paragraphs 11–16 explain what Meyrowitz means in paragraph 10 by the phrase "a complex code of symbols"?
4. Meyrowitz states in paragraph 8:

   Human development is based not only on innate biological stages, but also on patterns of access to social knowledge. Movement from one social role to another usually involves learning the secrets of the new status.

If you wanted to verify these inductive generalizations, what kinds of books or people would you consult? Could you verify them from your own observation and personal experience?

5. Do your observations and personal experience verify the thesis Meyrowitz develops, and do they confirm the evidence he presents?

Vocabulary Study

1. Is the difference between childhood and adolescence merely one of age, according to the definitions in your dictionary? Is the difference one of age merely for Meyrowitz?
2. What reference books in your library help to explain the phrase "Shirley Temple character" (paragraph 6)?
3. Why does Meyrowitz refer in paragraph 8 to "patterns of access to social knowledge" instead of merely to "access"? What does the word *patterns* mean?
4. How do paragraphs 15 and 16 explain the phrase "behavioral distinctions"?
5. How does paragraph 16 help to explain what Meyrowitz means in paragraph 17 by "formal reciprocal roles"? How does the final sentence of paragraph 18 explain this same phrase?
6. What is the difference between *mystery* and *mystification* (paragraph 17)?

Suggestions for Writing

1. Discuss the extent to which your own observation and personal experience give support to Meyrowitz's thesis.
2. Use your observation and personal experience to test the truth of one of the following statements:
   a. "The merging of childhood and adulthood is reflected in the shifting image of children in entertainment."
   b. "Children must read simple books before they can read adult books."
   c. "The world of children's books can be insulated to present kids with an idealized view of adulthood."
   d. "Television not only exposes adult secrets, it also exposes the secret of secrecy."

Edward H. Peeples, Jr.
. . . Meanwhile,
Humans Eat Pet Food

Edward H. Peeples, Jr., was born in 1935 in Richmond, Virginia. He attended the Richmond Professional Institute, the University of Pennsylvania, and the University of Kentucky, where he received his Ph.D. in 1972. He is associate professor of preventive medicine at Virginia Commonwealth University. In the sixties he gained knowledge of urban poverty as a social worker in Richmond and South Philadelphia. He has been a leader of the Richmond Human Rights Coalition and Council on Human Relations and is deeply concerned with the nutritional problems and medical care of poor people.

The first time I witnessed people eating pet food was 1
among neighbors and acquaintances during my youth in the
South. At that time it was not uncommon or startling to me
to see dog-food patties sizzling in a pan on the top of a stove
or kerosene space heater in a dilapidated house with no running
water, no refrigerator, no heat, no toilet and the unrelenting
stench of decaying insects. I simply thought of it as
the unfortunate but unavoidable consequence of being poor
in the South.

The second time occurred in Cleveland in the summer of 2
1953. Like many other Southerners, I came to seek my fortune
in one of those pot-at-the-end-of-the-rainbow factories
along Euclid Avenue. Turned away from one prospective job
after another ("We don't hire hillbillies," employers said), I
saw my nest egg of $30 dwindle to nothing. As my funds
diminished and my hunger grew, I turned to pilfering food
and small amounts of cash. With the money, I surreptitiously

purchased, fried and ate canned dog and cat food as my principal ration for several weeks.

I was, of course, humiliated to be eating something that, in my experience, only "trash" consumed. A merciless pride in self-sufficiency kept me from seeking out public welfare or asking my friends or family for help. In fact, I carefully guarded the secret from everyone, because I feared being judged a failure. Except for the humiliation I experienced, eating canned pet food did not at the time seem to be particularly unpleasant. The dog food tasted pretty much like mealy hamburger, while the cat food was similar to canned fish that I was able to improve with mayonnaise, mustard or catsup.

The next time I ate dog food was in 1956 while struggling through a summer session in college without income for food. Again, I was ashamed to admit it, fearing that people would feel sorry for me or that others who had even less than I would feel compelled to sacrifice for my comfort. I never again had to eat pet food. Later, while working as a hospital corpsman at the Great Lakes Illinois Naval Training Center in the late 1950's I had the opportunity to ask new recruits about their home life and nutrition practices. While I was not yet a disciplined scientist, I was able to estimate that about 5 to 8 percent of the thousands of young men who came to Great Lakes annually consumed pet foods and other materials not commonly thought to be safe or desirable for humans. Among these substances were baking soda, baking powder, laundry starch, tobacco, snuff, clay, dirt, sand and various wild plants.

My later experience as a public assistance caseworker in Richmond, a street-based community worker in South Philadelphia, and my subsequent travels and studies as a medical sociologist throughout the South, turned up instances of people eating pet food because they saw it as cheaper than other protein products. Through the years, similar cases found in the Ozarks, on Indian reservations and in various cities across the nation have also been brought to my attention.

While there do exist scattered scientific reports and commentary on the hazards and problems associated with eating such things as laundry starch and clay, there is little solid epidemiological evidence that shows a specific percentage of American households consume pet food. My experience and research, however, suggest that human consumption of pet food is widespread in the United States. My estimate, one I believe to be conservative, is that pet foods constitute a significant part of the diet of at least 225,000 American households, affecting some one million persons. Who knows how many more millions supplement their diet with pet-food products? One thing that we can assume is that current economic conditions are increasing the practice and that it most seriously affects the unemployed, poor people, and our older citizens.

There are those who argue that we do not have enough   7
hard data on the human consumption of pet foods. Must we wait for incontrovertible data before we seriously seek to solve the problems of hunger and malnutrition in America? I submit that we have data enough. Isn't it sufficient to know that one American child or a single elderly person in this bountiful land is reduced to eating the forage of animals or exposed to unknown toxic levels of mercury, lead or salmonella to know that something very extraordinary must be done?

Comment

The writer of an inductive argument must decide how much evidence is needed to draw a well-founded conclusion—to make the "inductive leap." There is, of course, no end to the amount of evidence that could be presented for a conclusion such as Peeples reaches in his final sentence; the writer makes the decision at some point in conducting an investigation that enough evidence has been found. The phrase "inductive leap" sometimes means that the writer has drawn a conclusion too soon, on the basis of incomplete evidence. Probably few writers are satisfied that they have found all the evidence needed to make the argument convincing to everyone. Like Peeples, they may feel it necessary to draw conclusions from a smaller amount of evidence because a current situation is growing critical and must be exposed at once. Notice that Peeples admits the limitation his personal experience imposes on his conclusions. He is careful to state this limitation and also the basis of his estimate—a conservative estimate, he notes—that about a million people in the United States eat pet food in significant amounts. If writers have wide and expert experience in their subject, as Peeples has, their experience alone may be sufficient to give weight to their conclusions. As in all inductive arguments, the conclusion Peeples reaches is probable only, not absolutely certain.

Questions for Study and Discussion

1. Why do people eat pet food, according to Peeples?
2. What is his purpose in writing, and where does he state it? What makes the essay inductive?
3. To what audience is he writing, and how do you know? Were he writing to public health officials only, would he approach the subject in a different way, or present different evidence?
4. How does Peeples qualify his conclusion that people who eat pet food are affected by it seriously—that is, how does he indicate the degree of probability that this is so?
5. Has Peeples persuaded you that the situation he describes is serious and that something must be done about it? If not, what other evidence would persuade you?

Vocabulary Study

1. Complete the following to show the meaning of the italicized words:
    a. His *disciplined* way of living was shown by
    b. A *conservative* action is one that
    c. An *incontrovertible* proof can never
    d. The *bountiful* harvest
2. Identify the denotative and connotative meanings of the following: paragraph 1: *sizzling, dilapidated, stench;* paragraph 2: *pilfering, surreptitious;* paragraph 3: *"trash";* paragraph 5: *cheaper;* paragraph 7: *extraordinary, forage.*

Suggestions for Writing

1. Write an essay that builds to a thesis through a series of obser-
    vations and experiences. Qualify your thesis by stating the lim-
    itations of your experience and knowledge of the subject.
2. Discuss an experience that resulted when you found yourself
    short of or without money. Discuss not only what you did but
    also what you learned about yourself and perhaps about other
    people.
3. Discuss how your ideas about people different from you in some
    way changed through experiences in a world different from that
    you grew up in. Use this experience to persuade a particular
    audience to change their thinking about these people.

Robin Roberts

Strike Out Little League

> Robin Roberts was born in Springfield, Illinois, in 1926. After
> his graduation from high school in 1944, he joined the Air Force
> Student Training Reserve Unit at Michigan State University,
> where he played basketball and baseball while he earned his
> Bachelor of Science degree. In 1946 he was named Michigan's
> Outstanding Basketball Player. Two years later he joined the
> Philadelphia Phillies and played with that baseball team until 1962.
> In 1976, he was made a member of the National Baseball Hall
> of Fame.

In 1939, Little League baseball was organized by Bert and   1
George Bebble and Carl Stotz of Williamsport, Pa. What they
had in mind in organizing this kid's baseball program, I'll never

know. But I'm sure they never visualized the monster it would grow into.

At least 25,000 teams, in about 5,000 leagues, compete 2 for a chance to go to the Little League World Series in Williamsport each summer. These leagues are in more than fifteen countries, although recently the Little League organization has voted to restrict the competition to teams in the United States. If you judge the success of a program by the number of participants, it would appear that Little League has been a tremendous success. More than 600,000 boys from 8 to 12 are involved. But I say Little League is wrong—and I'll try to explain why.

If I told you and your family that I want you to help me 3 with a project from the middle of May until the end of July, one that would totally disrupt your dinner schedule and pay nothing, you would probably tell me to get lost. That's what Little League does. Mothers or fathers or both spend four or five nights a week taking children to Little League, watching the game, coming home around 8 or 8:30 and sitting down to a late dinner.

These games are played at this hour because the adults 4 are running the programs and this is the only time they have available. These same adults are in most cases unqualified as instructors and do not have the emotional stability to work with children of this age. The dedication and sincerity of these instructors cannot be questioned, but the purpose of this dedication should be. Youngsters eligible for Little League are of the age when their concentration lasts, at most, for five seconds—and without sustained concentration organized athletic programs are a farce.

Most instructors will never understand this. As a result 5 there is a lot of pressure on these young people to do something that is unnatural for their age—so there will always be hollering and tremendous disappointment for most of these players. For acting their age, they are made to feel incompetent. This is a basic fault of Little League.

If you watch a Little League game, in most cases the 6

pitchers are the most mature. They throw harder, and if they throw strikes very few batters can hit the ball. Consequently, it makes good baseball sense for most hitters to take the pitch. Don't swing. Hope for a walk. That could be a player's instruction for four years. The fun is in hitting the ball; the coach says don't swing. That may be sound baseball, but it does nothing to help a young player develop his hitting. What would seem like a basic training ground for baseball often turns out to be a program of negative thoughts that only retards a young player.

I believe more good young athletes are turned off by the   7
pressure of organized Little League than are helped. Little Leagues have no value as a training ground for baseball fundamentals. The instruction at that age, under the pressure of an organized league program, creates more doubt and eliminates the naturalness that is most important.

If I'm going to criticize such a popular program as Little   8
League, I'd better have some thoughts on what changes I would like to see.

First of all, I wouldn't start any programs until the school   9
year is over. Any young student has enough of a schedule during the school year to keep busy. These programs should be played in the afternoon—with a softball. Kids have a natural fear of baseball; it hurts when it hits you. A softball is bigger, easier to see and easier to hit. You get to run the bases more and there isn't as much danger of injury if one gets hit with the ball. Boys and girls could play together. Different teams would be chosen every day. The instructors would be young adults home from college, or high-school graduates. The instructor could be the pitcher and the umpire at the same time. These programs could be run on public playgrounds or in schoolyards. I guarantee that their dinner would be at the same time every night. The fathers could come home after work and relax; most of all, the kids would have a good time playing ball in a program in which hitting the ball and running the bases are the big things.

When you start talking about young people playing base-   10 ball at 13 to 15, you may have something. Organize them a little, but be careful; they are still young. But from 16 and on, work them really hard. Discipline them, organize the leagues, strive to win championships, travel all over. Give this age all the time and attention you can.

I believe Little League has done just the opposite. We've worked hard with the 8- to 12-year olds. We overorganize them, put them under pressure they can't handle and make playing baseball seem important. When our young people reach 16 they would appreciate the attention and help from the parents, and that's when our present programs almost stop.   11

The whole idea of Little League baseball is wrong. There are alternatives available for more sensible programs. With the same dedication that has made the Little League such a major part of many of our lives, I'm sure we'll find the answer.   12

I still don't know what those three gentlemen in Williamsport had in mind when they organized Little League baseball. I'm sure they didn't want parents arguing with their children about kids' games. I'm sure they didn't want to have family meals disrupted for three months every year. I'm sure they didn't want young athletes hurting their arms pitching under pressure at such a young age. I'm sure they didn't want young boys who don't have much athletic ability made to feel that something is wrong with them because they can't play baseball. I'm sure they didn't want a group of coaches drafting the players each year for different teams. I'm sure they didn't want unqualified men working with the young players. I'm sure they didn't realize how normal it is for an 8-year-old boy to be scared of a thrown or batted baseball.   13

For the life of me, I can't figure out what they had in mind.   14

Comment

Roberts does not begin with general truths about boys and girls. He begins with and presents his specific experience and observations and draws limited conclusions from them. How much evidence he presents for these depends on how he views his reader. He clearly expects the reader to know from experience that eight-year-old boys are scared of hard balls, and that most adults who instruct the boys are unqualified; on other points he presents more evidence. In an inductive argument of this sort, depending on particulars of experience, the strength of the argument depends on the amount and variety. It depends, too, on the reputation of the author. Roberts has a claim to authority in writing about Little League baseball; an author with less impressive credentials may need to cite more particulars and verify them.

Questions for Study and Discussion

1. What audience does Roberts have in mind? Is his purpose to inform them of the situation, or to inform and persuade them to take action?
2. How does Roberts establish his authority on the subject? Does he make direct reference to his experience in baseball? Does he ask his audience to accept his views on the basis of his authority alone?
3. Roberts anticipates an objection sometimes called a *dilemma:* either we have Little League baseball, or we have no organized baseball for boys and girls. How does he "go between the horns" of this dilemma by suggesting a third possibility?
4. How might Roberts answer those who object that only parents with children playing Little League baseball currently have a right to judge the sport?

Vocabulary Study

1. Identify those words in the essay that you consider negative in connotation. Use your dictionary to find neutral words that could be substituted for them.
2. Use your dictionary to find antonyms—words opposite in their meaning—to the following. Use the antonyms in sentences of your own:
   a. restrict
   b. compete

c.   retard
d.   relax

Suggestions for Writing

1.   Discuss your experience with and attitude toward an organized sport like Little League baseball. Use this discussion to state the extent of your agreement or disagreement with Roberts on planned sports for children.
2.   Discuss how supporters of Little League baseball might answer the charges Roberts makes. Then discuss how Roberts might answer these people, given his statements in the essay.
3.   Write your own essay, using the title "Strike Out _____," to persuade your readers of the disadvantages of an organization or activity. Remember that you will not convince readers without strong evidence based on your experience and observations.
4.   Roberts discusses some mistaken ideas that adults have about children and adolescents. Discuss other such mistaken ideas that affect the lives of children in important ways—perhaps in school activities or home life.

Deductive Argument

Deductive arguments draw inferences or conclusions from statements assumed to be true or well-established factually. Here is an example:

> Since continuing economic growth keeps people working, and conserving natural resources is needed for such growth, conservation is needed to keep people working.

Such an argument says that *if* the first two statements (or premises) are true, the conclusion or inference drawn from the statements must be true also. Arranged formally, the same argument becomes the following *syllogism:*

> [*Major premise*] Continuing economic growth keeps people working.

> [*Minor premise*] Conserving natural resources is essential to continuing economic growth.

> [*Conclusion*] Conserving natural resources keeps people working.

In the next essay, Donald Kagan, arguing that military service is a moral obligation, presents his basic argument after briefly introducing the issue:

It would seem obvious that in a world of independent and sovereign states that come into conflict and threaten one another's vital interests—sometimes even existence itself—citizens who choose to remain in a particular country are morally obligated to serve in its armed forces when the need arises.

Kagan bases his argument on the premise that democracies "rely on the willingness of their citizens to accept the decisions that duly elected and appointed bodies and officials arrive at, even if they are wrong."

From this premise Kagan draws the conclusion that citizens must be willing to accept military service if elected officials mandate it. He considers his premise obvious enough to provide sufficient evidence for this conclusion; he presents no other.

Kagan's argument is deductive because he makes inferences from this premise alone. The remainder of the argument answers the objections that citizens need not accept mandates that violate conscience and that alternatives to military service meet the responsibility of citizenship. Kagan argues that citizens must accept mandates though they are free to protest them. He also argues that alternative service is morally unsatisfactory.

Writers of arguments know that not everyone will agree with their premises. For this reason they defend one or both of the premises through observations and facts in the course of the argument. Whether or not they defend the premises, the argument is deductive so long as the premises themselves provide the decisive evidence for the conclusion. Thus the writers may explain or illustrate one or both of the premises, but they do not draw inferences from examples or explanatory detail: the argument would be inductive if they did so.

Sometimes an obvious premise may be implied in the argument rather than stated explicitly. Kagan might have reduced his argument to the following statement:

> In a democracy, citizens who refuse to sign up for the draft are not acting responsibly.

The implied premise is that the responsible citizen in a democracy obeys the duly enacted laws even when these prove repugnant. As in the reduced argument or enthymeme just cited, the writer may not state an obvious premise. However, the reader may need to supply the premise and examine it carefully when weighing the soundness of the argument.

A deductive argument that is true in its premises and valid in its reasoning is considered to be sound. If the reasoning is faulty or the premises are untrue—if they are "glittering generalities" or statements that cannot be defended and do not cover all instances— the argument is unsound. Kagan's argument would be unsound if an opponent could disprove the major premise by showing that the survival of a democracy does not depend on exact observance of its laws by all its citizens.

Here is a valid argument:

> In a democracy those voters who reject the mandate of elected officials are irresponsible citizens.
>
> Some voters today reject the mandate of elected officials.
>
> These voters are irresponsible citizens.

The argument is logical because the process of reasoning is correct. An opponent, however, may consider this argument logical but nevertheless unsound because one or both of the premises are untrue. Compare the following invalid argument:

> In a democracy voters who accept the mandate of elected officials are responsible citizens.
>
> Some voters are not responsible citizens.
>
> These voters do not accept the mandate of elected officials.

The fault in reasoning arises from the minor premise and the conclusion. Clearly voters may accept the mandate of officials and yet be irresponsible. The first premise—the major premise—does not say that accepting the mandate is the sole test of responsible citizenship. The minor premise and conclusion assume that acceptance is the sole test and therefore they go beyond the major premise.

The tests of validity are complex—the subject of formal logic. Common sense sometimes can detect the error in invalid arguments like the above, but many deceptive arguments require a knowledge of these tests. Two simple points should be noted:

No conclusion can be drawn from two negative premises.

One of the premises must be affirmative to reach a valid conclusion.

The terms of the argument must not shift in meaning. Notice the shift in meaning that occurs in the following faulty argument:

Sick people are not happy people.

Bigots are sick people.

Bigots are not happy people.

The phrase *sick people* ordinarily refers to the physically ill. If the word *sick* in the minor premise refers to mental aberration, then the term has shifted in meaning. Bigots may very well be unhappy people, but not for the reason stated.

Donald Kagan
Military Service: A Moral Obligation

> Donald Kagan is a professor of history and classics at Yale University and the author of several books on the classical world. His essay on military service appeared in the *New York Times* on December 4, 1983. The issue of military service has often been argued with reference to particular wars—most recently the Vietnam War. Here, Kagan considers the nature of "moral obligation" in general.

The killing of 239 servicemen in Lebanon and the inva-   1
sion of Grenada have reminded Americans of the military's role in pursuit of the nation's purposes and once again have raised the question of the citizen's obligation to do military service when called upon. This question still is before us because of continuing controversy over a law requiring students seeking Federal aid to register for the draft.

It would seem obvious that in a world of independent   2
and sovereign states that come into conflict and threaten one
another's vital interests—sometimes even existence itself—citizens who choose to remain in a particular country are morally obliged to serve in its armed forces when the need arises.

Critics of this view appeal to a higher morality in which   3
an individual may refuse to serve if such service violates his
conscience. Some assert the right, even the duty, to refuse
service when they do not approve of the national policy that
leads to the need for military action, even though they do not
oppose serving when they approve the cause. To accept such
a claim would be to destroy all governments but especially
democracies, which rely on the willingness of their citizens to
accept the decisions that duly elected and appointed bodies
and officials arrive at, even if they are wrong.

That is not to say that citizens are morally obliged to ac-   4
cept the decisions of any country in which they live, no matter how wicked and despotic—only in legitimate ones. My
definition of a legitimate state is one that permits the open
advocacy of different opinions, the possibility of changing the
laws by peaceful means and, most important, emigration
without penalty. A regime that fails to meet these criteria imposes its will by force alone and has no moral claim on the
obedience of its subjects.

On the other hand, a nation that meets them has every   5
claim to its citizens' allegiance and especially to the service most
vital to its existence. When a citizen has become an adult and
has not chosen to leave the country, he tacitly approves of its
legitimacy and consents to its laws. He benefits from their
protection and has the moral obligation to obey them if he
wants to stay. To enjoy the enormous advantages provided
by a free society while claiming the right to ignore or disobey
the laws selectively, especially those essential to its survival and
most demanding of its citizens, is plainly immoral.

Some recusants are pacifists who refuse to fight regard-   6
less of the occasion. Their position, though it lacks the ab-
surdity of claiming the right of each citizen to conduct his

own foreign policy, is also deficient. Leaving the country would not solve their problem, since wherever they go they will find a state that will be prepared to use force in the national interest when necessary and will ask its citizens to do military service. One solution has been to refuse to serve and accept the legal penalty without complaint. Another has been to accept auxiliary service, such as in the medical corps, which, though dangerous, does not require killing. These responses prove sincerity and courage, but they do not satisfy the moral demands of citizenship. Pacifists in this imperfect world can pursue their beliefs only in free societies and only because their fellow citizens are willing to fight and protect them. There were no protected pacifists in Hitler's Germany and Stalin's Russia; there are none in Yuri V. Andropov's.

Pacifists are not alone in hating the need to kill. Most   7 American soldiers find it impossible to pull the trigger in their first combat experience and find it profoundly painful even later. Yet they do their duty, though there is no way to know if they dislike killing any less than those refusing to fight. A decent, free society is right to allow concern for personal conscience a place in its considerations and to afford special treatment to those who refuse to fight on plausible grounds of conscience. But those who accept such treatment must realize that they are getting a free ride and failing in their moral responsibility as citizens.

Comment

Kagan bases his argument in favor of military service on a belief about democracy and citizens. This belief he considers a given truth, requiring no defense. Most of his essay is given instead to rebuttal: Kagan introduces the arguments opposing military service one by one and answers them. In doing so, he informs the general reader about the issue.

In articles and editorials for periodicals with a wide circulation, writers usually assume that their audience is a general one. Because

Kagan is directing his argument to a general audience, he gives a full account of the issue, including the arguments of his opponents. Special audiences obviously do not require as much information as general audiences, though many writers provide it to be sure the facts and issues are correctly understood.

Questions for Study and Discussion

1. Kagan states his belief about democracy and citizenship in paragraphs 4 and 5. What is that belief, and how does Kagan explain it? How does he define *democracy*?
2. Is a "legitimate" state necessarily a "democratic" state? Could a state be legitimate without being democratic in its structure?
3. What behavior does Kagan consider "plainly immoral" (paragraph 5), and how is this belief related to his belief about citizenship?
4. How does Kagan define "the moral demands of citizenship" in paragraph 6?
5. Why does Kagan introduce the idea that "pacifists are not alone in hating the need to kill"? Is he making a concession to his opponents in making this point?

Vocabulary Study

1. What is the difference between an "independent" and a "sovereign" state (paragraph 2)? Can a state be independent without being sovereign?
2. Could the word *person* be substituted for the word *individual* in the first sentence of paragraph 3 without changing the meaning?
3. Could the word *quietly* be substituted for the word *tacitly* in the second sentence of paragraph 5 without changing the meaning?
4. What are synonyms of the words *recusant* and *pacifist*?

Suggestions for Writing

1. Argue your agreement or disagreement with Kagan on the issue of military service. State your own beliefs and explain them.
2. Discuss to what extent our society should "allow concern for

personal conscience a place in its considerations" and "afford special treatment" to recusants. Choose another contemporary issue—for example, tax resisters—for illustration.

Letters to the Editor: Rebuttal to Kagan

These two letters, written in answer to Kagan's essay on p. 271, appeared in the *New York Times* on December 11, 1983, only a week after his essay was published in the same paper. Like Kagan, the writers pursue the nature of "moral obligation" and how it affects military service.

To the Editor:

The citizen who according to Professor Kagan is morally obligated to do military service is male and 18 to 26 years old. No other is asked to do service of any kind. All Americans, he indicates, are given the right to dissent, but the select group earmarked for military service must be willing to risk their lives, forfeiting their right to dissent.

Professor Kagan appears to believe that, since the United States is a democracy, all decisions are made in a democratic manner. Unfortunately, this is not the case, particularly in regard to foreign policy.

And he plays on the "love it or leave it" theme when he makes the assumption that citizens who choose to remain in this country consent to its laws. People support some laws, are opposed to others and still wish to remain in the United States. Leaving is a difficult thing to do because one's coun-

---

Both letters first published in the *New York Times,* December 11, 1983. Reprinted by permission of Emily S. Guttchen and Phillip H. Hershberger.

try is not just laws and policies but loved ones, a culture and a home.

I was also struck by the anachronism of Professor Kagan's arguments. It is nuclear war, not some invading horde, that threatens our country's survival. The moral obligation of all United States citizens is to insist that their Government pursue policies designed to lessen tensions between the superpowers and support those forces in the third-world nations that are working toward a better life for their people rather than supporting repressive forces and using the Soviet threat as an excuse for doing so.

Americans must stop their Government from engaging in wars of intervention to protect vested interests—wars that carry the risk of escalating, by way first of tactical nuclear weapons and ultimately nuclear missiles, into all-out nuclear war. This is the highest moral obligation.

Emily S. Guttchen

To the Editor:

Donald Kagan's assertion that "pacifists can pursue their beliefs only in free societies and only because their fellow citizens are willing to fight and protect them" disregards what is to me, a conscientious objector who did alternative service as a volunteer, a key issue.

Professor Kagan does not see that the right to object to war is the *result* of objection. It is secured by the people who stand up and claim that right and by no one else.

Some believe that war objectors would serve in the military if threatened with alternatives of death, imprisonment or loss of livelihood. Many religious objectors to war, my German Church of the Brethren ancestors among them, suffered just such penalties in order to pursue their beliefs. It is that history of objection, and not the Marines in Beirut, from which I might be taking "a free ride," if in fact I am.

I believe we all do have a moral obligation to serve one

another, but because it is a moral obligation, my service must be outside the military.

Phillip H. Hershberger

Comment

The two letters written to the *New York Times* in response to Donald Kagan's essay attack his argument in different ways. Guttchen attacks Kagan's major premise—that democracies "rely on the willingness of their citizens to accept the decisions that duly elected and appointed bodies and officials arrive at, even if they are wrong." She also counters Kagan's assertion that citizens may leave a free country whose laws they cannot accept. Her attack on the "anachronism" of Kagan's argument is also an attack on the truth of the premises.

Hershberger, in turn, challenges Kagan's argument dealing with pacifists—an argument Kagan presents in answer to the objection that alternative service can also meet the moral responsibility of citizenship.

The two letters illustrate an important point about argumentation. Disagreement is often with the premises themselves rather than with the reasoning from premises to conclusion. In attacking Kagan's premises the writers use inductive evidence to show that facts do not support Kagan's premises. They use deductive arguments in presenting counter premises and definitions.

Questions for Study and Discussion

1. What evidence does Guttchen present in attacking the premise that governments depend on the willingness of citizens to obey laws? Does she use the same kind of evidence in attacking the "anachronism" of Kagan's argument?

2. How does Hershberger attack Kagan's argument concerning pacifists? How does his concluding paragraph attack Kagan's conception of moral obligation?

3. If you agree with Kagan, how would you answer the arguments presented in the two letters? If you disagree with Kagan, do you do so for the reasons stated in the letters?

Vocabulary Study

1. The words *presumption, presupposition, assumption,* and *premise* are close synonyms, yet each word has its special meaning and use. What information does your dictionary give about these special meanings?
2. Is the phrase "moral obligation" redundant—that is, are all obligations by definition "moral"? Or are there kinds of obligation that do not involve morality?

Suggestions for Writing

1. Write your own letter to Kagan—agreeing or disagreeing with his argument and stating why. In preparing to write, you should be clear in your mind about the kind of evidence you will present—inductive evidence consisting of facts, personal experience, or observations, or deductive evidence consisting of beliefs or given truths of your own.
2. Write a letter to the editor of a newspaper, disagreeing with an editorial or a letter and explaining why you disagree. Again, be clear about the kind of evidence you will present.
3. Write an argument on a current issue at your college—perhaps the financing of athletic programs or the reduction of electives and introduction of certain requirements. Answer one or more objections that might be raised to your argument, as Kagan does.

Rev. Timothy S. Healy, S. J.
In Defense of Disorder

Timothy S. Healy, S. J., is president of Georgetown University in Washington, D.C. A specialist in the poetry of John Donne, Reverend Healy previously taught English at Fordham University, and he also has served as vice chancellor for academic affairs at the City University of New York and on federal government commissions on education. His essay on student interruption of unpopular university speakers explores this specific issue and then moves on to the broader question of why universities exist.

Over the past weeks, the nation's colleges have taken a beating because of loudmouths who shouted down invited speakers. Eldridge Cleaver at Wisconsin, Ambassador Jeane Kirkpatrick at Berkeley and Sheik Ahmad Zaki Yamani at Kansas were the speakers, and the noise raised in their defense is only slightly less deafening than the shouts that drowned their speeches. No one in the academy approved or condoned the shouting: the clearest defense of the university as an open forum has come from university people themselves through the national associations that represent presidents, faculty members and students.

Whether or not they are aware of it, our critics misread our vulnerability to disruption. They seem to think that universities are orderly places, and if they aren't, presidents and trustees ought to make them so, even by force. Force is, however, our last and least resource, and order in the universities has seldom been more than skin-deep. We order our planning, our upkeep, our payroll and the lawns. But where our most serious work is done, messiness, not to say a kind of anarchy, is part of our nature.

Look first at our teaching. Our job is to put students in touch with beauty or thought and then watch what happens. A young mind seeing for the first time into Virgil, Plato or Burke undergoes an intellectual chain reaction that is uncontrollable. Great works and young minds are "fire and powder which as they kiss consume."

There is an anarchy in the being of our students. The chaos of living in a 20-year-old body translates into the 20-year-old's steady probing at authority. Most students at one time or another tangle with it, not because they want it removed, but because they want to see whether it will stand still long enough for them to measure themselves against it.

At times, the faculty, like parents, cry out in Shakespear-   5
ean eloquence:

> Let me not live . . . to be the snuff
> Of younger spirits, whose apprehensive senses
> All but new things disdain; whose judgments are
> Mere fathers of their garments; whose constancies
> Expire before their fashions.

But faculty, too, are caught up in our disorderly process. A
good class crackles with intensity. The professor knows the
long reach of his ideas and the challenge they put not only to
his students but to himself. He is also aware of how hard he
must crowd and pull to make student growth go as far as it
can. The wrestle of mind on mind fills both, and neither faculty member nor student has much time for the dull business
of keeping the world, even the world of the university, in good
trim. To learn and to teach are beautiful things, but at their
intense best, like laughter or pain, they distort.

The faculty knows also the messiness of research. Every   6
scholar who finds himself treading ground no one has trod
before feels as though he has been spun off his native planet
into a solitary and chaotic orbit of speculation, hypothesis and
doubt. Anarchy and loneliness go together. Scholarship in
which facts stay in line or ideas in order is either vulgariza-
tion or echo.

Our critics take as given the basic tidiness of govern-   7
ment, industry and the press, but authority within a university is tentative and dispersed. No one is completely in charge,
and no one should be. Academic decisions are made by faculties. Students want a large say in the conduct of their lives
on campus. Presidents and deans distribute the seven goods
of the university (people, space, money, books, equipment,
location and reputation) but are bigger fools than they look
if they confuse the ground they walk with the windy heights
where the young learn and grow.

That growth touches all of us. The faculty offer their ex-   8
perience and knowledge and the students their imagination
and energy. The shock between them remakes all our worlds,

including our democracy. Alfred North Whitehead's vision of the university as the smithy where a people's ideas and forms are rethought and recast in "the imaginative acquisition of knowledge" is still true. That vision doesn't work where premises or conclusions go untried or where a false neatness is forcibly laid on.

Because we are open in our process and open in our places, we are deliberately vulnerable to ill-aimed force, which can at times attack our own freedom. The very being of a university makes it easy to disrupt, and our centuries have taught us that we are weakly defended by policemen. A university's great gift is the grant of room for young and old to speculate, to dream, to rear great buildings of ideas. A second gift is an absolution from consequence should those ideas crash down about our ears. Unless the young learn firsthand how supple and strengthening our freedoms are, they will never learn to defend them. Imposed order is a poor teacher for any free people. 9

Our strong defense, on halcyon as on stormy days, is a discipline as old as man's mind. The worst of our errors are academic and intellectual and we can, given time, correct them. Correction comes not by crowd control, but by reason, by the slow, wearing rub of mind on mind. We live in a glass house that beckons the booby's stone, and none of the numerical barbed wire at the gates of admission can keep out boobies. All of us deal with disrupters, but we try to civilize them, or at least hold them at bay in the strong toils of talk, thought, persuasion. All of us know the acrid shame of failure whenever we must resort to force. We also know that authority alone can never lead a student out of "the prison of his days." 10

If America's colleges are to be roundly condemned because they feel the best way to handle disruption is to educate disrupters, then something of value to all of us will be lost. Our faculties have at least one large body of allies: the parents of their students. Parents know how hard it is for the young to grow without error, indeed how impossible. They 11 understand why colleges react so often with ambiguous patience. We who teach distrust force because we take the parentage of the mind seriously, because like parents we still at heart love our own.

Comment

Reverend Healy's argument is a mixed one. In paragraph 5 he states his conception of the ideal class and the ideal professor: "A good class crackles with intensity. The professor knows the long reach of his ideas and the challenge they put not only to his students but to himself." From this belief and others concerning the purpose and nature of education and the nature of twenty-year-old college students, he makes deductions and uses these to explain the behavior of students who disrupt speakers at college campuses. Reverend Healy combines his deductive argument with an inductive argument based on experience and observation—namely, that college administrations, trustees, and faculty cannot make universities tidy and well-behaved. He concludes with an appeal to the experience of the reader.

Questions for Study and Discussion

1. What does Reverend Healy tell us in paragraphs 3–5 about the purpose and nature of education and the nature of college students? How does he develop his ideas about education in paragraphs 8 and 9?
2. What conclusions does he draw about campus life and, in particular, disruption of speakers, from these ideas?
3. Why do college administrators, trustees, and faculty not have the power to control college life? Is Reverend Healy saying that anarchy is desirable or necessary? Is he saying that administrators and faculty should not discourage disruption of speakers?
4. What appeal to experience does he make to conclude the essay?

Vocabulary Study

1. What meanings of *order* does Healy explore in paragraphs 2 and 9? What is the meaning of *discipline* in paragraph 10? What

kind of order does he believe is possible and desirable on a college campus.

2. In what sense of the word is there "anarchy" in twenty-year-old college students?

3. What images and ideas do the words *wrestle* (paragraph 5), *smithy* (paragraph 8), and *rub* (paragraph 10) convey? How are these metaphors related in idea?

4. What meanings do the words *parent* and *parentage* have in paragraph 11?

Suggestion for Writing

Write an essay stating your views on one of the following issues. In the course of your essay explain your agreement or disagreement with Reverend Healy on what education can and should accomplish:

a. disrupting speakers on college campuses
b. appointing students to serve as college trustees
c. requiring college students to study a foreign language
d. permitting school prayer

George Bernard Shaw
On Experimenting with Animals

George Bernard Shaw (1856–1950) is best known for his many plays, including *Pygmalion, Major Barbara, Candida, Arms and the Man,* and *Saint Joan.* Shaw was also a social critic and political commentator—he was active in British social life and politics throughout his long life. His prolific writings cover a wide range of subjects including education, religion, penology, and militarism. His play *The Doctor's Dilemma* (1907) is a satirical picture

Reprinted by permission of The Society of Authors on behalf of the Bernard Shaw Estate.

of the British medical profession. In the long preface that Shaw
wrote for the play in 1911, he deals with still-current issues in
medicine and ethics—chief among them is vivisection, or the
dissection of living animals for the purpose of medical knowledge. The essay reprinted here is a section of this preface.

The right to know is like the right to live. It is funda-   1
mental and unconditional in its assumption that knowledge,
like life, is a desirable thing, though any fool can prove that
ignorance is bliss, and that "a little knowledge is a dangerous
thing" (a little being the most that any of us can attain), as
easily as that the pains of life are more numerous and constant than its pleasures, and that therefore we should all be
better dead. The logic is unimpeachable; but its only effect is
to make us say that if these are the conclusions logic leads to,
so much the worse for logic, after which curt dismissal of Folly,
we continue living and learning by instinct: that is, as of right.
We legislate on the assumption that no man may be killed on
the strength of a demonstration that he would be happier in
his grave, not even if he is dying slowly of cancer and begs
the doctor to despatch him quickly and mercifully. To get killed
lawfully he must violate somebody else's right to live by com-
mitting murder. But he is by no means free to live uncondi-
tionally. In society he can exercise his right to live only under
very stiff conditions. In countries where there is compulsory
military service he may even have to throw away his individual life to save the life of the community.

It is just so in the case of the right to knowledge. It is a   2
right that is as yet very imperfectly recognized in practice. But
in theory it is admitted that an adult person in pursuit of
knowledge must not be refused it on the ground that he would
be better or happier without it. Parents and priests may forbid knowledge to those who accept their authority; and social taboo may be made effective by acts of legal persecution
under cover of repressing blasphemy, obscenity, and sedi-
tion; but no government now openly forbids its subjects to
pursue knowledge on the ground that knowledge is in itself

a bad thing, or that it is possible for any of us to have too much of it.

But neither does any government exempt the pursuit of knowledge, any more than the pursuit of life, liberty, and happiness (as the American Constitution puts it), from all social conditions. No man is allowed to put his mother into the stove because he desires to know how long an adult woman will survive at a temperature of 500° Fahrenheit, no matter how important or interesting that particular addition to the store of human knowledge may be. A man who did so would have short work made not only of his right to knowledge, but of his right to live and all his other rights at the same time. The right to knowledge is not the only right; and its exercise must be limited by respect for other rights, and for its own exercise by others. When a man says to Society, "May I torture my mother in pursuit of knowledge?" Society replies "No." If he pleads, "What! Not even if I have a chance of finding out how to cure cancer by doing it?" Society still says, "Not even then." If the scientist, making the best of his disappointment, goes on to ask may he torture a dog, the stupid and callous people who do not realize that a dog is a fellow-creature, and sometimes a good friend, may say Yes, though Shakespeare, Dr. Johnson and their like may say No. But even those who say "You may torture *a* dog" never say "You may torture *my* dog." And nobody says, "Yes, because in the pursuit of knowledge you may do as you please." Just as even the stupidest people say, in effect, "If you cannot attain to knowledge without burning your mother you must do without knowledge," so the wisest people say, "If you cannot attain to knowledge without torturing a dog, you must do without knowledge."

Comment

One way of rebutting deductive arguments is to show that the argument is invalid—that the process of reasoning or inference from premises is faulty. Another way is to attack one or both of the premises, showing them to be false. Shaw does both. He first shows that the "unimpeachable" logic of animal experimenters would lead to acceptable conclusions that conflict with the laws of society (paragraph 1) and with accepted practices (paragraph 2). He then attacks the major premise, that the right to knowledge is "fundamental and unconditional"—showing it to be false (paragraph 3). Shaw reasons from experience in this passage, not from other beliefs or given truths of his own.

Questions for Study and Discussion

1. What do the laws of society forbid, and why are the practices of animal experimenters inconsistent with these laws?
2. What point is Shaw making in paragraph 2 about the right to knowledge?
3. In paragraph 3, how does Shaw disprove through an appeal to experience that knowledge is an absolute good?
4. Shaw builds to his thesis, "If you cannot attain to knowledge without torturing a dog, you must do without knowledge." What ways of attaining knowledge would be acceptable to Shaw?
5. Do you agree with Shaw's conclusion that we should not perform experiments that give pain to dogs or other animals? If you agree, do you for the same reasons? If you disagree, what beliefs form your own thinking of the issue?

Vocabulary Study

1. Would the following sentence have the same meaning as Shaw's original sentence? "It is fundamental and unconditional in its belief that knowledge, like life, is a desirable thing. . . ." Is an "assumption" the same thing as a "belief"?
2. What does Shaw mean by the word *unconditional*?

Suggestions for Writing

1. Discuss the position you think Shaw might have taken on one of the following issues—given his argument against animal experimentation:
    a.   testing experimental drugs on volunteers

b.   weapons testing near populated areas
c.   conscientious objection to military service
2.   Discuss your own view of the issues listed above, defending your own premises and conclusions and answering a possible argument of an opponent.

Robert J. White
A Defense of Vivisection

A neurosurgeon and neurophysiologist, Dr. Robert J. White received his M.D. degree from Harvard Medical School in 1953. He has practiced most of his professional life at Case Western Reserve University, in Cleveland, Ohio, where he directs neurosurgery at University Hospital and teaches in the School of Medicine. Dr. White developed several pioneering techniques in brain surgery and also developed the first isolated brain models for the purpose of experimentation. He describes some of these achievements in this essay, written in 1971 in response to a critical essay on vivisection.

The humanity which would prevent human suffering is a deeper and truer humanity than the humanity which would save pain or death in the animal.—Charles W. Eliot

The quotation above from that distinguished intellectual and former Harvard University president, written decades ago, continues to crystallize clearly the basic position of medical science toward the employment of animals in research and teaching. I would state it more simply: the alleviation of human suffering justifies the sacrifice of lower animals. Because

1

Reprinted from Robert J. White, "Antivivisection: The Reluctant Hydra," *The American Scholar,* Vol. 40, No. 3, Summer 1971. Copyright © 1971 by the United Chapters of Phi Beta Kappa. Reprinted by permission of the publishers.

this statement is as valid today as it was then, and yet has so little impact on the public conscience, I am almost reluctant to shed the mantle of clinical and professional detachment and take up the cudgels against that ill-defined, elusive Hydra— the antivivisection movement. To a degree, my inertia is also derived from my conviction that medical science has always seemed to assume a low-profile posture in justifying the utilization of lower animals for research and education (as it has so often done with other public health issues); it has invariably waited until one of those vigorous cyclic antivivisection campaigns, using the most advanced techniques in news management, has reached its apogee before attempting to combat the pernicious effects on public and congressional opinion. And then, unfortunately, it has employed almost exclusively its own scientific journals as the instruments for presenting its position to an already prejudiced audience. While the scientific community has lobbied successfully in congressional committees against restrictive legislation directed at medical research, it has neglected to present to the American public its case for the continuation of animal experimentation with sufficient force and clarity to eliminate the ever-present danger of government control of biological research through the limitation of animal availability and experimental design. The intelligent citizenry of this country must be educated not only regarding the already multiple advantages of medical research but, what is more important, the absolute necessity of continued proliferation of biological research.

Man, in a sense, has unwittingly painted himself into an ecological corner, and without the opportunity of biological testing in lower animals he may be unable to extract himself from his polluted environment. Acknowledging man's equally wanton disregard of animal life, as he has slowly but inevitably poisoned this planet (to say nothing of our careless attrition of individual species to the point of extinction), I do not intend that this essay should be, by any stretch of the imagination, construed as an indictment of the broad humanitarian movement; quite the contrary, for many of its objec- 2 tives, particularly in the ecological field, are not only most laudable but fully subscribed to by many within the scientific community. Rather, my proprietary interest here is to emphasize need for animal experimentation in neurological research. As a consequence, my confrontation is exclusively with those societies, collectively known as the antivivisection movement, whose single unifying principle is the almost religiously held tenet that it is morally wrong to use lower animals in medical research and teaching. Professor Saul Bevolson, in tracing the historical development of the antivivisection movement in this country, demonstrates that the movement, while spawned and nurtured by the humanitarian establishment, is, in reality, separate in organizational structure. Dr. Maurice Visscher has felt the necessity of characterizing the antivivisection movement as a spectrum with certain gradations of moral and ethical absoluteness with regard to man's right to sacrifice lower animal life for scientific knowledge and medical advancement. Thus, this philosophical spectrum is anchored at one end by the abolitionist who sees no justification under any circumstances for the employment of the nonhuman animal for scientific study, and at the other extreme by the regulatory antivivisectionists who would place external controls (obviously governmental) on medical research by limiting the type and number of animals utilized, and demanding review of the experimental methods with particular reference to purpose and duplication. Make no mistake, in spite of their highly publicized concern for the housing and veterinary care of research animals, the true thrust of these organizations is directed toward the eventual elimination from medical investigation and research of all nonhuman subjects.

As a concerned scientist and as a practicing neurosurgeon, I am simply unable to plumb the depths of a philosophy that places such a premium on animal life even at the expense of human existence and improvement. It would appear that this preoccupation with the alleged pain and suffering of the animals used in medical research may well represent, [3] at the very least, social prejudice against medicine or, more seriously, true psychiatric aberrations. Regardless of the social or psychiatric shortcomings of the antivivisectionists, it has always amazed me that the biological profession is forced into a position of periodically preparing defense briefs on animal experimentation (unfortunately appearing only in scientific journals) as a result of the Herculean efforts of these societies, while the meat-packing industry, which slaughters millions of animals annually, seldom if ever finds it necessary to defend its activities.

As I write this article, I relive my vivid experiences of   4
yesterday when I removed at operation a large tumor from the cerebellum and brain stem of a small child. This was a surgical undertaking that would have been impossible a few decades ago, highly dangerous a few years ago, but is today, thanks to extensive experimentation on the brains of lower animals, routinely accomplished with a high degree of safety.

The human brain is the most complex, the most superbly   5
designed structure known. Before it, all human scientific and engineering accomplishment pales. Our understanding of its intimate functions, such as intelligence and memory, is extremely limited. Even the more easily characterized capabilities of sensory reception and motor activity are only now being elucidated. Without the use of the experimental animal, particularly a species whose central nervous system is similar to that of man, we simply cannot decipher the mysteries of cerebral performance. Without this knowledge of brain function, we will never be able to develop new and improved methods for the treatment of neurological diseases, so many of which now must be placed in an incurable category. Even today the surgery of the brain is in its infancy, and on many occasions the critical tolerance between success and failure in human cerebral operations is narrow. Yet this gap can be significantly increased through properly oriented research. These serious considerations moved Dr. Harvey Cushing, the eminent brain surgeon, to remark, "Those who oppose the employment of animals for such purposes . . . leave us the only

alternative of subjecting our fellow man, as a lesser creature, to our first crude manipulations."

In a more personal sense, I have a score of my own to settle with these misguided societies that for decades have been attempting to confuse the public about the true purpose of animal experimentation by depicting the medical and veterinary scientist as the most cruel of men, seeking every opportunity to visit pain and suffering on defenseless laboratory creatures. The more aggressive of these organizations, which are committed to the total abolition of animal research, have recently installed me as their *célèbre terrible,* monster-scientist, perpetrator of abominable crimes. And thus I join the distinguished company of such legendary scientists as Claude Bernard, Louis Pasteur, Lord Lister, Victor Horsley and Alfred Blalock! Dr. Catherine Roberts herself has already prejudged my work and me by earnestly stating, "The details of his experiments are so horrifying that they seem to reach the limits of scientific depravity." Fortunately, my researches do not stand alone in her sweeping condemnation of medical science, for in the same article she described organ transplantation and profound hypothermia[1] as "life degrading scientific achievements." I am sure that she, as well as other staunch antivivisectionists, would be willing to include in this list: open-heart surgery, control of infection, surgical metabolism[2] and shock studies since literally thousands of animals were sacrificed in the development of these lifesaving techniques. In a sense, condemnation of these achievements amounts to condemnation of the most meaningful advances in medicine and surgery in the last thirty years.

What of our own experiments, which have evoked such vituperative treatment at the hands of the antivivisection press? Here are the "shocking" details.

6

7

---

[1]*profound hypothermia:* very low body temperature, induced in a part of the body to aid surgery
[2]*surgical metabolism:* problems of a surgical patient that are related to nutrition and physical and chemical processes

In 1964, we were successful for the first time in medical   8
history in totally isolating the subhuman primate brain outside of its body and sustaining it in a viable state by connecting it with the vascular system of another monkey or with a
mechanical perfusion circuit that incorporated engineering units
designed to perform the functions of the heart, lungs and
kidneys while simultaneously circulating blood to and from
the brain. We were overjoyed since scientists had attempted
to construct such a model surgically for the last one hundred
years without success. As late as the 1930s Dr. Alexis Carrel,
the Nobel laureate, with the collaboration of Colonel Charles
Lindbergh, had been able to support the viability of almost
all body organs in an isolated state with simple perfusion
equipment[3] that forcefully propelled nonsanguineous nutrient fluid[4] through the blood vessels of the separated tissue.
Only the nervous system, because of its complexity and deli-
cacy, escaped their magnificent scientific capabilities. Parenthetically, it should be mentioned that Dr. Carrel had his
problems with the antivivisectionists of his time.

With further refinements in operative technique, perfu-   9
sion/structural design and blood processing, we were able to
demonstrate normalization of intrinsic electrical activity and
metabolic performance of the isolated monkey brain for extended periods of time. We now had the methodology to un-
lock many of the subtle mysteries surrounding cerebral function
that heretofore had resisted all attempts at solution because
of the difficulties of neurogenically and vascularly isolating the
entire brain *in situ*.[5] What is perhaps of greater importance in
terms of understanding and treating neurological disease, we
could now easily impose on our brain models abnormal clinical states such as infarction,[6] circulatory arrest, infection and

---

[3] *perfusion equipment:* equipment designed to send fluid through or over a part of the
body or a specific organ
[4] *nonsanguineous nutrient fluid:* a non-blood nourishing fluid
[5] *neurogenically and vascularly isolating the entire brain in situ:* isolating the nerve tissue
and vessels of the brain at the site
[6] *infarction:* deprivation of blood in body tissue

malignancy with absolute control of environmental circumstances and with a real hope of elucidating their effects on brain tissue alone. Once the characteristics of these states were defined, these same models would be of inestimable value in developing new and meaningful therapeutic regimens aimed at eliminating these clinical disease states.

As we set about exploring and documenting the capabilities of the isolated brain in an atmosphere not unlike the conditions described for the fifth level in Michael Crichton's book, *The Andromeda Strain,* we gradually became aware of a growing public interest in the preparation, an interest that intensified after our success in transplanting the brain in the experimental animal in 1966. A succession of competent medical journalists visited our laboratories and subsequently prepared a number of highly informative and reasoned articles dealing with our investigative efforts. I personally have always approved of this kind of interchange. In spite of our best efforts to assist in the preparation of the textual material, however, an unreviewed and unauthorized article written by Orianna Fallachi appeared in *Look* (November 28, 1967), in which this well-known interviewer attempted to humanize the monkey by depicting it as a small child. This single article (or lengthy excerpts from it) has now enjoyed world-wide publication and translation. Besides her treatment of the monkey as a small patient, Miss Fallachi's detailed description of the preoperative preparation (including the induction of anesthesia) and her vivid portrayal of the isolated brain model apparently struck a sympathetic and responsive chord among the membership of the antivivisection societies in this country as well as throughout the world. Like Mary Shelley, Miss Fallachi had created a Doctor Frankenstein and an up-to-date monster, at least as far as the antivivisectionists are concerned. True, this tale has its amusing—if not outlandish—elements, but its overall effect is tragic, since Miss Fallachi's creations are not only as factitious as Mary Shelley's, but in reality the direct antithesis of the Frankenstein legend.

Admittedly, the nervous system is the most difficult body   11 organ system to investigate, not only because of its intrinsic complexity but also because, somewhere within its billions of cells and fibers, pain and suffering are represented. For this reason, the neurophysiologist is, on occasion, unable to avoid producing some discomfort in his animal when he is specifically studying pain in any or all of its complicated ramifications within the neural system. Actually, the isolated brain model is completely denervated[7] by virtue of the fact that all pain pathways have been surgically severed; consequently, this brain model enjoys a completely painless existence by all known physiological criteria.

Since the isolated brain is incapable of perceiving these 12 modalities, one can only wonder at the creditability and objectivity of the antivivisection prose, which has been so uncomplimentary in its descriptions of this subhuman research model.

The nervous system—the repository, so to speak, of pain 13 and suffering, but, more important, of the qualities and capabilities that uniquely distinguish an organism—is most critical to this discussion since direct surgical or electronic manipulation or chemical modification of this system in the experimental animal offers to the antivivisectionist the most logical area for condemnation of biological research. At issue here would not be the indiscriminate infliction of pain and suffering (these experiments are basically free of pain), but rather purposeful alteration of the innate behavior of the organism in order to advance our knowledge of emotion, memory and intelligence, with the final phase again being the interpretive extrapolation of this information to the human and to human mental functioning. As yet we have heard little from the antivivisectionists regarding the inappropriateness of these experiments with reference to animal welfare. It may be, however, that their historical fixation on the "twin sins" of pain and suffering in neurological investigation has blinded

---

[7] *denervated:* deprived of a nerve

them to the realities of modern experimental research. Just as
I must vigorously dissent from the antivivisection philosophy
(and the belief of certain physiologists) that the production
of some pain, no matter how minimal, is never justified, so
too I cannot conceive of the development of a valid argument
opposing behavioral research, if only for the simple reason that
mental illness cannot successfully be treated until mental performance is understood.

To circumvent the employment of nonhuman animals in   14
medical research, the antivivisection movement has recently
turned for assistance to science itself. It has been suggested
that many of the physiological and biochemical studies conducted on animals could be programmed for computer analysis and thereby reduce and eventually eliminate the need for
the living experimental preparations. Actually, computers, since
their inception, have been used in biological research and, with
their growing complexity, have markedly extended the fron-
tiers of investigation. If anything, computer availability has
contributed to the increasing demand for animals for research.

An equally unrealistic approach to the elimination of an-   15
imal experimentation has been based on the cell culture work
of Professor Sureyat Aygun, Director of the Bacteriological
Institute of the University of Ankara, and a leading antivivisection proponent. The theory here is that, with proper culture techniques, cells or embryos could eventually be developed
into entire organ systems. The technological advances and expense necessary to accomplish such a program to replace pre-
sent-day animal research facilities are unachievable. There is
no more need to seek alternatives to the use of lower animals
for medical research than to search for nonflesh substitutions
for meat in our diets. While it may well be true that ecological "facts of life" could eventually require the elimination of
certain endangered species from both the laboratory and
commercial market, there is nothing to suggest that some
suitable species cannot be substituted. Even Dr. Albert
Schweitzer recognized in his own unique philosophical scheme

of things that scientific experiments with animals were necessary for the alleviation of human ills.

The American public demonstrates its overwhelming 16 support of medical research by annually contributing millions of dollars through direct federal financing and private subscription; yet this same public is tragically unaware that progress in medical science is continually threatened by the antivivisection movement. At the urging of a small but determined group of antivivisectionists, the United States Congress is constantly considering legislation that, if enacted into law, will seriously restrict the freedom of individual scientists participating in medical research, in the same way that laws have so seriously hampered similar research in Britain. Since, through research grants to qualified individuals and institutions, the federal government provides the major financial support for medical investigation in this country, all laws affecting the conduct of such research are of paramount importance to the health of the entire citizenry. Unless American medicine and its allied biological professions cast off their mantles of detachment and undertake the responsibility of educating through established lines of communication our citizens to the necessities of medical research, the antivivisection movement may eventually win the day.

In the final analysis, there is no way that I can personally 17 resolve or even arbitrate the impasse that exists between the theology of the antivivisection movement and the immutable stance of practicality maintained by biological research, since like R. D. Guthrie, I believe that the inclusion of lower animals in our ethical system is philosophically meaningless and operationally impossible and that, consequently, antivivisection theory and practice have no moral or ethical basis.

Comment

White's essay is chiefly a rebuttal of his antivivisectionist opponents. In defending his experiments in neurophysiology, White argues the necessity of using animals. Underlying this defense is the belief that, in the words of Charles W. Eliot quoted at the start of the essay, "The humanity which would prevent human suffering is a deeper and truer humanity than the humanity which would save pain or death in the animal." White presents this belief as a given—not requiring defense. He notes his strong dissent from antivivisectionist beliefs; indeed he suggests that the failure to recognize its truth and "preoccupation with the alleged pain and suffering of the animals used in medical research" may be the result of "social prejudice against medicine" or mental aberration (paragraph 3). White's argument is thus a mixed one—deductive in its basic argument that animal experimentation serves a "deeper and truer humanity," inductive in its appeal to experience.

Questions for Study and Discussion

1. What practical reasons does White give for using animals in scientific research in general and neurophysiological research in particular?
2. What does White suggest are the alternatives to the use of animals?
3. At the start of his essay White states his basic belief or premise through the statement of Charles W. Eliot. Where does he later restate this belief? What reason does he give for not responding to the philosophy of his opponents?
4. Why does White make the motives of his opponents an issue? Does he believe his opponents have attacked his motives?
5. White focuses throughout on immediate needs and concerns in neurophysiology. At what points in the essay does he refer to the broader needs of people and society?

Vocabulary Study

Be ready to explain the following words and phrases and the use White makes of them:

a. paragraph 1: *crystallize, elusive Hydra, inertia, cyclic antivivisection campaigns, pernicious, proliferation*
b. paragraph 2: *ecological corner, wanton disregard, construed as an indictment, proprietary interest, spawned and nurtured, spectrum with certain gradations*

    c.   paragraph 3: *psychiatric aberrations, Herculean efforts*
    d.   paragraph 5: *critical tolerance, properly oriented research*
    e.   paragraph 7: *vituperative treatment*
    f.   paragraph 8: *viable state*
    g.   paragraph 10: *factitious, antithesis*
    h.   paragraph 11: *intrinsic complexity, ramifications, physiological criteria*
    i.   paragraph 12: *modalities*
    j.   paragraph 13: *repository, interpretive extrapolation*
    k.   paragraph 16: *mantles of detachment*
    l.   paragraph 17: *impasse*

Suggestions for Writing

1.   Discuss how White might deal with Shaw's central assumption in his attack on animal experimentation. Would he attack the truth of the assumption itself, or discuss the consequences of reasoning from this assumption, or possibly do both?

2.   Argue your agreement or disagreement with White on the same issue. Carefully note the extent of your agreement or disagreement.

Strategies of
Persuasion

Most arguments are directed to a particular audience and organized in light of that audience's knowledge and beliefs; in other words, most arguments are meant to be *persuasive*. We have seen that inductive arguments build particulars of experience and similar kinds of evidence to generalizations or conclusions; deductive arguments, on the other hand, proceed from premises and build to conclusions. But the order of ideas may sometimes be changed to fit particular audiences. Thus the conclusion of the argument may be stated at the beginning, as a way of focusing attention on the point of most concern. Or the essay may start with the least controversial statement (or premise), proceed to the more controversial, and end with the most controversial. The order of ideas does not affect the strength or soundness of the argument itself.

The persuasiveness of the inductive argument depends on the strength of the facts presented. George F. Will, in the inductive argument that follows, immerses his audience in the facts of a notorious episode—one that raises important questions about the situation of poor people in our cities. Will does not ask these questions directly: instead he gives a full account of what happened to a young

Harlem mother—stressing those details that dramatize the weakness of welfare systems.

The questions Will raises—in particular, what is a city's responsibility for the lives of the poor—might have been discussed theoretically, as in a sociology textbook. Will does discuss the issues theoretically toward the end of the essay, but he has no solution to offer for the plight of the poor, though he grants that cities must provide "a floor of support" of some kind. It is the intractable problem, for which no solution now exists, that he focuses on in his extended example. The example is indispensable to our understanding—especially so if we believe it is easy to assign blame in crimes of the poor, or that easy solutions are available.

Yet Will does something more: in dramatizing the episode, he allows the reader to imagine the situation of the young woman. This appeal to imagination is his most important persuasive device.

The writer has available numerous persuasive means. Will's essay illustrates dramatization, one of the most important. The satirist uses other means to persuade the audience to change its thinking on an issue or to take action. The satirist sometimes wants to awaken the conscience of the audience by appealing to shame and guilt. But appeals to conscience may take other forms; for example, writers also appeal to our common humanity. The essays in this section illustrate these many appeals.

George F. Will
On Her Own in the City

George F. Will was born in Champaign, Illinois, in 1941, and was educated at Trinity College, Oxford University in England, and Princeton University. Before becoming the Washington editor of *National Review* in 1971, he taught politics and worked as a congressional aide. He received the Pulitzer Prize for commentary in 1977, and is now a columnist for *Newsweek* and the *Washington Post*. His most recent book is *The Pursuit of Virtue, and Other Tory Notions* (1982).

When police, responding to her call, arrived at her East Harlem tenement, she was hysterical: "The dog ate my baby." The baby girl had been four days old, twelve hours "home" from the hospital. Home was two rooms and a kitchen on the sixth floor, furnished with a rug, a folding chair, and nothing else, no bed, no crib.

"Is the baby dead?" asked an officer. "Yes," the mother said, "I saw the baby's insides." Her dog, a German shepherd, had not been fed for five days. She explained: "I left the baby on the floor with the dog to protect it." She had bought the dog in July for protection from human menaces.

She is twenty-four. She went to New York three years ago from a small Ohio community. She wanted to be on her own. She got that wish.

She was employed intermittently, until the fifth month of her pregnancy, which she says was the result of a rape she did not report to the police. She wanted the baby. She bought child-care books, and had seven prenatal checkups at Bellevue Hospital. Although she rarely called home or asked for money, she called when the baby was born. Her mother mailed twenty-five dollars for a crib. It arrived too late.

When labor began she fed the dog with the last food in the apartment and went alone to the hospital. The baby was born on Wednesday. When she left Bellevue Sunday evening, the hospital office holding her welfare payment was closed. With six dollars in her pocket and a baby in her arms, she took a cab home. The meter said four dollars and the driver demanded a dollar tip. When she asked his assistance in getting upstairs, he drove off.

The hospital had given her enough formula for three feedings for the baby. Rather than spend her remaining dollar that night on food for herself and the dog, she saved it for the bus ride back to Bellevue to get her welfare money. Having slept with the baby on a doubled-up rug, she left the baby and the dog at 7 A.M. It was 53 degrees, too cold she thought to take the baby. She had no warm baby clothes and she thought the hospital had said the baby was ailing. She got back at 8:30 A.M. Then she called the police.

Today the forces of law and order and succor are struggling to assign "blame" in order to escape it. Her attorney and Bellevue are arguing about how she was released, or expelled, on Sunday evening. Welfare officials are contending with charges that they are somehow culpable for her failure to receive a crib before giving birth, and for her living conditions. (She was receiving payment of $270 a month; her rent was $120.) She has been arraigned on a charge of negligent homicide, but no one seems anxious to prosecute. Late in New York's U.S. Senate primary, Daniel P. Moynihan, talking like a senator prematurely, said that this case dramatizes weaknesses of the welfare system, and indicated that it also dramatizes the need for him in Washington. Perhaps.

But because cities are collections of strangers, they are, inevitably, bad places to be poor. Not that there are good places, but cities, being kingdoms of the strong, are especially hellish for the poor. Cities have their indispensable purposes, and their charms, not the least of which is that you can be alone in a crowd. But that kind of living alone is an acquired taste, and not for the weak or unfortunate. They are apt to learn that no city's institutions can provide protective supports like those of an extended family or real community. No metropolis can provide a floor of support solid enough to prevent the bewildered—like the woman from Ohio—from falling through the cracks.

Through those cracks you get an occasional glimpse of what George Eliot meant: "If we had a keen vision and feeling of all ordinary human life, it would be like hearing the grass grow and the squirrel's heartbeat, and we should die of that roar which lies on the other side of silence."

Questions for Study and Discussion

1. What details of the episode show why it is difficult to assign blame for the death of the child?
2. Is Will suggesting that everyone involved in the death was to blame—the mother, the hospital and welfare officials, the city as a whole—or is he saying that blame is difficult or impossible to define in this case?
3. What is the point of George Eliot's statement, and what is gained by concluding the essay with it? Would the statement be as effective if it introduced the essay?
4. How persuasive do you find the example? Do you have a so-lution for the plight of the woman? Are there other solutions Will might have presented?

Vocabulary Study

Give the meaning of the following words, in the context of the sentence in which each appears: *intermittently* (paragraph 4); *succor, arraigned, negligent homicide* (paragraph 7); *apt, extended, metropolis* (paragraph 8).

Suggestions for Writing

1. Will states in paragraph 8: "They are apt to learn that no city's institutions can provide protective supports like those of an ex-tended family or real community." Discuss what the details of the essay tell us about an "extended family" or "real commu-nity" by implication.
2. Discuss what you believe a city can and should do for a person like the woman Will describes. You may wish to discuss what responsibility a city has for the lives of poor people in general. State your reasons for the views that you hold.
3. Will states earlier in paragraph 8: "But because cities are col-lections of strangers, they are, inevitably, bad places to be poor." And he adds in the same paragraph: "Cities have their indis-pensable purposes, and their charms, not the least of which is that you can be alone in a crowd." Develop one of these ideas from your own experience or observation, or develop an idea

of your own about city or small-town life, giving one or more examples.

Wallace Stegner
The Gift of Wilderness

Wallace Stegner, who taught creative writing at Stanford University for many years, is the author of numerous essays, short stories, and novels. His writings have received numerous awards, including the O. Henry First Prize for Short Stories. Many of his books describe the American West. These include *Beyond the Hundredth Meridian, Gathering of Zion: The Story of the Mormon Trail,* and *One Way to Spell Man,* from which this essay on the American wilderness is excerpted.

Once, writing in the interests of wilderness to a government commission, I quoted a letter from Sherwood Anderson to Waldo Frank, written in the 1920s. I think it is worth quoting again. "Is it not likely," Anderson wrote, "that when the country was new and men were often alone in the fields and forest they got a sense of bigness outside themselves that has now in some way been lost . . . ? I am old enough to remember tales that strengthen my belief in a deep semireligious influence that was formerly at work among our people. . . . I can remember old fellows in my home town speaking feelingly of an evening spent on the big empty plains. It had taken the shrillness out of them. They had learned the trick of quiet."

I have a teenaged granddaughter who recently returned from a month's Outward Bound exposure to something like

1

2

wilderness in Death Valley, including three days alone, with water but no food, up on a slope of the Panamints. It is a not-unheard-of kind of initiation—Christ underwent it; Indian youths on the verge of manhood traditionally went off alone to receive their visions and acquire their adult names. I don't know if my granddaughter had any visions or heard the owl cry her name. I do know *she* cried some; and I know also that before it was over it was the greatest experience of her young life. She may have greater ones later on, but she will never quite get over this one.

It will probably take more than one exposure to teach her the full trick of quiet, but she knows now where to go to learn it, and she knows the mood to go in. She has felt that bigness outside herself; she has experienced the birth of awe. And if millions of Americans have not been so lucky as she, why, all the more reason to save intact some of the places to which those who are moved to do so may go, and grow by it. It might not be a bad idea to require that wilderness initiation of all American youth, as a substitute for military service. 3

I, too, have been one of the lucky ones. I spent my childhood and youth in wild, unsupervised places, and was awed very early, and never recovered. I think it must have happened first when I was five years old, in 1914, the year my family moved to the remote valley of the Frenchman River, in Saskatchewan. The town was not yet born—we were among the first fifty or so people assembled to create it. Beaver and muskrat swam in the river, and ermine, mink, coyotes, lynx, bobcats, rabbits, and birds inhabited the willow breaks. During my half dozen years there, I shot the rabbits and trapped the fur-bearers, as other frontier boys have done, and I can remember buying Canadian Victory Bonds, World War I vintage, with the proceeds from my trapline. I packed a gun before I was nine years old. But it is not my predatory experiences that I cherish. I regret them. What I most remember is certain moments, revelations, epiphanies, in which the sensuous little savage that I then was came face to face with the universe. And blinked. 4

I remember a night when I was very new there, when   5
some cowboys from the Z-X hitched a team to a bobsled and
hauled a string of us on our coasting sleds out to the Swift
Current hill. They built a fire on the river ice above the ford,
and we dragged our sleds to the top of the hill and shot down,
blind with speed and snow, and warmed ourselves a minute
at the fire, and plowed up the hill for another run.

It was a night of still cold, zero or so, with a full moon—   6
a night of pure magic. I remember finding myself alone at the
top of the hill, looking down at the dark moving spots of
coasters, and the red fire with black figures around it down
at the bottom. It isn't a memory so much as a vision—I don't
remember it, I *see* it. I see the valley, and the curving course
of the river with its scratches of leafless willows and its
smothered bars. I see the moon reflecting upward from a reach
of wind-blown clear ice, and the white hump of the hills, and
the sky like polished metal, and the moon; and behind or in
front of or mixed with the moonlight, pulsing with a kind of
life, the paled, washed-out green and red of the northern lights.

I stood there by myself, my hands numb, my face stiff   7
with cold, my nose running, and I felt very small and insig-
nificant and quelled, but at the same time exalted. Green-
land's icy mountains, and myself at their center, one little spark
of suffering warmth in the midst of all that inhuman clarity.

And I remember that evening spent on the big empty   8
plains that Sherwood Anderson wrote about. In June of 1915
my father took my brother and me with him in the wagon
across fifty miles of unpeopled prairie to build a house on our
homestead. We were heavily loaded, the wagon was heavy and
the team light, and our mare Daisy had a young foal that had
a hard time keeping up. All day we plodded across nearly
trackless buffalo grass in dust and heat, under siege from
mosquitoes and horseflies. We lunched beside a slough where
in the shallow water we ignorantly chased and captured a
couple of baby mallards. Before I let mine go, I felt the
thumping of that wild little heart in my hands, and that taught
me something too. Night overtook us, and we camped on the

trail. Five gaunt coyotes watched us eat supper, and later ser-
enaded us. I went to sleep to their music.

Then in the night I awoke, not knowing where I was.   9
Strangeness flowed around me; there was a current of cool
air, a whispering, a loom of darkness overhead. In panic I
reared up on my elbow and found that I was sleeping beside
my brother under the wagon, and that night wind was
breathing across me through the spokes of the wheel. It came
from unimaginably far places, across a vast emptiness, below
millions of polished stars. And yet its touch was soft, intimate, and reassuring, and my panic went away at once. That
wind knew me. I knew it. Every once in a while, sixty-six years
after that baptism in space and night and silence, wind across
grassland can smell like that to me, as secret, perfumed, and
soft, and tell me who I am.

It is an opportunity I wish every American could have.   10
Having been born lucky, I wish we could expand the opportunities I benefited from, instead of extinguishing them. I wish
we could establish a maximum system of wilderness preserves
and then, by a mixture of protection and education, let all
Americans learn to know their incomparable heritage and their
unique identity.

We are the most various people anywhere, and every seg-   11
ment of us has to learn all anew the lessons both of democracy and conservation. The Laotian and Vietnamese refugees
who in August 1980 were discovered poaching squirrels and
pigeons in San Francisco's Golden Gate Park were Americans
still suffering from the shock and deprivation of a war-blasted
homeland, Americans on the road of learning how to be lucky
and to conserve their luck. All of us are somewhere on a long
arc between ecological ignorance and environmental responsibility. What freedom means is freedom to choose. What
civilization means is some sense of *how* to choose, and among
what options. If we choose badly or selfishly, we have, not
always intentionally, violated the contract. On the strength of
the most radical political document in human history, democracy assumes that all men are created equal and that given

freedom they can learn to be better masters for themselves than any king or despot could be. But until we arrive at a land ethic that unites science, religion, and human feeling, the needs of the present and the claims of the future, Americans are constantly in danger of being what Aldo Leopold in an irritable moment called them: people remodeling the Alhambra with a bulldozer, and proud of their yardage.

If we conceive development to mean something beyond 12
earth-moving, extraction, and denudation, America is one of the world's most undeveloped nations. But by its very premises, learned in wilderness, its citizens are the only proper source of controls, and the battle between short-range and long-range goals will be fought in the minds of individual citizens. Though it is entirely proper to have government agencies—and they have to be federal—to manage the residual wild places that we set aside for recreational, scientific, and spiritual reasons, they themselves have to be under citizen surveillance, for government agencies have been known to endanger the very things they ought to protect. It was San Francisco, after all, that dammed Hetch Hetchy, it was the Forest Service that granted permits to Disney Enterprises for the resortification of Mineral King, it is Los Angeles that is bleeding the Owens Valley dry and destroying Mono Lake, it is the Air Force that wants to install the MX Missile tracks under the Utah-Nevada desert and in an ecosystem barely hospitable to man create an environment as artificial, sterile, and impermanent as a space shuttle.

We need to learn to listen to the land, hear what it says, 13
understand what it can and can't do over the long haul; what, especially in the West, it should not be asked to do. To learn such things, we have to have access to natural wild land. As our bulldozers prepare for the sixth century of our remodeling of this Alhambra, we could look forward to a better and more rewarding national life if we learned to renounce short-term profit, and practice working for the renewable health of our earth. Instead of easing air-pollution controls in order to postpone the education of the automobile industry; instead

of opening our forests to greatly increased timber cutting; instead of running our national parks to please and profit the concessionaires; instead of violating our wilderness areas by allowing oil and mineral exploration with rigs and roads and seismic detonations, we might bear in mind what those precious places are: playgrounds, schoolrooms, laboratories, yes, but above all shrines, in which we can learn to know both the natural world and ourselves, and be at least half reconciled to what we see.

Comment

This concluding section of Stegner's book draws conclusions from experiences and observations presented earlier. The account in this section focuses on his own experiences in the wilderness; these experiences are central to the thesis Stegner argues in the final paragraph: "We need to learn to listen to the land, hear what it says, understand what it can and can't do over the long haul. . . . To learn such things, we have to have access to natural wild land." Though Stegner is writing to a general audience, he is also addressing particular segments—especially those with the power to influence government policy on undeveloped land.

Questions for Study and Discussion

1. How does Stegner build the discussion to capture the interest and emotions of his audience? Does the essay build in emotion?

2. Why is the wilderness necessary to the success of American democracy? And why is conservation?

3. What does the discussion in paragraph 11 of the Laotian and Vietnamese refugees contribute to this discussion?

4. Why does Stegner express particular concern in paragraph 13 for the Western United States?

5. Is Stegner chiefly writing to inhabitants of the West and their representatives? What statements in the essay reveal the special audiences he has in mind?

6. Stegner uses his personal experiences to persuade his readers of the need for wilderness. What other means of persuasion does Stegner employ throughout the essay?

Vocabulary Study

1. Use reference books in your library to identify Sherwood Anderson and Waldo Frank.
2. Use the *New York Times Index, Facts on File,* and other reference sources to explain the following references:
   a. Outward Bound
   b. The Laotian and Vietnamese refugees in Golden Gate Park in August 1980
   c. the damming of Hetch Hetchy
   d. Disney Enterprises' Mineral King
   e. MX Missile tracks in Utah and Nevada
3. Look up the Alhambra in a reference book. What details explain Stegner's references in paragraphs 11 and 13?
4. What is an *ecosystem?* In what sense is a wilderness one?

Suggestions for Writing

1. Discuss an experience of your own that taught you how to "listen to the land" or taught you to appreciate the natural world. Use your discussion to make a point as Stegner does.
2. Stegner approaches current issues like oil and mineral exploration in national parks through the spiritual needs of individuals and American society in general. Discuss how convincing you find the essay and this evidence in particular.

E. B. White
The Decline of Sport
(A Preposterous Parable)

E. B. White, the distinguished essayist, humorist, and editor, was born in Mount Vernon, New York, in 1899. He was long associated with *The New Yorker* as writer and editor and also wrote for *Harper's Magazine* and other publications. His books include *Charlotte's Web* (1952) and *Stuart Little* (1945), both for children, and *One Man's Meat* (1943), *The Second Tree from the Corner* (1954), and *The Points of My Compass* (1962), collections of his essays. White died in 1985.

In the third decade of the supersonic age, sport gripped   1
the nation in an ever-tightening grip. The horse tracks, the ballparks, the fight rings, the gridirons, all drew crowds in steadily increasing numbers. Every time a game was played, an attendance record was broken. Usually some other sort of record was broken, too—such as the record for the number of consecutive doubles hit by left-handed batters in a Series game, or some such thing as that. Records fell like ripe apples on a windy day. Customs and manners changed, and the five-day business week was reduced to four days, then to three, to give everyone a better chance to memorize the scores.

Not only did sport proliferate but the demands it made   2
on the spectator became greater. Nobody was content to take in one event at a time, and thanks to the magic of radio and television nobody had to. A Yale alumnus, class of 1962, returning to the Bowl with 197,000 others to see the Yale-Cornell football game would take along his pocket radio and

pick up the Yankee Stadium, so that while his eye might be following a fumble on the Cornell twenty-two-yard line, his ear would be following a man going down to second in the top of the fifth, seventy miles away. High in the blue sky above the Bowl, skywriters would be at work writing the scores of other major and minor sporting contests, weaving an interminable record of victory and defeat, and using the new high-visibility pink news-smoke perfected by Pepsi-Cola engineers. And in the frames of the giant video sets, just behind the goalposts, this same alumnus could watch Dejected win the Futurity before a record-breaking crowd of 349,872 at Belmont, each of whom was tuned to the Yale Bowl and following the World Series game in the video and searching the sky for further news of events either under way or just completed. The effect of this vast cyclorama of sport was to divide the spectator's attention, over-subtilize his appreciation, and deaden his passion. As the fourth supersonic decade was ushered in, the picture changed and sport began to wane.

A good many factors contributed to the decline of sport. 3 Substitutions in football had increased to such an extent that there were very few fans in the United States capable of holding the players in mind during play. Each play that was called saw two entirely new elevens lined up, and the players whose names and faces you had familiarized yourself with in the first period were seldom seen or heard of again. The spectacle became as diffuse as the main concourse in Grand Central at the commuting hour.

Express motor highways leading to the parks and stadia 4 had become so wide, so unobstructed, so devoid of all life except automobiles and trees that sport fans had got into the habit of travelling enormous distances to attend events. The normal driving speed had been stepped up to ninety-five miles an hour, and the distance between cars had been decreased to fifteen feet. This put an extraordinary strain on the sport lover's nervous system, and he arrived home from a Saturday game, after a road trip of three hundred and fifty miles, glassy-eyed, dazed, and spent. He hadn't really had any relaxation and he had failed to see Czlika (who had gone in for Trusky) take the pass from Bkeeo (who had gone in for Bjallo) in the third period, because at that moment a youngster named Lavagetto had been put in to pinch-hit for Art Gurlack in the bottom of the ninth with the tying run on second, and the skywriter who was attempting to write "Princeton 0–Lafayette 43" had banked the wrong way, muffed the "3," and distracted everyone's attention from the fact that Lavagetto had been whiffed.

Cheering, of course, lost its stimulating effect on players, because cheers were no longer associated necessarily with the immediate scene but might as easily apply to something that was happening somewhere else. This was enough to infuriate even the steadiest performer. A football star, hearing the stands break into a roar before the ball was snapped, would realize that their minds were not on him, and would become dispirited and grumpy. Two or three of the big coaches worried so about this that they considered equipping all players with tiny ear sets, so that they, too, could keep abreast of other sporting events while playing, but the idea was abandoned as impractical, and the coaches put it aside in tickler files, to bring up again later.

I think the event that marked the turning point in sport and started it downhill was the Midwest's classic Dust Bowl game of 1975, when Eastern Reserve's great right end, Ed Pistachio, was shot by a spectator. This man, the one who did the shooting, was seated well down in the stands near the forty-yard line on a bleak October afternoon and was so saturated with sport and with the disappointments of sport that he had clearly become deranged. With a minute and fifteen seconds to play and the score tied, the Eastern Reserve quarterback had whipped a long pass over Army's heads into Pistachio's waiting arms. There was no other player anywhere near him, and all Pistachio had to do was catch the ball and run it across the line. He dropped it. At exactly this moment, the spectator—a man named Homer T. Parkinson, of 35 Edgemere Drive, Toledo, O.—suffered at least three other major disappointments in the realm of sport. His horse, Hiccough, on which he had a five-hundred-dollar bet, fell while getting away from the starting gate at Pimlico and broke his leg (clearly visible in the video); his favorite shortstop, Lucky Frimstitch, struck out and let three men die on base in the final game of the Series (to which Parkinson was tuned); and the Governor Dummer soccer team, on which Parkinson's youngest son played goalie, lost to Kent, 4–3, as recorded in the sky overhead. Before anyone could stop him, he drew a gun and drilled Pistachio, before 954,000 persons, the largest crowd that had ever attended a football game and the *second*-largest crowd that had ever assembled for any sporting event in any month except July.

This tragedy, by itself, wouldn't have caused sport to decline, I suppose, but it set in motion a chain of other tragedies, the cumulative effect of which was terrific. Almost as soon as the shot was fired, the news flash was picked up by one of the skywriters directly above the field. He glanced down to see whether he could spot the trouble below, and in doing so failed to see another skywriter approaching. The two planes collided and fell, wings locked, leaving a confusing trail of smoke, which some observers tried to interpret as a late sports score. The planes struck in the middle of the nearby eastbound coast-to-coast Sunlight Parkway, and a motorist driving a convertible coupé stopped so short, to avoid hitting them, that he was bumped from behind. The pileup of cars that ensued involved 1,482 vehicles, a record for eastbound parkways. A total of more than three thousand persons lost their lives in the highway accident, including the two pilots, and when panic broke out in the stadium, it cost another 872 in dead and injured. News of the disaster spread quickly to other sports arenas, and started other panics among the crowds trying to get to the exits, where they could buy a paper and study a list of the dead. All in all, the afternoon of sport cost 20,003 lives, a record. And nobody had much to show for it, except one small Midwestern boy who hung around the smoking wrecks of the planes, captured some aero news-smoke in a milk bottle, and took it home as a souvenir.

From that day on, sport waned. Through long, noncompetitive Saturday afternoons, the stadia slumbered. Even the parkways fell into disuse as motorists rediscovered the charms of old, twisty roads that led through main streets and past barnyards, with their mild congestions and pleasant smells.

8

Comment

Satire is an important kind of persuasive writing. An essay may be entirely satirical, as in E. B. White's satire on the American obsession with sports, or it may be satirical in part. The chief means of persuasion in satire is ridicule: the satirist makes fun of attitudes or behavior or holds them up to shame. The targets of social satire are foolish attitudes or behavior—social snobbery, pretentious talk, sloppy eating, and the like. Though amusing and sometimes even disgusting, these have no very serious consequences for the individual or for society. The targets of ethical satire are vicious attitudes and behavior that do have serious consequences—for example, racial or religious prejudice, dishonesty, hypocrisy deserving of shame. Social satire is always humorous; ethical satire may be humorous, as in many political cartoons like *Doonesbury,* but it is more often bitter or angry. Many satires like Twain's *Huckleberry Finn* contain elements of both types.

Some satirists are direct in their satire—their statements are angry and biting in their criticism. Others like E. B. White, James Thurber, and Art Buchwald depend on humorous understatement or exaggeration. These are forms of irony. An ironic statement generally implies more through inflection of voice or phrasing than the words actually say; sarcasm is a bitter kind of irony. You are being ironic when you smile or wink while saying something supposedly serious. Your smile or wink may express sarcasm. E. B. White depends on irony in his satire on American sports.

Questions for Study and Discussion

1.   What attitudes or habits is White satirizing in the America of late 1947, when this essay first appeared? Are the targets of the satire limited to attitudes and habits relating to sport, or does White have also in mind general attitudes and habits?
2.   Is the satire social or ethical? Is White satirizing merely foolish or, instead, vicious attitudes or behavior?
3.   To what extent does White depend on exaggeration or over-statement? Does he also use understatement?
4.   Names like "Dejected" can be satirical as well as humorous. Are they? Do you find other humorous names in the essay, and are they used satirically?
5.   White refers to the "high-visibility pink news-smoke perfected by Pepsi-Cola engineers." Why does he refer to "Pepsi-Cola" rather than to "U. S. Steel" or "Dow Chemical"?
6.   Do you think the essay describes attitudes toward sport and the behavior of sports fans in the eighties? Do you find the satire persuasive?

Vocabulary Study

1.   What is a "parable"? What does the subtitle "A Preposterous Parable" show about White's intention?
2.   Write a paraphrase of paragraph 2 or paragraph 6—a sentence-for-sentence rendering in your own words. Be sure to find substitutes for *proliferate, interminable,* and *over-subtilize* (paragraph 2), or *deranged, whipped,* and *drilled* (paragraph 6). Try to retain the tone of White's original paragraph.

Suggestions for Writing

1.   Identify the targets of White's satire and explain how you discover them in the course of reading.
2.   Discuss the extent to which White's predictions in 1947 have come true. Cite contemporary events and attitudes that support the predictions or that show White to be mistaken.
3.   Write a satirical essay of your own on a contemporary social or political issue. You may not discover the best strategy or tone until you have written several paragraphs. Revise your draft to make the strategy and tone consistent throughout.

Harvey and Nancy Kincaid
A Letter on Strip Mining

Harvey and Nancy Kincaid live with their seven children in Fay-
etteville, West Virginia, near Buffalo Creek. On February 26,
1972, a dam consisting of slag from the mines and owned by a
local coal company burst. The ensuing flood killed 125 people
and injured many thousands; most of the victims were coal miners and members of their families. In 1971 Mrs. Kincaid had
spoken about strip mining to the Congress Against Strip Mining, in Washington, D.C. Her letter was read before the West
Virginia State Legislature and it helped to pass the Anti-Strip-
Mining Bill. Mrs. Kincaid told an interviewer:

It used to be that the kids could keep fish, catfish, and minnows
in the creeks. Now you can see the rocks in the creek where the
acid has run off the mountains, off the limestone rocks. The rocks
in the creek are reddish-looking, like they're rusted. There's
nothing living in the creek now.

Gentlemen:

I don't believe there could be anyone that would like to   1
see the strip mines stopped any more than my husband and
myself. It just seems impossible that something like this could
happen to us twice in the past three and one half years of
time. We have been married for thirteen years and worked
real hard at having a nice home that was ours and paid for,
with a nice size lot of one acre. Over the thirteen years, we
remodeled this house a little at a time and paid for it as we
worked and did the work mostly ourselves. The house was
located about a quarter of a mile off the road up Glenco Hol-

low at Kincaid, Fayette County, West Virginia, where it used to be a nice, clean neighborhood.

Then the strippers came four years ago with their big machinery and TNT. I know that these men need jobs and need to make a living like everyone else, but I believe there could be a better way of getting the coal out of these mountains. Have you ever been on a mountaintop and looked down and seen about five different strips on one mountain in one hollow? 2

My husband owns a Scout Jeep and he can get to the top of the strip mines with the Scout. I would like to invite you to come and visit us sometime and go for a ride with us. It would make you sick to see the way the mountains are destroyed. 3

First they send in the loggers to strip all the good timber out and then they come with their bulldozers. If their engineers make a mistake in locating the coal they just keep cutting away until they locate the seam of coal. When the rains come and there isn't anything to stop the drainage, the mountains slide, and the spoil banks fall down to the next spoil bank and so on until the whole mountain slides. There is a small creek in the hollow and when the spring rains come, its banks won't hold the water. 4

So where does it go?—into people's yards, into their wells, under and into their houses. You have rocks, coal, and a little bit of everything in your yards. When the strippers came they started behind our house in the fall sometime before November. There was a hollow behind our house and we asked them not to bank the spoil the way they did, because we knew what would happen when the spring rains came. My father-in-law lived beside us and the property all ran together in a nice green lawn—four acres. 5

But the rains came in the spring and the spoil bank broke and the water and debris came into our property every time it rained. It would only take a few minutes of rain and this is what we had for three years. 6

Then the damage comes to your house because of so much 7

dampness. The doors won't close, the foundation sinks and cracks the walls in the house, your tile comes up off your floors, your walls mold, even your clothes in your closets. Then your children stay sick with bronchial trouble, then our daughter takes pneumonia—X-rays are taken, primary T.B. shows up on the X-ray. This is in July of two years ago. About for a year this child laid sick at home. In the meantime we have already filed suit with a lawyer in Oak Hill when the water started coming in on us, but nothing happens. For three years we fight them for our property—$10,000. The lawyer settles out of court for $4,500. By the time his fee comes out and everything else we have to pay, we have under $3,000 to start over with.

So what do we have to do? Doctor's orders, move out   8
for child's sake and health. We sell for a little of nothing— not for cash, but for rent payments, take the $3,000 and buy a lot on the main highway four miles up the road toward Oak Hill.

The $3,000 goes for the lot, digging of a well and a down   9
payment on a new house. Here we are in debt for thirty years on a new home built and complete by the first of September. We moved the first part of September and was in this house *one month* and what happens? The same strip company comes up the road and puts a blast off and damages the new house— $1,400 worth. When they put one blast off that will crack the walls in your house, the foundation cracked the carport floor straight across in two places, pull a cement stoop away from the house and pull the grout out of the ceramic tile in the bathroom. This is what they can get by with.

How do they live in their $100,000 homes and have a   10
clear mind, I'll never know. To think of the poor people who have worked hard all their lives and can't start over like we did. They have to stay in these hollows and be scared to death every time it rains. I know by experience the many nights I have stayed up and listened to the water pouring off the mountains and the rocks tumbling off the hills.

I remember one time when the strippers put a blast off   11 up the hollow a couple years ago and broke into one of the old mines that had been sealed off for 30 years. They put their blast off and left for the evening. Around seven o'clock that evening it started. We happened to look up the hollow, and thick mud—as thick as pudding—was coming down the main road in the hollow and made itself to the creek and stopped the creek up until the creek couldn't even flow.

The water was turned up into the fields where my hus- 12 band keeps horses and cattle. I called the boss and told him what was happening and the danger we were in and what did he say? "There isn't anything I can do tonight. I'll be down tomorrow." I called the agriculture and they told us, whatever we did, not to go to bed that night because of the water backed up in those mines for miles.

This is just some of the things that happen around a strip 13 mine neighborhood. But they can get by with it, unless they are stopped. Even if they are stopped it will take years for the trees and grass—what little bit they put on them—to grow enough to keep the water back and stop the slides.

Mr. and Mrs. Harvey Kincaid

Comment

The Swiss writer Henri Frédéric Amiel wrote in his journal: "Truth is the secret of eloquence and of virtue, the basis of moral authority." The Kincaids' great letter is an example of eloquence achieved through simple words that state facts plainly and exactly. Instead of reviewing the rights and wrongs of strip mining, Mr. and Mrs. Kincaid describe what happened to them and the land—in enough detail for the reader to imagine the life of people in the hollow. At the end of the letter they state the issue simply and without elaboration: "But they can get by with it, unless they are stopped."

Questions for Study and Discussion

1. The Kincaids state how their life was changed by strip mining. How do they show that their experiences were typical of people in the area?
2. Is the damage caused by strip mining the result of neglect or carelessness, or is it inherent in the process itself—given the details of the letter? Are the Kincaids mainly concerned with this question?
3. What is the central issue for them? Are they arguing against strip mining on moral grounds? Or are they concerned only with the practical consequences? What assumptions about the rights of individuals underlie their argument?
4. Are the Kincaids addressing a general or a specific audience? How do you know?
5. What is the tone of the letter, and what in the letter creates it? What do the various questions asked in the letter contribute?

Vocabulary Study

Consult a dictionary of American English or Americanisms on the exact meaning of the following words and phrases and explain their use in the letter: *hollow, strips, spoil banks, grout, pudding.*

Suggestions for Writing

1. Write a letter protesting an activity that has changed your life in some way. Let the details of the change carry the weight of your protest.
2. Look through magazines and newspapers for a defense of strip mining. You will find authors and titles in the *Reader's Guide to Periodical Literature*. Analyze the assumptions and reasoning of the writer. (For a general review of the debate, pro and con, see *Business Week*, November 4, 1972.)

Michaito Ichimaru
Nagasaki, August 9, 1945

As Michaito Ichimaru tells us in his essay, at the time of the nuclear bombing of Nagasaki he was a medical student in that city. Today he is a professor of medicine at the Nagasaki University School of Medicine. As a witness to the bombing he gives us an unusual and striking view of nuclear warfare. Ichimaru writes also from the viewpoint of a physician concerned with the contemporary world.

In August 1945, I was a freshman at Nagasaki Medical College. The ninth of August was a clear, hot, beautiful, summer day. I left my lodging house, which was one and one half miles from the hypocenter, at eight in the morning, as usual, to catch a tram car. When I got to the tram stop, I found that it had been derailed in an accident. I decided to return home. I was lucky. I never made it to school that day.

At 11 A.M., I was sitting in my room with a fellow student when I heard the sound of a B-29 passing overhead. A few minutes later, the air flashed a brilliant yellow and there was a huge blast of wind.

We were terrified and ran downstairs to the toilet to hide. Later, when I came to my senses, I noticed a hole had been blown in the roof, all the glass had been shattered, and that the glass had cut my shoulder and I was bleeding. When I went outside, the sky had turned from blue to black and the black rain started to fall. The stone walls between the houses were reduced to rubble.

After a short time, I tried to go to my medical school in Urakami, which was 500 meters from the hypocenter. The air dose of radiation was more than 7,000 rads at this distance but I could not complete my journey because there were fires everywhere. I met many people coming back from Ura-kami. Their clothes were in rags, and shreds of skin hung from their bodies. They looked like ghosts with vacant stares. The next day, I was able to enter Urakami on foot, and all that I knew had disappeared. Only the concrete and iron skeletons of the buildings remained. There were dead bodies every-where. On each street corner we had tubs of water used for putting out fires after the air raids. In one of these small tubs, scarcely large enough for one person, was the body of a des-perate man who sought cool water. There was foam coming from his mouth, but he was not alive.

I cannot get rid of the sounds of crying women in the destroyed fields. As I got nearer to school, there were black charred bodies, with the white edges of bones showing in the arms and legs. A dead horse with a bloated belly lay by the side of the road. Only the skeleton of the medical hospital remained standing. Because the school building was wood, it was completely destroyed. My classmates were in that build-ing attending their physiology lecture. When I arrived some were still alive. They were unable to move their bodies. The strongest were so weak that they were slumped over on the ground. I talked with them and they thought they would be O.K., but all of them would eventually die within weeks. I cannot forget the way their eyes looked at me and their voices spoke to me forever. I went up to the small hill behind the medical school, where all of the leaves of the trees were lost. The green mountain had changed to a bald mountain. There were many medical students, doctors, nurses, and some pa-tients who escaped from the school and hospital. They were very weak and wanted water badly, crying out, "Give me water, please." Their clothes were in rags, bloody and dirty. Their condition was very bad. I carried down several friends of mine on my back from this hill. I brought them to their houses using a cart hitched to my bicycle. All of them died in the next few days. Some friends died with high fever, talking de-liriously. Some friends complained of general malaise and bloody diarrhea, caused by necrosis of the bowel mucous membrane by severe radiation.

One of my jobs was to contact the families of the survivors. In all the public schools I visited, there were many many survivors brought there by the healthy people. It is impossible to describe the horrors I saw. I heard many voices in pain, crying out, and there was a terrible stench. I remember it as an inferno. All of these people also died within several weeks.

One of my friends who was living in the same lodging houses cycled back from medical school by himself that day. He was a strong man doing Judo. That night he gradually became weak but he went back to his home in the country by himself the next day. I heard he died a few weeks later. I lost many friends. So many people died that disposing of the bodies was difficult. We burned the bodies of my friends in a pile of wood which we gathered, in a small open place. I clearly remember the movement of the bowels in the fire.

On August 15, 1945, I left Nagasaki by train to return to my home in the country. There were many survivors in the same car. Even now, I think of the grief of the parents of my friends who died. I cannot capture the magnitude of the misery and horror I saw. Never again should these terrible nuclear weapons be used, no matter what happens. Only when mankind renounces the use of these nuclear weapons will the souls of my friends rest in peace.

Comment

Ichimaru writes about the Nagasaki bombing from the point of view of a participant, and he has chosen his details with care to communicate the horrors he witnessed. He builds to his thesis with an inductive method of development, like that of Peeples: details of the bombing build in intensity to the final horror—the burning of the bodies in an open place. The power of the essay comes in part from the simple way Ichimaru states the facts, with a brief occasional interpretation and commentary.

Questions for Study and Discussion

1. What details suggest the awesome power of the blast? Which details reveal the unusual effects?
2. What details does Ichimaru interpret or comment on? Would these details have the same impact without this commentary?
3. How different would the effect of the essay be if Ichimaru had begun with his thesis? How does the essay affect you? Does it change your thinking or your understanding of nuclear warfare?

Vocabulary Study

Connotative meanings are important in persuasive writing because of the emotion they convey. Find words in the essay that convey emotion, in addition to providing denotative meanings, and be ready to explain how they do so.

Suggestion for Writing

Use one of the periodical, newspaper, or essay and general literature indexes in your library to find an article or essay concerned with nuclear warfare—perhaps an article dealing with Hiroshima or Nagasaki, or one dealing with the recent controversy over nuclear disarmament. Analyze the article or essay to discover what persuasive means the writer employs. Then comment on the effectiveness of the essay—specifically, on whether it changed your mind on the issue, or failed to achieve its purpose.

Roger Rosenblatt
The Man in the Water

Born in 1940 in New York City, Roger Rosenblatt attended New York University and Harvard, where he later taught English. From 1973 to 1975, he was Director of Education for the National

Endowment for the Humanities, and from 1975 to 1978 was the literary editor of *New Republic*. Rosenblatt is a columnist for the *Washington Post*, has published essays in numerous magazines and journals, and is the author of *Black Fiction* (1974). His essay on an airplane crash in Washington, D.C., in the winter of 1982, shows his gift for stating in simple language important truths about contemporary events.

As disasters go, this one was terrible, but not unique, certainly not among the worst on the roster of U.S. air crashes. There was the unusual element of the bridge, of course, and the fact that the plane clipped it at a moment of high traffic, one routine thus intersecting another and disrupting both. Then, too, there was the location of the event. Washington, the city of form and regulations, turned chaotic, deregulated, by a blast of real winter and a single slap of metal on metal. The jets from Washington National Airport that normally swoop around the presidential monuments like famished gulls are, for the moment, emblemized by the one that fell; so there is that detail. And there was the aesthetic clash as well—blue-and-green Air Florida, the name a flying garden, sunk down among gray chunks in a black river. All that was worth noticing, to be sure. Still, there was nothing very special in any of it, except death, which, while always special, does not necessarily bring millions to tears or to attention. Why, then, the shock here?

Perhaps because the nation saw in this disaster something more than a mechanical failure. Perhaps because people saw in it no failure at all, but rather something successful about their makeup. Here, after all, were two forms of nature in collision: the elements and human character. Last Wednesday, the elements, indifferent as ever, brought down Flight 90. And on that same afternoon, human nature—groping and flailing in mysteries of its own—rose to the occasion.

Of the four acknowledged heroes of the event, three are able to account for their behavior. Donald Usher and Eugene Windsor, a park police helicopter team, risked their lives every time they dipped the skids into the water to pick up survivors. On television, side by side in bright blue jumpsuits, they described their courage as all in the line of duty. Lenny Skutnik, a 28-year-old employee of the Congressional Budget Office, said: "It's something I never thought I would do"—referring to his jumping into the water to drag an injured woman to shore. Skutnik added that "somebody had to go in the water," delivering every hero's line that is no less admirable for its repetitions. In fact, nobody had to go into the water. That somebody actually did so is part of the reason this particular tragedy sticks in the mind.

But the person most responsible for the emotional impact of the disaster is the one known at first simply as "the man in the water." (Balding, probably in his 50s, an extravagant mustache.) He was seen clinging with five other survivors to the tail section of the airplane. This man was described by Usher and Windsor as appearing alert and in control. Every time they lowered a lifeline and flotation ring to him, he passed it on to another of the passengers. "In a mass casualty, you'll find people like him," said Windsor. "But I've never seen one with that commitment." When the helicopter came back for him, the man had gone under. His selflessness was one reason the story held national attention; his anonymity another. The fact that he went unidentified invested him with a universal character. For a while he was Everyman, and thus proof (as if one needed it) that no man is ordinary.

Still, he could never have imagined such a capacity in himself. Only minutes before his character was tested, he was sitting in the ordinary plane among the ordinary passengers, dutifully listening to the stewardess telling him to fasten his seat belt and saying something about the "no smoking sign." So our man relaxed with the others, some of whom would owe their lives to him. Perhaps he started to read, or to doze, or to regret some harsh remark made in the office that morning. Then suddenly he knew that the trip would not be ordinary. Like every other person on that flight, he was desperate to live, which makes his final act so stunning.

For at some moment in the water he must have realized   6
that he would not live if he continued to hand over the rope
and ring to others. He *had* to know it, no matter how gradual the effect of the cold. In his judgment he had no choice.
When the helicopter took off with what was to be the last
survivor, he watched everything in the world move away from
him, and he deliberately let it happen.

Yet there was something else about the man that kept our   7
thoughts on him, and which keeps our thoughts on him still.
He was *there,* in the essential, classic circumstance. Man in
nature. The man in the water. For its part, nature cared nothing about the five passengers. Our man, on the other hand,
cared totally. So the timeless battle commenced in the Potomac. For as long as that man could last, they went at each
other, nature and man; the one making no distinctions of good
and evil, acting on no principles, offering no lifelines; the other
acting wholly on distinctions, principles and, one supposes,
on faith.

Since it was he who lost the fight, we ought to come again   8
to the conclusion that people are powerless in the world. In
reality, we believe the reverse, and it takes the act of the man
in the water to remind us of our true feelings in this matter.
It is not to say that everyone would have acted as he did, or
as Usher, Windsor and Skutnik. Yet whatever moved these
men to challenge death on behalf of their fellows is not peculiar to them. Everyone feels the possibility in himself. That
is the abiding wonder of the story. That is why we would not
let go of it. If the man in the water gave a lifeline to the people gasping for survival, he was likewise giving a lifeline to
those who observed him.

The odd thing is that we do not even really believe that   9
the man in the water lost his fight. "Everything in Nature
contains all the powers of Nature," said Emerson. Exactly. So
the man in the water had his own natural powers. He could
not make ice storms, or freeze the water until it froze the blood.
But he could hand life over to a stranger, and that is a power
of nature too. The man in the water pitted himself against an

implacable, impersonal enemy; he fought it with charity; and he held it to a standoff. He was the best we can do.

Comment

The Air Florida crash described occurred in Washington, D.C., on January 14, 1982, during the evening rush hour at a crowded bridge over the Potomac River. The event received wide coverage because of these circumstances and the extraordinary acts of heroism performed. Rosenblatt is doing more than describing these events: he wishes to persuade readers of an important truth. To do so, he must persuade them that the acts of the man in the water were indeed heroic, and much of his discussion toward the end of the essay is given to this point. Notice how appropriate the simple, direct style is to the subject and ideas of the essay. Rosenblatt presents the facts without overdramatizing them through colorful language. All the same, his simplicity of language is eloquent enough to bring the essay to a fitting emotional pitch:

> So the man in the water had his own natural powers. He could not make ice storms, or freeze the water until it froze the blood. But he could hand life over to a stranger, and that is a power of nature too.

Questions for Study and Discussion

1. Rosenblatt does not give us all the facts of the crash. What facts does he present, and what aspects does he emphasize?
2. Is Rosenblatt writing only to those readers familiar with the circumstances of the crash, or is he also providing information for those unfamiliar with what happened?
3. Rosenblatt builds from the details of the crash to reflections about it. In what order are these details presented? Is Rosenblatt describing the events in the order they occurred?
4. How does he explain the heroism of the man in the water, the helicopter police, and Larry Skutnik?
5. Rosenblatt builds to his thesis, instead of stating it toward the beginning of the essay. What is his thesis, and do you agree with it?

Vocabulary Study

1. How does the context of the final sentence in paragraph 4 help us to understand the reference to Everyman?
2. In what sense is Rosenblatt using the word *classic* in paragraph 7?
3. Does the word *power* have more than one meaning in paragraph 9?

Suggestions for Writing

1. Explain the following sentence in light of the whole essay: "If the man in the water gave a lifeline to the people gasping for survival, he was likewise giving a lifeline to those who observed him."
2. Explain the statement of Emerson, "Everything in Nature contains all the powers of Nature," in light of the final paragraph. Then illustrate it from your own experience.
3. First state the conception of heroism Rosenblatt presents in the essay. Then discuss the extent to which this conception fits an act of heroism you have observed, or accords with your idea of what makes a person heroic.
4. Discuss a recent event that taught you an important truth about people or life. Describe the event for readers unfamiliar with it, and build to your thesis as Rosenblatt does.

part five

Effective
Sentences

Sentence Style

The sentences you speak and write derive from the sentences you hear and read from day to day. The same is true of your vocabulary. But as you become aware of new words and new turns of phrase and special ways of giving ideas emphasis, you may modify your sentences and diction. Usually the change is slight, for habits of speaking and writing are established early and are not easy to change.

Since adding new words to your vocabulary is easier than changing the shape of your sentences, you usually pick up new words without realizing you have done so. It is harder to drop words you use habitually and to break habits of sentence construction that derive from speech patterns—habits that can sometimes make your written sentences confusing or inexpressive. The following statement is a transcription of spoken English:

> In the minor leagues we spent a lot of hours riding in buses, and they were so hot and you didn't have too many stops to eat. You ate poorly because you had bad meal money. We got $1.50 a day. But you were young. When I was with a class B league, I got a long distance call. My wife went to the hospital in labor. It was the first baby. I had to get home. The ticket was forty-

some dollars. We didn't have it between us—the manager, everybody. I got there a day late.—Studs Terkel, *Working*.

This highly informal statement is expressive despite the loose organization of the first sentence and the fragmented sound of the short sentences that follow. To convey meaning, speakers can depend on voice pitch and inflection. These are resources not available to the writer, however. Written sentences therefore must be tighter than the fragmented or run-on sentences often spoken. They must also have more structural variation to avoid the monotony that spoken sentences control by intonation.

Compare the statements of the baseball player of the previous excerpt with these from Joan Didion's essay on bureaucrats:

> Mere driving on the freeway is in no way the same as participating in it. Anyone can "drive" on the freeway, and many people with no vocation for it do, hesitating here and resisting there, losing the rhythm of the lane change, thinking about where they came from and where they are going. Actual participants think only about where they are. Actual participation requires a total surrender, a concentration so intense as to seem a kind of narcosis, a rapture-of-the-freeway. *The mind goes clean. The rhythm takes over.* A distortion of time occurs, the same distortion that characterizes the instant before an accident.—Joan Didion, "Bureaucrats" (italics added)

Didion in these sentences varies her sentences with considerable effect. The italicized short sentences make the impact they do because Didion uses them sparingly; each is suited in length to the ideas they express. Short sentences need not be as dramatic as these; the effect depends on the ideas they express.

At the same time, sentences that depart markedly from patterns of speech may sound stilted. In speech, you usually begin with the main idea and add to it supporting details and other modifiers, or link the main idea to another as Didion does in the passage above:

> Anyone can "drive" on the freeway, and many with no vocation for it do, hesitating here and resisting there, losing the rhythm of the lane change, thinking about where they came from and where they are going.

Because so many spoken sentences open with the main clause, variation from this pattern catches the reader's attention:

The closed door upstairs at 120 South Spring Street in downtown Los Angeles is marked OPERATIONS CENTER. In the windowless room beyond the closed door a reverential hush prevails. From six A.M. until seven P.M. in this windowless room men sit at consoles watching a huge board flash colored lights.

The looser sentence illustrated above is typical of informal writing today; the more dramatic "periodic" sentence (as in the second and third sentences just quoted) is typical of formal writing. So is dependence on the passive voice, as in these sentences from a book on information theory:

> Evidently nature can no longer be seen as matter and energy alone. Nor can all her secrets be unlocked with the keys of chemistry and physics, brilliantly successful as these two branches of science have been in our century. A third component is needed for any explanation of the world that claims to be complete. To the powerful theories of chemistry and physics must be added a late arrival: a theory of information. Nature must be interpreted as matter, energy, and information.—Jeremy Campbell, *Grammatical Man*

Each of us has an informal as well as a formal way of speaking—each appropriate to different occasions. You probably make adjustments in your spoken language without even realizing that you are doing so. Writing calls for more deliberate choices. Much writing today avoids the extremes of highly formal and highly informal English. General English is the term we give to a spoken and written standard that shares characteristics of both. It is much tighter than the spoken English quoted above, and at the same time it is looser than the formal sentences just quoted. It uses a plain vocabulary where possible, depending on technical words only when simpler words will not express the intended idea.

Most of the essays in this book, including Didion's essay which follows next, are illustrations of general English. Though Didion's sentences are tighter than the loose sentences of much spoken English, they convey the rhythm of ordinary speech—more often the rhythm of the active voice than the passive. Didion varies them to catch the pauses, interruptions, and nuances of talk.

In your writing, you can tighten your sentences as well as loosen them when you find it appropriate to do so. The discussions that follow suggest ways you can make your sentences more effective.

Joan Didion
Bureaucrats

Joan Didion has had a varied career in writing since her graduation from the University of California at Berkeley in 1956. She
has been an editor of *Vogue* and a columnist for *The Saturday
Evening Post;* she has also written screenplays, numerous essays,
and novels about contemporary American life including *Play It
as It Lays* (1971) and *The Book of Common Prayer* (1977). "Bureaucrats" shows her concern with urban problems today and, in
particular, her ironic view of the workings of government. It
is reprinted from *The White Album* (1979), a collection of
Didion's essays.

The closed door upstairs at 120 South Spring Street in   1
downtown Los Angeles is marked OPERATIONS CEN-
TER. In the windowless room beyond the closed door a reverential hush prevails. From six A.M. until seven P.M. in this
windowless room men sit at consoles watching a huge board
flash colored lights. "There's the heart attack," someone will
murmur, or "we're getting the gawk effect." 120 South Spring
is the Los Angeles office of Caltrans, or the California Department of Transportation, and the Operations Center is
where Caltrans engineers monitor what they call "the 42-Mile
Loop." The 42-Mile Loop is simply the rough triangle formed
by the intersections of the Santa Monica, the San Diego and
the Harbor freeways, and 42 miles represents less than ten
per cent of freeway mileage in Los Angeles County alone, but
these particular 42 miles are regarded around 120 South Spring
with a special veneration. The Loop is a "demonstration system," a phrase much favored by everyone at Caltrans, and is
part of a "pilot project," another two words carrying totemic
weight on South Spring.

The Loop has electronic sensors embedded every half-mile   2
out there in the pavement itself, each sensor counting the
crossing cars every twenty seconds. The Loop has its own
mind, a Xerox Sigma V computer which prints out, all day
and night, twenty-second readings on what is and is not
moving in each of the Loop's eight lanes. It is the Xerox Sigma
V that makes the big board flash red when traffic out there
drops below fifteen miles an hour. It is the Xerox Sigma V
that tells the Operations crew when they have an "incident"
out there. An "incident" is the heart attack on the San Diego,
the jackknifed truck on the Harbor, the Camaro just now
tearing out the Cyclone fence on the Santa Monica. "Out
there" is where incidents happen. The windowless room at
120 South Spring is where incidents get "verified." "Incident
verification" is turning on the closed-circuit TV on the con-
sole and watching the traffic slow down to see (this is "the
gawk effect") where the Camaro tore out the fence.

As a matter of fact there is a certain closed-circuit aspect   3
to the entire mood of the Operations Center. "Verifying" the
incident does not after all "prevent" the incident, which lends
the enterprise a kind of tranced distance, and on the day recently when I visited 120 South Spring it took considerable
effort to remember what I had come to talk about, which was
that particular part of the Loop called the Santa Monica
Freeway. The Santa Monica Freeway is 16.2 miles long, runs
from the Pacific Ocean to downtown Los Angeles through what
is referred to at Caltrans as "the East-West Corridor," carries
more traffic every day than any other freeway in California,
has what connoisseurs of freeways concede to be the most
beautiful access ramps in the world, and appeared to have been
transformed by Caltrans, during the several weeks before I went
downtown to talk about it, into a 16.2-mile parking lot.

The problem seemed to be another Caltrans "demonstra-   4
tion," or "pilot," a foray into bureaucratic terrorism they were
calling "The Diamond Lane" in their promotional literature
and "The Project" among themselves. That the promotional
literature consisted largely of schedules for buses (or "Dia-

mond Lane Expresses") and invitations to join a car pool via computer ("Commuter Computer") made clear not only the putative point of The Project, which was to encourage travel by car pool and bus, but also the actual point, which was to eradicate a central Southern California illusion, that of individual mobility, without anyone really noticing. This had not exactly worked out. "FREEWAY FIASCO," the *Los Angeles Times* was headlining page-one stories. "THE DIAMOND LANE: ANOTHER BUST BY CALTRANS." "CALTRANS PILOT EFFORT ANOTHER IN LONG LIST OF FAILURES." "OFFICIAL DIAMOND LANE STANCE: LET THEM HOWL."

All "The Diamond Lane" theoretically involved was re-   5
serving the fast inside lanes on the Santa Monica for vehicles carrying three or more people, but in practice this meant that 25 per cent of the freeway was reserved for 3 per cent of the cars, and there were other odd wrinkles here and there suggesting that Caltrans had dedicated itself to making all movements around Los Angeles as arduous as possible. There was for example the matter of surface streets. A "surface street" is anything around Los Angeles that is not a freeway ("going surface" from one part of town to another is generally regarded as idiosyncratic), and surface streets do not fall directly within the Caltrans domain, but now the engineer in charge of surface streets was accusing Caltrans of threatening and intimidating him. It appeared that Caltrans wanted him to create a "confused and congested situation" on his surface streets, so as to force drivers back to the freeway, where they would meet a still more confused and congested situation and decide to stay home, or take a bus. "We are beginning a process of deliberately making it harder for drivers to use freeways," a Caltrans director had in fact said at a transit conference some months before. "We are prepared to endure considerable public outcry in order to pry John Q. Public out of his car. . . . I would emphasize that this is a political decision, and one that can be reversed if the public gets sufficiently enraged to throw us rascals out."

Of course this political decision was in the name of the 6
greater good, was in the interests of "environmental improvement" and "conservation of resources," but even there the
figures had about them a certain Caltrans opacity. The Santa
Monica normally carried 240,000 cars and trucks every day.
These 240,000 cars and trucks normally carried 260,000
people. What Caltrans described as its ultimate goal on the
Santa Monica was to carry the same 260,000 people, "but in
7,800 fewer, or 232,200 vehicles." The figure "232,200" had
a visionary precision to it that did not automatically create
confidence, especially since the only effect so far had been to
disrupt traffic throughout the Los Angeles Basin, triple the
number of daily accidents on the Santa Monica, prompt the
initiation of two lawsuits against Caltrans, and cause large
numbers of Los Angeles County residents to behave, most
uncharacteristically, as an ignited and conscious proletariat.
Citizen guerrillas splashed paint and scattered nails in the
Diamond Lanes. Diamond Lane maintenance crews expressed fear of hurled objects. Down at 120 South Spring the
architects of the Diamond Lane had taken to regarding "the
media" as the architects of their embarrassment, and Caltrans
statements in the press had been cryptic and contradictory,
reminiscent only of old communiqués out of Vietnam.

To understand what was going on it is perhaps necessary 7
to have participated in the freeway experience, which is the
only secular communion Los Angeles has. Mere driving on
the freeway is in no way the same as participating in it. Anyone can "drive" on the freeway, and many people with no vo-
cation for it do, hesitating here and resisting there, losing the
rhythm of the lane change, thinking about where they came
from and where they are going. Actual participants think only
about where they are. Actual participation requires a total
surrender, a concentration so intense as to seem a kind of
narcosis, a rapture-of-the-freeway. The mind goes clean. The
rhythm takes over. A distortion of time occurs, the same distortion that characterizes the instant before an accident. It takes
only a few seconds to get off the Santa Monica Freeway at

National-Overland, which is a difficult exit requiring the driver to cross two new lanes of traffic streamed in from the San Diego Freeway, but those few seconds always seem to me the longest part of the trip. The moment is dangerous. The exhilaration is in doing it. "As you acquire the special skills involved," Reyner Banham observed in an extraordinary chapter about the freeways in his 1971 *Los Angeles: The Architecture of Four Ecologies,* "the freeways become a special way of being alive . . . the extreme concentration required in Los Angeles seems to bring on a state of heightened awareness that some locals find mystical."

Indeed some locals do, and some nonlocals too. Reducing the number of lone souls careering around the East-West Corridor in a state of mechanized rapture may or may not have seemed socially desirable, but what it was definitely not going to seem was easy. "We're only seeing an initial period of unfamiliarity," I was assured the day I visited Caltrans. I was talking to a woman named Eleanor Wood and she was thoroughly and professionally grounded in the diction of "planning" and it did not seem likely that I could interest her in considering the freeway as regional mystery. "Any time you try to rearrange people's daily habits, they're apt to react impetuously. All this project requires is a certain rearrangement of people's daily planning. That's really all we want."

It occurred to me that a certain rearrangement of people's daily planning might seem, in less rarefied air than is breathed at 120 South Spring, rather a great deal to want, but so impenetrable was the sense of higher social purpose there in the Operations Center that I did not express this reservation. Instead I changed the subject, mentioned an earlier "pilot project" on the Santa Monica: the big electronic message boards that Caltrans had installed a year or two before. The idea was that traffic information transmitted from the Santa Monica to the Xerox Sigma V could be translated, here in the Operations Center, into suggestions to the driver, and flashed right back out to the Santa Monica. This operation, in that it involved telling drivers electronically what they al-

8

9

ready knew empirically, had the rather spectral circularity that seemed to mark a great many Caltrans schemes, and I was interested in how Caltrans thought it worked.

"Actually the message boards were part of a larger pilot   10
project," Mrs. Wood said. "An ongoing project in incident management. With the message boards we hoped to learn if motorists would modify their behavior according to what we told them on the boards."

I asked if the motorists had.   11

"Actually no," Mrs. Wood said finally. "They didn't react   12
to the signs exactly as we'd hypothesized they would, no. *But.* If we'd *known* what the motorist would do . . . then we wouldn't have needed a pilot project in the first place, would we."

The circle seemed intact. Mrs. Wood and I smiled, and   13
shook hands. I watched the big board until all lights turned green on the Santa Monica and then I left and drove home on it, all 16.2 miles of it. All the way I remembered that I was watched by the Xerox Sigma V. All the way the message boards gave me the number to call for CAR POOL INFO. As I left the freeway it occurred to me that they might have their own rapture down at 120 South Spring, and it could be called Perpetuating the Department. Today the California Highway Patrol reported that, during the first six weeks of the Diamond Lane, accidents on the Santa Monica, which normally range between 49 and 72 during a six-week period, totaled 204. Yesterday plans were announced to extend the Diamond Lane to other freeways at a cost of $42,500,000.

Questions for Study and Discussion

1. What variations of sentence length do you find in paragraphs 1–6?
2. How many sentences in paragraphs 1–6 are built by addition of detail? How many are built by qualification and modification?

3. The greater the number of simple and compound sentences, the greater the informality of the essay. How informal is this essay?

4. Does Didion state her attitude toward Caltrans directly, or instead imply it through her details?

5. In what ways is the Los Angeles Freeway symbolic of Los Angeles life? Does Didion see the freeway as symbolic or representative of California or perhaps American life, generally?

Vocabulary Study

1. What is Didion saying about the word *verified* and the other forms of it she cites in paragraphs 2 and 3?

2. What points is she making about other special terms she discusses—for example, *surface street?*

3. Why does she use the word *proletariat* rather than *population* or *citizenry* in paragraph 6?

4. Why does she use the phrase *secular communion* instead of *being together*—"the only way of being together that Los Angeles has"—in paragraph 7?

5. Explain the italicized words:

   This operation, in that it involved telling drivers electronically what they already knew *empirically,* had the rather *spectral circularity* that seemed to mark a great many Caltrans schemes. . . .

6. Why does Didion give the following in capitals—CAR POOL INFO—instead of writing "car pool information"?

Suggestions for Writing

1. Didion is describing a different experience with bureaucracy from Nelson's ("The Desk," p. 26). Discuss the differences in the experiences and the conclusions reached about bureaucracy.

2. Use the traffic of your hometown or city to comment on its quality of life or atmosphere. Make your details as specific as you can.

3. Discuss an "improvement" that in your opinion has worsened the situation it was intended to make better. Describe the situation in detail.

Emphasis

Giving ideas exact emphasis requires attention to sentence co-ordination and subordination. When you *coordinate* you use the words *and, but, for, or, nor,* and *yet* to connect words, phrases, and clauses of the same weight and importance. The three opening clauses in the following sentence are independent and coordinate:

> The cold night had come, *and* Ukwane in the frosty grass was shivering, *yet* he sat for an hour keeping his patience, putting his hands into the cold blood of the springbok to trace veins to their source, prefacing all his answers with positive, qualifying re-marks.—Elizabeth Marshall Thomas, *The Harmless People*

To stress a close relation between ideas, the writer may coordinate clauses with semicolons, with or without connecting (or conjunc-tive) adverbs like *however* and *furthermore* or adverbial phrases:

> For us, the cave paintings re-create the hunter's way of life as a glimpse of history; we look through them into the past. But for the hunter, I suggest, they were a peep-hole into the future; he looked ahead.—J. Bronowski, *The Ascent of Man*

It is natural to come to astronomy straight from mathematics; after all, astronomy was developed first, and became a model for all the other sciences, just because it could be turned into exact numbers.—*The Ascent of Man*

When you *subordinate* you attach to independent clauses phrases and clauses that cannot stand alone. In the Thomas sentence above, the heavily stressed subordinate phrases that conclude the sentence contain specific details that explain the independent clause:

. . . yet he sat for an hour keeping his patience, putting his hands into the cold blood of the springbok to trace veins to their source, prefacing all his answers with positive, qualifying remarks.

English sentences often reserve the end of the sentence for the most important idea. This end-focus is evident in the stress given final words in speaking:

My wife's parents live in NEWark.

Even if another word in the sentence is stressed, the final word still receives a degree of stress:

My *WIFE'S* parents live in NEWark (my wife's parents, not my own parents)

This fact has important consequences for building sentences and varying them. It means that the speaker or writer can "load" the end of the sentence, adding ideas and details that cannot easily go at the beginning. You speak or write the following sentence without thinking about its structure:

(1) I know they won't come if they decide to go to Newark.

You would not say or write:

(2) That they won't come if they decide to go to Newark I know.

But you can open the sentence with a shorter complement:

(3) That they're coming I have no doubt.

Notice that the complement [*that*] *they won't come* in (1) contains a modifying subordinate clause *(if they decide to go to Newark)* and therefore cannot appear at the beginning of the sentence. The unmodified complement in (3)—*That he is coming*—can appear at the beginning. By contrast, complex modifiers can be added to the end of the sentence without difficulty:

> A school of minnows swam by, each minnow with its small individual shadow, doubling the attendance, so clear and sharp in the sunlight.—E. B. White, "Once More to the Lake"

Compound sentences, which coordinate independent clauses to emphasize their connection, can run on indefinitely:

> The height of the ginning season in that part of the country is early October, and in that time the loaded wagons are on the road before the least crack of daylight, the waiting is endless hours, and the gin is still pulsing and beating after dark.—James Agee, "Cotton"

This sentence might continue further. The familiar definition of a sentence as a complete thought is of no use in deciding when to end sentences of this kind. For the completeness of the thought lies in the mind of the speaker or writer, who seeks to emphasize each component idea and who alone knows when everything necessary has been said. At the same time, the emphasis or force diminishes for the reader if the sentence seems to run on or drift monotonously.

William Zinsser
Jury Duty

William Zinsser, who has taught at Yale University, was born in 1922 in New York City, and has written much about life there in numerous articles and books. He attended Princeton University, and later was a feature writer, film critic, and drama editor for the *New York Herald Tribune* and a columnist for *Look* and *Life*. His books include *Pop Goes America* (1966) and *On Writing Well* (1976).

Jury duty again. I'm sitting in the "central jurors' room" of a courthouse in lower Manhattan, as I do every two years, waiting to be called for a jury, which I almost never am. It's an experience that all of us have known, in one form or another, as long as we can remember: organized solitude.

The chair that I sit in is a little island of apartness. I sit there alone, day after day, and I go out to lunch alone, a stranger in my own city. Strictly, of course, I'm not by myself. Several hundred other men and women sit on every side, as closely as in a movie theater, also waiting to be called for a jury, which they almost never are. Sometimes we break briefly into each other's lives, when we get up to stretch, offering fragments of talk to fill the emptiness. But in the end each of us is alone, withdrawn into our newspapers and our crossword puzzles and our sacred urban privacy.

The room intimidates us. It is a dreary place, done in thirties Bureaucratic, too dull to sustain more than a few minutes of mental effort. On the subconscious level, however, it exerts a strong and uncanny hold. It is the universal waiting room. It is the induction center and the clinic; it is the assembly hall and the office where forms are filled out. Thoughts come unbidden there, sneaking back from all the other moments—in the army, at camp, on the first day of school—when we were part of a crowd and therefore lonely.

The mere taking of roll call by a jury clerk will summon back the countless times when we have waited for our name to be yelled out—loud and just a little wrong. Like every person whose job is to read names aloud, the jury clerk can't read names aloud. Their shapes mystify him. They are odd and implausible names, as diverse as the countries that they came from, but surely the clerk has met them all before. *Hasn't* he? Isn't that what democracy—and the jury system—is all about? Evidently not.

We are shy enough, as we wait for our name, without the extra burden of wondering what form it will take. By now we know most of the variants that have been imposed on it by other clerks in other rooms like this, and we are ready to answer to any of them, or to some still different version. Actually we don't want to hear our name called at all in this vast public chamber. It is so private, so vulnerable. And yet we don't want to *not* hear it, for only then are we reassured of our identity, really certain that we are known, wanted, and in the right place. Dawn over Camp Upton, 1943: Weinberg, Wyzanski, Yanopoulos, Zapata, Zeccola, Zinsser . . .

I don't begin my jury day in such a retrospective state. I start with high purpose and only gradually slide into mental disarray. I am punctual, even early, and so is everybody else. We are a conscientious lot—partly because we are so surrounded by the trappings of justice, but mainly because that is what we are there to be. I've never seen such conscientious-looking people. Observing them, I'm glad that American law rests on being judged by our peers. In fact, I'd almost rather be judged by my peers than judged by a judge.

Most of us start the day by reading. Jury duty is America's gift to her citizens of a chance to catch up on "good" books, and I always bring *War and Peace*. I remember to bring it every morning and I keep it handy on my lap. The only thing I don't do is read it. There's something about the room . . . the air is heavy with imminent roll calls, too heavy for tackling a novel that will require strict attention. Besides, it's important to read the newspaper first: sharpen up the old noggin on issues of the day. I'm just settling into my paper when the clerk comes in, around ten-twenty-five, and calls the roll ("Zissner?" "Here!"). Suddenly it is 1944 and I am at an army base near Algiers, hammering tin to make a hot shower for Colonel McCloskey. That sort of thing can shoot the whole morning.

If it doesn't, the newspaper will. Only a waiting juror knows how infinite the crannies of journalism can be. I read "Arrival of Buyers," though I don't know what they want to buy and have nothing to sell. I read "Soybean Futures," though I wouldn't know a soybean even in the present. I read classified ads for jobs that I didn't know were jobs, like "key-punch operators." What keys do they punch? I mentally buy

6

7

8

4bdrm 1½bth splt lvl homes w/fpl overlooking Long Island Sound and dream of taking ½ bath there. I read dog news and horoscopes ("bucking others could prove dangerous to-day") and medical columns on diseases I've never heard of, but whose symptoms I instantly feel.

It's an exhausting trip, and I emerge with eyes blurry and   9
mind blank. I look around at my fellow jurors. Some of them are trying to work—to keep pace, pitifully, with the jobs that they left in order to come here and do nothing. They spread queer documents on their knees, full of graphs and figures, and they scribble on yellow pads. But the papers don't seem quite real to them, or quite right, removed from the tidy world of filing cabinets and secretaries, and after a while the work-ers put the work away again.

Around twelve-forty-five the clerk comes in to make an   10
announcement. We stir to attention: we are needed! "Go to lunch," he says. "Be back at two." We straggle out. By now the faces of all my fellow jurors are familiar (we've been here eight days), and I keep seeing them as we poke around the narrow streets of Chinatown looking for a restaurant that isn't the one where we ate yesterday. I smile tentatively, as New Yorkers do, and they smile tentatively back, and we go our separate ways. By one-fifty-five we are seated in the jurors' room again, drowsy with Chinese food and American bore-dom—too drowsy, certainly, to start *War and Peace*. Luckily, we all bought the afternoon paper while we were out. Talk about remote crannies of journalism!

Perhaps we are too hesitant to talk to each other, to in-   11
vite ourselves into lives that would refresh us by being differ-ent from our own. We are scrupulous about privacy—it is one of the better gifts that the city can bestow, and we don't want to spoil it for somebody else. Yet within almost every New Yorker who thinks he wants to be left alone is a person des-perate for human contact. Thus we may be as guilty as the jury system of not putting our time to good use.

What we want to do most, of course, is serve on a jury.   12
We believe in the system. Besides, was there ever so out-

standing a group of jurors as we, so intelligent and fair-minded? The clerks have told us all the reasons why jurors are called in such wasteful numbers: court schedules are unpredictable; trials end unexpectedly; cases are settled at the very moment when a jury is called; prisoners plead guilty to a lesser charge rather than wait years for a trial that might prove them innocent. All this we know, and in theory it makes sense.

In practice, however, somebody's arithmetic is wrong, and one of America's richest assets is being dribbled away. There must be a better way to get through the long and tragic list of cases awaiting a solution—and, incidentally, to get through *War and Peace*.

13

Comment

Zinsser's first paragraph illustrates important kinds of sentence emphasis. The brief opening phrase—"Jury duty again"—which serves as a topic sentence, contrasts with the two longer sentences that follow. The first of these adds a series of qualifying clauses to the opening main clause:

> I'm sitting in the "central jurors' room" of a courthouse in lower Manhattan, as I do every two years, waiting to be called for a jury, which I almost never am.

The final sentence of the paragraph does the same, but with an important difference: the concluding phrase—"organized solitude"—complements the opening clause: "It's an experience that all of us have known." This concluding phrase gains special emphasis at the end of the sentence. In many of his sentences Zinsser takes advantage of this kind of terminal emphasis. But he uses this effect sparingly. His sentences have the ring of spoken sentences, depending on coordination and occasionally italics to convey vocal inflection:

> They are odd and implausible names, as diverse as the countries that they came from, but surely the clerk has met them all before. *Hasn't* he? Isn't that what democracy—and the jury system—is all about?

Questions for Study and Discussion

1. Which sentences in paragraph 5 are coordinate only? How many sentences consist of one introductory main clause, and one or more subordinate clauses? Do any of the sentences join subordinate to coordinate clauses?
2. Paragraph 6 contains a series of short emphatic opening sentences. Does Zinsser maintain this kind of emphasis in the rest of the paragraph?
3. How different is paragraph 7 from paragraph 6 in sentence construction? What use does Zinsser make of ellipsis? How much emphasis (through pitch and volume) should the parenthetical statements be given?
4. How much subordination do you find in paragraph 8? How many sentences are built through modification?
5. How does Zinsser establish a point of view and a dominant tone? Or do you find changes in tone throughout the essay?
6. Why would Zinsser "almost rather be judged by [his] peers than judged by a judge"?

Vocabulary Study

Write a sentence using each of the following pairs of words, and explain the difference between them. The first word in each pair is Zinsser's:

a. *fragments* (paragraph 2), *parts*
b. *intimidates* (paragraph 3), *threatens*
c. *bureaucratic* (paragraph 3), *governmental*
d. *uncanny* (paragraph 3), *strange*
e. *implausible* (paragraph 4), *unconvincing*
f. *vulnerable* (paragraph 5), *weak*
g. *scrupulous* (paragraph 11), *careful*
h. *bestow* (paragraph 11), *give*

Suggestions for Writing

1. Describe a waiting room and your feelings in it. Make your details specific, and use your description to make a comment about your general situation. Develop several of your sentences with modification, as Zinsser does. Where you can,

combine coordinate clauses with subordinate phrases and clauses.
2. Analyze two of the final paragraphs of Zinsser's essay, showing
    how coordination and subordination are used to give emphasis
    to particular ideas.

Michael J. Arlen
"Ring Around the Collar!"

Michael J. Arlen, the son of a famous writer, was born in London in 1930. Arlen wrote for *Life Magazine* from 1952 to 1956, and since 1966 he has been a commentator on television and American life for *The New Yorker*. His books include *The Living Room War* (1969), *Exiles* (1970), and *Passage to Ararat* (1975). The essay reprinted here reveals the keen observation and quiet humor that distinguish his writing.

This half-minute commercial for a laundry detergent called   1
Wisk appears fairly frequently on daytime and evening television. In a recent version, a young woman and a young man are shown being led down the corridor of a hotel by a bellman who is carrying suitcases. The hotel seems to be an attractive one—not very elegant but definitely not an ordinary motel. Similarly, the young man and woman are attractive, but with nothing either glamorous or working-class about their appearance. Perhaps he is a junior executive. And she is probably his wife, though there is nothing so far that says that the two people are married. Since the framework of the drama is a commercial, the assumption is that they *are* married. On the

From "Three Views of Women" from *The View from Highway 1* by Michael J. Arlen. Copyright © 1975, 1976 by Michael J. Arlen. This essay first appeared in *The New Yorker*. Reprinted by permission of Farrar, Straus and Giroux, Inc.

other hand, against the familiar framework of similar modern movie scenes, there is no such assumption; possibly it is the beginning of an adventure. Then, suddenly, the bellman drops one of the suitcases in the corridor; some of the contents of the suitcase spill out; the bellman crouches down on the corridor carpet to put the items back in. He notices one of the man's shirts and holds it up. "Ring around the collar!" he says accusingly; these words are then taken up in the kind of singsong chant that has become a feature of these ads. The man looks puzzled and let down. The woman examines the offending shirt and looks mortified and aghast. By now, whatever slight elegance or intimations of adventure may have existed at the beginning of the scene have totally disintegrated, and, indeed, have quickly re-formed themselves into the classic hubby-and-housewife focus of most television commercials. The wife admits her mistake—to the bellman and her husband—of having used an inadequate detergent, and the scene changes to what is apparently the laundry area of her house, where the wife (now back in her regular "wifely" clothes) discusses the merits of using Wisk when doing the family wash.

In a number of ways, this is the most noticeably irritating of the housewife commercials. There is a nagging, whiny quality to the "Ring around the collar!" chant which is almost a caricature of the nagging, whiny voices of earlier Hollywood and TV-commercial housewives but which deliberately stops before the point of caricature is reached. In the manner of certain other ads—especially those for aspirin and "cold remedies"—it is a commercial that expressly announces its own irritatingness. We are going to repeat and repeat and repeat, these commercials say, and we are going to grate on your nerves—and you are going to remember us. At times, this sales approach has been given various fine-sounding methodological names by advertisers, but essentially it is the voice of the small boy who wants something: I want, I want, I want, I want—and finally you give it to him. In this case, the small boy wants you to buy his detergent, and who is to tell him no?

On the level of anti-female condescension, the "Ring around the collar!" ad seems to go even beyond irritation. In most housewife commercials, the housewife is portrayed as little more than a simpering, brainless jelly, almost pathologically obsessed with the world of kitchen floors or laundry, or of the celebrated "bathroom bowl." But in the Wisk commercials the standard trivializing portrait is accompanied by quite unusual brutality. As if in a reverse Cinderella process, the young prince and his companion not only are stopped in their tracks by the hazard of the Dirty Shirt (and the curse cry of "Ring around the collar!") but, instantly, as if under a magic spell, are snatched from the hotel-palace and returned to their previous existence—she to profess folk-happiness among the laundry tubs, and he, presumably, to his northern New England sales route. Sex is back to what it used to be: the identityless woman in the traveling suit is replaced by the beaming housewife in housewifely attire. And it is all the result of *her* failure in not having properly attended to her husband's needs—in having exposed him to the scorn of the bellman who guarded the erotic corridor. The fable does not end in tragedy—for though Cinderella is back among the laundry tubs, she now has good magic on her side. But it has been a sobering experience.

Comment

As in Zinsser, in Arlen we hear someone talking to us. The sentences are close to the rhythms of spoken English, with emphasis indicated by italics to suggest the spoken idiom:

> Since the framework of the drama is a commercial, the assumption is that they *are* married.

Arlen might have written the following:

> Perhaps he is a junior executive, and she is probably his wife, though there is nothing so far that says that the two people are married.

In fact, he breaks the sentence to give particular emphasis to the second main clause:

> Perhaps he is a junior executive. And she is probably his wife. . . .

Arlen uses other means to gain emphasis. The colon in the following sentence focuses our attention on the series that follows. The concluding dash marks an emphatic break in idea and shows its importance:

> At times, this sales approach has been given various fine-sounding methodological names by advertisers, but essentially it is the voice of the small boy who wants something: I want, I want, I want, I want—and finally you give it to him.

Notice how careful Arlen is to give enough details of the advertisement so that the reader who has not seen it will understand his point. The presentation is economical and clearly focused.

Questions for Study and Discussion

1. What examples do you find in paragraph 3 of the kinds of emphasis just discussed?
2. How many formal transitions are there in paragraph 1? What transitional ideas do these express?
3. How soon in the essay do you discover the purpose of the description? Would you consider the essay more effective if Arlen had stated his purpose at the start?
4. What attitudes toward women and marriage is Arlen criticizing? Does he state all of these attitudes directly?
5. Do you agree with his interpretation of the commercial?

Vocabulary Study

Give the dictionary meaning of the following words and be ready to explain how each is used in the essay: *assumption, mortified, aghast, elegance, classic* (paragraph 1); *caricature, methodological* (paragraph

2); *condescension, pathologically, obsessed, trivializing, attire, erotic* (paragraph 3).

Sentence Study

1. Recast the following sentences to give terminal emphasis to the italicized words. Change the phrasing and punctuation as necessary:

   a. *"The hotel seems to be an attractive one*—not very elegant but definitely not an ordinary motel."

   b. "In the manner of certain other ads—*especially those for aspirin and "cold remedies"*—it is a commercial that expressly announces its own irritatingness."

   c. *"On the level of anti-female condescension,* the 'Ring around the collar!' ad seems to go even beyond irritation."

   d. *"Sex is back to what it used to be:* the identityless woman in the traveling suit is replaced by the beaming housewife in housewifely attire."

2. The following simple sentences are adapted from the originals in George Orwell's *The Road to Wigan Pier*. Combine each group into a single sentence, subordinating where possible, and using semicolons or colons only when necessary:

   a. Miners are changed from one shift to another. Their families have to make adjustments to these changes. These adjustments are tiresome in the extreme.

   b. If he is on the night shift he gets home in time for breakfast. He gets home in the middle of the afternoon on the morning shift. On the afternoon shift he gets home in the middle of the night. In each case, of course, he wants his principal meal of the day as soon as he returns.

   c. The rate of accidents among miners is high. It is high compared with that in other trades. Accidents are so high that they are taken for granted almost as they would be in a minor war.

   d. The most obviously understandable cause of accidents is explosions of gas. This cause is always more or less present in the atmosphere of the pit.

   e. The gas may be touched off by a spark during blasting operations. It may be touched off by a pick striking a spark from a stone. It may be touched off by a defective lamp.

And it may be touched off by "gob fires." These are spontaneously generated fires which smolder in the coal dust and are very hard to put out.

Suggestions for Writing

1. Discuss what attitudes toward women you find in other commercials for a detergent or another product. You may discover a variety of attitudes—even conflicting ones. Distinguish them, illustrating one or two of them through a careful choice of detail, and draw a conclusion from your analysis.

2. Analyze an ad or commercial for the image it conveys of men or children. Support your analysis through a careful choice of detail, and draw a conclusion from it.

3. Arlen suggests that the *Wisk* commercial appeals to a sense of guilt or shame in the housewife. Analyze the appeals you find in other detergent commercials or those of another product.

Parallelism

Words, phrases, and clauses that are similar in structure and perform the same function in a sentence are said to be *parallel:*

> We learned *to ski, to skate,* and *to toboggan.* (parallel phrases) We learned *that corn is a grain, that the tomato is a fruit,* and *that the potato is a plant tuber.* (parallel clauses)

In the same way, sentences in a paragraph may be parallel in structure:

> *You can watch* the judging of home-baked bread *or listen* to the latest rock group. *You can watch* free every day the teenage talent search *or pay* money to hear the same nationally known acts you can watch free on television.—Paul Engle, "The Iowa State Fair"

Parallelism makes the reader aware of the similarity in ideas. If the ideas are not similar, the parallel structure may seem awkward. Writers in the past often aimed for strict parallelism in sentences and paragraphs, to the point of using almost the same number of words in phrases and clauses. Modern writers, by contrast, favor a looser parallelism, and may vary the length of elements, to avoid a formal effect:

357

He watched Martin slip the lens into his pocket, he sighed, he struggled for something else to say, and silently he lumbered into his bedroom.—Sinclair Lewis, *Arrowsmith*

Margaret Mead and Rhoda Metraux
New Superstitions for Old

Margaret Mead (1901–1978), one of America's most distinguished anthropologists, was a curator of ethnology at the Museum of Natural History in New York City from 1926 to 1969. She also taught at Columbia and other universities, and participated in the work of numerous United States and United Nations agencies. She traveled widely and wrote about many cultures, including her own, in such widely read books as *Growing Up in New Guinea* (1930), *And Keep Your Powder Dry* (1942), and *Male and Female* (1949).

Rhoda Metraux was educated at Vassar, Yale, and Columbia, and has done field work in anthropology in many countries including Haiti, Mexico, Argentina, and New Guinea. She has been on the staff of various government agencies, and has also been a research associate at the Museum of Natural History. She and Margaret Mead worked together for many years, collaborating in the writing of *The Study of Culture at a Distance* (1953) and *Themes in French Culture* (1954).

Once in a while there is a day when everything seems to   1
run smoothly and even the riskiest venture comes out exactly right. You exclaim, "This is my lucky day!" Then as an afterthought you say, "Knock on wood!" Of course, you do not

really believe that knocking on wood will ward off danger. Still, boasting about your own good luck gives you a slightly uneasy feeling—and you carry out the little protective ritual. If someone challenged you at that moment, you would probably say, "Oh, that's nothing. Just an old superstition."

But when you come to think about it, what is a superstition?   2

In the contemporary world most people treat old folk   3 beliefs as superstitions—the belief, for instance, that there are lucky and unlucky days or numbers, that future events can be read from omens, that there are protective charms or that what happens can be influenced by casting spells. We have excluded magic from our current world view, for we know that natural events have natural causes.

In a religious context, where truths cannot be demon-   4 strated, we accept them as a matter of faith. Superstitions, however, belong to the category of beliefs, practices and ways of thinking that have been discarded because they are inconsistent with scientific knowledge. It is easy to say that other people are superstitious because they believe what we regard to be untrue. "Superstition" used in that sense is a derogatory term for the beliefs of other people that we do not share. But there is more to it than that. For superstitions lead a kind of half life in a twilight world where, sometimes, we partly suspend our disbelief and act as if magic worked.

Actually, almost every day, even in the most sophisti-   5 cated home, something is likely to happen that evokes the memory of some old folk belief. The salt spills. A knife falls to the floor. Your nose tickles. Then perhaps, with a slightly embarrassed smile, the person who spilled the salt tosses a pinch over his left shoulder. Or someone recites the old rhyme, "Knife falls, gentleman calls." Or as you rub your nose you think, That means a letter. I wonder who's writing? No one takes these small responses very seriously or gives them more than a passing thought. Sometimes people will preface one of these ritual acts—walking around instead of under a ladder or hastily closing an umbrella that has been opened inside a house—with such a remark as "I remember my great-aunt used to . . ." or "Germans used to say you ought not . . ." And then, having placed the belief at some distance away in time or space, they carry out the ritual.

Everyone also remembers a few of the observances of childhood—wishing on the first star; looking at the new moon over the right shoulder; avoiding the cracks in the sidewalk on the way to school while chanting, "Step on a crack, break your mother's back"; wishing on white horses, on loads of hay, on covered bridges, on red cars; saying quickly, "Bread-and-butter" when a post or a tree separated you from the friend you were walking with. The adult may not actually recite the formula "Star light, star bright . . ." and may not quite turn to look at the new moon, but his mood is tempered by a little of the old thrill that came when the observance was still freighted with magic.

Superstition can also be used with another meaning. When I discuss the religious beliefs of other peoples, especially primitive peoples, I am often asked, "Do they really have a religion, or is it all just superstition?" The point of contrast here is not between a scientific and a magical view of the world but between the clear, theologically defensible religious beliefs of members of civilized societies and what we regard as the false and childish views of the heathen who "bow down to wood and stone." Within the civilized religions, however, where membership includes believers who are educated and urbane and others who are ignorant and simple, one always finds traditions and practices that the more sophisticated will dismiss offhand as "just superstition" but that guide the steps of those who live by older ways. Mostly these are very ancient beliefs, some handed on from one religion to another and carried from country to country around the world.

Very commonly, people associate superstition with the past, with very old ways of thinking that have been supplanted by modern knowledge. But new superstitions are continually coming into being and flourishing in our society. Listening to mothers in the park in the 1930's, one heard them say, "Now, don't you run out into the sun, or Polio will get you." In the 1940's elderly people explained to one another in tones of resignation, "It was the Virus that got him down." And every year the cosmetics industry offers us new magic— cures for baldness, lotions that will give every woman radiant skin, hair coloring that will restore to the middle-aged the charm and romance of youth—results that are promised if we will just follow the simple directions. Families and individuals also have their cherished, private superstitions. You must leave by the back door when you are going on a journey, or you must wear a green dress when you are taking an examination. It is a kind of joke, of course, but it makes you feel safe.

These old half-beliefs and new half-beliefs reflect the 9 keenness of our wish to have something come true or to prevent something bad from happening. We do not always recognize new superstitions for what they are, and we still follow the old ones because someone's faith long ago matches our contemporary hopes and fears. In the past people "knew" that a black cat crossing one's path was a bad omen, and they turned back home. Today we are fearful of taking a journey and would give anything to turn back—and then we notice a black cat running across the road in front of us.

Child psychologists recognize the value of the toy a child 10 holds in his hand at bedtime. It is different from his thumb, with which he can close himself in from the rest of the world, and it is different from the real world, to which he is learning to relate himself. Psychologists call these toys—these furry animals and old, cozy baby blankets—"transitional objects"; that is, objects that help the child move back and forth between the exactions of everyday life and the world of wish and dream.

Superstitions have some of the qualities of these transi- 11 tional objects. They help people pass between the areas of life where what happens has to be accepted without proof and the areas where sequences of events are explicable in terms of cause and effect, based on knowledge. Bacteria and viruses that cause sickness have been identified; the cause of symptoms can be diagnosed and a rational course of treatment prescribed. Magical charms no longer are needed to treat the sick; modern medicine has brought the whole sequence of events into the secular world. But people often act as if this change had not taken place. Laymen still treat germs as if they were invisible, malign spirits, and physicians sometimes prescribe antibiotics as if they were magic substances.

Over time, more and more of life has become subject to the controls of knowledge. However, this is never a one-way process. Scientific investigation is continually increasing our knowledge. But if we are to make good use of this knowledge, we must not only rid our minds of old, superseded beliefs and fragments of magical practice, but also recognize new superstitions for what they are. Both are generated by our wishes, our fears and our feeling of helplessness in difficult situations. 12

Civilized peoples are not alone in having grasped the idea of superstitions—beliefs and practices that are superseded but that still may evoke compliance. The idea is one that is familiar to every people, however primitive, that I have ever known. Every society has a core of transcendent beliefs—beliefs about the nature of the universe, the world and man— that no one doubts or questions. Every society also has a fund of knowledge related to practical life—about the succession of day and night and of the seasons; about correct ways of planting seeds so that they will germinate and grow; about the processes involved in making dyes or the steps necessary to remove the deadly poison from manioc roots so they become edible. Island peoples know how the winds shift and they know the star toward which they must point the prow of the canoe exactly so that as the sun rises they will see the first fringing palms on the shore toward which they are sailing. 13

This knowledge, based on repeated observations of reliable sequences, leads to ideas and hypotheses of the kind that underlie scientific thinking. And gradually as scientific knowl- 14 edge, once developed without conscious plan, has become a great self-corrective system and the foundation for rational planning and action, old magical beliefs and observances have had to be discarded.

But it takes time for new ways of thinking to take hold,   15
and often the transition is only partial. Older, more direct beliefs live on in the hearts and minds of elderly people. And they are learned by children who, generation after generation, start out life as hopefully and fearfully as their forebears did. Taking their first steps away from home, children use the old rituals and invent new ones to protect themselves against the strangeness of the world into which they are venturing.

So whatever has been rejected as no longer true, as lim-   16
ited, provincial and idolatrous, still leads a half life. People may say, "It's just a superstition," but they continue to invoke the ritual's protection or potency. In this transitional, twilight state such beliefs come to resemble dreaming. In the dream world a thing can be either good or bad; a cause can be an effect and an effect can be a cause. Do warts come from touching toads, or does touching a toad cure the wart? Is sneezing a good omen or a bad omen? You can have it either way—or both ways at once. In the same sense, the half-acceptance and half-denial accorded superstitions give us the best of both worlds.

Superstitions are sometimes smiled at and sometimes   17
frowned upon as observances characteristic of the old-fashioned, the unenlightened, children, peasants, servants, immigrants, foreigners or backwoods people. Nevertheless, they give all of us ways of moving back and forth among the different worlds in which we live—the sacred, the secular and the scientific. They allow us to keep a private world also, where, smiling a little, we can banish danger with a gesture and summon luck with a rhyme, make the sun shine in spite of storm clouds, force the stranger to do our bidding, keep an enemy at bay and straighten the paths of those we love.

Comment

The contrasting ideas of the essay and the many examples encourage the parallelism of phrases and clauses:

> PHRASES: Sometimes people will preface one of these ritual acts—*walking around instead of under a ladder* or *hastily closing an umbrella that has been opened inside a house*—with such a remark as "I remember my great-aunt used to . . ." or "Germans used to say you ought not . . ." (paragraph 5)

The two quotations—both independent clauses—are also parallel in idea but not in their wording. In the following sentence, the similar wording underscores the similarity in idea:

> CLAUSES: *You must leave* by the back door *when you are going* on a journey, or *you must wear* a green dress *when you are taking* an examination. (paragraph 8)

Many sentences of the essay are *balanced* in this way—their phrases and clauses are of approximately the same length and wording and show the similarity in ideas. When parallelism is used to contrast ideas, the sentence is said to contain *antithesis:*

> The point of contrast here is *not between a scientific and a magical view of the world* but *between the clear, theologically defensible religious beliefs* of members of civilized societies and what we regard as the false and childish views of the heathen who "bow down to wood and stone" (paragraph 7).

The greater the balance and antithesis in sentences, the greater the formality of the writing. To avoid too formal an effect, writers vary the length of parallel phrases and clauses.

Questions for Study and Discussion

1. What sentences in paragraphs 6, 8, 10, and 13 contain parallel phrases? Are these phrases used to show similarity or difference? Are the wording and the length of the phrases the same?
2. What sentences in paragraphs 7, 11, and 13 contain parallel

clauses? Are these clauses used to show similarity or difference, and are the wording and the length the same?

3. Mead and Metraux discuss "the different worlds in which we live—the sacred, the secular and the scientific." What distinguishes the "sacred" from the "secular" world? And why is the "scientific" a different world from the sacred and the secular?

4. How does the distinction between the sacred, the secular, and the scientific world help Mead and Metraux define superstition? What is a superstition?

5. What is the order of ideas in the essay?

Vocabulary Study

1. Why do Mead and Metraux use the word *secular* instead of the word *everyday* to distinguish a different world and kind of belief?

2. How different is the definition of superstition in the essay from the definition in your dictionary? What do you think accounts for the difference, if any?

3. Explain the following: *derogatory term* (paragraph 4); *sophisticated home, evokes the memory* (paragraph 5); *freighted with magic* (paragraph 6); *theologically defensible* (paragraph 7); *contemporary hopes and fears* (paragraph 9); *exactions of everyday life* (paragraph 10); *transitional objects, laymen* (paragraph 11); *superseded beliefs and fragments* (paragraph 12); *evoke compliance, core of transcendent beliefs* (paragraph 13); *hypotheses* (paragraph 14); *ritual's protection or potency* (paragraph 16).

Suggestions for Writing

1. Discuss a superstition that you regularly observe. In the course of your essay, discuss the origin of the superstition, its effects on your thinking and behavior, and how much support these details give to Mead and Metraux on the nature of superstition.

2. Write an essay on one of the following statements, drawing upon your own experience and observations:

   a. "Actually, almost every day, even in the most sophisticated home, something is likely to happen that evokes the memory of some old folk belief."

b.   "We do not always recognize new superstitions for what they are, and we still follow the old ones because someone's faith long ago matches our contemporary hopes and fears."

Sentence Variety

Sentences need to be varied to avoid a sense of monotony. Thus a series of short simple sentences like the following will soon lose the reader's attention:

> You are watching coal miners at work. You realize momentarily what different universes people inhabit. It is a sort of world apart down there. One can quite easily go through life without ever hearing about that world. Probably a majority of people would even prefer not to hear about it.

Few people think or write in such a disconnected way. Here is the actual version of the sentences above:

> Watching coal miners at work, you realize momentarily what different universes different people inhabit. *Down there* where coal is dug it is a sort of world apart *which* one can quite easily go through life without ever hearing about. Probably a majority of people would even prefer not to hear about it.—George Orwell, *The Road to Wigan Pier* (italics added)

Orwell varied his sentences probably as most writers do—without much conscious attention. The italicized connectives come naturally to us as we speak or write: it is the disconnection in the first version

367

of the passage that is unnatural. Indeed, it takes some effort to write in so fragmented and disjointed a way. The rewritten sentences are not only monotonous but hard to understand because we must continually refocus our attention.

As a rule, the more varied the length and construction of our sentences, the less monotonous they are likely to be, and the more apparent the natural emphasis we wish to give our ideas. Notice the choices open to the writer in combining the following:

> You are watching coal miners at work. You realize momentarily what different universes people inhabit.

Orwell might have written:

> As you watch coal miners at work, you realize momentarily what different universes people inhabit.

Or:

> You realize momentarily what different universes people inhabit, as you watch coal miners at work.

Or:

> Watching coal miners at work makes one realize momentarily what different universes people inhabit.

These varied sentences achieve emphasis in different ways. In the first, the emphasis falls on the idea of different universes; in the second, on watching the miners at work. The third sentence gives the same emphasis to both ideas. Which sentence the writer chooses depends on what is emphasized in the whole paragraph or essay. And as Orwell's paragraph shows, the choice can depend on making the connection of ideas clear.

Russell Baker
The Beer Culture

> Russell Baker was born in 1925 in Loudon County, Virginia, and studied at Johns Hopkins University. He joined the staff of

the *Baltimore Sun,* and from 1954 to 1962 worked in the Washington office of the *New York Times.* Since 1963 he has written a column for the *Times,* in which the essay reprinted here first appeared. Baker writes humorously about all aspects of American life—its political life, urban life, and everyday experiences such as he discusses here. One of the pleasures of reading a columnist like Baker is that of discovering a special point of view and humor and enjoying it from column to column. Baker's essays have been collected in a number of books that include *All Things Considered* (1965), *Our Next President* (1968), and *So This Is Depravity* (1980). In 1979 Baker was awarded a Pulitzer Prize in journalism.

The people of Beer World are named Buck, Mike, Al and 1
Mac. There are no Algernons in Beer World, no Marmadukes, no Gaylords. Beer World has hair on its chest.

Yes, there are a few women in Beer World. They are 2
named Gladys, though there is one named Elvira. You have seen the woman who brings a tray of beer to Buck, Mike, Al and Mac while they are sitting in the beer parlor in their mackinaws being rugged and jolly? Of course you have seen her. That woman is Gladys.

You may also have seen Buck recently having his beer at 3
a distinctly sissified ski lodge in company with a lissome young woman. That woman is Elvira. Buck sometimes takes Elvira to these sissy places in order to experience the perfection of beer without sweating.

Buck often feels guilty after these perspiration-free out- 4
ings with Elvira, for in Beer World it is man's duty to heave and grunt until his pores open and let the honest body juices cascade freely. Only then does he truly deserve beer. Beer is the reward for manly toil in Beer World.

How often have you seen Buck, Mike, Al and Mac ex- 5
hausted at the end of an honest day's work on the firing squad, sleeves rolled up, shirt collars opened, perspiration dampening their cheeks as they labor to rid the world of malcontents, looters and sissies—how often have you seen them joyfully

throw down their tools as the sun sets, embrace each other merrily and tramp over to Gladys's place for their beer?

Now comes beer time. The beer has been created for Buck, Mike, Al and Mac in recognition of their labor, in recognition of all they do. The beer is for them. Not for Algernon. Not for Marmaduke and Gaylord. Someone will object that we never really see the boys putting in a full day's work on the firing squad, that all we ever see are the final few executions at sunset. But of course; in Beer World, sunset is the only time of day. The sun stands eternally in the setting position. Shortly after Buck, Mike, Al and Mac throw down their rifles, or their scythes or their big tractor-trailers, and receive their beer from Gladys, they tramp out into the sunset again and finish building a skyscraper so they can throw down their rivet guns and march back to Gladys's place for another round of well-earned beer.

Why does Buck occasionally sneak away to sissified places with Elvira to drink his beer in dry clothing? Surely Buck would rather be with Mike, Al and Mac arriving at Beer World's cottage by the lake in their plaid fishing shirts.

Of course, Buck would. It is much more fun racing to the refrigerator with Mike, Al and Mac and discovering four bottles of chilled beer than it is sitting across a table from Elvira. Is Buck—let us phrase the question as delicately as possible—is Buck soft on women?

The question is often raised by Mike, Al and Mac when they are all having dinner together in order to deserve a beer, or jogging twenty miles together just at sunset in order to earn the right really to enjoy a beer. Once they even asked Doc—Beer World's psychiatrist—to put Buck on the couch, give him a bottle of beer and find out if he was really one of the boys.

Doc had just finished whipping a massive superego down to size and was headed to Gladys's place for his beer when he conducted the examination. He pronounced Buck a perfectly normal beer guy with a slight woman problem.

It seems Buck had a mother, which is very rare in Beer

World. In his youth, "Old Moms," as Buck called her, used to send him to the corner saloon to buy her what she called "a bucket of suds." "Old Moms" had since been deported under Beer World's rigid legal code, which denies citizenship to most women, especially if, like "Old Moms," they sit around the house in dresses made from flour sacks drinking beer out of tin buckets.

The law was necessary because people like "Old Moms" created a bad image of Beer World, which wanted to be viewed as a sweaty but clean-cut place full of boys whose beer had fewer calories and whose mothers, if they must have mothers, wouldn't be caught dead wearing flour sacks. In short, Buck felt bad about the old lady's deportation; when he took Elvira out for beer, he was really taking out his mother who had learned to dress expensively and to drink her beer out of a glass.   12

Elvira actually despises beer and would much prefer a drink with Amaretto in it, but doesn't dare order it for fear Buck would accuse her of not being one of the boys and walk out of her life forever. The women of Beer World do not have much opportunity to get out for a good time. Elvira has often asked Gladys to go out and have some Amaretto with her, but Gladys is afraid that if the boys learned about it they would call her a sissy.   13

Comment

Baker satirizes not just the characters and situations in beer ads but also, in the phrase of Walker Gibson, their "tough talk." Gibson characterizes tough talk through its "short sentences, 'crude' repetitions of words, simple grammatical structures with little subordinating." The tough talker seeking a "tense intimacy with his assumed reader, another man who has been around." The tough talker favors "colloquial patterns from oral speech and . . . a high frequency of the definite article. He lets his reader make logical and other connections between elements" *(Tough, Sweet, and Stuffy)*. In short, tough talk is marked by the monotony of its sentences—the lack of variety that Baker is imitating.

Questions for Study and Discussion

1. The essay opens with three short simple sentences—all lacking modification. These illustrate one of the characteristics of Gibson's "tough talk." What other paragraphs also contain relatively simple or short sentences, compound or complex sentences?
2. How much " 'crude' repetition of words" do you find throughout the essay?
3. How often does Baker depend on "colloquial patterns from oral speech" and a "high frequency of the definite article"?
4. In imitating the tough talker through the style of the essay, Baker is characterizing the tough-talking advertiser. What does he gain satirically in imitating the speech of this person?
5. What does the essay reveal about the personality, outlook, and sense of humor of Russell Baker?
6. What satirical points is Baker making not only about beer ads but also about the "beer culture"? Is the essay closer to social satire than to ethical satire (p. 315)?
7. How effective do you find the satire?

Vocabulary Study

Baker depends on connotation—the associations and emotional auras of words—to convey the tone and attitudes about the beer culture. What do the following words mean? What connotations do they convey?

a. paragraph 3: *lissome*
b. paragraph 4: *cascade*
c. paragraph 5: *malcontents, sissies*
d. paragraph 10: *massive superego, slight woman problem*
e. paragraph 13: *Amaretto*

Suggestions for Writing

1. Compare Baker's treatment of beer ads with Michael J. Arlen's treatment of soap ads. Comment on the language and the tone of each essay and the presentation of a thesis.

2. Write a satirical essay on another series of ads depicting a different kind of world—perhaps the world of soda-drinking teenagers. Let your descriptive details and tone convey your thesis.

John Updike
Eclipse

As an undergraduate at Harvard, John Updike edited the humor magazine the *Lampoon*. In 1955 he joined the staff of *The New Yorker*, for which he continues to write poems, stories, and essays. Many of his stories and novels describe Shillington, Pennsylvania, where he grew up, and Ipswich, Massachusetts, where he now lives. His many novels include *Rabbit, Run* (the first of a series on the same character), *The Poor-House Fair, The Centaur, The Coup, Couples,* and most recently *The Witches of Eastwich.*

I went out into the backyard and the usually roundish spots of dappled sunlight underneath the trees were all shaped like feathers, crescent in the same direction, from left to right. Though it was five o'clock on a summer afternoon, the birds were singing good-bye to the day, and their merged song seemed to soak the strange air in an additional strangeness. A kind of silence prevailed. Few cars were moving on the streets of the town. Of my children only the baby dared come into the yard with me. She wore only underpants, and as she stood beneath a tree, bulging her belly toward me in the mood of jolly flirtation she has grown into at the age of two, her bare skin was awash with pale crescents. It crossed my mind that she might be harmed, but I couldn't think how. *Cancer?*

The eclipse was to be over 90 percent in our latitude and   2
the newspapers and television for days had been warning us
not to look at it. I looked up, a split-second Prometheus, and
looked away. The bitten silhouette of the sun lingered redly
on my retinas. The day was half-cloudy, and my impression
had been of the sun struggling, amid a furious knotted huddle of black and silver clouds, with an enemy too dreadful to
be seen, with an eater as ghostly and hungry as time. Every
blade of grass cast a long bluish-brown shadow, as at dawn.

My wife shouted from behind the kitchen screen door that   3
as long as I was out there I might as well burn the waste-
paper. She darted from the house, eyes downcast, with the
wastebasket, and darted back again, leaving the naked baby
and me to wander up through the strained sunlight to the
wire trash barrel. After my forbidden peek at the sun, the
flames dancing transparently from the blackening paper—yesterday's Boston *Globe,* a milk carton, a Hi-Ho cracker box—
seemed dimmer than shadows, and in the teeth of all the
warnings I looked up again. The clouds seemed bunched and
twirled as if to plug a hole in the sky, and the burning after-
image was the shape of a near-new moon, horns pointed down.
It was gigantically unnatural, and I lingered in the yard under
the vague apprehension that in some future life I might be
called before a cosmic court to testify to this assault. I seemed
to be the sole witness. The town around my yard was hushed,
all but the singing of the birds, who were invisible. The feathers
under the trees had changed direction, and curved from right
to left.

Then I saw my neighbor sitting on her porch. My neigh-   4
bor is a widow, with white hair and brown skin; she has in
her yard an aluminum-and-nylon-net chaise longue on which
she lies at every opportunity, head back, arms spread, pros-
trate under the sun. Now she hunched dismally on her porch
steps in the shade, which was scarcely darker than the light.
I walked toward her and hailed her as a visitor to the moon
might salute a survivor of a previous expedition. "How do
you like the eclipse?" I called over the fence that distin-

guished our holdings on this suddenly insubstantial and lunar earth.

"I don't like it," she answered, shading her face with a   5
hand. "They say you shouldn't go out in it."

"I thought it was just you shouldn't look at it."   6

"There's something in the rays," she explained, in a voice   7
far louder than it needed to be, for silence framed us. "I shut all the windows on that side of the house and had to come out for some air."

"I think it'll pass," I told her.   8

"Don't let the baby look up," she warned, and turned away   9
from talking to me, as if the open use of her voice exposed her more fatally to the rays.

Superstition, I thought, walking back through my yard,   10
clutching my child's hand as tightly as a good-luck token. There was no question in her touch. Day, night, twilight, noon were all wonders to her, unscheduled, free from all bondage of prediction. The sun was being restored to itself and soon would radiate influence as brazenly as ever—and in this sense my daughter's blind trust was vindicated. Nevertheless, I was glad that the eclipse had passed, as it were, over her head; for in my own life I felt a certain assurance evaporate forever under the reality of the sun's disgrace.

Comment

Updike's sentences create the mood of the essay—expressing a variety of impressions and ideas through their contrasting structure and length. The short sentences are particularly striking because Updike uses them sparingly:

> Though it was five o'clock on a summer afternoon, the birds were singing good-bye to the day, and their merged song seemed to soak the strange air in an additional strangeness. A kind of silence prevailed. Few cars were moving on the streets of the town.

Throughout the essay short sentences convey surprise or drama or a stark impression. Contrasting longer sentences like the first in the passage quoted usually provide explanation and connect facts and ideas; they suggest the slow process of reflection and the building of impressions:

> The town around my yard was hushed, all but the singing of the birds, who were invisible.

Questions for Study and Discussion

1. What contrasting length and structure do you find in the sentences of paragraph 2? How does this sentence variety help to create the mood of the experience?
2. How many of the sentences throughout the essay end with modifying phrases or clauses? Are these sentences less dramatic than the occasional short sentences?
3. How is the narrator's attitude toward the eclipse different from that of the woman on the porch and that of his wife? What idea emerges in the essay through these differences?
4. What does Updike mean by the statement, "I felt a certain assurance evaporate forever under the reality of the sun's disgrace"?

Vocabulary Study

Explain the following words and phrases:

a. paragraph 1: *dappled sunlight, crescent in the same direction*
b. paragraph 2: *split-second Prometheus*
c. paragraph 3: *the strained sunlight, cosmic court*
d. paragraph 4: *insubstantial and lunar earth*
e. paragraph 10: *brazenly*

Suggestions for Writing

1. Write an essay in which you show an event and develop a central idea or thesis through contrasting points of view. Build to a statement of that idea as Updike does.
2. Write an essay on one of the following topics. Let your details reveal your central idea or thesis. Do not state it explicitly:
    a. on watching a storm or snowfall
    b. on a sudden change in season
    c. on moving to a new neighborhood
    d. on entering a new school

part six

Effective Diction

Formal and informal writing share the basic word stock of English at all levels. But each also favors different kinds of words. The everyday words or colloquialisms of your speech are also the words that you probably use in your informal letters to friends. The following statement is typical of the informal style in newspaper columns and books today:

> The excitement of the rodeo comes not so much from the competition between the cowboys themselves as from the competition between man and animal. The fans, of course, are partisans; they root for their own species. The crowd always cheers when a cowboy wins even if they've never heard of the chap. But the animals must be good, or the contest will be no fun. The horses, bulls, steers, and calves are thus all bred and raised especially for their spunk.—Ray Raphael, *Edges*

As these sentences show, informal writing is much tighter than speech, though the informal style favors loosely strung, coordinated sentences. The familiar phrases and colloquial words, however, best mark the writing as informal.

Formal writing, by contrast, favors abstract words suited to the discussion of ideas. The following statement is typical of formal writing directed to a general reader:

> Lincoln was a pre-eminent example of that self-help which Americans have always so admired. He was not, of course, the first eminent American politician who could claim humble origins, nor the first to exploit them. But few have been able to point to such a sudden ascent from relative obscurity to high eminence; none has maintained so completely while scaling the heights the aspect of extreme simplicity; and none has combined with the attainment of success and power such an intense awareness of humanity and moral responsibility. It was precisely in his attainments as a common man that Lincoln felt himself to be remarkable, and in this light that he interpreted to the world the significance of his career.—Richard Hofstadter, *The American Political Tradition*

Much formal writing is usually directed to a particular audience familiar with the special terms or jargon that may be used:

> The grammar of English will generate, for each sentence, a deep structure, and will contain rules showing how this deep structure is related to a surface structure. The rules expressing the relation of deep and surface structure are called "grammatical transformations."—Noam Chomsky, *Language and Mind*

Much writing at the general level combines informal with formal features—sometimes a tight sentence structure with a highly informal vocabulary. The choices you make in your own writing depend upon your topic and audience. An abstract subject such as "grammatical transformations" sometimes invites a formal style, a concrete subject like the rodeo sometimes invites an informal style; and much depends also on what style you believe is suited to a particular audience. You know what is appropriate from what you read and hear, but styles usually are governed by use.

Every style also has its hazards. Formal sentences that depart too far from colloquial English become exceedingly hard to understand, and the injection of technical jargon is often inappropriate for a general audience:

> But already at a point in economic evolution far antedating the emergence of the lady, specialized consumption of goods as an evidence of pecuniary strength had begun to work out in a more

or less elaborate system—Thorstein Veblen, *Theory of the Leisure Class*

The formal style here invites other faults. This overprecise sentence, in which theoretical terms describe simple ideas, will give many readers trouble. "Pecuniary strength" means nothing more than having money. And by "specialized consumption of goods" Veblen means buying obviously expensive things, or in colloquial English, "putting on the dog."

In informal style overused phrases can make informal writing seem stale. The phrase "putting on the dog"—a popular colloquialism—loses its color in writing through over-familiarity. We refer to phrases of this kind as clichés. Informal sentence style can also be as troublesome. When most of the sentences are strung together loosely, the essay becomes monotonous. At its best, informal writing should remind us of the speech that varies its sentences patterns and does not drone.

Writing at all three levels contains metaphors and other figures of speech. In expressive writing such as the next essay by Annie Dillard on the coming of spring, metaphor may be highly colorful—expressing the special feelings and perceptions of the writer:

> This is the hoop of flame that shoots the rapids in the creek or spins across the dizzy meadows; this is the arsonist of the sunny woods. . . .

In informative writing, as in David R. Scott's description of his moon walk, figurative language is often not so obvious:

> The flowing moonscape, unmarred by a single jagged peak, reminds me of earth's uplands covered by a heavy blanket of fresh snow.

The essays that follow illustrate choices in diction open to you. There are no rules for deciding what style or what kind of diction is appropriate to particular subjects or audiences. A sense of appropriateness comes only with wide reading and the awareness that writers achieve different effects with different means and in no predictable ways.

Annie Dillard

Untying the Knot

Annie Dillard was born in 1945 in Pittsburgh and attended
Hollins College. A sensitive and close observer of nature, she lived
in the Roanoke Valley of Virginia for ten years and then moved
to Puget Sound in the Pacific Northwest. She has written three
books: *Tickets for a Prayer Wheel* (1974), a book of poems; *Pilgrim at Tinker Creek* (1974), for which she received a Pulitzer
Prize; and *Holy the Firm* (1978) a meditation.

Yesterday I set out to catch the new season, and instead   1
I found an old snakeskin. I was in the sunny February woods
by the quarry; the snakeskin was lying in a heap of leaves right
next to an aquarium someone had thrown away. I don't know
why that someone hauled the aquarium deep into the woods
to get rid of it; it had only one broken glass side. The snake
found it handy, I imagine; snakes like to rub against something rigid to help them out of their skins, and the broken
aquarium looked like the nearest likely object. Together the
snakeskin and the aquarium made an interesting scene on the
forest floor. It looked like an exhibit at a trial—circumstantial
evidence—of a wild scene, as though a snake had burst through
the broken side of the aquarium, burst through his ugly old
skin, and disappeared, perhaps straight up in the air, in a rush
of freedom and beauty.

The snakeskin had unkeeled scales, so it belonged to a   2
nonpoisonous snake. It was roughly five feet long by the
yardstick, but I'm not sure because it was very wrinkled and
dry, and every time I tried to stretch it flat it broke. I ended
up with seven or eight pieces of it all over the kitchen table
in a fine film of forest dust.

The point I want to make about the snakeskin is that, 3 when I found it, it was whole and tied in a knot. Now there have been stories told, even by reputable scientists, of snakes that have deliberately tied themselves in a knot to prevent larger snakes from trying to swallow them—but I couldn't imagine any way that throwing itself into a half hitch would help a snake trying to escape its skin. Still, ever cautious, I figured that one of the neighborhood boys could possibly have tied it in a knot in the fall, for some whimsical boyish reason, and left it there, where it dried and gathered dust. So I carried the skin along thoughtlessly as I walked, snagging it sure enough on a low branch and ripping it in two for the first of many times. I saw that thick ice still lay on the quarry pond and that the skunk cabbage was already out in the clearings, and then I came home and looked at the skin and its knot.

The knot had no beginning. Idly I turned it around in 4 my hand, searching for a place to untie; I came to with a start when I realized I must have turned the thing around fully ten times. Intently, then, I traced the knot's lump around with a finger: it was continuous. I couldn't untie it any more than I could untie a doughnut; it was a loop without beginning or end. These snakes *are* magic, I thought for a second, and then of course I reasoned what must have happened. The skin had been pulled inside-out like a peeled sock for several inches; then an inch or so of the inside-out part—a piece whose length was coincidentally equal to the diameter of the skin—had somehow been turned right-side out again, making a thick lump whose edges were lost in wrinkles, looking exactly like a knot.

So. I have been thinking about the change of seasons. I 5 don't want to miss spring this year. I want to distinguish the last winter frost from the out-of-season one, the frost of spring. I want to be there on the spot the moment the grass turns green. I always miss this radical revolution; I see it the next day from a window, the yard so suddenly green and lush I could envy Nebuchadnezzar down on all fours eating grass. This year I want to stick a net into time and say "now," as men plant flags on the ice and snow and say, "here." But it occurred to me that I could no more catch spring by the tip of the tail than I could untie the apparent knot in the snakeskin; there are no edges to grasp. Both are continuous loops.

I wonder how long it would take you to notice the regular recurrence of the seasons if you were the first man on earth. What would it be like to live in open-ended time broken only by days and nights? You could say, "it's cold again; it was cold before," but you couldn't make the key connection and say, "it was cold this time last year," because the notion of "year" is precisely the one you lack. Assuming that you hadn't yet noticed any orderly progression of heavenly bodies, how long would you have to live on earth before you could feel with any assurance that any one particular long period of cold would, in fact, end? "While the earth remaineth, seedtime and harvest, and cold and heat, and summer and winter, and day and night shall not cease": God makes this guarantee very early in Genesis to a people whose fears on this point had perhaps not been completely allayed. 6

It must have been fantastically important, at the real beginnings of human culture, to conserve and relay this vital seasonal information, so that the people could anticipate dry or cold seasons, and not huddle on some November rock hoping pathetically that spring was just around the corner. We still very much stress the simple fact of four seasons to school children; even the most modern of modern new teachers, who don't seem to care if their charges can read or write or name two products of Peru, will still muster some seasonal chitchat and set the kids to making paper pumpkins, or tulips, for the walls. "The people," wrote Van Gogh in a letter, "are very sensitive to the changing seasons." That we are "very sensitive to the changing seasons" is, incidentally, one of the few good reasons to shun travel. If I stay at home I preserve the illusion that what is happening on Tinker Creek is the very newest thing, that I'm at the very vanguard and cutting edge of each new season. I don't want the same season twice in a row; I don't want to know I'm getting last week's weather, 7 used weather, weather broadcast up and down the coast, old-hat weather.

But there's always unseasonable weather. What we think 8 of the weather and behavior of life on the planet at any given season is really all a matter of statistical probabilities; at any given point, anything might happen. There is a bit of every season in each season. Green plants—deciduous green leaves—grow everywhere, all winter long, and small shoots come up pale and new in every season. Leaves die on the tree in May, turn brown, and fall into the creek. The calendar, the weather, and the behavior of wild creatures have the slimmest of connections. Everything overlaps smoothly for only a few weeks each season, and then it all tangles up again. The temperature, of course, lags far behind the calendar seasons, since the earth absorbs and releases heat slowly, like a leviathan breathing. Migrating birds head south in what appears to be dire panic, leaving mild weather and fields full of insects and seeds; they reappear as if in all eagerness in January, and poke about morosely in the snow. Several years ago our October woods would have made a dismal colored photograph for a sadist's calendar: a killing frost came before the leaves had even begun to brown; they drooped from every tree like crepe, blackened and limp. It's all a chancy, jumbled affair at best, as things seem to be below the stars.

Time is the continuous loop, the snakeskin with scales 9 endlessly overlapping without beginning or end, or time is an ascending spiral if you will, like a child's toy Slinky. Of course we have no idea which arc on the loop is our time, let alone where the loop itself is, so to speak, or down whose lofty flight of stairs the Slinky so uncannily walks.

The power we seek, too, seems to be a continuous loop. 10 I have always been sympathetic with the early notion of a divine power that exists in a particular place, or that travels about over the face of the earth as a man might wander—and when he is "there" he is surely not here. You can shake the hand of a man you meet in the woods; but the spirit seems to roll along like the mythical hoop snake with its tail in its mouth.

There are no hands to shake or edges to untie. It rolls along the mountain ridges like a fireball, shooting off a spray of sparks at random, and will not be trapped, slowed, grasped, fetched, peeled, or aimed. "As for the wheels, it was cried unto them in my hearing, O wheel." This is the hoop of flame that shoots the rapids in the creek or spins across the dizzy meadows; this is the arsonist of the sunny woods; catch it if you can.

Comment

Metaphor is particularly appropriate to the ideas of this essay. Dillard uses the knotted snakeskin as a metaphor for existence. She makes her point directly: she can no more "catch spring by the tip of the tail" than she can untie the knot—"there are no edges to grasp. Both are continuous loops." She builds carefully to this statement, the full meaning emerging in the details of her account. The open feeling of spring stands for a larger experience: the sense of "open-ended time." Dillard wants to see the world anew at each moment, though she knows that experiences repeat themselves. That is why she does not want to "catch spring by the tip of the tail." It would fix the experience instead of keeping it open. Having explored these ideas, she can finish her analogy—"Time is the continuous loop"—and she thinks also of a divine power that is everywhere always. It is the oneness and at the same time the variousness of nature that she seeks to express through figurative language.

Questions for Study and Discussion

1. The power of nature, and its openness, are symbolized in many ways in the essay. How is it symbolized at the end?
2. Dillard moves from ordinary experience to the extraordinary. What words and phrases suggest the extraordinary and mysterious qualities of life as the essay proceeds?
3. What use does Dillard make of the Bible (Daniel 4:25) in paragraph 5?
4. In how many ways is the knotted snakeskin used in the essay?

That is, how many references do you find to entanglement and overlapping?

5. How does the author characterize herself through her response to the snakeskin and the world of Tinker Creek?

6. What use does Dillard make of personification?

Vocabulary Study

Write a paraphrase of the final paragraph, translating similes, metaphors, and other figures of speech into literal language.

Suggestions for Writing

1. Write about your feelings and thoughts concerning a season of the year. Focus your discussion on an object you associate with this season. You may want to explore the various qualities of the object and what these tell you about the season.

2. Develop one of the ideas of the essay from your point of view and personal experience.

Concreteness

To make an idea *concrete* is to make it exist for the reader through the senses. The statement "That car's a beauty!" expresses a general attitude and feeling but nothing more. If we want people to share our experience we must give particulars or details, as in this explanation of what California teenagers mean by the expression "low and slow, mean and clean":

> The car a lowrider drives—almost always a sedan produced by the General Motors Corporation—is also called a lowrider, or a ride. If it has been altered with conspicuous success—a multi-colored lacquer paint job, say, and metal-spoke wheels, and skimpy tires that seem to belong on a Datsun rather than a 1967 Chevrolet Impala, and a welded-chain steering wheel no bigger around than a 45-r.p.m. record—it is called a clean ride, or a bad ride. "Low and slow," lowriders sometimes say. "Mean and clean."— Calvin Trillin and Edward Koren, "Low and Slow, Mean and Clean"

Not all abstract ideas can be expressed through physical details. We can, however, show their application to experience or suggest how we came to the idea; or we can give the details that explain it.

In a discussion of the emotional makeup of human beings, Desmond Morris says that people enjoy exploring their emotions. Man, he says, "is constantly pushing things to their limit, trying to startle himself, to shock himself without getting hurt, and then signaling his relief with peals of infectious laughter." The abstract idea is here made specific; for we are told what people *do*. But Morris makes the idea even more concrete through the behavior of teenagers when their idols perform on stage. "As an audience, they enjoy themselves, not by screaming with laughter, but screaming with screams. They not only scream, they also grip their own and one another's bodies, they writhe, they moan, they cover their faces and they pull at their hair." From these details he draws a conclusion:

> These are all the classic signs of intense pain or fear, but they have become deliberately stylized. . . . They are no longer cries for help, but signals to one another in the audience that they are capable of feeling an emotional response to the sexual idols which is so powerful that, like all stimuli of unbearably high intensity, they pass into the realm of pure pain.—*The Naked Ape*

The idea has been made concrete. At the same time, we must be careful not to give more details than we need to make the idea clear. Writing can be so colorful—so crowded with details and descriptive words—that the reader is distracted from the main idea.

William G. Wing
Christmas Comes First on the Banks

William G. Wing was a veteran correspondent of the *New York Herald Tribune*. He is a specialist on natural resources and conservation, writing for *Audubon Magazine,* the *New York Times,* and other periodicals. This evocative essay shows how a popular subject can be written about freshly from a new and unusual point of view.

The Christmas sun rises first, in America, on trawlermen   1
fishing the undersea meadows of Georges Bank.

At the moment before sunrise a hundred miles east of Cape   2
Cod, the scene aboard a trawler is so unchanging it can be
imagined. The net has been hauled and streamed again. The
skipper is alone in the pilot house, surrounded by the radio-
telephone's racket and the green and amber eyes of electronic instruments, instruments that are supposed to tell him
not only where he is but where the fish are, too. But this is
only hope, not science. Despite the instruments, despite the
boat's resemblance to a plow horse, methodically criss-cross-
ing the meadow, her men are not engineers or farmers, but
hunters who seek their prey in the wilderness of the sea. The
trawlermen are, in fact, the last tribe of nomadic huntsmen
left in the East.

The skipper is alone, then, with a huntsman's anxieties: 3
the whereabouts of the prey, the uncertainties of the weather,
the chances of hitting a good market. On deck before him
the men are processing the catch just brought aboard. They
sit in a circle of brilliance, the deck lights reflecting from their
yellow and Daybrite-orange oilskins and from the brown curve
of the riding sail above. They sit on the edges of the pens,
holding the big white and silver fish between their knees, ripping with knives and tearing with hands, heaving the disem-
boweled bodies into a central basket. Nothing is visible beyond
the cone of light but the occasional flash of a whitecap or
comber. There is much noise, though—wind and water and
seabirds that have gathered in mobs for the feast of haulback.

There is an appropriateness to Christmas in this scene,   4
east of the sleeping mainland, so marked that it seems quaint.
The names of the trawlers themselves—*Holy Family, Immac-*
ulate Conception, St. Mary, St. Joseph—give the flavor. On the
engine room bulkhead of a trawler *Holy Cross,* beyond the
ugga-chugging Atlas diesel, is a painting of Christ at Geth-
semane. There is an appropriateness, too, among the men.
They share alike—equal shares of profit, equal shares of danger. To work together in such small quarters and stern con-

ditions requires a graciousness of spirit that is the essence of Christmas.

The sun is up and the pens are empty. As the deck is hosed ₅ down and the trash fish pitchforked overboard, the noise from the birds rises hysterically—barnyard sounds, shrieks, whistles, klaxon horns. Now the birds can be seen flying in a circle around the boat. Each can hold position for only a few moments beside the point where the remains of fish are washing over. Then it falls astern and has to come up to windward on the other side of the boat, cross ahead and fall backward to the critical point. The birds pumping up the windward side look like six-day bicycle riders, earnest and slightly ridiculous, but when they reach the critical point there is a miraculous moment of aerobatics as the birds brake, wheel and drop in the broken air.

Gulls snatch, gannets plunge, but the little kittiwakes bal- ₆ ance delicately, their tails spread like carved ivory fans. There is a column of descending, shrieking birds, a scintillating feathered mass. The birds revolving about the boat have made themselves not only guests at the feast but have formed the wreath as well.

Christmas Day has begun, but for the men it is time to ₇ sleep. They hose each other off and then disappear through the whaleback for a mug-up below. Boots and oilskins off, they will have a minute or two for a James Bond novel or a crossword puzzle in the bunks, braced against the elevator motions of the hull, not hearing the sounds of Niagara outside. Then the instant unconsciousness that seamen and children know. The skipper alone remains awake, watching Christmas come.

Christmas came first to men on lonely meadows. It will ₈ come first again to the men on the lonely meadows offshore, fishing the Bank in boats wreathed by seabirds.

Comment

The author tells us that he will seek to make the moment before the sun rises concrete: he will find images that convey the mood and experience of the moment. He does so in the details of the boat, the trawlermen, their relations—"equal shares of profits, equal shares of danger." The seabirds have an unexpected appropriateness, for they wreathe the boats in their circlings. Through careful selection of details, the author succeeds in his purpose; through his description, he is able to make a point without stating it directly.

Questions for Study and Discussion

1. What point is the author making through his description? Is it important to him where the Christmas sun first rises in America?
2. Is the order of details governed by space (moving from one part of the scene to another) or by time, or possibly both?
3. What details or qualities of the scene—stated and implied— suggest Christmas in some way?
4. Is the author saying that the life aboard the trawler and the relations between the men are different during the Christmas season or on Christmas day?
5. How does the author make transitions throughout the essay?
6. What is the point of the concluding comparison?

Vocabulary Study

For each of the following words, list at least two synonyms that suggest a more specific meaning or use. For example, *forecast* is more specific than *foretell* when referring to a weather prediction.

   a. *large*
   b. *small*
   c. *dirty*
   d. *clean*
   e. *law*
   f. *run*

Suggestions for Writing

1. Describe a scene at a particular moment—for example, the moment of impact in an automobile accident. Select details that

contribute to a central impression, but do not state the impression directly.

2. Describe a day of work, showing how the season of the year affects you and your fellow workers. Use your description to develop a thesis.

3. Describe an unusual day in your life—one that perhaps was spent in an unusual setting, away from home. Stress those feelings and details that made the day unusual and memorable.

Carol Bly
Great Snows

Carol Bly lives in her native Minnesota. She has been a visiting writer and lecturer at various schools in Minnesota, and has written short stories and poetry for *The New Yorker* and other magazines. Her essay on Minnesota winters appears in her collection of essays originally written for a newspaper in Madison, Minnesota—*Letters from the Country*.

> How strange to think of giving up all ambition!
> Suddenly I see with such clear eyes
> The white flake of snow
> That has just fallen in the horse's mane.
> —"Watering the Horse," by Robert Bly, *Silence
> in the Snowy Fields*

It is sometimes mistakenly thought by city people that grown-ups don't love snow. They think only children who haven't got to shovel it love snow, or only people like the von Fürstenburgs and their friends who get to go skiing in exotic places and will never backslope a roadside in all their lives: that is a mistake. The fact is that most country or small-town Minnesotans love snow. They relish snow in large inconvenient storms; they like the excesses of it, they like the threat of it, the endless work of it, the glamour of it.

Before a storm, Madison is full of people excitedly laying in food stocks for the three-day blow. People lay in rather celebratory food, too. Organic-food parents get chocolate for the children; weight watchers lay in macaroni and Sara Lee Cakes; recently-converted vegetarians backslide to T-bones. People hang around the large Super-Valu window and keep a tough squinty-eyed watch on the storm progress with a lot of gruff, sensible observations (just like Houston Control talking to the moon, very much on top of it all) like "Ja, we need this for spring moisture . . ." or "Ja, it doesn't look like letting up at all . . ." or "Ja, you can see where it's beginning to drift up behind the VFW." The plain pleasure of it is scarcely hidden.

That is before the storm. Then the town empties out as the farmers and their families take their stocks home before U.S. 75, Minnesota 40, and Lac Qui Parle 19 close up. During the storm itself heroism is the routine attitude. I remember once when the phone was out, before all the telephone lines went underground, and the power was off, our neighbor came lightly in his huge pack boots across the drift top, high up from our house level, like an upright black ant, delicately choosing his footing over the hard-slung and paralyzed snow waves. He looked as if he were walking across a frozen North Atlantic. He had come over to see if we were O.K. It was before snowmobiles, at −40 degrees a welcome gesture.

Then right after a storm we all go back uptown because we have to see how the town has filled. The streets are walled ten and eleven feet high. If they had had underground parking ramps in the pyramids this is what they'd have looked like, white-painted, and we crawl between the neatly carved clean walls. The horrible snow buildup is a point of pride. In 1969 a fine thing happened: the county of Lac Qui Parle imported a couple of gigantic snow-removal machines from Yellowstone Park. It cost several thousand dollars to get those monsters here; when they arrived our heavy, many-layered, crusted snow broke the machines—they couldn't handle it. With glittering eyes we sent them back to Yellowstone Park.

Snowdrifts in the bad years, as in 1969, force us to dump ⁵ garbage and nonburnables ever nearer the house, until finally in March there is a semicircle of refuse nearly at the front door. Even the German shepherd lowers his standards; the snow around the doghouse entrance is unspeakable.

If one has any kind of luck one garners comfort from great ⁶ weather, but if there is some anxious and unresolved part of one's inner life, snowfall and certainly snowboundness can make it worse. During the winter of 1968–69, the three doctors of our town prescribed between two and three times as much tranquilizing medicine as usual. And Robert Frost, despite being one of the best snow poets going, has an odd, recurring fretfulness about snow:

> The woods are lovely, dark and deep,
> But I have promises to keep

What promises? To whom? If we think about it it sounds moralistic and self-denying—a moral showing-off in some way. The nervousness is stronger, though, in "Desert Places":

> Snow falling and night falling fast, oh, fast
> In a field I looked into going past,
> And the ground almost covered smooth in snow,
> But a few weeds and stubble showing last.
>
> The woods around it have it—it is theirs.
> All animals are smothered in their lairs.
> I am too absent-spirited to count;
> The loneliness includes me unawares.

I am struck by the malaise of the word *absent-spirited*. It must mean—this joy in snow or fretfulness in snow—that whatever is providential and coming to each of us from within is sped the faster by snowfall.

Being out in a blizzard is not lovely. Nature then feels worse than inimical; it feels simply impersonal. It isn't that, like some goddess in Homer, she wants to grab and freeze your body in her drifts; it is that you can be taken and still the wind will keep up its regular blizzard whine and nothing has made a difference. In February of 1969 the fuel men couldn't get through for weeks; one midnight my husband and I had to transfer oil from a drum behind an old shed to our house tank. We did this in cans, load after load, crawling on all fours and rolling in the ravines between the drifts. It had some nice moments: every ten minutes or so we'd meet behind the old shed, when one returned an empty can and the other was coming away with a full one, and we'd crouch in the scoured place, leaning over the nasty, rusted, infuriatingly slow spigot of the oil tank there. Looking at each other, we saw we had that impersonal aspect of snow-covered people. It was peculiar to think that anyone behind those freezing, melting, refreezing eyebrows ever objected to an act of Congress or ever loved a summer woods or memorized the tenor to anything by Christopher Tye. Back inside, our job done, still cold and rough-spoken, still walking like bears, we studied the children in their beds.

To us in Minnesota a blizzard in itself is of no practical good, but it is interesting how useful blizzards can be. Ordinary snowfall, not moved into deep-packed areas by wind, runs off too quickly in the spring and can't be controlled for good use. The *Proceedings of the American Society of Civil Engineers* has essay after essay on uses of Rocky Mountain snowmelt. Twenty-five hundred years ago, and possibly even earlier, the Persians used deep-drifted snow for irrigation. They built their *qanats*. Qanats are brick-walled tunnels running from the snowfields of the Elburz and other mountain ranges of Iran to villages fifteen or twenty miles away. At a point in the mountains' water table still higher than the land level of the parched miles and miles to be irrigated, the arched brick tunnels were carefully sloped to keep the water moving. The "mother well" was 200 feet deep and deeper. These 22,000 tunnels (there were 30,000 in 1960 but 8,000 were not in working condition) had airshafts for fresh air and maintenance access every 50 to 60 yards. Darius took the qanat technique to Egypt in the 5th century B.C. Nothing could have been cultivated in three-fourths of the now-irrigated fields of Iran without the ancient qanats. Persia was the originator of melons, cucumbers, and pears.

This is just to give an idea of mankind's long use of heavily drifted snow. Since we don't *use* blizzards in western Minnesota, the question lingers: why the pleasure in great weather? As with children in thunderstorms, I think we all have a secret affair of long standing with the other face of things. Children want the parents and the police and the other irritating powers to have their measure taken; they want a change of justice; but it goes further: they have a secret affection for bad weather.

Storms, what is more, force us to look at nature closely, and that is never boring. All meetings of the Business Improvement Association and the Countryside Council and the play rehearsal committees stop in a blizzard. It is a help. Two things make nature lovely to people, I think: enforced, extended leisure in a natural place—which storms give us out here; and second, planning our own lives instead of just following along. The moment, for example, that someone finally decides not to take the promising job offered by Reserve Mining, for example, or the moment someone decides not to pad a travel-expense account at the Ramada is a moment in which ice and snow and bare trunks look better, less happenstance, less pointless. C. S. Lewis goes very far: he claims that the fact that we all agree on what is meant by *good* or *holy* (that is, no one thinks robbery or despoiling the land or depriving the poor is good) indicates that goodness and holiness are actually a normal, planned part of our universe—

perfectly natural to the species. He would not be surprised at all to see snow on a horse's mane all the better for having just worked out an ethical decision.

Comment

Carol Bly is expressing her feelings about snow through experiences she finds harder to interpret than to describe. Thus, having shown why "being out in a blizzard is not lovely," she finishes by describing how she and her husband, "still cold and rough-spoken, still walking like bears," watch their children in bed. In her final paragraphs, she explores various attitudes towards blizzards. But these statements seem to fall short of capturing their meaning. She ends the essay with ideas expressed by another writer about the world. His ideas perhaps will bring us a little closer to understanding the workings of the world.

Questions for Study and Discussion

1. What range of personal experiences does Bly present in the essay? And what are her various feelings?
2. Describing the experience of ancient Persians with snow, Bly illustrates "mankind's long use of heavily drifted snow." How does this reference to the long history of mankind help to convey her complex feelings?
3. How does Bly show that the "meaning" of the world is difficult both to describe and to interpret?
4. What is the point of C. S. Lewis's ideas and the statement about the sight of snow on a horse's mane?
5. What is the order of ideas in the essay? Why do you think Bly chose this order?
6. What concrete words and phrases develop the topic sentence of paragraph 2, "Before a storm, Madison is full of people excitedly laying in food stocks for the three-day blow"?
7. Bly often introduces an experience with a general characterization. The blizzard of 1969 "had some nice moments," she tells us in paragraph 7; then she describes these moments. What words and images convey her feelings about these moments?

Vocabulary Study

Give the denotative and connotative meanings—explain what things or ideas the words point to or name, and give what feelings or attitudes they suggest:

a. paragraph 2: *squinty-eyed, gruff*
b. paragraph 4: *glittering*
c. paragraph 6: *garners, fretfulness, moralistic, malaise*
d. paragraph 7: *inimical, nice*

Suggestions for Writing

1. Describe your own experiences with a series of snowfalls or some other natural occurrence. Use your description to suggest your own complex feelings and the ideas these experiences generate.
2. Families have their own ways of doing things—of celebrating birthdays and other anniversaries, of arguing and making up— that suggest different personalities. Suggest the personality of your own family through concrete details and experiences. Let the details reveal the qualities and the personality you have in mind. Don't name them directly.

Figurative Language

Much of our language is *figurative*—that is, not literal but metaphorical—sometimes without our realizing it is. Certain figures of speech may once have called a picture to mind but have become stale. Here are a few examples:

blaze of glory   *drunk with power*   *hard as nails*

The first of these is a *metaphor*—a figure of speech in which one thing is talked about as if it were something else. The metaphor does not tell us that glory is like a fire: it speaks of glory as if it were. "Drunk with power" is also a metaphor: it specifies that power acts like an intoxicant. "Hard as nails" makes the comparison directly through the word *as,* and we therefore call it a *simile.* Another important figure of speech is *personification,* which gives animate or human qualities to something inanimate or nonhuman:

The tree *cowered* in the storm.

Figurative language is one way of conveying our feelings about an object or experience.

In exposition and argument, figurative language can make an idea or attitude concrete and persuasive. It can be unobtrusive, and

398

at other times it can be dramatic, as in this description by a surgeon of the tools of his art:

> The scalpel is in two parts, the handle and the blade. Joined, it
> is six inches from tip to tip. At one end of the handle is a narrow
> notched prong upon which the blade is slid, then snapped into
> place. Without the blade, the handle has a blind, decapitated look.
> It is helpless as a trussed maniac. But slide on the blade, click it
> home, and the knife springs instantly to life. It is headed now,
> edgy, leaping to mount the fingers for the gallop to its feast.—
> Richard Selzer, *Mortal Lessons*

Metaphor, simile, and personification here are combined in a highly effective way; the description conveys the excitement of the surgeon as he holds the scalpel and prepares to use it.

David R. Scott

What Is It Like to Walk on the Moon?

David R. Scott was born in San Antonio, Texas, in 1932, where his father was serving as an Air Force brigadier general. Educated at West Point and MIT, Scott served in the Air Force as a jet pilot, and in 1963 began his training as an astronaut. He was one of the three who piloted the *Endeavour,* in the Apollo 15 mission to the moon, entering lunar orbit on July 29, 1971. Scott explored the lunar surface with James B. Irwin, while Alfred Worden remained in the command ship. The *Endeavour* returned to earth on August 7. The essay reprinted here gives a vivid account of his experiences on the moon, and shows how figurative language can serve in exposition.

Sixty feet above the moon, the blast of our single rocket 1
churns up a gray tumult of lunar dust that seems to engulf

Reprinted by permission of *National Geographic* and David R. Scott.

us. Blinded, I feel the rest of the way down "on the gauges." With an abrupt jar, our lunar module, or LM, strikes the surface and shudders to rest. We have hit our target squarely— a large amphitheater girded by mountains and a deep canyon, at the eastern edge of a vast plain.

As Jim Irwin and I wait for the dust to settle, I recall the twelve revolutions we have just spent in lunar orbit aboard our Apollo 15 spaceship *Endeavour*. Each two hours found us completing a full circuit of earth's ancient satellite—one hour knifing through lunar night, then sunrise and an hour of daylight. As we orbited, I found a particular fascination in that sector of the darkened moon bathed in earthshine. The light reflected by our planet illuminates the sleeping moon much more brightly than moonlight silvers our own night. The mountains and crater rims are clearly seen.

I will always remember *Endeavour* hurtling through that strange night of space. Before us and above us stars spangled the sky with their distant icy fire; below lay the moon's far side, an arc of impenetrable blackness that blotted the firmament. Then, as our moment of sunrise approached, barely discernible streamers of light—actually the glowing gases of the solar corona millions of miles away—played above the moon's horizon. Finally the sun exploded into our view like a visual thunderclap. Abruptly, completely, in less than a second, its harsh light flooded into the spaceship and dazzled our eyes.

As we looked into the early lunar morning from *Endeavour,* the moonscape stretched into the distance, everything the color of milk chocolate. Long angular shadows accentuated every hill, every crater. As the sun arched higher, the plains and canyons and mountains brightened to a gunmetal gray, while the shadows shrank. At full lunar noontide, the sun glared down upon a bleached and almost featureless world.

Now we have come to rest on the moon, and the last of the dust settles outside the LM. We throw the switches that convert this hybrid vehicle from spacecraft to dwelling. Thus begin our 67 hours of lunar residence. We are on a still and arid world where each blazing day and each subfreezing night stretch through 355 earth hours. We have landed in the bright morning of a moon day. When we depart, the sun will not have reached zenith.

It is sobering to realize that we are the only living souls on this silent sphere, perhaps the only sentient beings in our solar system not confined to earth. Though we have slipped the bonds of our home planet, we remain earthmen. So we keep our clocks set to Houston time and gear our lives to the 24-hour cycle we have always known.

Opening the top hatch for a preliminary reconnaissance, I peer out at a world seemingly embalmed in the epoch of its creation. Each line, each form blends into the harmonious whole of a single fluid sculpture. Craters left by "recent" meteorites—merely millions of years ago—stand out, startlingly white, like fresh scar tissue against the soft beige of the undulating terrain.

I steal a moment and glance straight up into the black sky where the crystalline sphere of earth—all blue and white, sea and clouds—gleams in the abyss of space. In that cold and boundless emptiness, our planet provides the only glow of color. For 30 minutes my helmeted head pivots above the open hatch as I survey and photograph the wonderland of the lunar surface. The incredible variety of landforms in this restricted area (on the moon, the horizon lies a scant mile and a half from a viewer) fills me with pleasant surprise. To the south an 11,000-foot ridge rises above the bleak plain. To the east stretch the hulking heights of an even higher summit. On the west a winding gorge plunges to depths of more than 1,000 feet. Dominating the northeastern horizon, a great mountain stands in noble splendor almost three miles above us. Ours is the first expedition to land amid lunar mountains. Never quickened by life, never assailed by wind and rain, they loom still and serene, a tableau of forever. Their majesty overwhelms me.

Eight years' training in lunar geology makes me instantly aware of intriguing details. A dark line like a bathtub ring smudges the bases of the mountains. Was it left by the subsiding lake of lava that filled the immense cavity of Palus Putredinis, on the fringes of Mare Imbrium, billions of years ago? Mare Imbrium, on whose edge we have landed, stretches across the face of the moon for some 650 miles. The celestial projectile that excavated it must have been huge—perhaps as much as 50 miles across—and it slammed into the moon with a velocity many times greater than that of a rifle bullet.

When we descend the ladder of the LM and step onto the moon's surface, Jim and I feel a gratifying sense of freedom. For five days we have been crammed into the tight confines of the spacecraft that brought us here. Now, all at once, we regain the luxury of movement. But, we quickly discover, locomotion on the moon has its own peculiar restrictions. At one-sixth of earth's gravity, we weigh only a sixth our normal poundage. Our gait quickly evolves into a rhythmic, bounding motion that possesses all the lightness and ease of strolling on a trampoline.   10

At the same time, since the mass of our bodies and personal gear—and hence, our inertia—remains unchanged, starting and stopping require unusual exertion. I learn to get under way by thrusting my body forward, as though I were stepping into a wind. To stop, I dig in my heels and lean backward.   11

To fall on the moon—and I did several times—is to rediscover childhood. You go down in slow motion, the impact is slight, the risk of injury virtually nil. Forsaking the adult attitude that regards a fall not only as a loss of dignity but also a source of broken bones, the moon walker—like a child—accepts it as yet another diversion. Only the clinging moon dust, the untoward demand on the oxygen supply occasioned by the exertion of getting up, pall the pleasure of a tumble. Personally I find the one-sixth gravity of the moon more enjoyable than the soothing weightlessness of space. I have the same sense of buoyancy, but the moon provides a reassuringly fixed sense of up and down.   12

As we unload and begin to assemble our equipment—in-   13

cluding the battery-powered four-wheeled Rover that will carry us across the moonscape at a jaunty six or so miles an hour— I gaze around at the plains and mountains that have become our world. My eyes trace a curiously contoured, totally alien wasteland. I scan the lofty mountains and feel a strange, indescribable emotion: No naked eye has ever seen them; no foot has ever trod them. I am an intruder in an eternal wilderness.

The flowing moonscape, unmarred by a single jagged peak, reminds me of earth's uplands covered by a heavy blanket of fresh snow. Indeed, the dark-gray moon dust—its consistency seems to be somewhere between coal dust and talcum powder—mantles virtually every physical feature of the lunar surface. Our boots sink gently into it as we walk; we leave sharply chiseled footprints. 14

Color undergoes an odd transformation here. Everything underfoot or nearby is gray, yet this hue blends gradually into the uniform golden tan that characterizes distant objects. And this small spectrum moves with the walker. Most of the scattered rocks share the same gray tint as the dust, but we find two that are jet black, two of pastel green, several with sparkling crystals, some coated with glass, and one that is white. As we advance, we are surrounded by stillness. No wind blows. No sound echoes. Only shadows move. Within the space suit, I hear the reassuring purr of the miniaturized machines that supply vital oxygen and shield me from the blistering 150°F. surface heat of lunar morning. 15

Any of a thousand malfunctions in a space suit or the LM could condemn an astronaut to swift death. Yet we have a quiet confidence in our own abilities, and boundless faith in the engineers and technicians who have fashioned the ingenious devices that transport and sustain us in space. Often, in the course of my stay on the moon, I recall the words of American poet Edwin Markham: "There is a destiny which makes us brothers; none goes his way alone." 16

At first we experience a troubling deception with perspective. Without the familiar measuring sticks of our native 17 planet—trees, telephone poles, clouds, and haze—we cannot determine whether an object stands close at hand or at a considerable distance, or whether it is large or small. Gradually our eyes learn to cope with the craters—mammoth, medium, and minuscule—that dot virtually every inch of the surface. And gradually the moon becomes a friendlier place. A thought occurs to me: Would human beings born on the moon be able to find their way among the trees and clouds of earth?

Each excursion on the lunar surface is planned to last seven hours, almost to the limit of a space suit's life-sustaining capabilities. We dig and drill into the surface, gather rocks and soil, take endless photographs. The photographs, it seems to me, provide us with a testament that transcends time, for we may be photographing the distant past of our own planet. The Rover functions impeccably as we ride from site to site, accumulating fragments of history. We bounce and pitch across omnipresent chuckholelike craters. The motion exactly resembles that of a small boat in a rough sea; so does the physical effect. Incredible as it seems, in the arid environment of the moon, seasickness could become an occupational hazard.   18

After each of our expeditions, we climb—sapped of energy—back into the LM. With its oxygen and food and water, it is a tiny artificial earth that comforts us in the void. Removing our space suits and attending to our housekeeping chores consumes two hours. For the first twenty minutes we are conscious of a pervasive odor, similar to that of gunpowder, from the moon dust we have tracked in. Our air-purifying system soon dispels the acrid scent, but the fine, adhesive dust clings to everything. Back on earth, no amount of cleaning will convert our space suits from the gray hue acquired on the moon to their once pristine and sparkling white.   19

The better to sleep, we create the illusion of night. We place opaque shades over the windows of the LM to exclude the harsh sunlight reflected from the moon's surface. Then we go through all the homey activities of sunset on earth, even to snapping on overhead lights. When finally we switch them off, we settle into hammocks. On earth, I have always found   20 hammocks uncomfortable. But here my 30-pound body adapts marvelously to the canvas crescent, and I easily fall into dreamless sleep.

Bounding along in the Rover on our third and final ex- 21 pedition, we begin to feel fully at home in our new habitat. The craters now seem familiar and help us gauge distances. And we venture across the horizon—the first astronauts ever to do so—without anxiety. Should the sophisticated Rover navigation system fail, we have a small cardboard sun com- pass fashioned by a technician in Houston—a frail instru- ment much shriveled by the savage lunar sunlight and coated with moon dust—that will give us our bearings. But our newfound confidence stems less from instruments than from the fact that we have come to know and understand our sur- roundings.

On our return we even dare a shortcut. The Rover bounces 22 between undulations and crater walls that mask our view of the LM for long minutes, but we emerge on target. Arriving at the LM, I experience a sense of impending loss. Soon I will leave the moon, probably forever. And, in a peculiar way, I have come to feel a strange affection for this peaceful, changeless companion of the earth.

As I mount the ladder for the last time, I halt and glance 23 back at the Rover. It seems poised and ready for its next task. And poised in that same eager attitude it could remain for thousands, perhaps millions of years—a driverless vehicle lost in the loneliness of this lifeless realm. Beside it, like staunch sentinels through the long millenniums, will hulk the LM de- scent stage and the assorted equipment of our mission. The vacuum of space, which knows only negligible decay, will confer upon all of it—even to the footprints we have left in the undrifting dust—a permanence akin to immortality.

The thought haunts us that the end of the Apollo flights 24 may mark man's last visit to the moon for a long time. Amer- ican manned exploration of deep space is scheduled for an in- definite hiatus. Most scientists have already suggested that, when it resumes, all effort should concentrate upon reaching

Mars and beyond. So our lunar artifacts—bypassed in the race to the planets—could remain undisturbed for eternity.

Clutching the ladder, I raise my eyes from the now-familiar moonscape to earth, glowing in the black heavens—that incredibly vivid sphere, so blue, so beautiful, so beloved. And so bedeviled: by ecological balances gone awry, by scattered starvation, by a shortage of energy that may motivate us to seek sources beyond our earth. Our Apollo crew believes that a technology capable of exploring space can and will help resolve such problems. We feel a sense of pride in the accomplishments of our program, yet we cannot escape a sense of deep concern for the fate of our planet and our species. This concern has led us to add certain items to the equipment we are leaving on the moon. The sum of these articles, we hope, will form a résumé of our era in the continuing story of the human race.   25

In eons to come, should astronauts from the deeps of space—from other solar systems in other galaxies—pass this way, they may find our spoor, our abandoned gear. A plaque of aluminum affixed to the deserted LM descent stage portrays the two hemispheres of our planet; upon it are engraved the name of our spacecraft, the date of our mission, and a roster of the crew. From these data, the equipment, and even the dimensions of our footprints, intelligent beings will readily deduce what kind of creatures we were and whence we came. We leave a piece of fauna—a falcon feather—and of flora—a four-leaf clover.   26

In a little hollow in the moon dust we place a stylized figurine of a man in a space suit and beside it another metal plaque bearing the names of the 14 spacemen—Russians and Americans—who have given their lives so that man may range the cosmos. Finally we deposit a single book: the Bible.   27

Our mission ends in fatigue and elation. Amazing success has rewarded the first extended scientific expedition to the moon. After debriefing and helping in the analyses of our findings, our crew disbands.   28

Now, two years later, I continue to work in the Lyndon   29
B. Johnson Space Center near Houston. Frequently I reflect
upon those three most memorable days of my life. Although
I can reconstruct them virtually moment by moment, sometimes I can scarcely believe that I have actually walked on the
moon.

Occasionally, while strolling on a crisp autumn night or   30
driving a straight Texas road, I look up at the moon riding
bright and proud over the clouds. My eye picks out the largest circular splotch on the silvery surface: Mare Imbrium.
There, at the eastern edge of that splotch, I once descended
in a spaceship. Again I feel that I will probably never return,
and the thought stirs a pang of nostalgia. For when I look at
the moon I do not see a hostile, empty world. I see the radiant body where man has taken his first steps into a frontier
that will never end.

Comment

To describe an experience entirely new to human beings, Scott
must refer to experiences with which we are familiar. Some of his
experiences are exactly like those on earth: the movement of the
Rover across the lunar surface "exactly resembles that of a small boat
in a rough sea; so does the physical effect." To fall on the moon is
to feel as we did as children, and Scott gives examples of that kind
of feeling. But not every feeling and experience has an exact equivalent on earth. Scott can suggest the "troubling deception with perspective," but he knows that the exact physical sensation cannot be
stated or described exactly: "A thought occurs to me: Would human beings born on the moon be able to find their way among the
trees and clouds of earth?" As his frequent resort to simile shows,
we depend on figurative language to express new experiences, feelings, and insights: "Beside it, like staunch sentinels through the long
millenniums, will hulk the LM descent stage, and the assorted
equipment of our mission."

Questions for Study and Discussion

1. To what does Scott implicitly compare the weightlessness experienced on the lunar surface? What other such experiences does he describe through comparisons?
2. What sights not previously experienced by human beings does he describe, and how does he?
3. What aspects of the total experience does he stress the most? Why do you think he does?
4. Had he been writing to an audience of future astronauts, how might the description and exposition have been different?
5. Does Scott develop a thesis, or instead describe an experience without drawing conclusions?

Vocabulary Study

1. Give the dictionary meaning of the following words. Then explain how Scott uses the word figuratively:
   a. "*blotted* the firmament" (paragraph 3)
   b. "*dazzled* our eyes" (paragraph 3)
   c. "the shadows *shrank*" (paragraph 4)
   d. "a world seemingly *embalmed*" (paragraph 7)
   e. "totally *alien* wasteland" (paragraph 13)
   f. "a *testament* that transcends time" (paragraph 18)
   g. "the *homey* activities of sunset on earth" (paragraph 20)
   h. "the *radiant* body" (paragraph 30)
2. The phrase "the shadows *shrank*" is an example of personification: the inanimate shadows are given animate or human qualities. What other examples of personification do you find in the essay?
3. Metaphors that do not immediately call a picture to mind or strike us as being comparisons are sometimes called "submerged" or "buried" metaphors. They become submerged through long and frequent use:

   > So we keep our clocks set to Houston time and *gear* our lives to the 24-hour cycle we have always known.

   Find several examples of such metaphors in the essay.
4. The following sentence makes a literal comparison of the

moonscape to the color of milk chocolate. Rewrite the sentence, turning the literal comparison into metaphor:

> As we looked into the early lunar morning from *Endeavour*, the moonscape stretched into the distance, everything the color of milk chocolate.

5. Use your dictionary to investigate the etymology of the following words—that is, their origin. Then write a sentence for each, stating what the etymology contributes to your understanding of the words as used by Scott: *"firmament* (paragraph 3); *reconnaissance* (paragraph 7); *mantles* (paragraph 14); *mammoth* (paragraph 17).

Suggestions for Writing

1. Describe a recent experience in several paragraphs, in as literal a language as possible. Then rewrite one of these paragraphs, substituting metaphorical for literal language where possible. In an additional paragraph, discuss the changes that the addition of metaphorical language provides.

2. Narrate and describe an experience that would be strange to a particular audience. Assume that this audience knows nothing about the circumstances, equipment, or world of this experience, and therefore needs them explained or described. Focus on those aspects of the experience that you consider most significant or revealing, since you will not be able to explain or describe them all.

Tone

The tone of a statement expresses the attitude or feeling of a speaker or writer. The tone of the following statement is immediately clear:

> Man is, of all quadrupeds, at once the most vain and the most idiotic. A genuine popinjay, whatever that may be, is as a shrinking violet compared to him. He cannot imagine himself save as at the center of situations. He never opens his mouth without talking of himself.—H. L. Mencken, "The Eternal Male"

Mencken's blunt statement expresses his astonishment and exasperation. He says exactly what he means—in contrast to this ironic statement in which the words imply more than they actually say:

> Already architectural designers are toiling to find ways out of the technical trap represented by sealed buildings with immovable glass, ways that might let in some of the naturally cool air outside. Some have lately come up with a remarkable discovery: the openable window. Presumably, that represents progress.—Frank Trippett, "The Great American Cooling Machine"

410

The designers of sealed buildings, the writer implies, are not very bright if they are making so obvious a discovery as the openable window. The final comment is plainly sarcastic.

Other statements are harder to interpret, particularly in writing. If you heard a person exclaim "What a tragedy!", you would know immediately whether the person is expressing pain, anger, sarcasm, wonder, or bewilderment. If you come upon the exclamation in a piece of writing, however, you would have to examine its context or setting to discover the writer's tone. The following statement by Mark Twain on the novelist James Fenimore Cooper is ambiguous out of context:

> Cooper's eye was splendidly inaccurate.

The sentences that follow show that Twain is not praising Cooper. Here is the whole passage:

> Cooper's proudest creations in the way of "situations" suffer noticeably from the absence of the observer's protecting gift. Cooper's eye was splendidly inaccurate. Cooper seldom saw anything correctly. He saw nearly all things as through a glass eye, darkly. Of course a man who cannot see the commonest little everyday matters accurately is working at a disadvantage when he is constructing a "situation."

In writing your own essays, you will probably adopt a tone without much consideration. In revising your draft, you might discover shifts in tone that you did not intend, or you might find ambiguous words or statements. Your reader will need help with these shifts and ambiguities. The solution is to clarify your feelings or attitudes, as H. L. Mencken does in the following passage:

> Some time ago I put in a blue afternoon re-reading Joseph Conrad's "Youth." A *blue* afternoon? What nonsense! The touch of the man is like the touch of Schubert. One approaches him in various and unhappy moods: depressed, dubious, despairing; one leaves him in the clear, yellow sunshine that Nietzsche found in Bizet's music.—"Joseph Conrad"

William Aiken
Hanging Out and Looking Good

William Aiken is a poet, essayist, and social critic who teaches poetry at the University of Lowell in Massachusetts. He has published articles in the *Wall Street Journal* and the *Christian Science Monitor,* where his essay reprinted here appeared in 1984. Provincetown and Truro are towns on Cape Cod, Massachusetts.

My son, Matthew, has just turned 15 and arrived at that   1
time when children like to hang out where people are cheerful. As you may know, that is not home.

The days of selling home-picked berries at the beach are   2
gone. (I kept him at that for three years, but he objected to my taking half the profits.) Now he wants to work with stainless-steel machines—dishwashers and gas pumps. No more of this berry-basket stuff.

In the course of my recent belated education I have learned   3
that 15-year-olds will clean up houses as a surprise for pleasant strangers, but they don't want to clean the house for me. They go for holistic personalities, which they find at ice cream parlors or in houses down the street. During this new age of the public persona the big trick is not to grow fretful. You want to project a smiley face, pretend you're an aerobics teacher. It gets hard.

Fifteen is the time when kids are too young to drive, and   4
yet they want to go certain places. You may not want them to go, but you don't want them to hitchhike, either. As a result of such dilemmas you begin to perfect various levels of

First published in the *Christian Science Monitor,* November 28, 1984. Reprinted by permission of William Aiken.

grumpiness. As Matthew pops out his plans for any given day I keep thinking there is something he should be doing around the house, but I can't think what it might be.

I was going over his new summer schedule, scratching my head as my mind drifted back to my own vivid past raising chickens. After pumping gas for six hours in the morning he figures the rest of the day is his, so he's off to *town:* to dive for quarters off MacMillan Wharf, go water-skiing in Provincetown Harbor, walk around town pricing silver bracelets, have a slice of pizza, and join the breakdancers at Union Square.

Listening blankly to his adventures, I feel I'm in some kind of parental limbo of the '80s: almost ready to go out and have a good time—but not quite. I still find myself waiting by the phone and can't really seem to set out for anywhere. I watch the underlying happiness of my 15-year-old as he scales the heights of adolescence, and I keep thinking maybe he'll drop me a rope. But as he wanders farther and farther from his backyard I become more and more homebound. I have begun to take up stamp collecting again. I do these little garbage things around the house.

One day I decided to slip into a disguise and follow my son up to Provincetown. I have some costumes from the '50s that I still occasionally wear, and I was going over these in my closet, confident that in Provincetown no one would notice. The last time I walked down Commercial Street there was a man dressed as a lobster in front of the Wreck Club who kept an eye on passers-by through his claws. No one paid any attention. Besides, I have this underlying certainty that no young person has looked at me for years.

So I got to town, parked my car, and walked down to the center. Nothing much seemed to be happening, just people moving along in short pants and sequins. As I looked around through my new reflecting glasses I noticed a ring of young people in front of the Town Hall playing hackensack—popping this leather thing around on their feet. Suddenly I realized that one of them was my son. Dressed in a mesh T-shirt, he was playing hackensack in front of the Town Hall.

There they all were—all his friends—with their smiles and   9
their faces and their stainless-steel presences. And there I was, all bent over in my tattered overcoat, dreaming of lobster suits. It suddenly occurred to me that while I was in disguise, my 15-year-old had decided to go public. Like a small corporation that had gotten itself together and become a dazzling new entry on the Exchange, he was "hanging out and looking good." He saw me and waved. There are certain things a disguise will never cover.

I walked back to my car, which I had left at a foodstore   10
where there's free parking for customers, and a nine-year-old says, "That'll be $3, mister." "Your store didn't have any Sure-Gel so I had to go downtown," I say. "That'll be $3."

I pay up and drive slowly back to Truro. It was almost   11
time for my walk in the marsh.

Comment

Aiken writes informally about his relationship to his fifteen-year-old son. The tone of his essay is shaped by his attitude toward his son and also toward his audience—by the relationship that he establishes in his opening paragraph. This audience is a general one, needing some details but not others about Matthew and his world. Aiken's gentle humor arises from the understatement of his feelings, particularly at the end. This understatement is one source of the quiet irony that characterizes the whole essay.

Questions for Study and Discussion

1. Irony is possible when the writer and the audience share certain experiences and facts. What does Aiken assume his audience knows about the towns of Cape Cod, Massachusetts? What

other facts and what experiences does he assume his audience possesses? In general, what shared ironies does Aiken develop in the whole essay?

2. How would you define the attitude and feelings of Aiken toward Matthew and his world? What are his feelings at the end of the essay—on the Provincetown street and in the foodstore parking lot?

3. Is Aiken developing a thesis or merely describing personal experiences and feelings?

4. How would you characterize the writer of these experiences? What qualities of personality and outlook emerge in the telling of what happened?

Vocabulary Study

What do the following words, phrases, and sentences contribute to the tone of the essay?

a. paragraph 3: *my recent belated education, a smiley face*
b. paragraph 6: *some kind of parental limbo of the '80s*
c. paragraph 9: *stainless-steel presences, "hanging out and looking good"*

Suggestions for Writing

1. Write about experiences with a younger or older brother or sister or relative that define your relationship. Don't state this relationship directly. Let your details reveal it.

2. Aiken ends his essay with an embarrassing experience. Write about an embarrassment of your own and its consequences. Use the episode to make a point about yourself or people in general.

Frank Deford
Beauty and Everlasting Faith—Local Level

Frank Deford was born in Baltimore in 1938, and was educated at Princeton, where he edited *The Daily Princetonian* and the humor magazine *The Tiger*. A senior writer for *Sports Illustrated,* he has written on tennis, basketball, roller derbies, and the Miss America contest. His books include *Cut 'n' Run* (1973) and *The Owner* (1976). In the essay printed here, a section from a chapter of his book *There She Is* (1971), he is describing the preliminary contest in Wilson, North Carolina, for the state title.

The judging formally begins with the Saturday luncheon at the Heart of Wilson Motel. Dr. Vincent Thomas, the head of the judges' committee, welcomes all the judges, and is himself thereafter always introduced as "Dr. Vincent," by Jerry Ball, the well-known "dean of beauty-pageant judges." Jerry has sent two state queens on to become Miss America, and judged in states as far away as Alaska. Jerry is joined on the jury by Mrs. Judy Cross, who was Most Photogenic at Miss North Carolina a few years ago, and by Mrs. Marilyn Hull, a former Miss New Jersey. She is married, as so many beauty queens are, to an athlete. Her husband is Bill Hull, a former Kansas City Chief. The other two judges are Jim Church, chairman of the board of the North Carolina Jaycees, and Bob Logan, Charlotte sales manager for Fabergé, the beauty products concern. It is a hot-shot panel for any local Pageant.

The eight contestants keep a wary eye out as they sit down to lunch and make sure to reach for the correct implements. The judges, however, show no interest whatsoever in what eating tools are being utilized. They are genial and pleasant; the girls could be dispensing peas with a knife for all they seem to care about such formalities.

Doris's hat tumbles off. She does not realize it has gone, which is not surprising, since hats are as foreign to these girls as bustles or U.S. Army fatigues would be. Judi has a hat on for exactly the second time in her life. The first time was when she was in another beauty pageant. There are speeches and everyone in attendance is introduced. Then the room is cleared, and a table set up for the judges at the far end. It is time for the serious interviewing. Officially, the girls in any *Miss America* Pageant are not graded on their interviews. Actually, it is the underside of the iceberg that determines the winner.

The girls are directed to another room where, one by one, they will be funneled toward the judges. Following an interview, the contestant will proceed on to another room for a sort of debriefing. The judges arrange themselves and pour coffee. The men must concentrate to do their best, for the South Carolina-Duke basketball game is just starting on TV, and their hearts all lie there. Jerry Ball presides in the middle, like a Chief Justice, a leader among equals, and everyone agrees that there will be no set order to the questioning, just "catch as catch can."

Dr. Thomas sits at the other end of the room with a stop watch. Jerry says, "All right, Dr. Vincent, bring in the first young lady." The girls have been assigned an order in which they will present their talents in the show; they visit the judges in the same order. Rita Deans is first. Like all the others, she has her little hat on and carries a handbag, and she walks, as she has been taught, in the proper manner. This is an unfamiliar gait for all the girls and makes them resemble the little dogs on the Ed Sullivan Show, who have outfits on, are balanced precariously on their hind feet, and take desperate little steps to keep from pitching forward.

Rita, seated, is straightforward and demure. She assures the panel that her fourteen-year Sunday School record is not in any danger of being jeopardized by a victory tonight. The judges spring what is considered as a controversial question: what does Rita think of coed college dormitories? Rita thinks awhile. "Well, I haven't formed an opinion about that," she finally says. Mrs. Butner has instructed the girls to answer that way whenever they feel that they are unsure of an answer. The judges nod and agree that Rita would be unwise, indeed, to venture into unknown philosophical territory.

Sharon Shackleford is next. Talkative anyway, she seems especially garrulous when juxtaposed to Rita. "You've got to pull the plug on her," a judge says upon her departure. Wendy Formo, the third contestant, makes the best approach of all. Over six feet tall, she cannot help walking like a normal person. Also, she shuffles a question about Vice President Agnew beautifully, and the panel is obviously impressed. "It reminds you," Jim Church says. "I always liked that Jeanne Swanner."   7

Bob Logan asks, "What time is it?"   8

Jerry answers, "About the end of the first quarter."   9

Peggy Murphy, recovered from the flu, is next, and for her, the judges reach back for a classic old standard of a question: what kind of person do you think you are yourself? There is one stock answer to this question, which every girl ever in a beauty pageant has always provided. In so many words, it is: that I am naturally a shy, thoughtful person, but I love a good time on occasion. Also, I am nuts about people. Peggy is close enough.   10

The interviewing is now halfway through, so the judges stand and reach for some coffee. Doris comes in. She is in yellow, with a matching handbag that she sets on the rug by the side of her chair. She banters back the usual polite preliminaries, and then one of the judges asks her if she believes there is a generation gap. "Yes, I definitely believe there is one," Doris replies firmly. All the judges sit up and cock their heads. The regular answer to this question is that there certainly isn't one around my house, where everyone works to understand each other better. Doris proceeds. "Ours is the first generation brought up with the threat of the hydrogen   11 and atom bombs, and the first generation to have grown up with television as a major force in our lives. I really don't even believe it is surprising that there is a gap. Maybe we should only be surprised that there is not more of one."

The judges nod sagely, and to test her further, pull an-   12
other old chestnut out of the fire. All right, what about coed dorms? Doris backs down here; she comes out with the company line. "It may be fine for other people," she says, "but I can certainly see enough of the opposite sex on dates and other things." Doris has inserted a proper amount of righteous indignation in her voice by the end of her speech. The judges draw a breath, relieved not to have a genuine revolutionary on their hands. They are spent, though, so they ask her if she has any questions for them.

Gay Butner has informed the girls that they may be faced   13
with this request, and to have a question on stand-by. "Yes," Doris says, "I'd like to know why you're still interested in judging. Does it keep you closer to our generation and help close the gap for you?" Yes, the judges agree, yes, it certainly works that way for them.

Time is up; the panel smiles and thanks her; and Doris   14
is hardly out of the door when Jerry slams his hand down. "She came through like 'Gangbusters,' " he exclaims. "She took everything we threw at her and came right back."

"A live cookie," Jim Church says.   15

Vince Thomas goes to fetch Judi. She comes in, smiling   16
broadly, wearing her aunt's bright orange sleeveless dress. She talks enthusiastically, almost conversationally, from the moment she deposits herself in the chair before the judges. It is as if she has been doing this all her life. Judi is restrained only by what she keeps reminding herself, to keep her hands anchored in her lap and not to say "you know." She is bright and cheery and carries the judges along with her. "Learn to gain control over the interview," Gay has told all the girls. "Give a brief answer, then lead into another area that you particularly like to talk about."

That advice was like giving Judi a license to steal. She   17 and all the other modern Southern belles are born and bred in this briar patch. In Atlantic City a few months later, Phyllis George, Judi's temperamental and verbal kin, babbled on with such dazzle about her pet crab and her dog that the most serious thing that the judges found time to ask her was whether or not she liked beer—and Phyllis even side-stepped that one, and went rambling right on, absolutely stunning the judges from start to finish of the interview. Judi's footwork is proportionately as good at the Heart of Wilson Motel, but she slows down and twice permits the judges time to reach into the portfolio of controversial questions.

First, they want to know if Judi endorses drugs. Well, she doesn't. Then Marilyn Hull remembers Doris. "Do you think there is a generation gap?" she asks. Judi pauses but for a second, then replies: "I don't think there's any more gap now than there's ever been." The judges nod, and then they want to know if she might have a question for them.   18

Judi has come loaded for that bear. "What is your idea of a Miss Wilson?" she rips back at them.   19

A girl with poise, the judges solemnly agree.   20

"Now, do you have any other question you would like to ask us?" Jerry asks. This is a formality, like drop-over-sometime-and-see-us, but Judi tears into it at face value. "Do you think there is a generation gap?" she asks. Marilyn fields the answer, uneasily, and this time Jerry does not ask Judi if she has another question to ask. "I'm afraid Dr. Vincent is signaling that our time is up," he informs her. Judi thanks everyone and leaves. As soon as she is out of the room, the judges start marveling about her performance. "Imagine," one says, "we asked if she had another question, and she did." There is a first time for everything.   21

They are still chuckling at Judi's effervescence as Rose Thorne comes in. She expresses a solid opposition to coed dorms, and then Connie Whisenant finishes up by voicing displeasure at those college students who had participated in the Vietnam Moratorium.   22

Outside the room Doris and Judi are already comparing   23

notes. It is immediately obvious to each that her rival was not disappointed; at the least, neither felt she had done poorly. Judi is stunned to learn, though, that Doris has actually said that there is a generation gap. Was she right? Was that the correct answer that the judges were fishing for? Anyway, it only reinforces Judi's growing opinion. By the time she goes home to put her hair up in curlers, and to affix false eyelashes for the first time in her life, Judi Brewer is absolutely convinced that Doris Smith is the only thing that stands between her and Miss Wilson 1970.

Comment

In this early section of his book on Miss America, Frank Deford describes the preliminary interview in the local Miss America contest in Wilson, North Carolina. In succeeding sections he describes the events that followed. The judges of the local contest are old hands and have long memories; one of them mentions Jeanne Swanner, Miss North Carolina of 1963, who sometimes emcees local contests. The chapter from which this section is taken focuses on Doris Smith and Judi Brewer, who became finalists for first and second place.

Deford's attitude toward Miss America is suggested by his opening comment in the book: "Maligned by one segment of America, adored by another, misunderstood by about all of it, Miss America still flows like the Mississippi, drifts like amber waves of grain, sounds like the crack of a bat on a baseball, tastes like Mom's apple pie, and smells like dollar bills." He is obviously concerned with the values the contest represents. In the section printed here, he is direct about how the contest affects the participants. "Over six feet tall," he says about Wendy Formo, "she cannot help walking like a normal person." And he has similar things to say about how the girls act on the advice of Mrs. Butner, a woman from Rocky Mount who has been tutoring them. Another important indication of tone is the incongruity he stresses: the girls are forced to walk and sit in uncomfortable ways; their answers to questions are also forced. Deford need not comment directly on their situations. His sympathy for them shapes his attitude and therefore his tone; so does his complex attitude toward the contest and the idea of "Miss America." Tone is revealed unmistakably in exaggeration as in understatement—if the author prefers not to state his or her attitude directly. The details selected for emphasis can be equally revealing.

Questions for Study and Discussion

1. How does Deford's choice of details stress the incongruous? How do his comparisons to Army fatigues, bustles, and little dogs make the incongruities vivid to us?
2. Does he express or imply the same attitude towards all the girls in the contest? To what extent is his sympathy toward them qualified by his attitude toward the values represented by or implied in the contest?
3. What are those values, and what details best reveal them?
4. How sympathetic is Deford toward the judges? Is it his view that the panel is "hot-shot," or is he giving someone's opinion of it?
5. What does Deford mean by the statement that "it is the underside of the iceberg that determines the winner"? How does he illustrate the statement?
6. Does Deford resort to understatement or irony, or does he depend solely on the details to create tone?
7. How does he establish and maintain a consistent point of view in the whole essay? What is the order of ideas?
8. What are your feelings toward the contestants and the judges? How much were they shaped for you by Deford?

Vocabulary Study

Identify words and phrases that you would classify as slang (such as "hot-shot") and determine their use in the essay, in particular their contribution to the overall tone. If this slang is no longer current, suggest how the statements might be reworded to convey the same tone.

Suggestions for Writing

1. Describe a contest in which you participated. Focus on the behavior and attitude of the judges or the participants, and use

your discussion to reveal your attitude toward the contest. Choose vivid details that best reveal the values represented by or implied in the contest.

2. Discuss what you think Deford is saying or implying about the contest. Consider his details about the judges as well as about the contestants.

3. Rewrite a part of this essay from the point of view of one of the contestants. Allow her attitude toward the judges and the contest itself to emerge in the details she selects and the feelings she expresses.

Usage

Each of us has a formal and informal vocabulary. We use each vocabulary on different occasions, often without much thought. On formal occasions like weddings, funerals, and job interviews, you use a vocabulary different from that at home or with friends. Though judgments about vocabulary vary from one group of people or one part of the country to another, people do agree on what is extremely formal and informal—the language of insurance policies and that of television comedy and sports writing, for example.

Consider the following formal and informal statements:

In defying nature, in destroying nature, in building an arrogantly selfish, man-centered, artificial world, I do not see how man can gain peace or freedom or joy. I have faith in man's future, faith in the possibilities latent in the human experiment: but it is faith in man as a part of nature, working with the forces that govern the forests and the seas; faith in man sharing life, not destroying it.—Marston Bates, *The Forest and the Sea*

He sailed up to me, and then cut to my left for the sidelines, with a little grunt, and I could hear the *shu-shu* of his football

424

trousers as he went by, and the creak of his shoulder pads.—
George Plimpton, *Paper Lion*

The vocabulary of the first passage is formal—abstract words and
phrases like *faith in the possibilities latent in the human experiment*
expressing abstract ideas. In the second passage, the colloquial or
everyday conversational phrases like *sailed up* and *cut to my left* contribute to the informality.

Vocabulary and sentence structure work together to make a piece
of writing formal or informal. In the first passage the tight parallelism and the opening periodic sentence (a sentence that builds to
the core idea) creates a highly formal effect. In the second the loose
coordination is characteristic of everyday informal conversation.
However, formal English is not limited to ideas, nor is informal
English limited to concrete experiences. Formal English often deals
with specific concrete ideas and experience and uses a simple vocabulary. Informal English often deals with ideas in concrete language
and in sentences containing looser parallelism.

Slang and jargon associated with particular jobs or activities are
common in informal speech and writing. Slang describes colorful,
sometimes short-lived, expressions peculiar to a group of people.
Jargon consists of the technical words specific to a trade or profession. Assembly-line workers and telephone and automobile repair-
men have their own special language—in particular, special terms
and expressions. So have teenagers, jazz musicians, college professors, and baseball fans. This special language is less common in formal speech and writing, mainly because the audience for that writing
is usually a general one. Expressions associated with rock music will
be understood by a special audience of rock fans, but a general audience will need an explanation.

As in Art Buchwald's following comic series of letters, awareness of usage often begins when a piece of writing creates an un-
intended impression or effect. Unless you know your audience will
be a special one, you will do best to think of it as general—repre-
senting many backgrounds and interests. This advice bears especially on diction, for vocabulary gives readers the most trouble—
especially inexact, ambiguous words and phrases.

Art Buchwald
Job Hunting

Art Buchwald was born in Mount Vernon, New York, in 1925,
and was educated at the University of Southern California. During the Second World War he served in the Marine Corps. He
has written for many newspapers; his satirical columns have been
collected into many books. His chief target has been the Washington scene but he has also written about contemporary social
problems.

Vice President of Development
Glucksville Dynamics
Glucksville, California

DEAR SIR,

I am writing in regard to employment with your firm. I
have a BS from USC and PhD in physics from the California
Institute of Technology.

In my previous position I was in charge of research and
development for the Harrington Chemical Company. We did
work in thermonuclear energy, laser beam refraction, hydrogen molecule development, and heavy-water computer data.

Several of our research discoveries have been adapted for
commercial use, and one particular breakthrough in linear
hydraulics is now being used by every oil company in the
country.

Because of a cutback in defense orders, the Harrington
Company decided to shut down its research and development department. It is for this reason I am available for immediate employment.

Hoping to hear from you in the near future, I remain

Sincerely yours,
EDWARD KASE

DEAR MR. KASE,

We regret to inform you that we have no positions available for someone of your excellent qualifications. The truth of the matter is that we find you are "overqualified" for any position we might offer you in our organization. Thank you for thinking of us, and if anything comes up in the future, we will be getting in touch with you.

Yours truly,
MERRIMAN HASELBALD
Administrative Vice-President

Personnel Director
Jessel International Systems
Crewcut, Mich.

DEAR SIR,

I am applying for a position with your company in any responsible capacity. I have had a college education and have fiddled around in research and development. Occasionally we have come up with some moneymaking ideas. I would be willing to start off at a minimal salary to prove my value to your firm.

Sincerely yours,
EDWARD KASE

DEAR MR. KASE,

Thank you for your letter of the 15th. Unfortunately we have no positions at the moment for someone with a college education. Frankly it is the feeling of everyone here that you are "overqualified," and your experience indicates you would be much happier with a company that could make full use of your talents.

It was kind of you to think of us.

HARDY LANDSDOWNE
Personnel Dept.

To Whom It May Concern
Geis & Waterman Inc.
Ziegfried, Ill.

DERE SER,
    I'd like a job with your outfit. I can do anything you want
me to. You name it Kase will do it. I ain't got no education
and no experience, but I'm strong and I got moxy an I get
along great with peeple. I'm ready to start any time because
I need the bread. Let me know when you want me.

Cheers
EDWARD KASE

DEAR MR. KASE,
    You are just the person we have been looking for. We
need a truck driver, and your qualifications are perfect for us.
You can begin working in our Westminister plant on Monday. Welcome aboard.

CARSON PETERS
Personnel

Comment

Buchwald writes in a clearly satirical voice when he writes in
his own person. He is not writing in his own person in these letters, but we do hear him indirectly—in the language he has given
the correspondents. Buchwald's humor arises in the changes we see
in Kase's letters and in the situation itself. Humor must develop out
of real problems in the world we know: we will not find humor
long in invented qualities and situations. Those problems may be
serious—the problem Buchwald deals with is a serious one today.
We can laugh with Buchwald because we are laughing not at Kase
but at ourselves and at the dilemma of our world.

Questions for Study and Discussion

1. How do Kase's letters change in language? What are the most important changes? What changes do you notice in sentence structure?
2. What situation is the source of Buchwald's humor? What exactly is he satirizing?
3. What do Kase and his correspondents reveal about themselves in the impressions they give of themselves?

Vocabulary Study

Find substitutes for the formal diction in the letters to Kase. Discuss how their substitution would change the humor or point of the letters.

Suggestions for Writing

1. Write three letters of application for the same job. Change your language to give a different impression of yourself. Use these letters to make a satirical point, as Buchwald does.
2. Write an exchange of letters like Buchwald's, satirizing a current social problem through them. Fit the language of each letter to the character and attitude of the writer.

Michael Demarest
The Fine Art of Putting Things Off

Michael Demarest was born in Long Island, New York, in 1924, and was educated in England at Rugby and Oxford. Since World War II, when he served in the U.S. Merchant Marine, he has

Reprinted by permission from *Time*, The Weekly Newsmagazine; copyright Time, Inc.

written for newspapers and magazines. He has been associated
with *Time* as a foreign correspondent, editor, and senior writer.
He won the John Hancock Award in 1973 for financial and
business reporting, and the J. C. Penney University of Missouri
Award for his 1974 *Time* cover story on American pets. Demarest is a member in good standing of the Procrastinators' Club
of America, Inc.

"Never put off till tomorrow," exhorted Lord Chester-   1
field in 1749, "what you can do today." That the elegant earl
never got around to marrying his son's mother and had a bad
habit of keeping worthies like Dr. Johnson cooling their heels
for hours in an anteroom attests to the fact that even the most
well-intentioned men have been postponers ever. Quintus
Fabius Maximus, one of the great Roman generals, was dubbed
"Cunctator" (Delayer) for putting off battle until the last possible *vinum* break. Moses pleaded a speech defect to rationalize his reluctance to deliver Jehovah's edict to Pharaoh.
Hamlet, of course, raised procrastination to an art form.

The world is probably about evenly divided between de-   2
layers and do-it-nowers. There are those who prepare their
income taxes in February, prepay mortgages and serve precisely planned dinners at an ungodly 6:30 P.M. The other half
dine happily on leftovers at 9 or 10, misplace bills and file for
an extension of the income tax deadline. They seldom pay
credit-card bills until the apocalyptic voice of Diners threatens doom from Denver. They postpone, as Faustian encounters, visits to barbershop, dentist or doctor.

Yet for all the trouble procrastination may incur, delay   3
can often inspire and revive a creative soul. Jean Kerr, author
of many successful novels and plays, says that she reads every
soup-can and jam-jar label in her kitchen before settling down
to her typewriter. Many a writer focuses on almost anything
but his task—for example, on the Coast and Geodetic Survey
of Maine's Frenchman Bay and Bar Harbor, stimulating his
imagination with names like Googins Ledge, Blunts Pond, Hio
Hill and Burnt Porcupine, Long Porcupine, Sheep Porcupine
and Bald Porcupine islands.

From *Cunctator's* day until this century, the art of post- 4
ponement had been virtually a monopoly of the military
("Hurry up and wait"), diplomacy and the law. In former times,
a British proconsul faced with a native uprising could comfortably ruminate about the situation with Singapore Sling in
hand. Blessedly, he had no nattering Telex to order in machine guns and fresh troops. A U.S. general as late as World
War II could agree with his enemy counterpart to take a
sporting day off, loot the villagers' chickens and wine and go
back to battle a day later. Lawyers are among the world's most
addicted postponers. According to Frank Nathan, a nonpost-
poning Beverly Hills insurance salesman, "The number of at-
torneys who die without a will is amazing."

Even where there is no will, there is a way. There is a 5
difference, of course, between chronic procrastination and
purposeful postponement, particularly in the higher echelons
of business. Corporate dynamics encourage the caution that
breeds delay, says Richard Manderbach, Bank of America
group vice president. He notes that speedy action can be embarrassing or extremely costly. The data explosion fortifies those
seeking excuses for inaction—another report to be read, another authority to be consulted. "There is always," says Manderbach, "a delicate edge between having enough information
and too much."

His point is well taken. Bureaucratization, which flour- 6
ished amid the growing burdens of government and the greater
complexity of society, was designed to smother policymakers
in blankets of legalism, compromise and reappraisal—and
thereby prevent hasty decisions from being made. The cen-
tralization of government that led to Watergate has spread to
economic institutions and beyond, making procrastination a
worldwide way of life. Many languages are studded with
phrases that refer to putting things off—from the Spanish
mañana to the Arabic *bukra fil mishmish* (literally "tomorrow
in apricots," more loosely "leave it for the soft spring weather
when the apricots are blooming").

Academe also takes high honors in procrastination. 7

Bernard Sklar, a University of Southern California sociologist who churns out three to five pages of writing a day, admits that "many of my friends go through agonies when they face a blank page. There are all sorts of rationalizations: the pressure of teaching, responsibilities at home, checking out the latest book, looking up another footnote."

Psychologists maintain that the most assiduous procrastinators are women, though many psychologists are (at $50-plus an hour) pretty good delayers themselves. Dr. Ralph Greenson, a U.C.L.A. professor of clinical psychiatry (and Marilyn Monroe's onetime shrink), takes a fairly gentle view of procrastination. "To many people," he says, "doing something, confronting, is the moment of truth. All frightened people will then avoid the moment of truth entirely, or evade or postpone it until the last possible moment." To Georgia State Psychologist Joen Fagan, however, procrastination may be a kind of subliminal way of sorting the important from the trivial. "When I drag my feet, there's usually some reason," says Fagan. "I feel it, but I don't yet know the real reason." 8

In fact, there is a long and honorable history of procrastination to suggest that many ideas and decisions may well improve if postponed. It is something of a truism that to put off making a decision is itself a decision. The parliamentary process is essentially a system of delay and deliberation. So, for that matter, is the creation of a great painting, or an entrée, or a book, or a building like Blenheim Palace, which took the Duke of Marlborough's architects and laborers 15 years to construct. In the process, the design can mellow and marinate. Indeed, hurry can be the assassin of elegance. As T. H. White, author of *Sword in the Stone,* once wrote, time "is not meant to be devoured in an hour or a day, but to be consumed delicately and gradually and without haste." In other words, *pace* Lord Chesterfield, what you don't necessarily have to do today, by all means put off until tomorrow. 9

Comment

Demarest's sentences and diction are mostly formal, although his essay deals with everyday experiences. He does not chat with us about the art of putting things off: he prefers to deal with the subject seriously. But the serious point he has to make about procrastination does not prevent him from being humorous, as his frequent play on words shows: "Even where there is no will, there is a way." Thus the formality of the language invites us to consider Demarest's ideas seriously, but he manages to avoid a sober attitude toward the subject, toward his reader, and toward himself.

Questions for Study and Discussion

1. Demarest mixes abstract with concrete words, often for humorous effect. What examples of this mixed diction can you cite?
2. Why does Demarest refer to visits to the barber, the dentist, and the doctor as "Faustian encounters"?
3. What point is he making about bureaucratization? Is he making this point seriously?
4. What points is he making about putting things off?
5. What shifts in tone do you notice, and how are they managed?

Vocabulary Study

1. Identify words in the essay that you would expect to find in formal speech and writing. State what words might be used in their place in informal speech and writing.
2. Use your dictionary to find out whether the following pairs of words are different in meaning or in level of usage or possibly both. The first word in each pair is Demarest's:
   a. *ruminate* (paragraph 4), *ponder*
   b. *echelon* (paragraph 5), *ranks*
   c. *reappraisal* (paragraph 6), *revaluation*
   d. *rationalizations* (paragraph 7), *excuses*
   e. *assiduous* (paragraph 8), *hard-working*
   f. *truism* (paragraph 9), *platitude*

Suggestions for Writing

1. Demarest distinguishes two classes of people in his second paragraph. Describe your attitude toward putting things off and state the class you belong to and why you do.

2. Organize an essay for a specific audience on one of the following statements. Use your experience and observations to qualify it or to support it fully:

    a. "The best liar is he who makes the smallest amount of lying go the longest way—who husbands it too carefully to waste it where it can be dispensed with."—Samuel Butler

    b. "One of the most striking differences between a cat and a lie is that a cat has only nine lives."—Mark Twain

    c. "One can never pay in gratitude; one can only pay 'in kind' somewhere else in life."—Anne Morrow Lindbergh

    d. "You might as well fall flat on your face as lean over too far backward."—James Thurber

Glossary

allusion: An indirect reference to a presumably well-known literary work or an historical event or figure. The phrase "the Waterloo of his political career" is a reference to Napoleon's disastrous defeat at the Battle of Waterloo in 1815. The allusion implies that the career of the politician under discussion has come to a dramatic end.

analogy: A point-by-point comparison between two unlike things or activities (for example, comparing writing an essay to building a house) for the purpose of illustration or argument. Unlike a comparison (or contrast), in which the things compared are of equal importance, analogy exists for the purpose of illustrating or arguing the nature of one of the compared things, not both.

antithesis: The arrangement of contrasting ideas in grammatically similar phrases and clauses (*The world will little note, nor long remember, what we say here, but it can never forget what they did here*—Lincoln, *Gettysburg Address*). See *parallelism*.

argument: Proving the truth or falseness of a statement. Arguments are traditionally classified as *inductive* or *deductive*. See *deductive argument* and *inductive argument*. Argument can be used for different purposes in writing. See *purpose*.

autobiography: Writing about one's own experiences, often those of growing up and making one's way in the world. The autobiographical

435

writings of Mary E. Mebane and Maya Angelou describe their childhood in the South.

balanced sentence: A sentence containing parallel phrases and clauses of approximately the same length and wording (*You can fool all the people some of the time, and some of the people all the time, but you cannot fool all the people all of the time.*—Lincoln).

cause and effect: Analysis of the conditions that must be present for an event to occur *(cause)* and of the results or consequences of the event *(effect)*. An essay may deal with causes or with effects only.

classification and division: *Classification* arranges individual objects into groups or classes (Jonathans, Winesaps, Golden Delicious, and Macintoshes are types of apples). *Division* arranges a broad class into subclasses according to various principles (the broad class *apples* can be divided on the basis of their color, use, variety, or taste). There are as many divisions as principles of division or subclassification.

cliché: A once-colorful expression made stale through overuse *(putting on the dog, mad as a wet hen)*.

coherence: The sense, as we read, that the details and ideas of a work connect clearly. A paragraph or essay that does not hold together seems incoherent.

colloquialism: An everyday expression in speech and informal writing. Colloquialisms are not substandard or "illiterate" English. They are common in informal English and occur sometimes in formal English.

comparison and contrast: The analysis of similarities and differences between two or more persons, objects, or events (A and B) for the purpose of a relative estimate. The word *comparison* sometimes refers to the analysis of similarities and differences in both A and B. *Block comparison* presents each thing being compared as a whole (that is, if the comparison is between A and B, then features a, b, c of A are discussed as a block of information, then features a, b, c of B are compared to A in their own block of information). *Alternating comparison* presents the comparable features one by one (a, a, b, b, c, c).

complex sentence: A sentence consisting of one main or independent clause, and one or more subordinate or dependent clauses *(The rain began when she stepped outside)*.

compound sentence: A sentence consisting of coordinated independent clauses *(She stepped outside and then the rain began)*.

compound-complex sentence: A sentence consisting of two or more main or independent clauses and at least one subordinate or dependent clause *(She stepped outside as the rain began, but she did not return to the house)*.

concrete and abstract words: Concrete words refer to particular objects, people, and events (Benedict Arnold, Franklin Delano Roosevelt, the Rocky Mountains); abstract words refer to general shared qualities (cowardice, courage, beauty). Concrete writing makes abstract ideas perceptible to the senses through details and images.

concreteness: Making an idea exist through the senses. Writing can and should be concrete at all three levels—informal, general, and formal. See *concrete and abstract words*.

connotation: Feelings, images, and ideas associated with a word. Connotations change from reader to reader, though some words probably have the same associations for everybody.

context: The surrounding words or sentences that suggest the meaning of a word or phrase. Writers may dispense with formal definition if the context clarifies the meaning of a word.

coordinate sentence: A sentence that joins clauses of the same weight and importance through the conjunctions *and, but, for, or, nor,* or *yet,* or through conjunctive adverbs and adverbial phrases *(however, therefore, nevertheless, in fact)*.

deductive argument: Reasoning from statements assumed to be true or well-established factually. These statements or assumptions are thought sufficient to guarantee the truth of the inferences or conclusions. In formal arguments they are called premises. A valid argument reasons correctly from the premises to the conclusion. A sound argument is true in its premises and valid in its reasoning. See *enthymeme, syllogism*.

definition: Explaining the current meaning of a word through its etymology or derivation, its denotation, or its connotations. Denotative or "real" definitions single out a word from all of other words (or things) like it by giving *genus* and *specific difference*. Connotative definitions give the associations people make to the world. See *connotation*.

description: A picture in words of people, objects, and events. Description often combines with narrative and it may serve exposition and persuasion.

division: See *classification and division*.

enthymeme: A deductive argument that does not state the conclusion or one of the premises directly. The following statement is an enthymeme: *Citizens in a democracy, who refuse to register for the draft, are not acting responsibly.* The implied premise is that the responsible citizen obeys all laws, even repugnant ones.

essay: A carefully organized composition that develops a single idea or impression or develops several related ideas or impressions. The word sometimes describes a beginning or trial attempt which explores the central idea or impression instead of developing it completely.

example: A picture or illustration of an idea, or one of many instances or occurrences that is typical of the rest.

exposition: An explanation or unfolding or setting forth of an idea, usually for the purpose of giving information. Exposition is usually an important part of persuasive writing. Example, process analysis, causal analysis, definition, classification and division, and comparison and contrast are forms of exposition.

expressive writing: Essays, diaries, journals, letters, and other kinds of writing which present personal feelings and beliefs for their own sake. The expressive writer is not primarily concerned with informing or persuading readers.

figure of speech: A word or phrase that departs from its usual meaning. Figures of speech make statements vivid and capture the attention of readers. The most common figures are based on similarity between things. See *metaphor, personification, simile.* Other figures are based on relationship. See *allusion. Metonymy* refers to a thing by one of its qualities (*the Hill* as a reference to the United States Congress). *Synecdoche* refers to a thing by one of its parts (*wheels* as a reference to racing cars). Other figures are based on contrast between statements and realities. See *irony.* Related to irony is *understatement,* or saying less than is appropriate ("Napoleon's career ended unhappily at Waterloo"). *Hyperbole* means deliberate exaggeration ("crazy about ice cream"). *Paradox* states an apparent contradiction ("All great truths begin as blasphemies"—G. B. Shaw). *Oxymoron,* a kind of paradox, joins opposite qualities into a single image *(lake of fire).*

focus: The limitation of subject in an essay. The focus may be broad, as in a panoramic view of the mountains, or it may be narrow, as in a view of a particular peak. For example, a writer may focus broadly on the contribution to scientific thought of scientists from various fields, or focus narrowly on the achievements of astronomers or chemists or medical researchers, or focus even more narrowly on the achievements of Albert Einstein as representative of twentieth century science.

formal English: Spoken and written English, often abstract in content, with sentences tighter than spoken ones, and an abstract and sometimes technical vocabulary. See *general English* and *informal English.*

general English: A written standard that has features of informal and formal English and avoids the extremes of both. See *formal English* and *informal English.*

image: A picture in words of an object, a scene, or a person. Though visual images are common in writing, they are not the only kind. Images can also be auditory, tactile, gustatory, and olfactory. Keats's line "With beaded bubbles winking at the brim" appeals to our hearing and taste as well as to our sight. His phrase "coming musk-rose" appeals to our sense of smell. Images help to make feelings concrete.

implied thesis: The central idea of the essay, suggested by the details and discussion rather than stated directly. See *thesis.*

inductive argument: Inductive arguments reason from particulars of experience to general ideas—from observation, personal experience, and experimental testing to probable conclusions. Inductive arguments make predictions on the basis of past and present experience. An argumentative analogy is a form of inductive argument because it is based on limited observation and experience and therefore can claim probability only. Analysis of causes and effects is inductive when used in argument.

"inductive leap":   Making the decision that sufficient inductive evidence (personal experience, observation, experimental testing) exists to draw a conclusion. Sometimes the writer of the argument makes the leap too quickly and bases his conclusions on insufficient evidence.

informal English: Written English, usually concrete in content, tighter than the loose sentences of spoken English, but looser in sentence construction than formal English. The word "informal" refers to the occasion of its use. A letter to a friend is usually informal; a letter of application is usually formal. See *formal English* and *general English.*

irony: A term generally descriptive of statements and events. An ironic statement says the opposite of what the speaker or writer means, or implies that something more is meant than is stated, or says the unexpected *(He has a great future behind him)*. An ironic event is unexpected or is so coincidental that it seems impossible *(The fireboat burned and sank).*

jargon: The technical words of a trade or profession (in computer jargon, the terms *input* and *word processor)*. Unclear, clumsy, or repetitive words or phrasing, sometimes the result of misplaced technical words *(He gave his input into the decision process).*

loose sentence: A sentence that introduces the main idea close to the beginning and concludes with a series of modifiers *(The car left the expressway, slowing on the ramp and coming to a stop at the crossroad).* See *periodic sentence.*

metaphor: An implied comparison which attributes the qualities of one thing to another (the word *mainstream* to describe the opinions or activities of most people).

mixed metaphor: The incongruous use of two metaphors in the same context *(the roar of protest was stopped in its tracks).*

narrative: The chronological presentation of events. Narrative often combines with description and it may serve exposition or persuasion.

order of ideas: The presentation of ideas in a paragraph or an essay according to a plan. The order may be *spatial,* perhaps moving from background to foreground, or from top to bottom, or from side to side; or the order may be *temporal* or chronological (in the order of time). The presentation may be in the order of *importance,* or if the details build intensively, in the order of *climax.* The paragraph or essay may move from *problem* to *solution* or from the *specific* to the *general*. Some of these orders occur together—for example, a chronological presentation of details that build to a climax.

parallelism: Grammatically similar words, phrases, and clauses arranged to highlight similar ideas *(There are neighborhoods of nations . . . There are streets where, on January nights, fires burn on every floor of every house . . . There are meadows and fields*—Mark Helprin). See *antithesis*.

paraphrase: A rendering of a passage in different words that retain the sense, the tone, and the order of ideas.

periodic sentence: A sentence that builds to the main idea *(Building speed as it curved down the ramp, the car sped into the crowded expressway)*. See *loose sentence*.

personification: Giving animate or human qualities to something animate or inhuman (The sun *smiled* at the earth).

persuasion: The use of argument or satire or some other means to change thinking and feeling about an issue.

point of view: The place or vantage point from which an event is seen and described. The term sometimes refers to the mental attitude of the viewer in narrative. Mark Twain's *Huckleberry Finn* narrates the adventures of a boy in slave-owning Missouri from the point of view of the boy, not from that of an adult.

premise: see *syllogism*.

process: An activity or operation containing steps usually performed in the same order. The process may be mechanical (changing a tire), natural (the circulation of the blood), or historical (the rise and spread of a specific epidemic disease such as bubonic plague at various times in history).

purpose: The aim of the essay as distinguished from the means used to develop it. The purposes or aims of writing are many; they include expressing personal feelings and ideas, giving information, persuading readers to change their thinking about an issue, inspiring readers to take action, giving pleasure. These purposes may be achieved through description, narrative, exposition, or argument. These means may be used alone or in combination, and an essay may contain more than one purpose.

reflection: An essay that explores ideas without necessarily bringing the exploration to completion. The reflective essay can take the form of a loosely organized series of musings or tightly organized arguments.

satire: Ridicule of foolish or vicious behavior or ideas for the purpose of correcting them. *Social satire* concerns foolish but not dangerous behavior and ideas—for example, coarse table manners, pretentious talk, harmless gossip. George Bernard Shaw's "Arms and the Man" is a social satire. *Ethical satire* attacks vicious or dangerous behavior or ideas—

religious or racial bigotry, greed, political corruption. Mark Twain's *Huckleberry Finn* is an ethical satire.

simile: A direct comparison between two things *(A growing child is like a young tree)*. See *figure of speech, metaphor.*

simple sentence: A sentence consisting of a single main or independent clause and no subordinate or dependent clauses *(The rain started at nightfall).*

slang: Colorful and sometimes short-lived expressions peculiar to a group of people, usually informal in usage and almost always unacceptable in formal usage *(nerd, goof off).*

style: A distinctive manner of speaking and writing. A writing style may be plain in its lack of metaphor and other figures of speech. Another writing style may be highly colorful or ornate.

subordinate clause: A clause that completes a main clause or attaches to it as a modifier (She saw *that the rain had begun; When it rains,* it pours).

syllogism: The formal arrangement of premises and conclusion of a deductive argument. The premises are the general assumptions *(All reptiles are cold-blooded vertebrates, All snakes are reptiles)* from which particular conclusions are drawn *(All snakes are cold-blooded vertebrates).* This formal arrangement helps to test the validity or correctness of the reasoning from premises to conclusion. See *deductive argument.*

symbol: An object that represents an abstract idea. The features of the symbol (the fifty stars and thirteen horizontal stripes of the American flag) suggest characteristics of the object symbolized (the fifty states of the Union, the original confederation of thirteen states). A sign need not have this representative quality: a green light signals "go," and red light "stop" by conventional agreement.

thesis: The central idea that organizes the many smaller ideas and details of the essay.

tone: The phrasing or words that express the attitude or feeling of the speaker or writer. The tone of a statement ranges from the angry, exasperated, and sarcastic, to the wondering or approving. An ironic tone suggests that the speaker or writer means more than the words actually state.

topic sentence: Usually the main or central idea of the paragraph that organizes details and subordinate ideas. Though it often opens the paragraph, the topic sentence can appear later—in the middle or at the end of the paragraph.

transition: A word or phrase *(however, thus, in fact)* that connects clauses and sentences. Parallel structure is an important means of transition.

unity: The connection of ideas and details to a central controlling idea of the essay. A unified essay deals with one idea at a time.

Index